THE EUROPEAN UNION AND TERRORISM

The European Union and Terrorism

edited by

David Spence

JOHN HARPER
PUBLISHING

The European Union and Terrorism

Published by John Harper Publishing
27 Palace Gates Road
London N22 7BW, United Kingdom.

www.johnharperpublishing.co.uk

ISBN 978-0-9556202-0-1

Printed and Bound in Great Britain by Cromwell Press Ltd.

TABLE OF CONTENTS

ANNEXES

PREFACE

A common European approach to fighting terrorism is essential. Technology, with its speed and sophistication, and terrorists willing to attack wherever and whenever they think they will get maximum results negate traditional national borders. Nor do the effects of terrorism stop at borders: they can affect people or infrastructure in many countries. We must therefore work together at local, national, EU level, and with our international partners, to face this challenge and protect our citizens. Working together has enabled the EU to adopt a common definition of a terrorist offence or a terrorist-related offence. This has built mutual trust between Member States and made it easier for police and intelligence services to work together.

The European Union has achieved much in the last half century. We must ensure it continues to face the challenges ahead. Today security is the new challenge for Europe. We must act resolutely against those who threaten our security. As European Union Commissioner for Justice, Freedom and Security I believe that the debate and development of counter-terrorism policy must be kept active. This book brings together key thinkers and is a welcome analysis of terrorism challenges. David Spence has succeeded in giving us a timely and thoughtful complement to the terrorism debate.

The EU has been developing a counter-terrorism policy in which Member States fight terrorism together with equal determination, commitment and in full respect for human rights and fundamental freedoms as laid down in the European Convention on Human Rights and the Charter of Fundamental Rights of the European Union. A number of important initiatives have been taken along four main tracks: prevention, protection, prosecution and responding if an attack occurs.

Security is not an add-on but interconnected to other work. This book rightly looks across the spectrum and considers, for example, the challenge of understanding violent radicalisation. The Commission has proposed measures to interrupt terrorists' finances. Protecting critical infrastructure – our roads, airports, electricity plants, bridges – is also key. Here the European Union works with both international and private partners. Measures at European level to aid prosecution, such as the European Arrest Warrant, ensure terrorists can be prosecuted across Europe. If an attack does occur the EU requires a well-organised and effective response to minimise casualties and quickly bring the situation under control.

All our action in the fight against terrorism is based on the absolute primacy of the rule of law. We fight terrorism by the law and within the law. Fighting terrorism is about preserving our most fundamental and cherished human rights and this means that we must uphold these human rights with every step we take. Our policies must be proportionate and effective. I am Commissioner also for Fundamental Rights. I believe these two issues – fighting terrorism and protecting individuals' rights – sit well within my portfolio as we must consider them together. Comment and debate surrounding counter-terrorism measures and policy is necessary, including, as in the case of this volume, the airing of ideas and interpretations which may be contentious. This book provides thoughtful insight into the issues involved.

Franco Frattini
Vice-President of the European Commission
Commissioner for Justice, Freedom and Security

FOREWORD

Numerous publications have been written on terrorism for experts and laymen alike, and the same is true of America's 'War on Terror'. Given the current international security environment, this trend will likely continue. However, only a few have ventured to write specifically about the European Union and terrorism. Although separately the policy areas have each rightfully received extensive scrutiny, book-length analyses of how the European Union as an actor is approaching and dealing with terrorism are scarce. This comes as no surprise, of course, for the Maastricht Treaty creating the EU was only signed in 1992 and the contours of a common security and defence policy started to emerge less than a decade ago. The horrendous events of 11 September 2001 and subsequent attacks on European soil have inevitably served to speed up this policy process. They have also served to catalyse member state cooperation in the domain of justice and home affairs, a traditional reserve of national governments, but one in which international cooperation is crucial if transnational terrorism is to be successfully countered.

The Geneva Centre for the Democratic Control of Armed Forces (DCAF) therefore welcomes this new book, *The European Union and Terrorism*, a timely publication which cogently documents and critiques the European Union's response to terrorism thus far. The publication is the latest DCAF contribution to the topic of terrorism. Already in 2002, Ambassadors Theodor Winkler and István Gyarmati edited *Post-Cold War Defence Reform: Lessons Learned in Europe and the United States*, which addressed the post-9/11 world. The following year, DCAF devoted a chapter of its yearbook, *Challenges of Security Sector Governance*, to 'US "Homeland Security" Reforms in the Aftermath of 9/11'. In 2005, DCAF published *Combating Terrorism and Its Implications for the Security Sector* and *Facing the Terrorism Challenge: Central Asia's Role in Regional and International Cooperation*. Both publications sought to tackle the questions, issues and dilemmas for the security sector posed by terrorism. That same year, DCAF was a co-organiser of a conference on contemporary security sector governance issues, which focused on terrorism and at which David Spence was the keynote speaker.

In addition to filling a gap in the literature, by examining both internal and external policy, *The European Union and Terrorism* also expands the areas of work which DCAF has conducted on the EU from an emphasis on security and defence issues into the domain of justice and home affairs. Both of these policy sectors are crucial for effective counter terrorism and indispensable aspects of security sector governance, an area of policy to which the EU is increasingly contributing as a major donor in cooperation with the United Nations. Reflecting this broadened focus, another publication, *The European Union and Security Sector Reform*, jointly edited by David Spence and myself, also appears shortly.

Dr. Philipp H. Fluri
Executive Director
DCAF Brussels

The Geneva Centre for the Democratic Control of Armed Forces (DCAF) is an international foundation, with 45 states and the canton of Geneva in membership, that was established by the Swiss government in October 2000. Its mission is to promote good governance and reform of the security sector in accordance with democratic standards. www.dcaf.ch

ABOUT THE CONTRIBUTORS

Note: All the authors write in a personal capacity and the opinions expressed may not be attributed to the institutions for which they work.

Arjen Boin is the Director of the Stephenson Disaster Management Institute and an associate professor at the Public Administration Institute, at Louisiana State University. He writes on institutional design, leadership and crisis management. His publications include *Crafting Public Institutions* (2001, Lynne Rienner), *The Politics of Crisis Management* (2005, Cambridge University Press) and *Governing after Crises* (2008, Cambridge University Press).

Fraser Cameron is Director of the EU-Russia Centre. He is also Director of EuroFocus-Brussels, an adjunct professor at the Hertie School of Governance in Berlin and Senior Advisor at the European Policy Centre (EPC), and at the European Institute for Asian Studies, Brussels. Having previously been a British diplomat, he worked for the European Commission from 1990 until 1 January 2006, being closely involved in policy issues related to the external relations of the EU. He has published widely on European affairs, his most recent book being *An Introduction to EU Foreign Policy* (Routledge, 2007).

Mirjam Dittrich is a criminal intelligence analyst at Interpol headquarters in Lyon. From 2002 to 2006 she worked as a policy analyst at the European Policy Centre in Brussels where her area of expertise was counter-terrorism, radicalisation and EU foreign policy.

Magnus Ekengren is Senior Lecturer at the Swedish National Defence College and was previously Deputy Director of the Policy Planning Unit of the Swedish Ministry for Foreign Affairs. His main research interests are in the fields of European foreign and security policy and the Europeanisation of the nation-state. Recent publications include *The Time of European Governance* (2002, Manchester University Press).

Kim Eling is First Secretary in the Permanent Delegation of the European Commission to the international organisations in Geneva. He was responsible for relations between the European Commission and the United Nations in the area of counter-terrorism between 2001 and 2003, and was subsequently responsible within the European Commission for the Kimberley Process for conflict diamonds, of which he chaired the Working Group on Monitoring from 2003 to 2006.

Florian Geyer is a lawyer and Research Fellow at the Justice and Home Affairs Unit of CEPS, the Centre for European Policy Studies in Brussels. He was previously Senior Research Assistant at the Institute for European Constitutional Law at the University of Trier. He has published on topics including the European Arrrest Warrant, EU police and judicial cooperation, Commission strategy in the Area of Freedom, Justice and Security, and extraordinary rendition.

Hans Nilsson is head of division on judicial cooperation in the general secretariat of the Council of the European Union. He is also a professor at the
College of Europe in Bruges where he teaches on EU justice and home
affairs matters.

Mark Rhinard is Senior Researcher at the Swedish Institute of International
Affairs, Stockholm, where he conducts research on European security questions. He has been a postdoctoral researcher at Leiden University, The
Netherlands, and earned his PhD from Cambridge University, England. His
recent publications include studies of EU internal security matters, agenda
setting in Europe, the role of the EU as a global actor, and EU implementation and compliance.

David Spence is Political Counsellor at the European Commission's
Delegation to the international organisations in Geneva. He has been lecturer in politics at the Sorbonne, head of European training in the UK's Civil
Service College and secretary of the Commission's task force for German
unification. He has also worked in the Commission on ESDP and terrorism
and was head of training for the Commission's external delegations. He has
edited all three editions of *The European Commission* (John Harper, 3rd
edition, 2006) and was co-editor (with Brian Hocking) of *Foreign Ministries
in the EU: Integrating Diplomats* (Palgrave, 2005).

*The editor would like to express his particular thanks to Suying Lai, without whose
efforts as sub-editor this book would never have seen the light of day.*

Introduction: International Terrorism – the Quest for a Coherent EU Response

David Spence

The challenges of the new terrorism for EU policy[1]

Europe sent mixed messages in response to 9/11 and its aftermath. European governments and the EU institutions were confronted by several fundamental issues. Was there now a terrorist threat to all EU Member States? Should there be a specific EU response to 9/11? Or were national responses adequate to the task of expressing public sympathy with the United States and galvanising public acceptance for supportive action? Retrospectively, with a preening EU formally committed to the fight against terrorism through a series of declarations and new policies, these may seem irrelevant questions. But, overriding all the practical issues was the fact that 9/11 challenged Europe's ability to respond coherently by raising issues for national sovereignty, EU values, and European integration itself. Thrust onto the public agenda before governments and publics had made up their minds on the existential matters, 9/11 required rapid reflection on the future of the EU as a coherent global actor. Responding to 9/11 was initially about demonstrating political commitment. If the early rhetoric seemingly hinted at a robust practical stance, policy in the medium term came to focus largely on a series of legal and administrative developments rather than the kind of 'robust' approach, which might have pleased the United States. Being 'robust' and proactive presupposed strong and undisputed leadership within the EU. And this, in turn, implied not only clear political will, but readiness to forget internecine quarrels between the EU institutions and between the proponents of supranational and intergovernmental procedures.

Thus, Europe's initial inability to rise to the implicit challenges should come as no surprise. The history of the expansion of EU competence into new policy areas has always been characterised by disputes between Member States and EU institutions about the effective and desirable locus of policy making. The EU was not able to articulate an immediate robust response for its Member States, quite simply because there was no joint counter-terrorism strategy in place, despite some thirty years of cooperation on terrorism within the 'Trevi Group', the regular meetings of officials responsible for terrorism issues set up under European Political Cooperation in the 1970s, and despite years of cooperation in a CFSP committee on terrorism (COTER).[2] There had also been regular meetings in troika format with key international partners for whom terrorism was a priority issue, such as the US and India. So, the EU was not uninformed of the issues and the threats.

The EU initially offered condolences and political support to the US. Within a relatively fast time frame it then incorporated new, terrorism-focussed elements into existing policies and legislation. But the term 'counter-terrorism' was absent from the EU discourse. It was deemed a national responsibility, despite, as a British minister later stated to a sceptical House of Lords select committee, 'the fact that these issues cross all three Pillars of the European Union is a particular challenge for us'.[3] A coordinated, multidisciplinary response was needed, yet the EU Member States did not feel constrained to create a counter-terrorism policy matching the EU's economic and political weight in the world and the expectations of its partners, not least the US. Time showed, however, that the terrorism threat was not diminishing, and the growing realisation of European vulnerability began to produce a distinctive EU contribution to the fight against terrorism. The attacks of September 2001 were followed in March 2004 and July 2005 by successful terrorist attacks in Madrid and London, and there were also attacks on European targets in Turkey, Morocco and Saudi Arabia as well as single incidents such as the assassination of Dutch filmmaker Theo van Gogh. And there were revelations of other planned attacks within the European Union.

All these events led within the EU to rapid enhancement of police and judicial cooperation between Member States against all forms of cross-border crime, including terrorism. Terrorist attacks against targets in other parts of the world such as those in Indonesia (Bali and Jakarta), Tunisia (Djerba) and Russia (Beslan and Moscow) also served to catalyse the process by creating a permissive context for radical measures. Most importantly, however, the increasing terrorist threat and its impact on international relations raised consciousness in the EU of two clear needs: first, to employ national, intergovernmental and supranational policy toolboxes in a coherent fashion; and, second, to create a distinct political alternative to America's 'war on terror'. Reflection on such policy departures proved the harbinger, if not catalyst, of an acceleration in the development of an enhanced European Security and Defence Policy with a 'European Security Strategy' reflecting new parameters in terms of threat perception and international security. But, it must be admitted that the EU nevertheless remained slow in creating a substantive European policy of counter-terrorism. Six years later, the policies in place in 2007 encompassing prevention of terrorism, capturing terrorists, keeping the most dangerous weapons out of their hands, ensuring the safety of Europe's critical infrastructure and dealing satisfactorily with the root causes of radicalisation, show the EU is in the forefront of sensible governmental reaction. This may still remain far from an ideal strategy, but it is 'light years' away from the initial floundering which characterised Europe in the weeks after 9/11.

Responsibility for implementation of policy remains with Member States, and while this may be rightly so, Member State action has proved uneven and uncoordinated. If the EU has become active in all the relevant areas, the fact that practical action remains in the hands of national authorities means over-all preparedness is not optimal and that policy remains reactive. Again, this is understandable. Proactive policy-making at EU level would be resented by some national authorities – even those who plead for more coordination. Coordination there is, but it remains at the level of information sharing, whereas an authoritative European locus of policy making and practical action might arguably be more helpful to the overall counter-terrorist endeavour[4], as the EU's counter-terrorism coordinator frequently stressed, though he was unable to get Member States to agree a more substantial policy before his departure in March 2007 (see below). This illustrates the problems arising from a form of cognitive dissonance in national policy-makers; committed rhetorically to action by the EU, they are more often than not constrained by national mindsets. Policy remains national and thus frequently duplicated in practice by different national administrations. Even if national means to thwart attacks are enhanced, there still remains a need to improve the ratio of warnings to effective prevention and it is likely that the necessary information provision and sharing will prove to be optimal for all EU Member States if it occurs at EU level, rather than at individual national level. There was and there remains a need for concerted EU response, but national reticence still arguably slows proactive policy-making.

Meeting the challenges

Yet, on the more positive side, EU commitment to countering terrorism has certainly strengthened over time, not only owing to Europe's own experience in Madrid in 2004 and London in 2005, but also because of the belated realisation that Europeans face a real international terrorist threat against them rather than solely against their American allies. Such realisation helped Europe identify challenges. The devastatingly successful suicide attacks against US embassies in East Africa in 1998 and the *USS Cole* in 2000, added to a list of spectacularly botched attempts, were for US officials clear warnings, long before 9/11, that, in time, one such attempt in the US or in Europe would not be botched, unless heightened vigilance prevented it. History proved them right. But, the US, so went the previous unspoken assumption in Europe, sidled into a 'war on terror' as a result of 'the deep solipsism of US security policy in the 1990s'[5], with which few in Europe could identify. Yet, if America's history of intervention abroad, whether covert or overt, had understandably led to a violent backlash, the blame fell on the West in general. So, the US was clearly not the only target for the new international terrorism and though the close military partners of the US (including Australia in Indonesia) were the first to suffer, the potential threat to all European countries could not be ignored. The backlash was directed against liberal democracy worldwide, as the Dutch and the Danes were graphically to learn. Strange that the realisation was so slow in coming, for the Europeans were formally warned at every troika meeting with the US from the mid-1990s on, and the number of thwarted attacks in Europe surely demonstrated clearly to publics and politicians alike that American warnings were by no means scaremongering.[6]

But creating concerted responses posed clear challenges to policymakers. It questioned the basics of political commitment at European level – not only to the quest for a coherent EU response but also to harmonious relations with its partner, ally and yet rival, the United States. (Fraser Cameron reviews the issues in chapter 6.) And a different challenge lay in the profound questions posed for European integration itself: what was the reality behind the rhetoric of the EU's 'common foreign and security policy'? Was there any content to it, or was it 'procedure as a substitute for policy', as many had argued? Indeed, an existential question was whether 'civilian-power Europe' was the desired end-state of European integration or whether EU states were now ready to endow the EU organisations with the ability to share their monopoly of the use of force, whether at home or abroad.

9/11 and its aftermath were actually to prove a catalyst for three new dimensions of EU governance. First, further integration in some of the most sensitive policy areas of European nation states took place – policies on security, justice and internal affairs evolved fast, as Hans Nilsson and Boin et al demonstrate in chapters 3 and 4. Second, the existing impetus for a European Security and Defence Policy accelerated, forcing the EU to question, if not change, both its self image and its role as an international actor. Finally, the EU was incited to review its institutional relationships with other regional organisations. The by-product of these three dimensions of governance was ever-tighter relations between the EU and the UN.[7] Kim Eling describes in chapter 5 the specific emergence of the EU's pivotal role in focussing the attention of the better-endowed UN nations on ways in which they might assist the creation and consolidation of good security governance in the less well-endowed states. The EU's targeted assistance at the behest of the UN Security Council demonstrated that effectiveness depended not on the Europeans' national capacity but on a comprehensive European approach to international relations with terrorism the prime motivator. The unspoken realisation was the hollowness of the myth of the independent capacity of nation states, which politicians everywhere were reluctant to admit. Nation states of course retained the monopoly on the legitimate use of force at home, but in practical reality national borders and varying national capacity to act tempered the notion that national sovereignty was more than simply a principle of international law. The sovereignty of states had arguably become little more than a legal principle. The EU states had been consciously compromising it in practice for fifty years, and the sovereignty of weak states in the developing world was also being undermined in significant new ways. Their sovereignty came increasingly to be subjugated to a greater good, the 'responsibility to protect' as liberal democracy viewed the sovereignty-based impunity of failed and rogue states as increasingly questionable.[8]

The problem was that if sovereignty might no longer be practically operational or actually desirable, the notion could hardly be jettisoned without full-scale reform of the international system. Here, the stumbling block was that the sovereignty of some failed states was religiously defended by other states whose liberal democratic credentials (China and Russia) were disputable. Efforts by the then UN Secretary-General, Kofi Annan, to review the costs and benefits of the UN system did not change the prerogatives of

UN Security Council members. As it turned out, the idea that the responsibility to protect was a generally acceptable normative and operational principle thus remained compromised in practice, since action in practice focussed on zones where individual states had interests.

The UK Prime Minister, Tony Blair, argued a different case. He had, he said:

> been reaching for a different philosophy in international relations from the traditional one which has held sway since the treaty of Westphalia in 1648; namely, that a country's internal affairs are for it, and you don't interfere unless it threatens you, or breaches a treaty, or triggers an obligation of alliance [though] regime change alone could not be and was not our justification for war [in Iraq]. Our primary purpose was to enforce UN resolutions over Iraq and WMD.[9]

There was however at the EU level no practical sign of a readiness to go beyond rhetoric and move away from the underpinning of the Westphalian system.

Defining the 'new' terrorism?

Al-Qaida had not really invented a 'new' terrorism. Its methods, in the end, hardly differed from old-style terrorism, bar the increase in the terrorists' own suicides and the mass-casualty factor. Yet, international terrorism did pose new challenges. Like previous forms of terrorism, it was as threatening as it was untraceable; but the novelty lay in the absence of specific demands and the fact that its command structure was not hierarchical, or exclusively cell-based, but predicated rather on voluntary emulation by disciples who were often not even specifically recruited – despite the claim of one of Al-Qaida's leaders to the contrary.[10] It was also not open to negotiation in the familiar ways. One could not assume the terrorists were rational in any Western sense of the term. If a key requirement of Al-Qaida was that the West should remove itself from Muslim lands, in particular from Jerusalem and the large Arab states, and that it should suffer for the pain allegedly inflicted on Muslim peoples, these issues were never adumbrated in terms of the bargaining familiar to states threatened by 'traditional' terrorism; no territory liberated from foreign control in exchange for peace and non-violence, no bargaining for release of prisoners, no trade-off between an end to the ban in France on headscarves and a reduction of the terrorist threat. There was no offer of any kind to negotiate on either side, even if there have been indications that a minimum demand would be for 'the West' to leave Saudi Arabia and the Israelis to leave Jerusalem. Neither is likely to happen, and there would in any case likely be a large number of additional requirements. The 'new' terrorism was still about audacity, still about evoking a major 'gasp' response in a public concerned for its own safety, but significantly both the terrorists and their Western opponents perceived the situation as zero-sum – and no acceptable table existed to accommodate negotiators. The 'new' terrorism was not, of course, the first to be 'bargainless'. There had been several cases of bargainless terrorism before. One example was the Aum Shinrikyo sect's attack with Sarin gas on the Tokyo underground in March 1995, preceded by its use of anthrax in the summer of 1993 and biological weapons in 1990 at Tokyo airport and against US bases in Yokohama and Yokusaka.

Though it sounded academic, there were (and remain), problems arising from the absence of a generally accepted definition of terrorism. Attempts to reach one in negotiations at the UN on a comprehensive convention on terrorism have continued to founder, largely because of the reluctance in many countries to accept a definition that would simultaneously legitimise Israeli action in Palestine, while maintaining the rights of 'freedom fighters' to fight. The UK's Terrorism Act defined terrorism as 'the use or threat of serious violence against persons or serious damage to property, designed to influence the government or intimidate the public or a section of the public … for the purpose of advancing a political, religious or ideological cause'. The EU's definition focuses on what terrorist groups do, as opposed to what terrorism is.[11] According to the EU definition, a terrorist group is 'a structured organisation … of more than two persons, acting in concert to commit terrorism offences. The EU's legislation requires that 'each Member State shall take the necessary measures to ensure the following offences, defined according to its national law, which are intentionally committed by an individual or a group against one or more countries, their institutions or people with the aim of intimidating them and seriously altering or destroying the political, economic or social structures of a country, will be punishable terrorist offences'[12] , the latter defined to cover perpetrators of all offences in the UN conventions.

National rhetoric and practice

Embarrassingly, at the end of 2001, as the EU called for universal ratification of all UN conventions against terrorism, not all Member States of the EU had actually ratified them. The EU was in the curious position of advocating ratification to others, while its own house was not quite in order. But, the problem, in any case, is that if a state is not a party to the relevant UN conventions, little really can be done. A threat from non-state actors could not be prevented by all the state-signed conventions in the world. Al-Qaida and other such non-state actors are not, in sum, treaty-bound; they rub their unbound hands in amusement. There has, however, been a clear evolution of European conceptions of security, as Magnus Ekengren sets out in chapter 1, even if there often remains national reticence to draw operational conclusions for European policymaking from the widely recognised irrelevance of classical distinctions between internal and external security.

At first there was apparent readiness at national level to provide a firm and clear response to the challenges of the new 'hyper-terrorism'[13], but declarations cost the EU Member States little. National capacities actually to do something varied according to historical experience with domestic terrorism. Some states had no provision in their criminal legislation explicitly mentioning terrorism. The G8's four European members did, as did Spain and Portugal. The UK's Terrorism Act of 2000 was the largest piece of terrorism legislation in Europe's national arsenals. Some Member States had had little or no experience with terrorism. When the Finns held the presidency in 2002, its foreign ministry representative in the EU's CFSP counter-terrorism committee (COTER) was head of a terrorist section in his capital with a staff of none. His UK counterpart had twenty-five staff before 9/11 and more than eighty some months after. Others, in particular the 'G5' (France, Germany, Italy, Spain and the UK) were ready for a robust national response, both in foreign and domestic policy. Over time, the French hard-line domestic policy was actually to become a model which others both envied and loathed. Despite the fact that the major international attacks occurred in America, Spain and the UK, and that France had carefully dis-tanced itself from the US's most radical interventions, its Interior Minister Nicolas Sarkozy expressed the French fear of the worst. He openly sup-ported and implemented 'offensive harassment' and 'active intolerance' against the potential domestic terrorist threat. Even so, some in other European states began to find the French model attractive as time went by and more terrorist threats emerged.[14] But this was arguably a sideshow to the fight against international terrorism of the Al-Qaida variety, though it would not be the first time that an international threat provided the where-withal, if not the inspiration, for separate and dissociated domestic policy.

In January 2005 the Dutch government allocated 400 million euros to boost its national intelligence service, the AIVD, by 10 percent to more than 1000 staff and increase national and military police services, simultaneously planning a general toughening of the law enforcement environment – a clear response to a new domestic environment created by the madcap and despi-cable killing of a Dutch filmmaker.[15] Likewise, in May 2006 Denmark announced the creation of a new intelligence unit, the Centre for Terror Analysis, an interministerial department inspired by the UK's Joint Terrorism Analysis Centre. Denmark had actually only once been the target of Islamic terrorism, in an attack on an office of North West Orient Airlines in 1985. The (Palestinian) perpetrators had subsequently been found in Sweden and sentenced to life imprisonment in 1989. It was threats arising throughout the world from the 'Danish cartoons' affair of early 2006 that doubtless prompted these measures. In the UK, in May 2007, the Home Office was split in two, with the creation of an Office for Security and Counter-terrorism responsible for anti-terrorism policy, immigration and the security services and a Ministry of Justice with control of probation, pris-ons and prevention of re-offending. In the Sunday Telegraph of 21 January 2007, Home Secretary John Reid was quoted to the effect that there would be 'no sacred cows when it comes to protecting security and administering justice', but whether this meant a more open attitude to the creation or strengthening of EU mechanisms remained a moot point. Importantly, it underlined that one response to the new awareness of the interaction between the external and internal threats should be a separated approach to the two sides of the terrorist coin.

EU rhetoric and practice

Descriptions of EU policy customarily point to the swift EU reaction to 9/11. True, in its immediate response to the September 2001 attacks the EU announced strong political support for the US. It immediately began lobby-ing other governments to accelerate the long overdue ratification of the then twelve (now sixteen) United Nations conventions and protocols on terror-ism, to implement UN Security Council Resolution 1373 on Threats to

International Peace and Security Caused by Terrorist Acts (28 September 2001) and to support the signature of a new comprehensive convention against terrorism. There was also strong Member State support for the military operations in Afghanistan, which began on 7 October 2001, based on Security Council Resolution 1368.[16] Individually, some EU and NATO Member States (but not NATO as such) contributed to the US led 'coalition of the willing' to combat the Al-Qaida network and to end the Taliban regime in Afghanistan. Demonstrating European unity with the US, NATO's article 5 had been invoked on 12 September 2001 and implemented on 2 October once the external nature of the 9/11 terrorism had been demonstrated. But significantly, the Europeans' offer of assistance to the US, initially resisted by the Germans, Norway, Belgium and the Netherlands, but not the French, was regarded by the US as an expression of political and diplomatic solidarity rather than as an important military and operational support.[17] There was token NATO 'backfill' cover of US territory as US forces moved to Afghanistan, but as Deputy Defence Secretary Paul Wolfowitz put it, 'if we need collective action, we will ask for it, but we do not anticipate that at the moment'[18], while another US official commented that the Europeans 'were desperately trying to give us political cover and the Pentagon was resisting it'.[19]

Naturally, the most involved ally, the UK, was able to offer three distinct advantages: British troops were already operative in the region through joint exercises in the Gulf; they benefited from a 'special relationship' with the US, in particular the intelligence-sharing which others (not least the EU organs themselves) coveted; and their military systems had a high degree of interoperability with those of the US.[20] But British national action did not imply EU commitment, just as 'backfill' operations did not imply readiness on the part of the US to involve NATO nations in the serious military operations in Afghanistan and thereby diminish American ability to act without resort to NATO's committees of officials. Did the EU draw the conclusion that EU-NATO relations needed urgent enhancement? NATO's ambassadorial committee, the NAC, claimed that it did. 'NATO and the EU are exploring ways to enhance cooperation to combat terrorism', it claimed.[21] One looks in vain for practical evidence.

The EU did, however, begin to adopt a series of policies flanking the 'hard power' of the US. It set aside increasingly large sums for technical anti-terrorism assistance abroad, security sector reform, WMD operations and peace-building in general – all signs of a form of international 'actorness' which differentiated it from the United States, as Eling records in chapter 5. But European countries could not accept the Bush administration's view that the 'war' on terror included threatening violent action not only against the nebulous and amorphous forces of extremist groups, but also against states on every continent. American admonitions and threats of robust intervention to governments potentially holding weapons of mass destruction did not wash in Europe. President Bush's speech on 1 June 2002, with its announcement of a preventive war doctrine, was coolly welcomed, even if EU declarations and meetings on terrorism meanwhile abounded.

The EU's policy dilemmas

The absence of an EU counter-terrorism strategy before 9/11 is understandable. A succession of treaty changes during the 1990s had left the EU with a Byzantine system of differentiated decision-making. Neither a state nor an international organization, it defied simple definition. As Jacques Delors, former European Commission President, put it, the EU was an 'unidentified political object'.[22] This was reminiscent of Shonfield's characterisation of the EU some thirty years before as a 'journey to an unknown destination'.[23] Some matters directly relevant to the security of the EU's common territory and assets (such as intelligence collection and sharing, and the running of police forces, military and civil defence and disaster response) had remained a purely national responsibility, while matters falling within the collective EU framework could be handled in at least three significantly different procedural contexts.[24]

When it came to practical policy-making, Member States found the European Commission and the EU's first pillar to be the repository of legal competence for most of the necessary flanking policies, and it was EU-US relations, particularly between the Commission and various parts of the US administration, that were to flourish. National politicians and officials were justifiably rueful; national responses might have been simpler in principle, but the problem was that they were inadequate in practice, given the size and cross-border nature of the problem. The historic European Community (EC) – the 'first pillar' – covers those areas where Member States have ceded sovereignty to the Union. In relation to security threats and peace building, the most important areas are those relating to external economic and financial programmes and assistance, and the extensive areas of civil protection, air and sea transport, information security and data protection, described in detail by Boin et al in chapter 4. In the Common Foreign and Security Policy (CFSP) – the 'second pillar' – Member States coordinate their national foreign policies but retain sovereignty over decision making in most areas. There was considerable debate from the Maastricht (1993) through the Amsterdam (1997) to the Nice (2000) treaties surrounding the EU's ability to ensure a European contribution to world security and the instruments it might wield towards that end. Much was achieved on the reach, salience, instruments and procedures of Europe's international policy, but the basic flaws in political will, institutional capacity and the financial instruments available remained a source of stress to the EU's foreign policy system.[25]

Justice and Home Affairs (JHA) activity, now called Justice, Liberty and Security (JLS) – the EU's 'third pillar' – provides the essential internal legal framework for anti-terrorist cooperation, a framework increasingly shifting to first pillar competence, in implementation of frequent political commitments to 'communitarise' the third pillar, i.e. to switch from intergovernmentalism to the supranational 'Community method'. The Commission has a lead role as policy planner and proposer of legislation in the third pillar, including essential legislation to combat organised crime and terrorism within the European Union. This is a complex area of cooperation on sensitive issues surrounding identity, finance and the use of instruments to combat organised crime and terrorism. Member States have been reluctant to agree to policies which risk undermining national legal systems and procedures, fearing the potential for placing their own overall security at stake. States with no specific anti-terrorist legislation welcomed the luxury of European legislation drafted and negotiated in Brussels, thus largely escaping domestic debate and dissension. The Council Framework Decision on Combating Terrorism, introduced immediately after 9/11 by the Commission, was meant to provide a coordinated EU level policy that could fill the national gaps.

As to Europe's second pillar, the CFSP, the EU's intergovernmental coordination of national foreign policy orientations, has seen considerable progress, including the extension of CFSP to ESDP. Yet EU Member States still regard the sensitive areas of foreign, security and defence policy as central to their notion of national sovereignty. They resist the pooling of sovereignty, which characterises the economic and other internal policy areas or foreign trade. They remain particularly allergic to placing any control of the resources devoted to security, or of specific operational decisions, in collective European hands. And this national reticence is compounded by significant differences in foreign policy culture, experience and expectations within Member States.[26] The EU's Member States might be said to resemble 'dodgem cars' at the fun fair – all on the same track but lurching in different directions.[27] Importantly, however, they increasingly abstain from 'lurching' all of the time. Usually, they concert their policies. They coordinate closely in regular meetings of senior diplomats and foreign ministers, prepared by a welter of CFSP working groups or in the framework of regional or functional working groups. The resulting shared objectives and policy tools actually constitute 'European' policy, the result of a 'go-kart' race, rather than 'the dodgems' – still perhaps going round in circles, but all players on the same track and attempting to avoid clashes, rather than seeking or suffering frequent crashes. There is no doubt that the 'dodgem' model was telling in the 1990s. But, after 9/11, notwithstanding policy over Iraq and disputes over the relevance of NATO, this was less the case. Indeed, the speed on the track and the degree of shared purpose in avoiding clashes has clearly increased.

Coordinating policy on terrorism was to prove a catalyst for generally increased EU foreign policy capability. The threat of the 'new' terrorism contributed to the strengthening of ESDP, engendering the EU Security Strategy (ESS), prepared by the High Representative for CFSP, Javier Solana, and adopted by the European Council in December 2003.[28] The ESS was the key structuring innovation in the evolution of ESDP. It identified terrorism as a key threat to the European Union and a prime field for action. It linked terrorism to other key threats, including state failure, regional conflicts, proliferation of WMD and organised crime. Thirty months after 9/11 came the Madrid attacks in March 2004, which also spurred the EU and its Member States to further accelerate development of ESDP to encompass the fight against terrorism. The conceptual framework adopted by the European Council in November 2004 (see annex 5) stressed four main areas where ESDP could provide a European contribution: prevention, protection, consequence management and support to third countries. Significantly, of course, while CFSP and ESDP set this overall framework, it is important to register that they were not the sole repositories of policy-making competence with regard to terrorism. As Eling, Dittrich and Boin et al describe in detail in chapters 2, 4 and 5, and as mentioned above, the European Community pillar provided the main policy toolbox, a fact that was a bone of inter-bureaucratic contention within the EU institutions and to which this introductory chapter returns below.

CFSP had had a difficult first decade after its introduction in 1993, but had begun rapid institutional development after the Treaty of Amsterdam and the 13 November 1999 decision of the WEU Ministerial Council to transfer its crisis management functions to the European Union. It was thus significant that the increasing practical operations in the security field were given strategic underpinning with the European Security Strategy. In the ESS, unlike in the American security strategy which place greater weight on the military dimension of the fight against terrorism, the emphasis was on conflict prevention rather than preventive military engagement. In any case, it was too early for the EU to undertake major military operations. NATO remained in the lead in the Balkans with air operations against the Milosevic regime, operation Essential Harvest for collecting arms from Albanian fighters in Macedonia and operation Amber Fox for protecting election monitors there. But, as EU foreign policy making developments moved ever faster, probably owing to 9/11, its military operations were not totally inspired by the threat of terrorism. International humanitarian concerns provided the formal justification for proactive policy. Nevertheless, the reigning terrorism-inspired permissive consensus for EU action abroad doubtless led to creative and pro-active policy making.[29] The EU's stance in foreign affairs was hardly contested by public opinion, which seemed more ready to accept concerted EU action abroad than it was to accept it at home. Slowly the deployment of new police and military crisis-management instruments changed the nature of the EU as an international actor.[30]

Thus, if the threat of terrorism was not the prime cause, it so changed the international security environment, that there was clearly a demand for more 'Europe' in international security affairs. By 2006, the European Union was conducting simultaneously 10 operations with around 10,000 men and women serving in them. The global reach and scope of these different operations were striking. They covered three continents and stretched from 'pure' military operations, through security-sector reform and institution building to police and rule of law missions. Their impact was significant. From Aceh to Rafah, and from Kinshasa to Sarajevo, the EU provided support for peace and stability, with 2007 witnessing two new major missions in Kosovo and Afghanistan. The policy context for these developments was the fillip to EU security governance after 9/11 created by the debate on security in the 2002-2003 European Convention and the consequent Draft European Constitution, in which the security field, ESDP, was set to expand apace.

The overriding issue was how each of the three EU pillars could tackle the relevant internal and external aspects of security; in practice whether and how a single decision-making centre in the EU under stronger and more consistent leadership could wield the appropriate instruments in each of the pillars. The EU's mission in the world was at stake. The 9/11 attacks had proved a reminder that external enemies could strike from within, that even the richest and most peaceful 'homelands' were not immune, and that defence could not be achieved with the classic, state-level tools of security alone. Though there is clearly not a simple, causal link, there is no doubt that the post 9/11 political context proved to be not only a permissive environment for the emergence of a European foreign minister post and the smartening up of the EU's external and internal security 'act'. The draft constitution also set out new parameters for European integration to accelerate, including a significant 'solidarity clause' providing for a joint response to threats against individual Member States, which, while not specifying the tools to be used in 'solidarity' clearly echoed article V of the North Atlantic Treaty.

The expansion from CFSP to ESDP posed many other issues of principle. What, for example, was the value of the theoretical monopoly of the legitimate use of force at nation-state level, when the threat came from outside and then from non-state actors? And how could the billiard-ball model of international relations fit into a context where the threat from abroad was not from another state, but from what became known as the swamp of terrorist groups – a swamp in need of clearance, but which was geographically hard to pinpoint? And what was the nature of the increasing foreign policy coordination? The fact was that the big EU players were attempting to make the running for the others, if not going it alone. Indeed, the image that remained in the public mind was the farcical emergency prime ministers' dinner in London following 9/11. It was not a formal EU meeting. Indeed it was one to which most European prime ministers were not invited, though the High Representative for the CFSP was; others were seemingly self-invited and had to scramble for a seat at the table.[31] The fear was clearly that absence from the core policy-making group would relegate states to permanent follower status, and this posed the perhaps obvious question of whether this was a trend that was to become the norm.

Practical response – EU measures and cross-pillar plans

In preparing policy responses to 9/11, the EU faced the challenge of bringing together a wide array of possible instruments from the three pillars. This was no mean task, for all the policy-making centres involved also do other things and have conflicting priorities. EU activities were reviewed in each field in a succession of Council meetings involving foreign, interior, finance, transport, environment and telecommunications ministers. The resulting action to combat terrorism, both domestically and abroad, extended across a very broad spectrum, underlining the multifaceted nature both of the security threat itself and of the EU's arsenal of relevant policies. The main lines of action were broken down into a series of measures addressing cooperation within the EU and relations between the EU and other countries, including tracking, detaining and prosecuting terrorists; denying terrorists financial and material resources; encouraging, supporting and technically assisting third countries in tackling terrorism; and addressing the social and political resources drawn on by terrorist and criminal networks.

On the external policy side there was:

–   implementation of UN Security Council Resolution 1373 targeting through EU external funding priority third countries where counter-terrorist capacity or commitment to combating terrorism needed to be enhanced;

- enhanced bilateral cooperation with the United States and Canada, including the appointment of liaison officers to the EU from both countries and mutual visits between Eurojust and Canada and the USA;

- signature by Europol of a Strategic Cooperation Agreement with the United States on 4 December 2001 and a further specific agreement on 20 December 2002 allowing for the transfer of personal data;

- introduction of anti-terrorism clauses in agreements with third countries;

- an international policy on weapons of mass destruction and creation of a personal representative of the EU High Representative for CFSP, Javier Solana;

- a centralised system of information exchange;

- enhanced cooperation between Member States on a common list of international terrorist organisations;

- strengthened external border checks;

- exchange of information on visas;

- freezing of international terrorists' property and reducing the access of terrorists to financial resources through an EU strategy on the suppression of terrorist financing;

- protecting the security of international transport;

- identifying international factors contributing to recruitment to terrorism, both within the EU and abroad, and developing a long-term strategy to address them.

Internally, there was:

- agreement on a common definition of terrorist offences for criminal law purposes;

- stepping up mutual assistance between police and justice authorities in the Member States and provision for improved joint investigation between national police forces, strengthened cooperation between anti-terrorist units and the creation of an anti-terrorism unit within Europol[32];

- the creation of coordinated judicial agencies (Eurojust);

- improving the Schengen Information System (SIS) by giving the intelligence services access to parts of its data and simplifying procedures to improve use of the SIS in the fight against terrorism;

- agreement and legislation on a European Arrest Warrant (formally adopted on 27 December 2001[33]), dispensing with traditional extradition procedures and expediting the arrest and transfer of suspects;

- improved cooperation between judiciary and prosecutors' offices;

–   coordination of critical infrastructure protection at EU level;

–   enhancing the capacity of Member States to deal with the conse-
    quences of a terrorist attack;

–   measures combating bio-terrorism.

All these policy areas were grouped together in the form of a 'living document', the EU Action Plan to combat terrorism. The EU's first pillar in fact
covered the bulk of the counter-terrorist policy areas detailed in the succession of action plans and roadmaps which provide the milestones in six years
of concentrated anti-terrorist activity after September 2001.[34] In some cases,
as Nilsson describes in chapter 3, such as the European Arrest Warrant,
preparatory work to propose an EU policy had been done by the
Commission prior to 9/11. It had been a question of waiting for the time to
be politically ripe for a formal legislative proposal to be made. Thus, seeds
of further integration had already been sown, though the work was accelerated and repackaged in the weeks following the attacks. Later, it became
clear that some Member States were guilty of inadequate implementation
into national law, a weakness of 'decisions' as opposed to Community regulations, which become law without national redrafting, but were currently
impossible in the justice and home affairs framework. Indeed, eleven
Member States made errors of transposition and the German Constitutional
Court, for example, turned down a Spanish request in July 2005 on the
grounds that the legal base for a specific extradition was flawed.

The Commission proposed a register and database of persons, groups
and entities providing full information, including on convictions, and a
Council Decision aimed at broadening the exchanges of information on convictions for terrorist offences and cooperation between Member States,
Europol and Eurojust. Work in the Forum on Organised Crime Prevention
was undertaken in partnership with the private sector and in liaison with
Europol, the EU's police office, which was to receive extra powers to tackle
cross-border crime and team up with national forces on investigations.
Europol had been established in 1999. Based in The Hague, it had a budget
of 63.4 million euros by 2006 and a staff of more than 500. Its mandate was
to enhance cooperation between national police forces in counter-terrorism,
drugs and counterfeiting and provide analysis, technical support, and
exchange of information. Its powers are arguably too limited. In December
2006 the Commission therefore proposed an extension of Europol's remit to
cover all serious crimes affecting two or more Member States and enabling
it to take part in joint investigations. Until then, Europol had only been able
to tackle cases where it was proven from the start that an organised crime
group was involved. Under the Commission's proposals, EU officials would
support and assist, but not arrest suspects. Europol would be allowed to
create more databases to share information between police across the EU on
issues such as monitoring militant Islamist web sites. The proposal was also
to turn Europol into an EU agency financed by the EU budget instead of by
Member State contributions. Most of these proposed changes are actually
part of existing, but largely unratified protocols or in the draft European
Constitution[35], but the Commission's view was that it was vital to adapt
Europol's structure and mandate to the new challenges of terrorism and
serious cross-border criminality.

Improvement of the Schengen Information System (SIS) has included improved access for Eurojust, Europol and Member States' security services to the SIS, improved search capability on the basis of incomplete data, access to vehicle registration records and extended access to the files of authorities which issue residence permits. To block the international movement of the guilty and facilitate their arrest, and to stem illegal immigration, an EU Border Agency (FRONTEX) was established. There was agreement to include bio-metric identifiers in EU travel documents and visas granted to non-EU nationals. In addition, the EU created a Visa Information System (VIS) to check visa applications against terrorism watch lists, which pleased the US authorities no end.[36] For some Member States this did not go far enough. The Treaty of Prüm (Schengen III), signed on 27 May 2005, was one result.[37] This further increased cross border cooperation on terrorism, organised crime and illegal immigration and was the forerunner of a Commission proposal to do the same throughout the EU.[38]

By late 2003 US demands on countries enjoying visa-free access for their citizens to the USA to introduce machine-readable passports with bio-data had been causing practical problems for many European governments. Ironically, the US extended the deadline for its bio-metric passport requirement on more than one occasion. Thirteen European countries, making up about 80 percent of all overseas visa waivers and two-thirds of all visa waiver travellers, would have missed the proposed deadlines and the US's own passports actually did not yet meet the standards required of other visa waiver states. Another issue was air transport protection. US proposals to place armed air marshals on flights and to transfer large quantities of personal data on passengers for US intelligence screening were seen by many as objectionable.

Leadership, inter-pillar coordination and integrated intelligence: the EU Counter-Terrorism Coordinator

Strong police and intelligence coordination was in its infancy in the EU at the time of 9/11, just as the European Security and Defence Policy was still young. It had been established barely a year before 9/11. Javier Solana's passage from Secretary General of NATO to Secretary General of the EU Council of Ministers and the Franco-British initiative at St. Malo had taken place just four years before. But, the opening of intra-European borders, global markets and global communications had facilitated the movement of people and goods internally, and one of the many dilemmas facing an effective EU response to terrorism was that terrorists were able to profit from the same rights to freedom of movement and establishment as the EU's citizens themselves. So, in a sense, the EU was half a domestic polity, providing rights but not providing for obligations and not creating automatic control by civil authorities of the misuse of these rights. Likewise, Europe's new-found role as an international security actor implied a concomitant need for Europe to improve security and intelligence coordination. But national decision-makers did not yet perceive this need. After 9/11 the need for coordination was felt both within the EU organisations, between the EU and Member States and between the EU and third countries, especially the US.[39] The EU also required a clear strategy and respected leadership, able to make sense of the myriad potential policy inputs and to communicate purpose to governments, the EU institutions and citizens. But all these 'needs' involved areas where governments remained sensitive; where they were reticent to see power seep away to the EU by default. There are four parts of the EU which might have a claim to be the embryo of a European intelligence service: the Joint Situation Centre (SITCEN), the Intelligence Division of the European Military Staff (INTDIV), the European Union Satellite Centre (EUSC) and Europol. Despite their potential to provide intelligence, only lip service is paid to the potential role of the 130 European Commission Delegations outside the EU and the numerous crisis mechanisms and early warning centres within the Commission.[40]

A first step towards improving intelligence sharing was taken with the agreement to expand the Joint Situation Centre within the Council Secretariat. The objective was for the Union to develop integrated analysis of the terrorist threat by bringing together experts from both the intelligence and security services, and from both outside and inside the EU. The move was not without debate about where the locus of intelligence gathering should be placed. The UK led other Member States in believing that EU activity should be based on the principle of its being a support to Member States, rather than a question of approaching the issue of international terrorism at what for others might be the 'appropriate' international level. As a UK minister responsible for terrorism affairs put it:

> we do want increased cooperation, information-sharing and we want to make ourselves as effective as we can be in fighting the terrorist threat … what we do not want is the origination of intelligence at European Union level … we have to be careful to avoid European wide institutions wanting to create something fresh that comes simply from a European perspective rather than necessarily a bringing together of the information, skills and expertise that Member States have to offer.[41]

This view prompts doubts as to whether the SITCEN could ever represent an efficient pooling of intelligence. EU 'intelligence' may, in the end, be simply limited to upgrading the minimal intelligence available to some Member States (Austria, Belgium, Greece, Ireland etc.), while those with sophisticated national intelligence gathering (and contacts with American intelligence agencies), such as the G5 (France, Germany, Italy, Spain, UK – all bar Spain G8 members, and all with long histories of domestic terrorism) fight shy of genuine intelligence sharing across all members of the EU. There were several alternative proposals. At the European Council of 19 February 2004, an Austrian-inspired, Belgian-supported project for a European Intelligence Agency (EIA) was floated – but nipped immediately in the bud. After the Madrid attacks of 11 March, which left 191 victims dead, the EIA idea was revived, only to receive another stake through the heart, while G5 states in fact met separately at the headquarters of the General Commissioner for Information in Spain.[42] Meanwhile, the much canvassed cooperation between law enforcement agencies remained outside formal EU structures in the so-called Berne Group, originally created in 1968, and of which the anti-terrorist working group became, in 2004, a forum for contacts between national intelligence services. Europol also made regular reports to EU justice ministers on the work of its own counter-terrorism task force and its European network for the protection of public figures set up by the Council in November 2002. The European Police Chiefs Task Force, though demonstrating 'dedication and enthusiasm'[43], was hampered by lack of access to the relevant third pillar working group, the Article 36 Committee, until it was gradually granted in 2004. As a senior UK civil servant put it, 'if we are going to have a comprehensive EU approach, there comes a time when there has to be some linkage with the formal structures. Maybe it is simply a process of evolution that has brought us to this point'.[44] This was almost four years after 9/11. By 2007, however, as intelligence services began to fear a wave of Al-Qaida attacks in Europe, the first meeting of the 'international network of anti-terrorist magistrates' was held in Paris on 8 March, gathering around fifty senior magistrates from nine countries. The aim was to accelerate international cooperation. Senior judges such as Jean-Louis Bruguière of France and Baltasar Garzon of Spain participated. The meeting also brought together representatives from Indonesia and Morocco in addition to France, Germany, Belgium, Spain, the Netherlands, the United Kingdom and the United States. This 'Paris Group' was set to become a light and permanent structure for discussion of counter-terrorism problems, but it was outside the EU institutional framework.

Notwithstanding these various endeavours, the 19 February 2004 European Council had tasked Solana with a report on intelligence capacity. The terrorist attack in Spain took place the following month. Solana's proposal was to increase intelligence sharing among national security services and to expand the role of the EU Situation Centre. Some Member States had called for the EU to create a European FBI or CIA to boost intelligence sharing, but Solana's idea was to enhance existing cooperation rather than create new EU bodies, though he did propose the appointment of a special representative for terrorism. Formally, this idea was first invoked in a SITCEN think piece presented three days before the Madrid bombing in which Solana stressed the lack of EU efficiency in the overall response to terrorism and lamented the low level of implementation of European agreements on, for example, the creation of investigatory teams in cooperation with Europol or the coordination problems between the many European actors and instruments. Solana pointedly underlined that specific first pillar areas were also in need of enhanced cooperation, such as transport. This justified a cross pillar approach under a counter-terrorism coordinator – clearly necessary, but since it was apparent that what was meant was an appointment outside the Commission framework, it was welcomed neither in the relevant Commission services nor by Commissioner Vitorino and his successor Frattini.

What was needed was an individual with vision, a broad strategic view, knowledge of the intricacies of the EU's three pillar system and the ability to engage the support of all governments, gain the respect of their civil servants and those of the EU institutions and a readiness to collaborate with those parts of the private sector where the security of infrastructure was already routine. The danger was the appointment of an individual with none or only some of these characteristics, for it was clear that respect from the constituencies involved would be key to the success of the coordination operation itself. This, in turn, would provide a sound basis for policy advocacy and successful negotiation across the pillars and abroad for the inclusion of EU objectives in agreements with other states and international organisations. Solana initially envisaged that the post would go to a civil servant, but finally chose a personality with more political profile. In a letter to the Irish EU presidency, Solana said he expected the coordinator to take action in three main areas: to present proposals aimed at better organising and streamlining the work of the EU secretariat on the fight against terrorism, to prepare proposals for better EU coordination between EU councils of ministers and their preparatory bodies, and to maintain regular contacts with Member States so as to ensure coordination between EU and national action. Dutch politician, Gijs de Vries, a former deputy interior minister, was appointed the EU's first counter-terrorism coordinator[45], a job described by a British Minister as 'an awesome task'.[46] The priority was to 'chase, drive and really push' the EU Action Plan, which the Commission incidentally believed was already doing tolerably well. De Vries' appointment came a full two and a half years after 9/11. His task became one of monitoring and reporting on EU action against terrorism in areas ranging from intergovernmental matters, such as intelligence cooperation, to first pillar concerns such as border security and the fight against the financing of terrorism. The Commission had been cautious about the idea of a special representative for terrorism and had not advocated the appointment of a terrorism coordinator, whether in the Commission or outside. Some of the Commission's senior staff were keen on a higher profile, but caution was the leitmotiv. It exemplified familiar modesty in the CFSP area under Commissioner Patten, who later stated that:

> some of my staff... would have preferred me to have made a grab for foreign policy, trying to bring as much of it as possible into the orbit of the Commission. This always seemed to me to be wrong in principle and likely to be counterproductive in practice. Foreign policy should not in my view... be treated on a par with the single market. It is inherently different.[47]

That may be true, but as far as terrorism was concerned, the pertinent issue was whether an anti-terrorism strategy was actually 'foreign' policy or not. After all, the policy instruments lay in the first pillar and it was only after 2004 that CFSP/ESDP began to carve out a role in the area. By that time there was a growing perception in the Commission that the Council Secretariat was continually proposing structures and policies which tended to put the first and third pillars at the service of the second, by locating policy initiative and coordination within the Council Secretariat and Solana's Policy Unit. So, a chance had clearly been missed by the Commission to put political responsibility where the anti-terrorism toolbox actually resided, just as a chance had been missed earlier to establish a workable cross-pillar structure, headed by a personality fulfilling the criteria for success mentioned above.

De Vries resigned in March 2007. He had not had an easy time. In the absence of the mooted Constitution's fusion of the external policy making structures, there exists the curious situation whereby the terrorism coordinator is the public face of EU counter-terrorism measures, plans and attends high-level meetings with foreign governments and monitors progress on the EU's action plan, but has no right to propose legislation, which is a

Commission prerogative. De Vries could also not oblige governments to act. He even had no express right to call an emergency meeting of Justice Ministers – a task incumbent on the Presidency of the day. Since the High Representative's role as per the Amsterdam Treaty of 1997 is to 'assist' the Presidency, such, normally, would be the role of his personal representative, so this should not be surprising. Yet it clearly reduced the potential to lead and strengthen concerted EU action.

Nevertheless, it would be wrong to assume that there was and is no concerted action. There has been notable progress. There now exist EU strategies on terrorism and on radicalisation and recruitment, for example, though how much these new policy areas can be attributed to the terrorism coordinator or to presidencies and the relevant Commissioners and their staff is a moot point. De Vries stated that his retirement from the job had nothing to do with a report by the European Parliament, which criticised both his reticence to give evidence concerning the complicity of some EU governments in illegal CIA activities in Europe and the general lack of transparency surrounding his functions.[48] His colleague responsible for WMD, Annalisa Giannella, was clearly more successful in raising the profile of her post and expanding both her staff and competence. The scope and cross pillar nature of De Vries' post was perhaps more of a political challenge than the specific task of WMD coordination, for terrorism cut across many policy areas jealously guarded by Member States or the Commission. It is also worth considering that Giannella was an official and an astute insider. She knew the Machiavellian institutional game well. De Vries, on the other hand, was parachuted into his post with no experience of the zero-sum game for competence played out within the EU institutions and between them and Member States. These deficiencies might not have been so important had the Constitution been ratified and had Solana and his personal representatives entered the Commission, dual-hatted as Member States had intended and thus able to command the support of the various contributing policy-making bodies. In short, a truly strategic approach to the fight against terrorism required a different power base, different structures and better-positioned leadership. In addition, the EU's contribution to the fight against terrorism, while considerable, was nonetheless hampered by the vacillations of changing presidencies, the three pillar system and rival centres of power within the EU. As the advocates of the Constitution argued, all these features stymie effective leadership across the board, not least in counter-terrorism, where dispersion of effort is tantamount to abdication of responsibility.

US pressure and the European permissive context

The US's forceful reactions after 9/11 put pressure on the EU to demonstrate its own seriousness and efficiency, not just in tackling the new mass-impact terrorism, but in contributing to global security.[49] This was not so straightforward as it might seem. European states had clear and outspoken differences of view with the US. Whether it was threat analysis, operational priorities, or even basic attitudes to human rights and other values, there were different perceptions, perhaps hitherto discreetly ignored but now firmly on the policy agenda, as Cameron details in chapter 6. While policy rapprochement was the requirement and the stated desire on both sides, its achievement was not a foregone conclusion. Indeed, the American decision in 2003 to launch military action against Iraq exposed the EU to its most painful political split for many years, for it took place without a UN mandate and with an embarrassingly limited coalition of partners. When Germany's Chancellor Schröder argued that attacking Iraq might 'destroy the international coalition against terrorism', he was perhaps exaggerating, yet the gradual defection of Europeans' support for American action in Iraq and the quagmire the US found itself in by 2007, showed that his intuition was largely correct.

Some Europeans ('old' Europe, as Defence Secretary Rumsfeld put it) based their policy on insights and historical experience. They were openly unhappy with policy without forethought for the long-term implications.[50] The resulting split within the transatlantic alliance never fully mended. In 2007, politics in France, the leader of Western resistance to US policy, was dominated by preparations to change its president, but its policy stance on Iraq was not an issue. In addition, the French drew the lesson from 9/11 that EU capacity for crisis operations, rather than NATO's, should be strengthened. The diverse responses to 9/11 were thus a pointer to profound divergences of view over transatlantic cooperation, not least in the NATO framework, and contributed to the strengthening of an independent ESDP and a weakening of NATO. Indeed, an increasingly held view in diplomatic circles was that:

> by declaring a situation of collective defence and failing to follow up, I fear that we (NATO) may have undermined Article 5 forever; and therefore, I think that NATO has suffered as an alliance.[51]

The Euro-Atlantic rift was thus profound. American academics and think tanks regaled public opinion with the idea that the Europeans (apart from the British and a few rather insignificant allies of the US) were softies, that 'Europeans were from Venus' as one American put it, while 'Americans were from Mars'.[52] As for European views on US policy, the most significant criticism of US policy was that it totally misjudged European declarations of solidarity after 9/11. Sympathy was not empathy, and continued European support for the 'war' on terrorism was not the foregone conclusion the Bush administration perhaps took it to be in the autumn of 2001.

Despite the fact that some European states were also the objects of hatred and armed defiance, as evidenced both by the number of foiled attempts and by the successful attacks in Madrid and London, most Europeans did not support the idea of war against potential developers of weapons of mass destruction. And in those countries where governments decided on such action, public opposition grew rapidly, as it also became increasingly clear that states cooperating with the US were now at risk by association with and support for US action. This compounded alleged historical complacency before – if not direct responsibility for – the social and economic tribulations of the Islamic world. There was perhaps 'a gap between the self-image of standing firm for liberty, democracy, international law and peace, while conducting policies characterised by inconsistency on free trade, the support of tyrants, economic imperialism, playing fast and loose with international law and, when necessary, being ready, willing and able to use violence'.[53]

The issue areas for the EU thus became twofold: what should Europe do differently to tackle terrorism and related challenges in its own interests; and if, where and when should it take a stand in relation to the USA. Whatever the school of opinion, European politicians came to believe that the only way forward was to be clearer about Europe's own security philosophy and policy, as well as a great deal more effective in pursuing it. This political response broadly reflected public opinion across Europe. The perception had largely been that 'old-style' terrorism remained the threat in most European states. Since 1996 surveys had shown a slow but steady increase in feelings of insecurity across the EU until, after 9/11, for most Europeans maintaining peace and security, combating terrorism, and fighting organised crime and drug trafficking were priorities close in order of importance to tackling unemployment and poverty.[54] A survey of EU and US opinion in the autumn of 2002 showed little difference between British, French, German, Italian and US respondents when it came to their concern about the possibility of terrorist attacks in their countries.[55] If, by Spring 2006, priorities seemed to have changed, and the European public appeared disabused with American policy, the permissive environment for anti-terrorism measures in the crucial post 9/11 period still existed. Eurobarometer reported on the one hand that the prime concern was now unemployment for around 49 percent of the population, while crime, the economic situation and healthcare were deemed most important by 18-23 percent. Terrorism worries equalled worries about diminishing pensions, a priority for only 10 percent of respondents.[56] Yet, at the same time, 80 percent of respondents separately supported expanded EU decision-making for 'the fight against terrorism'.[57]

Thus, seemingly, the permissive context for enhanced counter-terrorism measures remained, but there was undoubtedly increased public concern about the costs of counter-terrorism measures in foregone rights and liberties. An EU-US Passengers Data Agreement with the US had been reached after eighteen months of haggling and a good deal of US pressure (fines and loss of landing rights) in December 2003, but it was much debated, both within the Commission and in the European Parliament, where it was rejected in March 2004. The Parliament objected both to not being consulted on the agreement and to the extent of the information to be transmitted, which covered 34 categories of information about flights originating in the EU, including the transfer of names, credit card details and telephone numbers of travellers to the US. This may have been deemed vital for counter-terrorism, but it was anathema to human rights activists. The issue ended in the European Court with a decision nullifying the agreement in May 2006, to which Member States responded by adopting the agreement again, this time as a security measure. It had after all been agreed by the governments of the Member States and the US, and it had been found illegal by the Court on the grounds of its emanating from a wrongly selected legal base. The Court ruled that because information in passenger records is collected by airlines for their own commercial use, the EU could not legally agree to provision of the data to American authorities for public security purposes. Predictably, discussions from October 2006 between the EU and the US proved difficult. They presaged long EU negotiations on a new EU/US agreement planned for mid-2007.

Other measures introduced as part of overall EU/US policy included the blocking of the international movement of suspects. Reconciling this with the protection of the innocent proved complex and problematic. And on aviation security, the EU had no trouble in backing initial US pressure for better baggage security and passenger screening.[58] Yet, when airlines were hit by rocketing insurance premiums and sought help, effectively in the form of reinsurance from national governments, the European Commission was exercised by the need for such support to be time-limited, minimalist and devoid of hidden subsidies. The Commission had also to ensure that European airlines fearful they would be driven to the point of closure by their losses were not improperly bailed out. Competition and state aids policy were thus involved. The cross-pillar implications of seemingly sensible security measures were thus considerably complicated.

Consequences, crises and the threat of mass destruction

Managing the consequences of terrorist attacks potentially concerns a large number of Community programmes, originally created for maintenance and restoration of vital services in situations of crisis affecting the EU itself – in the transport and energy sector, security of supplies, energy reserves, the use of civilian and military airspace or the European Global Positioning System (GPS) and the GALILEO satellite system.[59] In these sectors, and even more so in the information-technology (IT) sector, the issue of protection of critical infrastructure such as telecommunications and the Internet have received increasing attention.[60] The European Commission's proposal for a European Critical Infrastructure Warning Information Network was a first step in the preparatory work to establishing a European Programme for Critical Infrastructure Protection.[61] It was a key strategy document, following former Commissioner and French foreign minister Barnier's 2006 report on intervention in crises outside the EU.[62] They are both discussed in chapter 4. Member States need to strengthen the identification, control and interception of illegal trafficking in WMD materials, including their support for international initiatives aimed at disrupting WMD networks, the interception of illegal WMD shipments and measures to enhance controls of WMD related material in the EU, including the transit and transhipment of sensitive materials. This involves common policies related to criminal sanctions for illegal export, brokering and smuggling of such material[63], not to mention investigating the rumours of 'lost' small nuclear devices.[64] These issues, in turn, assume basic policies are in place on detection, traceability and control of weapons accessible to terrorists such as explosives, detonators and radioactive sources including precursors, implying new and upgraded databases and use of advanced technologies such as satellite (GALILEO) and enhanced Radio Frequency Identification Device (RFID).

Following the adoption of an EU WMD strategy in 2003 to combat state and non-state proliferation, a centre for WMD monitoring and enhancement of consistent implementation of the WMD strategy was created early in 2007 in the Council Secretariat under the authority of Solana's special representative for WMD, a post also created in 2003. Annalisa Giannella, who holds the post, is responsible for coordinating input on the EU's WMD strategy and endeavours to provide a European response to UN Security Council Resolution 1540 on measures to combat nuclear terrorism, though much of the initial spadework was done in the Commission's DG for External Relations.[65] Considerable sums of EU money have been committed in the G8's 'ten plus ten over ten' initiative, whereby the Europeans were to donate ten billion dollars to match the US ten billion over a ten year period. This initiative was established as an Action Plan at the G8 summit in Kananaskis on 27 June 2002 to facilitate the dismantling of former Soviet WMD installations and retrain otherwise unemployed scientists. Because of their relative poverty, they were deemed at risk of accepting offers from terrorist high bidders for their scientific services.

Finally, in the field of bio-terrorism, as discussed in Chapter 4, the Commission has maintained that tackling bio-terrorism requires specific health security measures. Health and security communities were seemingly not communicating as efficiently as they might. The Commission argued that the EU and Member States should accelerate the implementation of a Health Security Strategy addressing in particular the adoption of a general EU Emergency Preparedness Plan, joint emergency planning and response exercises, an agreed risk incidence classification scale, and most crucially, ensuring the mutual availability of adequate stocks of medicines and vaccines. A European Centre for Disease Prevention and Control (ECDC) was established in 2005 and now prioritises the coordination of efforts to improve surveillance, notification, response, assistance, communication and laboratory capacity on health security matters.

Addressing the financial and material resources of terrorism

As the world's largest trading partner and development assistance donor, the European Union helps other governments tackle organised crime and terrorism – and is prepared to withdraw assistance from governments which refuse to do so. It spends around €400 million in targeted assistance programmes to reinforce UN objectives and uses its leverage in trade and cooperation with third countries by linking this to implementation of standards for cooperation on terrorism, human rights and non-proliferation. Conditionality was underlined by the agreement reached in 2002 at the Seville European Council on the inclusion of an 'EU counter-terrorism clause' in the Association and Co-operation Agreements between the EU and other states and reinforced in the European Declaration on Combating Terrorism of 25 March 2004. The clause has been included in a number of agreements concluded since then.[66] It provides for cooperation in preventing and repressing terrorist acts, as required by UN Security Council resolution 1373, and on sharing information and expertise. A clear weakness, however, is that the anti-terrorism clause is technically regarded as 'non-essential', meaning that it dos not necessarily lead to suspension of agreements and its application is further limited in that it only covers recognition of international conventions to which the signatory states are party and for which they have actually implemented legislation and corresponding regulations. This standard clause commits parties to:

agree to cooperate in the prevention and suppression of terrorist acts ...
in particular in the framework of the full implementation of Resolution
1373 of the UN Security Council and other relevant UN resolutions,
international conventions and instruments ... by exchange of information on terrorist groups, their support networks in accordance with
international and national law and by exchanges of views on means
and methods used to counter terrorism, including in technical fields
and training, and by exchange of experiences in respect of terrorism
prevention.[67]

The European Union accounts for 40 percent of world gross domestic
product and a high proportion of global financial transactions. The freezing
of funds or other financial assets and economic resources of those involved
in terrorism is thus key. Several legal instruments had been adopted in the
wake of 9/11 under Title V of the TEU. But, the lists of terrorist organisa-
tions/assets needed to become operational and reactive on a 'real time' basis
and they needed to be streamlined. The Commission advocated the establishment of a new coordination mechanism for the exchange of information
– a clearing house mechanism – where law enforcement, judicial authorities
and intelligence services would meet to enhance mutual trust and exchange
operational intelligence enabling each to perform its duty properly. Europol
and Eurojust became fully involved, together with national intelligence and
law enforcement networks. Priorities cover recruitment to terrorist organisations, identification of sleeping cells, their financial powerbases in civil
society and their external connections. Thus tighter controls on transactions
are now contributing significantly to restriction of the financial resources of
terrorism. Suspect bank accounts totalling some hundreds of millions of
euros have been frozen.[68]

As Eling describes in chapter 5, the EU supports United Nations guidelines[69] and supervises implementation of the 2001 Financial Action Task
Force on Money Laundering (FATF) of the Organisation for Economic Cooperation and Development (OECD). The latter's remit was extended in
2001 beyond money laundering to include measures against terrorist financing. The eight FATF special recommendations required governments to
ratify and implement UN instruments, criminalise the financing of terrorism
and associated money laundering, freeze and confiscate terrorist assets,
report suspicious transactions, assist third countries with implementation,
and review and upgrade domestic legislation in certain areas.[70] The
Commission ensures ratification and implementation of all relevant UN
instruments and decisions and the FATF recommendations by EU members,
and there has been significant progress, not only towards implementing
decisions of the United Nations and the FATF, but also in corresponding
measures at the EU level. The November 2001 EU Directive on Money
Laundering was upgraded to include terrorist acts, and a regulation regarding the freezing of funds of terrorist organizations was also adopted in
December 2001.[71] On 28 February 2002 the Justice and Home Affairs Council
reached a common understanding on the draft Framework Decision on the
execution in the European Union of orders on the freezing of property or
evidence. The purpose was to establish the rules under which a Member
State was to recognize and execute in its territory a freezing order issued by

a judicial authority of another Member State. A special committee was set up to review policy at frequent intervals.

Conclusion: security and terrorism as catalysts in the integration process

A common theme of the European response to terrorism has been the need to tackle the 'sources of terrorism' as well as terrorism itself. Terrorist networks have deep roots in weak states and draw social and political capital from societies where there is unresolved conflict, social upheaval or economic stagnation. In addition, there are sources of terrorism that are internal to the EU, such as the radicalisation of a section of the Muslim community. As Dittrich shows in chapter 2, terrorism has widened its recruitment base and solidified its hallmark method of attacking large numbers of vulnerable citizens. In demonstrating its disregard for justice and fairness it has wittingly provoked the unfortunate signs of a backlash against Islam itself and against the 15 to 20 million peaceful Muslims living in Europe today, a figure that has grown rapidly from a base of only 800,000 in 1950. Foreseeing the threats and providing security demand a coherent approach to the internal and external ramifications of identifying these sources. The European Strategy for Combating Radicalisation and Recruitment was a timely response, which, in tasking in 2006 both the CFSP working group on terrorism (COTER) and the third pillar Terrorism Working Group (TWG) with the development of a consolidated strategy, demonstrated the inextricable link between the EU's pillars and the similar symbiotic nature of the external/internal security dimension. In doing so, it led to greater integrated European policy-making.

Another key theme in the analysis of threat is state weakness – or in some extreme cases the absence of any functioning state at all. Afghanistan's link with both terrorist and crime networks, for example, has been well documented. If weak states breed terrorism, they also throw up problems of organised crime. In the Afghan case, along with the threat of terrorism goes the fact that most of Europe's heroin originates in Afghanistan and enters Europe along trafficking routes through Central Asia and the Western Balkans, where organised crime contributes to erosion and collapse from within and forms a breeding ground for terrorism. So border controls and concerted immigration policies are called for. Facing the terrorism threat again poses issues which cross the pillars and require a level of coordination that make a European response inescapable.

A further, related, theme is the manner in which, in the Western Balkans for example, the prospect of EU membership has acted as a powerful driver for reform.[72] The strongest EU influence on other countries has undoubtedly been the pre-accession process. Enlargement has added 12 states to the EU-15 at the time of 9/11, mostly post-Communist. Clearly, the prospect of EU membership is a powerful incentive for reform in the Western Balkans, as it has been throughout the twelve. The Stabilisation and Association Process (SAP), introduced by the EU for the Western Balkans in 1999[73], was designed, more explicitly than any previous EU strategy, to bring security problems in the region under control and to pre-empt new conflict through a combination of material aid and political incentives – notably the prospect (albeit long-term) of eventual full EU membership. There was thus a strong security rationale. And it can also be found in the EU's Barcelona Process, the latest embodiment of a long-standing Euro-Mediterranean dialogue with states in North Africa and the Middle East.[74] Policy again crosses all the pillar divides and lies at the intersection of domestic and international security. Indeed, the EU's assistance programmes and structured agreements with most countries, while not designed primarily for or billed as security-building programmes, militate against the conditions which breed and spread terrorism by promoting social and economic development, drawing states into profitable international economic cooperation, improving education, cultural standards and transparency, and in general fostering and consolidating democracy and good governance. At the end of 2006, new guidelines for the granting of development aid became part of the conditionality of the 10th European Development Fund. The Commission now drafts country strategies including governance profiles, which form the basis of incentive programmes for recipient states. Terrorism is obviously not the explicit focus, but the criteria include human rights, rule of law and general criteria linked to the liberal democratic values assumed to form the basis of a society in which there is no recourse to terrorism.

Thus, two major conclusions must be that the EU commands a formidable range of potential instruments to combat terrorism and that a new found recognition of the practical interlinkage between internal and external security, coupled with readiness to envisage proactive policy within the EU, are important conditioning factors in Europe's endeavour to rise to the terrorist challenge. The fight against terrorism has brought about far-reaching cooperation and highlighted the growing security rationale behind many of the EU's policies, inducing the EU down the track of further European integration. In setting out the EU's achievements in the fight against terrorism, the chapters in this book set out how and why this has come about.

Endnotes

1   Key publications on the EU and terrorism include: J. Monar and D. Mahncke (2006) *International Terrorism: A European Response to a Global Threat?* Brussels: Peter Lang; C. Hill (2004) 'Renationalising or Regrouping? EU Foreign Policy Since 11 September 2001', *Journal of Common Market Studies*, Vol. 42, No. 1, pp 143-63; M. Dittrich 'Muslims in Europe: Addressing the Challenges of Radicalisation', EPC Working Paper No. 23, 24 March 2006; M. Dittrich (2005) 'Facing the Global Terrorist Threat: A European Response', EPC Working Paper No. 14, 14 January 2005; T. Delpech (2002) 'International Terrorism and Europe', Chaillot Paper No 56, Institute for Security Studies; D. Keohane (2005) 'The EU and Counter-terrorism', Centre for European Reform; K. von Hippel (2005) *Europe Confronts Terrorism*, Palgrave; *Political Quarterly*, (2002), vol. 73, special issue; A. Adam (2006) *La lutte contre le terrorisme : Etude comparative Union européenne – Etats-Unis*, l'Harmattan; O. Bures (2006) 'EU Counterterrorism Policy: a Paper Tiger?', *Terrorism and Political Violence*, 18, pp. 57-78.
2   The equivalent third pillar group, the Terrorism Working Group (TWG), was created much later.
3   Hazel Blears, Home Office Minister, House of Lords (2004) 'EU Counter-terrorism Activities'. Minutes of evidence, Select Committee on the EU, Wednesday 8 December 2004, Questions 361-399.
4   This, inter alia, was the message of a report by former Commissioner Michel Barnier 'For a European Civil Protection Force', EuropeAid, 2006.
5   C. Hill (2003) *The Changing Politics of Foreign Policy*, Palgrave, p.133.

6   T. Delpech (2002) 'International Terrorism and Europe', Chaillot Paper No 56, Institute for Security Studies, pp. 16-20. (Delpech 2002: 16-20)

7   See D. Spence (2007) 'EU Diplomacy and Global Governance' in A. Cooper, B. Hocking and W. Maley (eds.) *Worlds Apart: Exploring the Interface between Governance and Diplomacy*, Tokyo, UN University Press.

8   For a history of the concept see 'Making Idealism Realistic: The Responsibility to Protect as a New Global Security Norm', Address by Gareth Evans, President of the International Crisis Group, to launch Stanford MA Program in International Policy Studies, Stanford University, 7 February 2007.

9   Speech given by PM Tony Blair in Sedgefield, UK, justifying military action in Iraq and warning of the continued threat of global terrorism. Reprinted in the *Guardian*, Friday March 5, 2004.

10   *The Economist*, 15 March 2006 'Inside Al Qaeda's Brain: Al-Qaeda bigwig admits to many wicked deeds'.

11   13 June 2002 Council Framework Decision on combating terrorism, OJ L 164, 22 June 2002.

12   For a discussion of the issues, see J. Gearson 'The Nature of Terrorism', in *Political Quarterly*, 2002.

13   F. Heisbourg, (2003) *Hyperterrorisme: La Nouvelle Guerre*, Fondation pour la Recherche Stratégique, Paris: (Odile Jacob: Paris, 2003).

14   'Europe and Terrorism: The French Lesson', *Economist*, 13 August 2005.

15   Ian Buruma (2006) *Murder in Amsterdam: The death of Theo van Gogh and The Limits of Tolerance*, Penguin.

16   UN Security Council Resolution 1368, on threats to international peace and security caused by terrorist acts, 12 September 2001.

17   See M. A. Smith (ed.) *Where is NATO Going?*, in particular the chapter by D. Brown, 'The War on Terror Would Not be Possible without NATO: a critique'. Routledge, 2006, pp. 23-43.

18   Ibid p 27.

19   Quoted in D. Benjamin and S. Simon (2006) *The Next Attack, The globalisation of Jihad*. Hodder and Stoughton, p 297.

20   T. Delpech (2002) 'International Terrorism and Europe', Chaillot Paper No 56, Institute for Security Studies, p. 22.

21   NATO M-NAC 2 (2001) 158, 6 December, 2001.

22   J. Delors (2001) 'Where is the European Union Heading?', speech in the United States, 20 March 2001.

23   A. Shonfield (1972) *Europe: Journey to an Unknown Destination*, Penguin.

24   For a detailed analysis of the 3 pillar system see P. Demaret (1994) 'The Treaty framework' in D. O'Keeffe and P. Twomey (eds.) *Legal Issues of the Maastricht Treaty*. London: Chancery Law, p. 3.

25   For a description and critique of these developments see S. Everts (2002) *Shaping a Credible EU Foreign Policy*, London: Centre for European Reform; D. Spence (2006) 'The Commission and CFSP' in D. Spence (ed.) *The European Commission*, 3rd edition, London: John Harper; C. Gourlay (2006) 'Community Instruments for Civilian Crisis Management' in A. Nowak (ed.) *Civilian Crisis Management: the EU Way*, Chaillot Paper no. 90, European Institute for Security Studies, June 2006.

26   For a description of foreign policy cultures and the role of national foreign ministries in EU affairs see B. Hocking and D. Spence (eds.) *Foreign Ministries in the European Union: Integrating Diplomats*, Palgrave.

27   I am grateful to Chris Hill for this analogy.

28   J. Solana 'A Secure Europe in a Better World: European Security Strategy', European Council, Brussels, 12 December 2003.

29   C. Hill (2004) 'Renationalising or Regrouping? EU Foreign Policy Since 11 September 2001', *Journal of Common Market Studies*, Vol. 42, No. 1, pp 143-63

30   For a recent analysis see A. Nowak (ed.) *Civilian Crisis Management: the EU Way*, Chaillot Paper no. 90, European Institute for Security Studies, June 2006.

31   At British PM Blair's invitation, France's President Chirac and Germany's Chancellor Schröder were to follow up their much criticised, separate pre-Ghent European Council meeting on 20 October, with a dinner in London, but Italy and Spain insisted on participating (they were G5 members) as did Belgium, which held the Presidency, and the Netherlands. See 'Guess Who Was Not Coming to Dinner' and 'Better Late than Never' (the latter referring to Italian PM Berlusconi who arrived after the main course in London), *The Economist*, 10 November 2001.

32   See the Europol Internet site at URL <http://www.europol.net>.

33 On the European Arrest Warrant see Laeken European Council, 'Extradition will no longer be necessary between EU Member States', European Union Factsheet: 'The fight against terrorism'.

34 Though for a sceptical view see H. Brady and D. Keohane (2005) 'Fighting Terrorism: the EU Needs a Strategy not a Shopping List', Centre for European Reform.

35 'Europol to Become a More Effective EU Agency to Help Police Cooperation between the Member States', Commission Press Briefing: IP/06/1861, 20 December 2006.

36 Permanent Delegation of the European Commission to the USA, 'The EU, the US and the Fight against Global Terrorism', Eufocus, May 2005, page 3.

37 Convention on the stepping up of cross border cooperation, particularly in combating terrorism, cross-border crime and illegal immigration.

38 Commission Proposal for a Council decision on the improvement of police cooperation between the Member States of the European Union, especially at the internal borders and amending the Convention implementing the Schengen Agreement (Com(2005) 317), 18 July 2005.

39 For an in-depth analysis of the issues see S. Duke (2006) 'Intelligence, Security and Information Flows in CFSP', Intelligence and National Security, vol. 21, no. 4, pp. 604-630.

40 On the crisis management and civil protection capacity of the Commission see Boin et al in D. Spence (2006) The European Commission, 3rd edition, John Harper. For a detailed description and defence of the case for greater coordination rather than a new intelligence agency, see B. Müller-Wille (2004) 'For Our Eyes Only? Shaping an Intelligence Community within the EU', Occasional Paper no. 50, European Institute for Security Studies.

41 Hazel Blears, see endnote 3 above.

42 A. Diaz (2005) 'Crisis and Reform of the European Intelligence Services: A National or a European Challenge?', ECPR 2005 Workshop on Crisis and Politics.

43 see endnote 3.

44 ibid.

45 See 'EU's Mr. Terrorism', European Voice, 1-14 April 2004.

46 see endnote 3.

47 C. Patten (2005) Not Quite the Diplomat: Home Truths about World Affairs, Allen Lane, p. 225.

48 See 'Mr. Terrorism to Give up his Post', Agence Europe, 13 February 2007.

49 National Commission on Terrorist Attacks, The 9/11 Commission Report: The Full Final Report of the National Commission on Terrorist Attacks Upon the United States, Norton, 2004. For a rebuttal of many of the official US arguments, see D.R. Griffin, The 9/11 Commission Report: Omissions and Distortions, Arris, 2004.

50 Schröder was not alone, since it was President Chirac who took the lead in opposing US military action in Iraq. Significantly, while Chirac drew little criticism in France but was lambasted by Americans who even threatened to stop eating French cheese, Schröder was immediately attacked both in the US and Germany. See S. Erlanger (2002) 'Schröder Rebuked by US in Iraq War', International Herald Tribune, 17/18 August 2002.

51 Quoted in N. Bensahel (2002) 'The Counterterror Coalitions: Cooperation with Europe, NATO and the European Union; in J. Kitfield, 'NATO Metamorphosis' in National Journal 34/6 9 Feb 2002: 376-380. For an insightful review of all the divergences of view see R. E. Rupp (2006) NATO after 9/11: An Alliance in Continuing Decline, Palgrave; A. Deighton (2002) 'The Eleventh of September and Beyond: NATO', Political Quarterly, pp 119-134.

52 R. Kagan (2002) 'Power and Weakness', Policy Review, no. 113, June-July, p. 1.

53 K. Booth and T. Dunne (2002) Worlds in Collision: Terror and the Future of World Order, Palgrave, p. 3.

54 See European Commission, Eurobarometer 58, March 2003 and Eurobarometer 59, July 2003.

55 Pew Research Centre for the People and the Press, 'Americans and Europeans differ widely on foreign policy issues: Bush's ratings improve but he's still seen as unilateralist', Washington,17 April 2002.

56 Eurobarometer main concerns http://ec.europa.eu.int/public_opinion/archives/eb/eb65/Presentation.

57 Eurobarometer 'The Future of Europe', May 2006, p. 40.

58 European Commission, Directorate-General for Energy and Transport, 'Air safety & air security', http://europa.eu.int/comm/transport/air/safety/index.en.htm.

59 See European Commission, www.europa.eu.int/comm/transport/air/singlesky

60 European Commission, 'Activities of the European Union Information Society', www.europa.eu.int/pol/infso/index;

61 Proposal for a directive of the council on the identification and designation of European Critical Infrastructure and the assessment of the need to improve their protection COM(2006) 787 final Brussels, 12.12.2006.

62 Michel Barnier 'For a European Civil Protection Force', EuropeAid, 2006.

63 A succinct history of Commission and EU involvement in the WMD issues can be found in House of Lords, minutes of evidence taken before the select committee on the European Union (sub-committee c) EU strategy on non-proliferation of weapons of mass destruction, Tuesday 18 January 2005.

64 Russian General Alexander Lebed made an allegation to this effect, see Delpech, p. 26.

65 A succinct list of WMD, in particular NRBC, cases leading to arrests can be found in J-L. Marret (2005) *Transnational Jihadist Networks and 'Weapons of Mass Destruction*, monograph, Fondation pour la Recherche Stratégique.

66 Seville European Council, 21-22 June 2002, Presidency Conclusions, Annex V (note 17). See also F. Perpiña-Robert, 'EU Presidency Statement on Counter-Terrorism: Resolution 1373: Summary: Speaking points for the presentation by the European Union in the meeting of the Counter-Terrorism Committee with the EU', New York, 23 Apr. 2002; and 'Report of the European Union to the Security Council Committee established pursuant to resolution 1373 (2001) concerning counter-terrorism', and UN Security Council document S/2001/1297, 28 Dec. 2001.

67 EU Counter-Terrorism Clauses: assessment Council of the European Union, 11 May 2005, (Partially Declassified) 14458/2/04.

68 See, for example, Permanent Delegation of the European Commission to the USA, 'The EU, the US and the Fight against Global Terrorism', *Eufocus*, May 2005, p. 4.

69 The Counter-Terrorism Online Handbook, a collaborative effort of the 24-member Counter-Terrorism Implementation Task Force (CTITF) of the UN is available at www.un. org/terrorism/cthandbook

70 See Financial Action Task Force on Money Laundering, 'Special Recommendations on terrorist financing', www1.oecd.org/fatf

71 The scope of Directive 91/308/EEC on prevention of the use of the financial system for the purpose of money laundering was extended in Directive 2001/97/EC of the European Parliament and the Council, approved on 19 November 2001 and issued on 4 December 2001.

72 See M. Caparini (2004) 'Security Sector Reform in the Western Balkans', *SIPRI Yearbook* 2004 (note 7).

73 The SAP offers the possibility for the 6 countries of the region (Albania, Bosnia and Herzegovina, Croatia, FYROM, Serbia and Montenegro) to sign a new kind of agreement, i.e., a Stabilisation and Association Agreement with the EU, opening up concrete EU accession perspectives for the first time, as the EU did for Central and East European countries in 1998 with the launch of the enlargement process and the opening of accession negotiations. See European Commission, 'EU in Southeast Europe: the Stabilisation and Association Process', URL <http://www.eudelyug.org.

74 On the Barcelona Process, or Euro-Mediterranean Partnership, see http://europa.eu.int/comm/external_relations/euromed. The Euro-Mediterranean Partnership has since 1995 built up a substantial set of cooperation activities, ranging from political dialogue, through trade liberalisation, economic reform and infrastructure networks to culture, education and the movement of people. It is based on a comprehensive approach to security and the principle that cooperation and co-ownership are the best way to promote reform and to deal with the root causes of the terrorist threat. It includes EU-financed activities to promote exchange of best practice and training to help police and judicial authorities.

1. Terrorism and the EU: The Internal–External Dimension of Security

Magnus Ekengren

Introduction

The introductory chapter to this book sets out how the threat of international terrorism has been a catalyst for considerable change in EU foreign and security policy. The need for transnational prevention and protection against terrorism led the Union to adopt a new pro-active foreign policy stance, complete with policies to use the EU's extensive first pillar tools such as technical assistance to countries unable to implement commitments on counter-terrorism or to demonstrate sound internal governance.

However, other threats have also compelled the Union to develop new responsibilities and tools, allowing it to go beyond its soft power capacity and actually intervene in more robust fashion abroad. As chapter 6 sets out in detail, in the last few years the Union has given assistance to those affected by the Asian tsunami, supported the US authorities during the Hurricane Katrina disaster, and coordinated water-carrying aircraft to fight forest fires in Southern Europe and rescue teams in Turkey and Morocco after earthquakes. The EU has sent military peacekeeping missions to Bosnia and the Democratic Republic of Congo, taken measures to prevent the further spread of avian influenza and coordinated EU member states' efforts in bringing home thousands of refugees after the war in Lebanon in the summer of 2006. All of these exciting new policy departures were, of course, not a response to the challenges of international terrorism. But they were important evidence of a fast-growing capacity of potential use in the anti-terrorism policy arsenal. In his early days as High Representative for the CFSP, Javier Solana used to say that the EU was moving at the speed of light. He cannot be gainsaid. The list of EU activities is growing at an extraordinary pace. It provides striking evidence both that the new security agenda is truly global[1] and that EU capacities are incontestably cross-pillar. Indeed, EU policies and instruments of protection have had a hard time keeping up with growing demand, as the evolving anti-terrorism roadmap amply illustrates.[2]

Unfortunately, the many tragic events since the beginning of the 1990s have forced the EU onto the defensive, with development of security policies triggered conspicuously by 'events'. Experience in the Balkans led to a European Security and Defence Policy (ESDP) for *external* crises, backed up with a military and civil crisis management capability and new organs. '9/11' led to the intensification of EU *internal* security efforts, flanked by a raft of external policies designed to assist others achieve legislative and operational effectiveness. The result, in 2007, is that almost every area of cooperation in all three EU pillars has a security plan, a security committee and a network for rapid communication and reaction. The events in Madrid on 11 March 2004 led to the adoption of the 'Solidarity Declaration' on mutual support for the prevention of terrorism and aid in the event of terrorist attack on EU territory.[3] The Asian tsunami disaster in December 2004 resulted in closer consular EU cooperation and the establishment of civilian teams for *international* rescue missions, including a far-reaching set of new proposals from former Commissioner and French foreign minister Michel Barnier to take these capabilities further (Barnier Report). The bomb attacks in London in July 2005 led to closer EU cooperation on intelligence. This was resisted by some, as Spence points out in the introductory chapter, but moves are nevertheless afoot to give practical implementation to a programme for the protection of critical infrastructure in Europe.[4]

The issue, of course, is whether the Union has tended to fall into the same traps as its member states; basing its defence on the last crisis (or war) and making a strong distinction between internal and external security.[5] In fact, most of the external actions listed above were predicated on the existence of EU instruments initially created for 'internal' crisis management. The problem for effective joined-up policy-making is that new global tasks are often managed with ad hoc arrangements. Owing to lack of capacity for external civilian crisis, it was the *enlargement* department (and budget line) of the EU Commission that took the lead for EU support to affected candidate states during the flooding of Central Europe in 2002. For similar reasons, EU responsibility for the safety of EU citizens abroad was 'invented' and developed *during* the acute phases of the tsunami disaster.[6]

The 2003 European Security Strategy declared that 'internal and external aspects are indissolubly linked'.[7] However, the implications for EU protection were not reflected in policy-making, analysis and institutional arrangements, and this despite the fact of the existence of a 'situation centre' in the Council Secretariat and several 'crisis rooms' in the Commission with the task to provide comprehensive threat and risk outlooks. It is widely acknowledged that there is great potential in a more efficient combination of the EU's external and internal crisis management capacities.[8] Indeed, the future development of the ESDP and the Solidarity Clause in the draft Constitutional Treaty[9] are the commitment by member states to create the framework for the EU to regain the international initiative and thus shape transnational security in an innovative and strategic manner. It is a task perhaps historically never so crucial, given today's shortcomings in civilian crisis management and traditional uses of warfare and arms in Iraq and elsewhere.

It is with this background that this chapter examines some central policy implications of the internal/external security interface for EU protection policies of relevance to the terrorist threat. The chapter presents a conceptual framework for the analysis of EU security providing theoretical background to explain why the internal-external distinction has had such a strong influence on policy planning. The chapter then sketches a global approach to EU security in terms of concentric circles, in contrast to a perspective based on a division between national views of 'home' and 'abroad'. This approach throws light on implications for responses to international terrorism, whether they fall into ESDP or the EU's civil protection capabilities. It also discusses future implications for the draft Constitution's Solidarity Clause and the need for new thinking on the required national military capacities for implementation of the clause. The aim is to pin-point key challenges which must be overcome if a more efficient EU role in the protection of Europe's core values and, not least, its citizens, is to be achieved.

From the internal-external divide to circles of security

The EU between national and international security – the potential tools of counter-terrorism

The Union has always essentially been a transboundary security project. For the first forty years of its existence, it promoted inter-state security through a system of networks that crossed state borders. External security relations among member states were turned into 'domestic' European politics. Now – in an era of transboundary threats, both man-made and natural – the task is to create a common defence and security through similar networks beyond the internal-external divide. Yet, concepts and frameworks have generally leaned hard on *national* security analysis to engender analysis of supranational security. There has consequently been an unhelpful distinction between internal 'desecuritisation' of relations between EU member states[10] and external Common Foreign and Security Policy (CFSP), analysed in the context of international security dynamics.[11] This division is not surprising. It originates in the tradition of territorial security and border defence, itself inspiring the practical division of the EU's pillar structure. The second pillar (CFSP/ESDP) contrasts, formally and analytically, with the 'internal' security domains of the first pillar (civil protection, health etc.) and the third pillar (justice, police, border control).[12]

But the key issue is the extent to which a line between external and internal security can be drawn for a political entity with two key definitional components: no distinct territorial definition and conscious erosion of borders for the purpose of inter-state security. What is inside and what is outside the Union in terms of external and internal EU security is an area requiring renewed analytical attention.[13] This section combines domestic and international perspectives on EU security and sketches the contours of a European security field stretching from inside the EU beyond its borders; a field definable as a sequence of concentric circles of different concerns and dynamics, rather than on the basis of a strict distinction between internal and external security. In this way, the approach builds upon and extends earlier conceptual attempts such as those associated with an 'enlarged European security space',[14] the 'internal' European security area[15] or 'sub-regional institutional security frameworks'.[16] It also relates to studies of

Europe's increasingly decentralised decision making and metaphors such as 'olympic rings'.[17] All of the policy areas discussed under the term 'security' are, of course, part of the uncited toolbox against terrorism.

Theories on the dissolution of boundaries between internal and external *national* security have marked out a new transboundary 'field of security' in Europe.[18] Here, the role of the EU is often described as a 'platform' for negotiations between the security agencies of the member countries, such as the police and military forces.[19] The roles of national actors are changing; both the police and the military forces are now increasingly oriented towards the common task of 'internal' European security. This has led to security analysis and planning being preoccupied with crisis situations and the prevention of conflicts and international crime rather than traditional war.[20] EU measures are gradually leading to a Europeanisation of the national obligation to protect citizens. The challenge to current theory, therefore, is to make sense of the EU as more than just a platform: it now possesses both internal and external safety and security instruments of its own. Consequently, the EU increasingly reflects the characteristics of a *domestic* system that could be understood by using theories of system and societal vulnerability, i.e. major disturbances on society (system effects).[21]

What is the *international* security threat to the EU? The confusion provoked by this kind of question is due to the fact that traditionally the EU has not been conceived of as an international security entity; it has, for example, no collective defence in the traditional sense.[22] Nor has it been analysed conceptually as an actor pursuing an active security policy. There have, of course, been analyses of the EU as an emerging actor in the broadly defined system of security governance, but these analyses cover the EU as an external actor, not as an actor with internal security problems.[23] Thus, 'security policy' has been adjudged to remain within the competence of the EU member states (or to be managed in other organisations such as the North Atlantic Treaty Organisation). The EU has most frequently been viewed as an outcome or reflection of the considerations of actors organising for other concerns. Its success was that it created security by not discussing security. The consequence is that the EU has, until recently, lacked its own international security identity. This causes difficulties for attempts to capture in theoretical language the explicit and active EU security role taking shape today. Thus, the evolution of ESDP since 1999 has been interpreted as 'the end of territorial defence' for the EU.[24] But the EU's security identity cannot be defined by negations alone and the overlap between 'internal' and 'external' dimensions of EU security needs further definition. What values, systems, 'functions' or even territory do 'internal' and 'external' policies aim to protect from terrorism?

Internal and external security: common objects of protection

Over the years, new security referent objects have evolved incrementally within the Union as a result of its growing field of competence. The gradual expansion of the tasks of the EU institutions, in particular the Commission's, have obliged them to assume growing responsibility for safeguarding and protecting the EU's core functions. New policy competences have thereby emerged. One way to capture the *who, what* and *from what* EU security is protecting is a review of what the Union has considered to constitute a 'crisis' throughout its history and the expansion of the notion of what should be safeguarded for the common good at the EU level.

Since the 1950s the EU has in fact provided *national* security.[25] In the 1970s and 1980s, economic welfare and stability came to be perceived as a critically important object for EU members to secure jointly. A crisis for the functioning of the common market and the institutional and legal measures taken to uphold the 'four freedoms' of intra-European exchange became an EU crisis.[26] By focusing on safeguarding the vital flow of resources for the welfare and identity of EU member states, the Union in effect took steps towards transnational societal security.[27] In the 1990s, the outbreak of war and violence in the Balkans also forced EU leaders to define this external crisis as a potential crisis for the Union itself. The value of peace and stability in the neighbourhood – the 'near abroad' – was added to the EU's core goals, and the aim of protecting peace and the safety of civilians was thus no longer geographically limited to the EU member states. Consequently, the reference to security for the Union became the same both within and outside its borders: to secure states or ethnically based groups against threats from each other. Thus a threat or event that undermines peace and stability in the wider Europe also presents a potential crisis for the EU itself.

The concept of *human security*[28] has also been added to the aims of European security, a development underlined by the fact that natural disasters increasingly became perceived as EU crises. The Commission and its directorate-general (DG) for humanitarian aid (ECHO) gave high priority to helping Turkey when the country was hit by two earthquakes in 1999.[29] If early practices set a precedent for future EU crisis management, EU security policy might increasingly cover humans in grave international crises, wherever they occur.[30]

The 1990s saw a new development in internal EU safety. The BSE crisis in 1996 was a serious threat to the common market and at the same time to the safety of European consumers. The EU had to reconcile the protection of both aspects of the growing multidimensional character of its referent object of security.[31]

These various events in the recent history of the EU's security are by no means all related to 'terrorism'. But the methods and instruments to deal with them are easily transferable to the anti-terrorism toolbox. As Spence underlines in the introduction to this book, the events of 11 September 2001 began a chain of policy responses with 'EU citizens' as a clear referent object of security. The Solidarity Clause proposed in the draft Constitution constituted further confirmation by declaring that the EU aim should be to 'protect democratic institutions and the civilian population' not only from terrorist attack but also in the event of natural or man-made disasters (Article I-43).[32] Thus, the referent object of security is not just infrastructure or flow of essential services such as water, electricity supply and communications, but the ability to govern society and to articulate political goals – *functional* security areas.[33]

This historical overview shows how the Union has come to play a security role in four 'core' areas transcending the external-internal divide. It demonstrates how the EU now protects fundamental values such as peace and stability (both within the EU and the near abroad), the European economy and the safety of people and society wherever these are under threat. The EU has developed its policies for the protection of these fundamental EU values.[34] The EU's role in the four core areas embraces all the security concepts referred to above: national, societal, human and functional.

Figure 1 illustrates how the Union security role has evolved over the years in the form of the protection of these four 'core areas'. The figure depicts the chronological evolution beginning with the inner circle. It also depicts the geographical extension of the Union's security commitment, ranging from member states in the inner circle to anybody in need of protection in the outer area.

Figure 1. *The four core areas for EU security.**

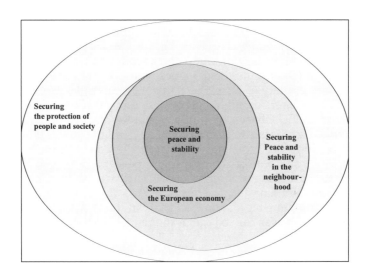

* The figure was first presented in Ekengren, M., Matzén, N., Svantesson, M. (2006) *The new security role of the European Union: transnational crisis management and the protection of Union citizens*, EUCM report 2, ACTA 35 B 2006, Stockholm: National Defence College, p.25.

EU actions in circles of European security

The circle approach can be translated into descriptions of specific security complexes. For instance, the Union has responded to its neighbours not only as a traditional security actor, but mainly by extending its internal system of governance through enlargement and through the integration of external actors into joint policy-making processes and the fostering of an enlarging security community.[35] The consequence is a blurred boundary between 'outsiders' and 'insiders' in many EU security initiatives such as security sector reform.[36] In the light of earlier CFSP history, the capabilities developed for the ESDP will probably be used primarily in the areas bordering the EU.[37]

These areas are defined not only by the incidence of transboundary threats and risks, such as terrorism, but also by expanding economic and security networks – the EU's now traditional method of crisis and conflict prevention. The networks include first pillar systems to minimize societal vulnerabilities and prepare for emergencies. The main task of the new military and civilian capabilities of the ESDP is formally to manage crisis and conflict outside the borders of the EU.[38] But, and this is significant, while the intention is to make the EU better-equipped as an 'international' security actor, it is doing this in the same territory for which it is attempting to build a 'domestic' European infrastructure through *inter alia* the Solidarity Clause on terrorism. Forthcoming enlargements and the 'European neighbourhood policy'[39] only underline the need for a concentric circle approach in an EU security space steadily moving east and southwards.

Further away from the Union heartland, the security identity of the EU is also gradually changing character. The Union is a hybrid structure. It is at once an international organisation and a would-be polity. Its aim is both the protection of EU and universal values wherever they are threatened in the world and the safety of EU citizens in a more narrow sense.[40] Closer to the core, EU security crises might best be defined by threats to free trade and EU citizens or the EU Charter of Fundamental Rights. Further out, crisis might be provoked by threats to international law and the values embodied by the United Nations.[41] According to the draft EU Constitution, ESDP missions should be carried out for the purpose of peacekeeping, conflict prevention and the strengthening of international security in accordance with the principles of the UN Charter.[42] Thus, the EU's first independently launched military operation – Operation ARTEMIS in the Democratic Republic of the Congo, in 2003 – was carried out at the request of the UN (under a Chapter VII resolution).[43]

If early practice, involving UN requests and mandates, come to set the precedent for future ESDP operations, EU security might increasingly encompass all people involved in a grave international crisis – as the circle approach predicts.[44] The evolving security role of the EU might then perhaps best be characterised as that of a regional body for the implementation of UN decisions. Thus, the 'outer' EU security circle would equate with international security, and there would – by definition – exist no external security dimension in relation to which internal security could be distinguished.

The conclusion, therefore, is that the internal-external divide has to a large extent lost its importance as an analytical concept and as a political guideline for EU security action. The initial plan for the deployment of EU battle groups was 'within a geographical radius of 6000 kilometres from Brussels'. The obvious analytical implication of this kind of definition of European security is the concentric circle approach presented above. But what are the policy and operational implications?

Implications for ESDP

EU level

ESDP has given rise to fundamental discussions about how to develop a more global EU concept that would seek to combine external and internal approaches more closely. This is thought to be essential if ESDP is to be successful and proactive.[45] The EU's security answer to the September 2001 attacks in the USA was non-military in nature. The focus was on legal measures and crisis management capacities that exist in all three EU pillars. In practice, this made the EU responsible for 'internal' and 'external' non-territorial security. In general, the events of 9/11 started a process which has led the EU to rethink its previous demarcation lines between trade, aid, diplomacy and the new crisis management capacities created under the ESDP. Discussions on whether or not to include the capacities of the EU's third pillar, Justice and Home Affairs – for example, in the areas of personnel and threat identification – signalled a development towards a broad transboundary security approach to the ESDP. For internal as well as external security reasons, many observers argued that there was an urgent need for better coordination between non-military ESDP activities, work under the Justice and Home Affairs pillar and the European Commission. It was also suggested that security thinking might be 'mainstreamed' into other areas of EU cooperation as well.[46] Most of these issues still remain to be solved.

The Union's strength both as a crisis manager and as a provider of an effective, coordinated response to terrorism lies, above all, in the possibility of gathering together the full range of instruments that it has acquired over the years. Just as it will be difficult to separate internal from external security policy aspects, so will it probably be difficult to separate non-political aid instruments from protection activities with a security-political dimension. Such dilemmas need rapidly to be addressed. The EU's credibility will crystallise through the development of new and innovative networks beyond the individual pillars of the EU system. To be really successful in crisis management and counter-terrorism, the EU must find ways to bridge the pillar structure, which currently militates against effective coordination of the various resources at EU disposal. Already, international crisis management instruments have developed within the EU's first pillar in the form of coordination by CIVCOM and the Commission's Rapid Reaction Mechanism (RRM).[47] The cross-pillar coordination that has already begun will help to break down the divisions between external and internal policies of protection. Yet, the challenge of different principles for decision-making in each pillar will remain. Some analysts predict that CFSP crisis management in the long run will remain intergovernmental due to weak incentives for member states to delegate to supranational organs.[48] Others, in contrast, show how the institutionalisation of EU protection policies in some sectors is leading to more supranational solutions.[49] In this perspective the long term potential for an all-embracing decision-making system for EU protection needs to be envisaged. This would standardise decision-making structures between pillars.[50]

Another important factor for ESDP is the general transition (both in the

USA and in Europe) from expressing the combating of terrorism in terms of war, foreign policy and diplomacy to an emphasis on prevention of 'extremism', fighting crime of a domestic political nature and practical international cooperation (police cooperation, intelligence, etc). This could mean greater focus on the civilian elements of ESDP, but also on the need for closer links between ESDP and other EU instruments, such as the Solidarity Clause, Commission assistance and advice to other countries about prevention etc.

Developments continue apace in the broader security policy areas where the Commission and Community lead the work. These developments include civil and legal cooperation and, of course, the enlargement of the EU and cooperation with neighbouring countries (in reality the EU's best ESDP and CFSP). In today's circumstances, it is perhaps not a European foreign minister that will be most missed, but rather a European interior minister. The EU's first Counter-Terrorism Coordinator, Gijs de Vries, had great difficulties in getting member states to keep up with the rapidly increasing legal cooperation and the joint efforts against organised crime and terrorism (where many EU proposals have already been made, but have only been implemented to a limited extent). Legislation varies greatly in the 27 countries. Cooperation with other countries must be improved.

National level

To a greater degree than EU level coordination, perhaps, effective capability depends on member states being prepared to break down or redefine corresponding barriers on the home front: barriers between internal vulnerability and external defence, between defence and police forces, military and civilian intelligence agencies, between defence, justice and foreign ministries, and between defence policy, emergency planning and rescue agencies.[51] All of these barriers originate from a strong distinction between internal and external security. Not surprisingly, therefore, some observers conclude that the evolving relationship of EU institutions with member states is the key dimension for efficient ESDP instruments.[52]

Ability is not just about having material resources to hand; it is also – as in the 1950s – about being ready to think in new ways and with new priorities. Currently, ESDP capability is unlikely to be greater than the contributions by member states, so the extent to which EU security policy is intertwined with national security, though a national issue, is clearly crucial to CSFP. Nowhere is this more clearly illustrated than in the EUFOR operation in Bosnia-Herzegovina, which replaced NATO's SFOR in December 2004. One reason the EU Police Mission (EUPM) in Bosnia (starting in 2003) received such a strong response to its request for national experts in organised crime was the great interest in the issue amongst justice ministries and police forces in member states. It was understood at an early stage that the drug smuggling and crime syndicates, which threaten the EU's major cities, are best countered by action on the ground in the Balkans.[53] The managerial issue was how much security the member states could achieve at home for money invested in the Balkans through the EU.

Member states have differing views on issues in joint operations of central importance to the dismantling of the internal-external divide. For example, there are ongoing discussions about the extent to which there should be strict demarcation between military and police tasks in EUFOR operations. The Council and the Commission distinguish EU police operations (Council responsibility) from support for capacity-building of police forces abroad (Commission funding). And member states have emphasised that in Bosnia, the EU will only be regarded as a key actor if it demonstrates good coordination. Certain countries have made moves to place the EU Commission under the authority of ESDP, in practice the EU Special Representative. Others have maintained that the objective of the Union has always been to turn European security policy into EU domestic policy. On the latter basis, attempts should be resisted to subordinate what they see as the engine for the whole process – the EU Commission – to the infrastructure for Union foreign policy making in the second pillar.[54]

Security, and thus both the response to terrorism internally and externally and ESDP itself, stretches minds beyond the internal-external divide. It requires policy analysis based not only on long-term vision, the original purpose of the Council's Policy Planning and Early Warning Unit, but also unified concepts that give direction and impetus to both national and European perspectives. The current establishment of multinational *EU battle groups* is one indication of the capabilities required for future global security, as is the increased cooperation between police forces and intelligence agencies within EU countries. Yet, there is still much thinking to be done about the political and strategic use of such resources both abroad and at home.

Implications for the Solidarity Clause

The Solidarity Clause was adopted in March 2004 after the Madrid bombings as a political declaration.[55] The clause builds on the fundamental character of the Union and contains a range of forward-looking elements, which contribute to the removal of boundaries between EU internal and external security and between crisis management and defence. The clause was initially developed in the European Convention's Defence Working Group in 2002-2003.[56] It states that:

'The Union shall mobilise all the instruments at its disposal, including the military resources made available by the Member States, to:

– prevent the terrorist threat in the territory of the Member States;
– protect democratic institutions and the civilian population from any terrorist attack;
– assist a Member State in its territory, at the request of its political authorities, in the event of a terrorist attack;
– assist a Member State in its territory, at the request of its political authorities, in the event of a natural or man-made disaster.'

The instruments required for realisation of the Solidarity Clause are being developed at a great rate. Today there are no less than 25 to 30 systems led by the Commission and Council Secretariat in Brussels for information, early warning, rapid reaction, coordination and mutual support for everything from rescue services and the spread of infectious diseases to natural catastrophes and preventive measures in unstable regions.[57]

The Solidarity Clause can in this perspective be seen as an all-embracing umbrella over systems that already exist. In many respects this change reflects the changed security thinking and security sector reforms that have been implemented in many member countries. All these systems will, unfortunately, be tested sooner or later and then the question that will arise is: what responsibility does the EU actually have, given the new capabilities and systems that have been built up in the Union? This is a debate that, for reasons of effectiveness and democracy, should be taken up now – before the crisis. Moreover, it is reasonable to accept that any possible activation of the Solidarity Clause is dependent on two factors: which country is affected and what sort of catastrophe occurs.

The clause also brings to the fore several central issues addressed by the theoretical section of this chapter: Whose security? What will the EU secure? What constitutes a crisis for the EU? What is the EU providing security against? Does EU security apply to democracy and institutions in member states and/or at the EU level and to the member states or the EU's population? What made the bomb attacks in Madrid an EU crisis? Why was the clause not invoked in the case of the London Underground bombings in the summer of 2005?[58] These add up to a number of 'when', 'where' and 'how' questions.

When? What should be the deciding factor in mobilising EU instruments? Could a request for help come from EU institutions? Does one EU state have the right to decide that another is at risk of being attacked, and thus invoke the clause? Bearing in mind that the clause is already in force, in the form of a political declaration, to what extent is an attack on one member state an attack on all? Is it possible to envisage the clause being put into effect, if a member state considers itself threatened by terrorists? Could such a state demand mobilisation of 'all' EU instruments to counter the threat?

Where? The clause applies to efforts within the Union's territory, not beyond. Territorial integrity was the goal of nation states. Will the integrity of societal functions be the goal of EU defence? The Solidarity clause can take the EU a step closer to a new sort of transnational societal defence of the civilian population and democratic institutions. This 'total' EU defence could be seen as distinct from collective territorial defence as well as traditional EU conflict prevention. Finally, is the EU an emerging defence union rather than simply a defence alliance – and what do publics in the militarily non-aligned EU states understand and desire? Whatever the answers to these somewhat rhetorical questions, there can be no doubt that however elusive a successful defence union might be, it would certainly consolidate a European identity.

How? The clause emphasises the need for capabilities embracing all sectors – including military resources. The thinking is that, in the long term, member states should move in the same direction in their defence policy in order to meet the new terrorist threat. The assumption is that, today, member states are converging in terms of values and have reached a sufficient degree of integration in terms of cooperative networks. Another condition for the clause to be successful is that preventive measures and national infrastructures are coordinated to the point that member states can act jointly at times of crisis. This readiness to act can, to a limited extent, be legislated for through the EU, but must be based on a long-term common viewpoint and on the development and consolidation of new forms of cooperation within the EU. Practical requirements for the clause include a new transnational, cross-sector EU infrastructure of 'working networks' between member states in the protection field. These should include national public administrations as well as the civilian community, private business and voluntary organisations, the military, police forces, the judiciary and intelligence agencies. Discussions are underway as to how such cooperation can best be achieved. Thinking has included the idea of 'EU preparedness guidelines' as a basis for an all-encompassing European societal defence.[59] Other far-reaching questions are how EU candidate countries and neighbouring countries can best be involved in this process, and what links there should be between the EU, the USA and Russia in these matters.

More than perhaps any other EU instrument, the clause has the potential to contribute to the dissolution of the boundary between internal civil protection for emergencies and external crisis management for security, whether these are terrorist-inspired or natural catastrophes.[60] The clause could be interpreted as bridging the two main views coexisting so far on the *finalité* of EU defence: collective defence through military alliance, on the one hand, and security through networks on the other. An EU defence within expanding European security circles is more easily reconciled with European integration's traditional role of creating a long-term zone of peace (a security community), in contrast to the defence of territory for its own sake. The latter is more closely associated with traditional military instruments of power, which could be detrimental to relations with certain third countries and to the image of the EU as a security model. The EU could thus become a defence power while simultaneously avoiding a new and potentially destabilizing balance-of-power relationship with neighbouring regions. The EU candidate states could be involved, and neighbouring and other states would be allowed to participate as far as possible. The clause could prove, in time, to be a model for other parts of the world, and developed with similar regional systems into an interlinked global defence network to combat network-based global terrorism.

The clause legally codifies the external-internal interface by formally recognising EU security, where the functions of democratic institutions are to be safeguarded and populations are to be protected. Compared to the case of the traditional nation state, functional specification acquires a relatively stronger position than territorial delimitation as a basis of EU security and defence, thus further weakening the rationale for a dividing line between internal and external EU security, in practice as well as in analytical terms.

Implications for EU Civil Protection

EU civil protection cooperation also demonstrates the Union's expanding concern for protecting 'people', 'property' and 'democratic institutions'. Civil protection cooperation first began in the mid-1980s, largely as the result of a Commission push for more coordination to manage natural disasters internal to the Union. The then-commissioner for environment affairs argued strongly that his directorate-general should do more in the wake of forest fires and heat waves in Southern Europe. Several Council resolutions adopted since 1985 approved the move toward joint training and an exploration of resource sharing. A legal basis for the actual deployment of such resources, however, did not come until 2001.

The 11 September attacks led to the creation of a Community 'mechanism' for the compilation and use of member state resources, not only for natural disasters but also terrorist attacks.[61] In cautioning the increase of the EU's external role through ESDP, member states ensured that the mechanism could be used to coordinate events both inside and outside the EU[62] – a seemingly straightforward affair in principle, though the elaboration of a transboundary capacity in practice was more cumbersome than expected.

The Community civil protection mechanism covers the response phase of a disaster. It involves pooling civil protection resources amongst the 27 EU member states plus 3 non-EU states – Iceland, Liechtenstein, and Norway. Member states are obliged to 'identify in advance intervention teams which might be available for such intervention'.[63] Moreover, the 'member state in which the emergency has occurred shall notify those member states which may be affected by the emergency'[64] along with the European Commission. Member states committed themselves to make available civil protection intervention teams of up to 2,000 persons at short notice by 2003.[65] Community civil protection activities are managed by a unit for civil protection in the Commission's directorate-general for the environment. Monitoring and coordination of disasters takes place through the Monitoring and Information Centre (MIC), which operates a 24/7 communication and rapid alert network between member states called the Common Emergency Communication and Information System (CECIS).[66]

This Community mechanism not only strengthenes the EU's competence in civil protection, which is vital for the inner-EU response to terrorism. It also pools resources potentially available for use abroad. The EU, operating through pillar I, has thus acquired an explicitly external role in civil protection alongside its traditional internal role. The question soon arose as to whether the Community mechanism might also be deployed as part of pillar II's ESDP. The Feira European Council in June 2000 agreed that the civilian crisis management component of ESDP should include civil protection. After several years of negotiation, the Commission and the Council agreed on a joint declaration in 2003 setting out how the Community mechanism might be employed for an ESDP mission.[67] It has since been employed several times.

After 9/11 more than 1,000 rescue workers from the member states were co-ordinated through the mechanism for missions across the Atlantic.[68] The MIC has launched requests for assistance in connection with the oil accident caused by the *Prestige* tanker off the Spanish coast in the autumn of 2002[69], which resulted in ships, aircraft, equipment and experts from different participating countries being put at the disposal of the Spanish, Portuguese and French authorities. The mechanism was also used to supply high capacity pumps during the floods in France in December 2003 and in February 2004, when Morocco was hit by an earthquake. In 2006 the mechanism was used for the first time in a war situation when it helped member states evacuate their citizens from Lebanon and coordinated European experts for the education of locals to clean up the oil spill caused by Israeli bombing.

Several capacities were tested in these first EU interventions. The added value in comparison with the system of bilateral requests for assistance lies in its provision for more consolidated and, in principle, faster and more precise response. The mechanism was shown to perform well as a clearing house for assistance, though a number of technical problems emerged. These related mainly to communication problems between the various national teams.[70] Many of the problems seem to have originated in a mindset still strongly shaped by a distinction between internal and external security. Although the formal mandate to use civil protection tools outside Union territory now exists, implications for operational planning in practice are not as well implemented as one might expect or wish.

The Internal–External Challenge

FLOODINGS 2002. On 14 August 2002, Czech president Vaclav Havel phoned Commission president Romano Prodi – at that time on vacation in his home town of Bologna – to explain the acute flooding situation in Central Europe.[71] Prodi travelled immediately to Prague and promised that the Union would assist the Czech Republic. Contacting most of the high-level civil servants in the Commission (largely from DG Environment and DG Enlargement), Prodi called them back from vacation to coordinate the assistance of EU member states and put together an EU aid package for the affected areas. One of the first to be contacted was the head of unit for the Czech Republic team at directorate-general for enlargement at the European Commission.[72] Later that same day, Czech Republic authorities made a formal request to the MIC of DG Environment to activate the Community mechanism. The request prioritised portable dryers, floating pumps, and electric submersible pumps. It was notified by the MIC to the competent national authorities.

Some EU states used other mechanisms for assistance in addition to the MIC. Others went ahead with bilateral contacts even while the MIC was trying to coordinate activities. This led to confusion at the European level, 'rather than better coordination'.[73] Member states were free to send whatever resources they had available, rather than those sought by the requesting country. This led to the major problem that some of the assistance could not be used by the Czech Republic.[74] Embarassingly, but significantly in terms of the implications of non-coordination, Czech foreign minister Stanislav Gross announced on 14 August that, while grateful for the aid, he believed some of it was unnecessary. He emphasised that assistance with reconstruction was, by that point, a higher priority.[75] By 21 August, the Czech Republic had received assistance in the form of dryers, pumps, blankets, stoves, disinfectants, hygienic materials, generators, emergency grants, personnel and other humanitarian items from twenty countries. Throughout the disaster, Commission president Romano Prodi was closely involved, reiterating the fact of the wider Europe's 'solidarity with the victims of the flooding'.[76] After several days, a Commission delegation including commissioners Margot Wallström, Günter Verheugen, and Michel Barnier visited Prague and Germany to assess the damage; the largest ever visit by a Commission delegation at this level for a civil protection incident. It displayed a concern, in the words of one Commission official, for an EU response to disasters '*wherever* they happen' (italics added).[77]

TSUNAMI 2004. Within hours of the tsunami in 2004, the Commission's directorate-general for environment began collecting information and critical intelligence for dissemination through the MIC. As with any use of the civil protection mechanism, however, no action could proceed without a formal request from the country concerned. For external deployment of the mechanism, a further approval needed to be granted from the current holder of the EU's rotating presidency.[78] The Sri Lankan government made a formal request to the MIC while the Dutch presidency formally agreed the use of the mechanism.[79] The MIC notified all EU states (and the five other participants in the Community mechanism at the time) of the appeal from Sri Lanka through the MIC's rapid alert network.[80] The receiving countries were later broadened to include Indonesia and the Maldives, in addition to Sri Lanka and Thailand.[81]

After several days the Union was forced to take on a new responsibility that had never been included in its crisis preparation, namely to support and evacuate EU citizens affected by the tsunami. The Dutch presidency focused considerable attention on this task.[82] The MIC took part in the inter-consular telephone conferences organised by the presidency aimed at coordinating the evacuation efforts in Thailand. The result of these conferences was a new request by the MIC to member states, stipulating the need for medical assistance and search and rescue teams for European citizens.[83] In the aftermath of the crisis, the Union admitted its shortcomings and lack of imagination. The Union had been prepared to assist its own citizens in its territory and to aid third-country nationals hit by catastrophes, but there had been no operational planning for help to EU citizens abroad.

The Commission subsequently attempted to remedy these shortcomings. It launched a consultation process with the member states on the development of the existing civil protection tools into a broader instrument addressing prevention, preparedness and response to disasters.[84] The Commission proposed that member states should declare their 'firm commitment' to cooperate with each other in delivering civil protection assistance and the reinforcement of EU coordination capacities, such as an 'operational planning capacity' of the MIC of the Commission and a common function on site with the formal authority to coordinate the assistance. The idea was to make the MIC more able to mobilise military means, hire equipment not obtained by member states, and promote a system of specialised national modules for European use. The Commission argued that these standby modules should be deployed 'quasi-automatically' on the request of an 'appropriate European authority'.[85]

In their response, many member state authorities emphasised the need to respect national sovereignty and the principles of subsidiarity. They warned against any reform that did not strengthen the added value of the EU capacity. On this view the role of the EU was first and foremost to provide coordination support to national interventions. There was thus support for proposals to improve the MIC. There was also a broad consensus on the need to strengthen the Union's capacity in the area of prevention, preparedness and information to the public.

But most member states hesitated to adopt the idea of creating a standby capacity for mutual European assistance, not least because they thought the composition of national and European teams needed to be as flexible as possible in a situation where future disasters were 'unknown'. Different compositions were needed for different interventions and teams should be composed of personnel working with emergencies on a daily basis. The idea of a flexible modular system could, according to some member states, be further discussed.[86]

These differences of view led to the so-called Barnier report of Spring 2006 suggesting the establishment of a standing European civil protection force – unfortunately named 'Europe aid', which was already the name of the Commission directorate-general responsible for management of aid and technical assistance abroad. The European civil protection force was proposed to be put under the authority of a new Council for Civil Security (Conseil de Sécurité Civile) and supported by permanent sites around the globe for the fast provision of assistance.[87] First signs are that the proposal has not been favourably received by national ministries. As with the ESDP, the challenge lies in transcending the internal-external divide. Divergences on policy can be seen as an expression of the tensions between the need for common action, practical sector specific needs and the ideal of national sovereignty. [88]

Implications for National Armed Forces

The ability of EU member states to provide for military assistance to internal protection will be decisive in defining the EU's potential to transcend the internal-external security boundary. But the issue of military activities within a European state raises important and sensitive questions. An important example of national policy is provided by the three Nordic EU countries – Finland, Sweden and Denmark. Here the issue of the use of military assistance in domestic counter-terrorism activities has been discussed, and with interesting consequences. The emerging new internal role of the Nordic armed forces is a significant example of the national reforms needed for the implementation of the EU's Solidarity clause, which calls upon the member states to make available 'military resources'. Again, the closer internal–external interface makes the development of the EU's security policies increasingly dependent on the contributions of the member states. In order to put the national resources requested at the disposal of the EU, governments must fundamentally rethink the traditional division of roles between the police and the military.

Traditionally, EU member states have adopted many different solutions for providing and regulating these functions.[89] In all of the Nordic countries historically there has been a strict division between the military's defence of the state border and national security on the one hand and the maintenance of order by the police on the other. In the aftermath of 11 September 2001, however, the Nordic governments began to re-examine their legal frameworks with regard to the use of military assistance to combat terrorist attacks on their territory.

Finland's 1980 act on the provision of assistance by the defence forces to the police allows military assistance to be given only in cases where the resources of the police are inadequate. After 11 September 2001, a commission established to consider the act proposed amendments in areas related to combating terrorism. Under the proposal, the police can ask the Ministry of the Interior to request assistance from the Ministry of Defence. The two ministers together decide whether this type of assistance ought to be provided. The naval and air force units of the defence forces can then be put at the disposal of the police, provided the nature of the terrorist threat calls for these resources.[90] The 2004 amendment to the 1980 act also specifies the conditions for military assistance. The police may receive assistance from the armed forces in order to prevent or avert certain criminal acts as specified in the Finnish Criminal Code. In emergency situations when there is a 'serious' and 'direct' threat to 'particularly important' functions of society, the police force's request for assistance can be made directly to the top military command.[91] In the Finnish government's strategy for national preparedness, the basic functions of society are defined as 'state leadership, external capacity to act, the nation's military defence, internal security, functioning of the economy and society, securing the livelihood of the population and its capacity to act, and their ability to tolerate a crisis'.[92]

Military assistance by the Swedish armed forces to the police has not been permitted since 1931, when the military opened fire on a strike demonstration in Ådalen and several participants were killed. In 2003 the Swedish Ministry of Justice published the report of a government commission on the implications of the attacks of 11 September 2001, suggesting legal reforms to enable military assistance.[93] The report proposed that, on the request of the police or coastguard, the armed forces could intervene against non-state actors with the degree of force necessary to avert immediate danger to the safety of the state or to human life or to prevent extensive destruction of property. The commission suggested that the government could deploy the armed forces to combat an armed attack against the Swedish state even if the attack did not emanate from a foreign state. This opened a new field in which the armed forces could be used: military assistance would be allowed in cases of large-scale terrorist attacks threatening the security of the state. Less serious terrorist attacks that could be classified as armed attacks against the security of the state would continue to be a matter for the police. Currently, the Swedish armed forces may respond to surprise attacks against the Swedish state by a foreign state without awaiting a decision by the government. The report suggested that this condition should also apply in the event of threats from terrorists.[94] The proposed bill did not, however, obtain political support. Instead, a new commission proposed the framing of a new act to regulate the conditions for military assistance to the police in the event of a major terrorist act on (Sweden's) democracy beyond the current capacity of the police.[95] The new legislation was adopted by parliament in June 2006. In the framework of the EU Solidarity clause on terrorism, the Swedish government predicts that military support for civilian crisis management, including the police, will most likely concern the provision of nuclear, biological and chemical expertise, logistics and command resources.[96]

One of the tasks for the Danish armed forces, according to the 2001 defence forces act, is assistance to the civilian authorities, including both assistance in rescue operations and assistance to the police.[97] The guiding principle is that military units providing assistance are subordinated to the command of the requesting authority and should obey the latter's rules of engagement. There are no particular statutory limitations concerning the character of the assistance. According to the act, among the assets that could be provided by the armed forces are helicopters and boarding expertise. The Danish police do not possess their own helicopters, and it is primarily the Royal Danish Navy that could provide boarding expertise to the police. Danish law does not exclude assistance for combating organized crime. Decisions on this kind of assistance are taken jointly by the ministries of Justice and Defence.[98]

Conclusion: towards a new type of transnational security community?

This chapter has elaborated a concept of European security in concentric circles as an aid to understanding the new landscape for EU protection policies. By putting the ESDP, the Solidarity clause, EU civil protection and national armed forces in this landscape it reveals key questions concerning the need for reform in a way impossible for approaches constrained by the theoretical premise of an internal-external security divide.

Viewed over the last five decades, the transformation of European security into increasingly wider circles is nothing new. In the 1950s the European Community helped the West European states to think ahead in terms of common security through transnational cooperation. With the EU's transcending of national internal-external boundaries, Western Europe emerged as a security community: defined by Karl Deutsch as a group of people integrated to the point where there is a 'real assurance that the members of that community will not fight each other physically, but will settle their disputes in some other ways'.[99] For the European security community, there was no sharp division between 'internal' and 'external' security. The community faded away the further one moved from its centre.

The current challenge is to try again to make the most of innovative thinking on security, and the key is to think and act beyond the internal-external divide. In the 1950s the European Union was able to transcend the division between external and domestic security for its member states by generating cooperation and community through transnational networking. Fifty years later, it has begun to dissolve the boundary between external and internal EU security by expanding its internal safety, police and defence cooperation to neighbouring areas and linking it to the EU's contribution to international security. This chapter examines some of the clearest and most visible signs of this development. It also shows that much remains to be done. Yet, notwithstanding the need for further analysis and policy development, the trans-governmental security and safety cooperation that has evolved since September 2001 and been codified by the Solidarity clause on terrorism, has the potential to provide the EU with an opportunity to take the lead again in the creation of post-national security systems and communities.

As in the case of Europe's security community, the new EU security role does not imply the transformation of Europe into a state. It is also unlikely to be based on a military defence alliance. Instead, the Solidarity clause and the ESDP point to a Union fostering a new type of regional security identity. The question is whether the EU will manage to deepen the European security community into a secure European community – a homeland defence à l'européenne. A secure community could tentatively be defined as 'a group of people that is integrated to the point where there is real assurance that the members of that community will assist each other to protect their democratic institutions, their civilian populations and the core functions of their societies and governments'.[100] Such a new form of security community would make no clear distinction between internal and external security. And it is precisely in this light that the emerging new European- and perhaps transatlantic-secure community order can have important implications for the EU's policies against terrorism.

Endnotes:

1   Duke, S., The Elusive Quest for European Security (Macmillan: Basingstoke, 2000); Van Ham, P. and Medvedev, S., Mapping European Security after Kosovo (Manchester University Press: Manchester, 2002).
2   See also, Boin, A., Ekengren, M., Rhinard, M. (eds) (2006) 'Special Issue: Protecting the Union: The Emergence of a New Policy Space', Journal of European Integration, Vol. 28, No 5, December.
3   European Council, 'Declaration on combating terrorism', Brussels, 25 Mar. 2004, URL <http://ue.eu.int/ueDocs/cmsUpload/79635.pdf>.
4   Commission Green Paper on a European Programme for Critical Infrastructure Protection, COM (2005) 576 final, Brussels, 17.11.2005.
5   Lagadec has frequently made this point. See for example Lagadec, P., and Guilhou, X.,: 'Katrina': Quand les crises ne suivent plus le script', Préventique-Sécurité, n° 88, Juillet-août 2006, pp. 31-33. Also Henri Quarantelli, Arjen Boin, Patrick Lagadec : 'Trans-System Ruptures: The New Disasters and Crises of the 21st Century and the Implications for Planning and Managing', in R. Dynes, H. Quarantelli, H. Rodriguez, Handbook of Disaster Research, Springer, September 2006.
6   Ekengren, M., Matzén, N., Svantesson, M. (2006) The new security role of the European Union: transnational crisis management and the protection of Union citizens, EUCM report 2, ACTA 35 B 2006, Stockholm: National Defence College. See more on the these two cases in section on 'Implications for EU civil protection' below.
7   Council of the European Union, 'A secure Europe in a better world: European Security Strategy', Brussels, 12 Dec. 2003.
8   Duke, S. and Ojanen, H. (2006) 'Bridging Internal and External Security: Lessons from the European Security and Defence Policy', Journal of European Integration, Vol. 28, No 5, December.
9   European Union (2004) 'Treaty establishing a Constitution for Europe.' Official Journal of the European Union, C 310, 16 December 2004, p. 32. Adopted as a political declaration in the aftermath of the Madrid train bombings in 2004.
10   Buzan, B., Wæver, O. and de Wilde, J., Security: A New Framework for Analysis (Lynne Rienner: London, 1998).
11   Ginsberg, R. H., The European Union in World Politics: Baptism of Fire (Rowman & Littlefield: Lanham, Md., 2001); and Smith, M. E., Europe's Foreign and Security Policy: the Institutionalization of Cooperation (Cambridge University Press: Cambridge, 2004).
12   Winn, N. and Lord, C., EU Foreign Policy Beyond the Nation State: Joint Actions and Institutional Analysis of the Common Foreign and Security Policy (Palgrave: Basingstoke, 2001); and Hill, C., 'The capability-expectations gap, or conceptualising Europe's international role', eds S. Bulmer and A. Scott, Economic and Political Integration in Europe: Internal Dynamics and Global Context (Blackwell: Oxford, 1994).
13   Walker, R. B. J., Inside/Outside: International Relations as Political Theory (Cambridge University Press: Cambridge, 1993); Wæver, O. et al., Identity, Migration and the New Security Order in Europe (Pinter: London, 1993); and Sjursen, H., 'Security and defence', eds W. Carlsnaes, H. Sjursen and B. White, Contemporary European Foreign Policy (Sage: London, 2004), p. 62.
14   Lenzi, G., 'Defining the European security policy', ed. J. Zielonka, Paradoxes of European Foreign Policy (Kluwer: The Hague, 1998), pp. 111-14.
15   Wæver, O., 'The EU as a security actor: reflections from a pessimistic constructivist on post-

sovereign security orders', eds Kelstrup and Williams, *International Relations and the Politics of European Integration: Power, Security and Community* (Routledge: London, 2000), pp. 250-94.

16 Jørgensen K. E. (ed.), *European Approaches to Crisis Management* (Kluwer Law: The Hague, 1997), p. 211.

17 Browning, C. (2005) 'Westphalian, Imperial, Neomedieval: The Geopolitics of Europe and the Role of the North', in C. Browning (ed.) *Remaking Europe in the margins* (London: Ashgate).

18 Bigo, D., 'When two become one: internal and external securitisations in Europe', eds Kelstrup and Williams, *International Relations and the Politics of European Integration: Power, Security and Community* (Routledge: London, 2000), pp. 171-204; and Bigo, D., 'The Möbius ribbon of internal and external security(ies)', eds Albert, Jacobson and Lapid, *Identities, Borders, Orders: Rethinking International Relations Theory* (University of Minnesota Press: Minneapolis, Minn., 2001), pp. 91-116.

19 Bigo, 'When two become one' (note 18), p. 183.

20 Bigo, D., *Polices en Réseaux: l'Expérience européenne* [Police in networks: the European experience] (Presses de la Fondation nationale des sciences politique: Paris, 1996); and Mitsilegas, V., Monar, J. and Rees, W., *The European Union and Internal Security: Guardian of the People?* (Palgrave: Basingstoke, 2003).

21 Jervis, R., *System Effects: Complexity in Political and Social Life* (Princeton University Press: Princeton, NJ, 1997).

22 Sjöstedt, G., *The External Role of the European Community* (Saxon House: Farnborough, 1977); and Whitman, R. G., *From Civilian Power to Superpower? The International Identity of the European Union* (Macmillan: Basingstoke, 1998).

23 Kirchner, E. (2006) 'The Challenge of European Union Security Governance', *Journal of Common Market Studies,* 44 (5), pp 947-68.

24 Gärtner, H., 'European security: the end of territorial defense', *Brown Journal of World Affairs*, vol. 9, issue 2 (winter/spring 2003).

25 Technically speaking, the European Union has only existed since 1992. We take the history of the European Communities since 1952 into account as well.

26 See chapter 4 in this book by Boin, A., Ekengren, M., Rhinard, M.

27 Buzan, B., Wæver, O. and de Wilde, J., *Security: A New Framework for Analysis* (Lynne Rienner: London, 1998); Møller, B. (2001) 'Global, National, Societal and Human Security, A General Discussion with a Case Study from the Middle East', Paper presented at the 4th Pan-European Conference at the University of Kent at Canterbury, UK, 8-10 September 2001.

28 Paris, R. (2001) 'Human Security: Paradigm Shift or Hot Air?', *International Security*, 26,2: 87-102.

29 Ekengren, M., and Ramberg, B. (2003) 'EU Practices and European Structure of Crisis Management: A Bourdieuian Perspective on EU Foreign Policy – The cases of Earthquakes in Turkey and Reconstruction of Kosovo, 1999' Paper presented at ECPR Conference, September 2003 Canterbury, UK.

30 It is perhaps significant that 'A Human Security Doctrine for Europe' recently was proposed as a doctrine for Europe's security capabilities. (Kaldor, M., *A Human Security Doctrine for Europe, The Barcelona Report of the Study Group on European Security*. Presented 10 November 2004, led by Professor Mary Kaldor in 2003 at the request of EU Secretary-General Javier Solana. Online. Available HTTP: <http://www.lse.ac.uk/Depts/global/> (accessed 6 October 2005).)

31 Grönvall, J. (2000) *Managing Crisis in the European Union: The Commission and 'Mad Cow' Disease*, Stockholm: CRISMART/Swedish National Defence College, p. 89; and Grönvall (2001) 'Mad Cow Disease: The Role of Experts and European Crisis Management,' in Rosenthal, U., Boin, A. and Comfort, L. (eds), *Managing Crises: Threats, Dilemmas, Opportunities*. Springfield: Charles C Thomas.

32 European Union (2004) 'Treaty establishing a Constitution for Europe.' Official Journal of the European Union, C 310, 16 December 2004, p. 32.

33 Sundelius, B. (2005) 'Disruptions – Functional Security for the EU', in Elbe, S., Luterbacher, U., Missiroli, A., Sundelius, B. and Zupi, M. (2005) *Disasters, Diseases, Disruptions: a new D-drive for the EU*, Chaillot Paper, no. 83, September.

34 Boin, Arjen, Ekengren, M., Rhinard, Mark (2006) *Functional Security and Crisis Management Capacity in the European Union*. Report, No B 36 ACTA-series, National Defence College, Stockholm, p. 20. This characterisation of an EU crisis builds on a classical crisis definition according to which a crisis should be understood as a 'serious threat to (...) fundamental values and norms of a social system (...)' (Rosenthal, 't Hart and Charles 1989).

35 Filtenborg, M. S., Gänzle, S. and Johansson, E., 'An alternative theoretical approach to EU

foreign policy: network governance and the case of the Northern Dimension initiative', *Cooperation and Conflict*, vol. 37, no. 4 (2002), pp. 387-407.
36 Hänggi, H. and Tanner, F. (2005) *Promoting security sector governance in the EU's neighbourhood*, Chaillot Paper, No 80, July, Paris: Institute for Security Studies.
37 On the basis of the growing collection of case studies of the EU's external actions it is safe to conclude that the CFSP has been politically strongest within ('collective at any cost') and on the EU's frontiers. See Piening, C., *Global Europe: The European Union in World Affairs* (Lynne Rienner: London, 1997). This development has been underlined as a consequence of the extended cooperation with candidate states in the 1990s. See Friis, L. and Murphy, A., 'The European Union and Central and Eastern Europe: governance and boundaries', *Journal of Common Market Studies*, vol. 37, no. 2 (1999), pp. 211-32.
38 See Treaty of Amsterdam, 2 Oct. 1997, <http://www.europarl.eu.int/topics/treaty/pdf/amst?en.pdf>; European Council, 'Presidency conclusions', Helsinki, 10-11 Dec. 1999, URL <http://europa.eu.int/council/off/conclu/dec99/dec99_en.htm>; European Council, 'Conclusions of the Presidency', Santa Maria da Feira, 19-20 June 2000, URL <http://www.europarl.eu.int/summits/fei1_en.htm>; and European Council, Gothenburg, 15-16 June 2001, URL <http://europa.eu.int/comm/gothenburg_council/index_en.htm>.
39 Commission of the European Communities, 'Communication from the Commission: paving the way for a new neighbourhood instrument', Brussels, 1 July 2003, COM (2003) 393 final, URL <http://europa.eu.int/comm/world/enp/document_en.htm>.
40 Whitman, R. G., 'The fall, and rise, of civilian power Europe?', Paper presented at the Conference on the European Union in International Affairs, National Europe Centre, Australian National University, 3-4 July 2002; and Manners, I., 'Normative power Europe: a contradiction in terms?', *Journal of Common Market Studies*, vol. 40, no. 2 (2002).
41 Haaland Matlary, J., 'Human rights', eds Carlsnaes, Sjursen and White (note 13), pp. 141-54. On the EU Charter of Fundamental Rights see URL <http://www.europarl.eu.int/charter/>.
42 United Nations, 'Charter of the United Nations', URL <http://www.un.org/aboutun/charter/>.
43 Ulriksen, S., Gourlay, C. and Mace, C., 'Operation Artemis: the shape of things to come?', *International Peacekeeping*, vol. 11, no. 3 (autumn 2004), pp. 508-25.
44 It is perhaps significant that 'a human security doctrine for Europe' was recently proposed as a doctrine for Europe's security capabilities. Study Group on Europe's Security Capabilities, 'A human security doctrine for Europe', Barcelona Report of the Study Group on Europe's Security Capabilities, London School of Economics and Political Science, Centre for the Study of Global Governance, London, 15 Sep. 2004, URL<http://www.lse.ac.uk/Depts/global/Publications/HumanSecurityDoctrine.pdf>.
45 Duke, S. and Ojanen, H. (2006) 'Bridging Internal and External Security: Lessons from the European Security and Defence Policy', *Journal of European Integration*, Vol. 28, No 5, December. *Protecting Europe – Policies for enhancing security in the EU*, International Conference organised by The Security & Defence Agenda, 30 May 2006, Brussels. 'Session four: Is Europe getting the politics of security right?'
46 See Dwan, R., 'Capabilities in the civilian field', Speech at the Conference on the European Union Security Strategy: Coherence and Capabilities, Working Group 2, Capabilities, Swedish Institute of International Affairs, Stockholm, 20 Oct. 2003, http://www.sipri.org/contents/conflict/nonmilitary.htm>,
47 Boin, A., Ekengren, M., Rhinard, M. (2006) 'Chapter 18: The Commission and Crisis Management', in D. Spence (ed.) *The European Commission*, London: John Harper Publishing.
48 See Wolfgang Wagner (2003) 'Why the EU's Common Foreign and Security Policy will remain Intergovernmental: a rationalist institutional choice analysis of European crisis management policy, *Journal of European Public Policy* 10: 4, pp. 576-595.
49 Boin, A., Ekengren, M., Rhinard, M. (eds) (2006) *Protecting the European Union – Policies, sectors and institutional solutions*, Report, Swedish National Defence College, October.
50 Ekengren, Magnus (2002) 'EU som civil krishanterare – nätverksbyggare eller aktör?', i S. Myrdal (red) *EU som civil krishanterare*, Säkerhetspolitiska rådet, Utrikespolitiska Institutet, Stockholm. See also the proposals of former Commissioner and French foreign minister, Michel Barnier: Barnier Report (2006) *For a European Civil Protection Force: Europe Aid*. Independent report commissioned by the Austrian Presidency (Spring 2006) and Commission President José Manuel Barroso. Delivered May 2006.
51 Sundelius, B., 'The seeds of a functional security paradigm for the European Union', Paper

presented at the Second Pan-European Conference on EU Politics of the ECPR Standing Group on European Union Politics., Bologna, 2004.
52 Smith, M. E., *Europe's Foreign and Security Policy: the Institutionalization of Cooperation* (Cambridge University Press: Cambridge, 2004).
53 See Dwan, R., 'Capabilities in the civilian field', Speech at the Conference on the European Union Security Strategy: Coherence and Capabilities, Working Group 2, Capabilities, Swedish Institute of International Affairs, Stockholm, 20 Oct. 2003, URL
54 The bureaucratic wrangling involved is discussed in D. Spence 'The Commission and CFSP' in D. Spence (ed) *The European Commission*, John Harper Publishing, 2006.
55 de Wijk, R., 'Civil defence and solidarity clause: EU homeland defence', Paper prepared for the Directorate-General for Research of the European Parliament, Brussels, 5 Jan. 2004.
56 Ekengren, M. and Larsson, S., *Säkerhet och försvar i framtidens EU: an analys av försvarsfrågorna i det europeiska konventet* [Security and defence in the future EU: an analysis of the defence questions in the European convention], Report no. 2003:10 (Swedish Institute of European Policy Studies (SIEPS): Stockholm, 2003), URL <http://www.sieps.se/_eng/forskning.htm>. See also the SIEPS Internet site at URL <http://www.sieps.se/>.
57 Boin, A., Ekengren, M., Rhinard, M. (2006) 'Chapter 18: The Commission and Crisis Management', in D. Spence (ed.) *The European Commission*, London: John Harper Publishing.
58 ibid.
59 Ekengren, M. (2006) 'New Security Challenges and the Need for New Forms of EU Co-operation – the Solidarity Clause and the Open Method of Coordination', *European Security*, Vol. 15, No. 1, 89-111.
60 de Wijk, R., 'Civil defence and solidarity clause: EU homeland defence', Paper prepared for the Directorate-General for Research of the European Parliament, Brussels, 5 Jan. 2004.
61 Ekengren, M., Matzén, N.,, Rhinard, M., Svantesson, M. (2006) 'Solidarity or Sovereignty? EU Cooperation in Civil Protection', *Journal of European Integration*, Vol. 28, No 5, December.
62 Duke, S. and Ojanen, H. (2006) 'Bridging Internal and External Security: Lessons from the European Security and Defence Policy', *Journal of European Integration*, Vol. 28, No 5, December.
63 Council of the European Union (2001) Council Decision of 23 October 2001 establishing a Community mechanism to facilitate reinforced co-operation in civil protection assistance interventions, Article 3. 2001/792/EC, Official Journal of the European Union, L 297, 15 November 2001, pp. 7-11.
64 Article 2. Ibid.
65 These commitments were made at the European Council meeting in Göteborg in June 2001.
66 CECIS is linked with a number of other networks operating in different sectors, including those dealing with radiological, health, and biological-chemical disasters. See *Communication from the Commission on Reinforcing the Civil Protection Capacity of the European Union*, Brussels, 25 March 2004, COM(2004)200 final, pp. 11-12.
67 Joint Declaration (2003) Joint Declaration by the Council and the Commission on the use of the Community Mechanism in Crisis Management referred to in Title V of the Treaty on the European Union of 29 September 2003, Internal Document.
68 de Wijk, R., 'Civil defence and solidarity clause: EU homeland defence', Paper prepared for the Directorate-General for Research of the European Parliament, Brussels, 5 Jan. 2004.
69 Personal interview with an official from the Commission's civil protection unit, directorate-general for environment, 13 February 2003 (a).
70 Woodbridge, J. (2002) Civil Protection Against Terror Attacks: testing EU cooperation, *European Security Review*, (ISIS), 2002(15), pp. 7-8.
71 Personal interview with an official from the Commission's directorate-general for enlargement, 13 February 2003 (b).
72 Personal interview with an official from the Commission's directorate-general for enlargement, 13 February 2003 (b).
73 Woodbridge, J. (2002) Civil Protection Against Terror Attacks: testing EU cooperation, *European Security Review*, (ISIS), 2002(15), pp. 7-8.
74 Personal interview with a member of the Commission's civil protection unit, directorate-general for environment, 11 February 2003 (a).
75 Radio Free Europe/Radio Liberty (2002, August 15) transcript of broadcast found on Relief Web (available at: http://www.reliefweb.int/w/rwb.nsf, accessed February, 2003).
76 Commission (2002a) Commission expresses solidarity with victims of floods, Press Release IP/02/1220, Brussels, 15 August 2002.
77 Personal interview with a member of the Commission's civil protection unit, directorate-general for environment, 11 February 2003 (a).

78   For further assessment of the general procedures of the MIC within the directorate-general for environment, see Boin, Ekengren & Rhinard (2006).

79   Commission (2005) EU Civil protection assistance in South East Asia, Memorandum, MEMO/05/6, Brussels, 11 January 2005.

80   Commission (2005) Commission's civil protection mechanism takes effective measures to coordinate technical assistance in South Asia, Press Release IP/05/4, Brussels, 5 January 2005.

81   Commission (2004) The European Commission coordinates EU civil protection support to catastrophe areas in South Asia, Press Release IP/04/1544, Brussels, 31 December 2004.

82   Commission (2004) European Commission mobilises the Civil Protection Mechanism for victims of the earthquake and tsunami in South Asia, Press release IP/04/1543, Brussels, 27 December 2004.

83   Commission (2005) EU Civil protection assistance in South East Asia, Memorandum, MEMO/05/6, Brussels, 11 January 2005.

84   European Commission, *Consultation on the future instrument addressing prevention of, preparedness for and response to disasters: Issue Paper*, 31 January 2005, Brussels. Commission, Directorate General Environment, Directorate A. ENV. A.5. – Civil Protection. http://www.europa.eu.int/comm/environment/civil/consult_new_instrument.htm. Accessed on 20-02-2006.

85   Ibid. p. 11.

86   European Commission, *Consultation on the future instrument addressing prevention of, preparedness for and response to disasters: Questionnaire*, Brussels. Commission, Directorate General Environment, Directorate A. ENV. A.5. – Civil Protection, 2005.

87   Barnier Report (2006) For a European Civil Protection Force: Europe Aid. Independent report commissioned by the Austrian Presidency (Spring 2006) and Commission President José Manuel Barroso. Delivered May 2006.

88   Ekengren, M., Matzén, Nina, Rhinard, Mark, Svantesson, Monica (2006) 'Solidarity or Sovereignty?' pp. 472-473.

89   The French Gendarmerie Nationale is made up of paramilitary forces and is organized under the Ministry of the Interior. Austria, Belgium, Greece (to a certain extent), Italy and Luxembourg have similar forces. All these forces are specialized in terms of training, equipment (often comprising heavy weaponry, armed vehicles, etc.) and lines of command for tasks that straddle the border between internal order and security and external security – e.g., the Italian Arma dei Carabinieri is responsible for certain military operations as well as for 'internal' civilian tasks, such as maintaining order. In some countries the forces are under the control of the defence ministry, in others, of the interior ministry. In some states (e.g., Italy) the authority, chain of command and rules of engagement change depending on the particular task. See Benyon, J. et al., *Police Forces in the European Union* (University of Leicester, Centre for the Study of Public Order: Leicester, 1994); and Stålvant, C.-E., 'Questioning the roles of the military and police in coping with functional security: some assertions about national variations and their impacts', Paper presented at the Second Pan-European Conference on EU Politics of the ECPR Standing Group on European Union Politics, Bologna, Italy, 24-26 June 2004.

90   Finnish Prime Minister's Office, Finnish Security and Defence Policy 2004, Government Report no. 6/2004 (Prime Minister's Office: Helsinki, 2004), URL <http://www.vnk.fi/vn/liston/vnk.lsp?r=88862&k=en>, pp. 127-28.

91   Republic of Finland, Hallituksen esitys Eduskunnalle laiksi puolustusvoimien virka-avusta poliisille annetun [Government proposition to parliament concerning amendment of the act on the provision of assistance by the defence forces to the police], Government proposition to parliament no. 187/2004, 8 Oct. 2004, URL <http://www.finlex.fi/linkit/hepdf/20040187/>.

92   Finnish Ministry of Defence, Government resolution on securing the functions vital to society and strategy for securing the functions vital to society, Helsinki, 27 Nov. 2003, URL <http://www.defmin.fi/index.phtml/page_id/369/topmenu_id/7/menu_id/369/this_topmenu/368/lang/3/>, p. 5.

93   Swedish 11 September Commission, Vår beredskap efter den 11 September [Our preparedness after 11 September], Statens Offentliga Utredningar no. 2003:32 (Swedish Ministry of Justice: Stockholm, 2003), URL <http://www.regeringen.se/sb/d/108/a/424>.

94   Swedish 11 September Commission (note 93), pp. 24-25.

95   Swedish Support Inquiry, *Polisens behov av stöd i samband med terrorismbekämpning* [The police's need for support in connection with combating terrorism], Statens Offentliga Utredningar no. 2005:70, (Swedish Ministry of Justice: Stockholm, 31 Aug. 2005), URL <http://www.regeringen.se/sb/d/108/a/48806/>.

96 Bjurner, A., 'The development of the European Security and Defence Policy', Statement in the Committee on Foreign Affairs, Swedish Parliament, 20 Apr. 2004, p. 10.

97 Kingdom of Denmark, Lov om forsvarets formål, opgaver og organisation m.v. [Act on the defence force's aims, tasks and organization, etc.], Act no. 122, 27 Feb. 2001, URL <http://www.retsinfo.dk/_GETDOCI_/ACCN/A20010012230-REGL>.

98 Mäkelä, J. (Lt Com.), 'Combating terrorism in Nordic countries: a comparative study of the military's role', C?level thesis, Swedish National Defence College, Stockholm, May 2003, URL <http://bibliotek.fhs.mil.se/publikationer/uppsatser/2003/chp0103/>.

99 Deutsch, K. W. et al., *Political Community and the North Atlantic Area: International Organization in the Light of Historical Experience* (Princeton University Press: Princeton, NJ, 1957).

100 Ekengren, M. (2007) 'From a European Security Community to a Secure European Community – Tracing the New the Security Identity of the EU', in: H.B. Brauch et al. (eds.) *Globalization and Security Challenges* (New York: Springer Verlag).

2. Radicalisation and Recruitment: The EU Response

Mirjam Dittrich

Introduction

This chapter reviews the factors contributing to violent radicalisation and examines the European Union' s short- and long-term policies to hinder terrorist recruitment. It might be thought that this is a straightforward, descriptive task based on a review of symptoms in an attempt to categorise identifiable causes in individual cases, with a subsequent appraisal of EU countermeasures. Yet, it is not so straightforward. First, whilst violent radicals are exploiting and misusing Islam as a framework for recruiting terrorists, the overwhelming majority of the 15 to 20 million Muslims living in Europe are law-abiding citizens who condemn these attacks. Using Islam as a way of justifying terrorism is an abuse of their faith. To attempt to analyse the phenomenon of violent radicalisation should therefore in no way be understood as equating an entire community with a small militant minority. Second, analysts concur that such reviews often reveal but partial truths (von Hippel, 2002); listing identifiable causes, while clearly necessary, confounds the analyst by simply revealing the multiplicity of potential causes.

It is, however, certain that the growing tendency in some quarters to equate an entire community with a small militant minority is a growing political concern. Increased Islamophobia means increased cultural isolation and a consequent negative impact on social integration. So, if the risk is misleading extrapolation from potential root causes in the search for policy guidance, there is clearly a need to distinguish between believers, religious fundamentalists, religious conservatism and violent radicalisation. Terrorism has disparate and complex causes, which experts and government officials need to address. Identifying the sources of violent radicalisation and the reasons for an individual's choice to become a terrorist are without doubt a major pre-condition for identifying possible solutions.

While there are external factors, such as the war in Iraq, the revelations about mistreatment of prisoners at Abu Ghraib or the Israeli-Palestinian conflict, there are also domestic issues such as the headscarf debate, the socio-economic situation of young Muslims or, more generally, the failure of integration policies. Yet drawing conclusions from analyses of these issues is far from simple. Arguments involving the catalyst of external events in a process of radicalisation resulting from social alienation and economic background are complex. Terrorists come from all walks of life and include relatively prosperous and seemingly well integrated individuals. Indisputably, however, international events often do provide stimulus and inspiration. Many young Muslims equate the 'war on terror' with a perceived war on Islam. They claim common cause with suffering brethren in the Palestinian territories, Iraq, Chechnya and elsewhere.[1]

Terrorists and suicide bombers now include ethnic Europeans and Muslim women, which makes it increasingly difficult to develop a 'terrorist profile' or even adequate theories to explain the patterns of terrorist recruitment. Theo Van Gogh was murdered by a young, Dutch speaking, well educated Muslim born in the Netherlands. The leaders of the German Al-Qaida cell which carried out the 9/11 attacks were neither poor nor socially disadvantaged, and the terrorists who carried out the 7 July 2005 bombings in London were British born and apparently well integrated.[2] The arrest on 10 August 2006 by UK police of 24 people in connection with a terrorist plot to detonate liquid explosives smuggled in carry-on luggage on transatlantic airliners, involved detention of mainly British citizens of Pakistani descent. Thus, irrespective of their socio-economic background, some – whether expatriate engineers studying in Germany, young Arabs living in the banlieues of Paris or second-generation Pakistanis living in the UK – find their calling in religious extremism and violent radicalism.

The difficulties for the analyst are thus equal to the difficulties facing law enforcement and intelligence agencies in identifying potential terrorists. Indeed, the London bombings added a new dimension to the contemporary terrorist threat. For the first time in Europe, 'home-grown' terrorists – young British-born Muslim men – committed suicide attacks. Some of the terrorists involved in the Madrid attacks in March 2005 were also seemingly well-integrated into Spanish society and might well have been radicalised while living in Europe. Clearly, an increasing number of young Muslims are finding a spiritual home within the most radical forms of Islam. So, if, in the short and medium term, improving security and intelligence cooperation is essential, there can be no doubt that longer-term solutions will require both understanding the root causes and addressing the issues involved. The problem, however, was summed up well by Javier Solana when he said that: 'there is a fanatical fringe who are beyond political discourse. But it is nourished by a pool of disaffection and grievance. Where these grievances are legitimate they must be addressed, not just because this is a matter of justice but also because "draining the swamp" depends on it.'[3] The dilemma for European policymakers is the resulting obligation to walk a narrow path between ensuring the security of the Union against further terrorist activity, confident prediction that addressing the threat from the fanatical fringe will be sufficient and yet still guaranteeing the rights and civil liberties of Europe's citizens. New counter-terrorism measures must respect human rights, if they are not to backfire.[4]

Growing radicalisation and root causes

Numbers and networks

What makes Al-Qaida so dangerous is that it no longer functions as a

closely interlinked network, but acts rather as a sort of 'franchising organisation'. In addition, Al-Qaida has always sought to be a vanguard for the *umma*[5],
mobilising popular support through spectacular attacks that serve as an
example. Its ideas find fertile ground throughout the world, as they increasingly become a militant ideology. Terrorist cells and individuals all over the
world operate in the name of Al-Qaida without being linked in any substantial way to its leader, Bin Laden, or his immediate circle. They simply follow
his methods. Cells operate in loose-knit networks, with connections across the
world. Many have considerable local autonomy to carry out attacks without
central command.[6] And there are spontaneous cells, appearing with no central direction. One aim of groups operating with a cell structure is prevention
of any one member or group from knowing who the leaders and other groups
are. So, the existence of autonomous, self-structuring cells makes such groups
more difficult to infiltrate and less easy to trace. The current violent jihadist
terrorist threat is also diverse and difficult to categorise. It includes self-facili-
tating or so called home-grown terrorists, fighters returning from Iraq, individuals connected to established fighting groups like the Salafist Group for
Call and Combat (GSPC), the Moroccan Combatant Group (GICM), or
Jemaah Islamiyah (JI), and individuals with direct links to Al-Qaida. There is
little evidence of an overarching organizational structure for the violent jihad
in Europe.

It is thus difficult to determine how many 'radicals' exist in Europe. But,
according to counter-terrorism officials, their number is certainly growing.
Time Magazine reported that in 2004, French police had discovered that 150
of the 1,600 mosques and prayer halls in the country were under the control
of extremist elements, and 23% of the French converts to Islam identified
themselves as Salafists. There are as many as 20 different hard-line Islamic
groups operating in the Netherlands and, in recent years, the UK has been
home to as many as 3,000 veterans of Al-Qaida training camps. In Germany,
according to the Federal Office for the Protection of the Constitution,
approximately 30,600 people are members of Islamist organisations, of
whom an estimated 300 or so are regarded as 'dangerous', because of their
contacts with terror organisations. Significantly, also, around 3,000 are considered willing to use violence but have no proven links to terrorist activities so far. After 9/11, in a move against 20 religious groups, the German
government conducted more than 200 raids and banned three radical
Islamic organisations (i.e. Kalifatsaat, Al-Aksa e.V., and Hizb-ut-Tahrir).[7]
Such interventions may bring some satisfaction to the authorities, but an
alarming ICM poll in the UK published in March 2004 found that 13% of
British Muslims surveyed would 'regard further attacks by Al-Qaida or
similar organisations on the US as justified'.[8]

In sum, while there are no precise figures on the number of extremists in
Europe, what can be observed is that before 9/11 members of radical groups
tended to be older and linked to the Afghan wars. This changed after 9/11.
Today there is increasing involvement of young people in extremist groups
interacting through family links and friends. Muslim youth in a number of
European countries including France, Germany, Belgium, the Netherlands
and the UK, most commonly respond to the question of what causes radicalisation by expressing a lack of respect and acknowledgment from society,
identity crisis, feelings of victimisation or inferiority and misguided under-

standing of Islam – all traits which can be easily exploited.[9] They are traits which can also be identified and traced, for there are practical steps an individual must take to become involved in terrorism, and it is this behaviour which the authorities need to identify and trace through community policing, effective monitoring of the internet and controlled travel to conflict zones.

Target groups and sites

European converts to Islam

European converts to Islam have also become a cause of concern. The threat they could pose was highlighted by the arrest of Richard Reid, a British citizen who converted to Islam and was found guilty of attempting to blow up a flight from Paris to the US in 2002. An increasing number of young Europeans from working-class backgrounds are converting to Islam. Kepel writes: 'Even if jihadist militants make up a tiny minority of this fresh group of enthusiasts, converts are of great concern to security services, because insurgents who choose not to display their faith overtly can easily elude the authorities. For this reason, the security services have begun increasing attention on converts.'[10] And, as Roy argues, converts seemingly do not turn towards fundamentalism because of the Iraq war, but because they feel excluded from Western society. This is especially true of the many converts from the Caribbean islands, both in France and the UK. 'Born again' Muslims, or converts, are rebels in search of a cause. They find it in the dream of a virtual, universal *umma*, in the same way that the ultra-leftists of the 1970s (the Baader-Meinhof Group and the Italian Red Brigades) justified their terrorist acts in the name of the 'world proletariat' and 'Revolution' with no preoccupation either with immediate consequences or with the end results.[11] However, at the same time European converts are often involved in integrating Islam into their host country, and significantly, while they tend to be more rigid and radical in the interpretation of their faith, it is difficult to judge whether they pose a more serious security threat than other groups.

The role of the internet

The internet plays a key role in the radicalisation process and has become one of the most important tools for Al-Qaida to spread its message and recruit young Muslims for the global jihad. It has created a sense of belonging to a global, virtual *umma*. There are large numbers of jihadi websites containing videos and photographs of terror attacks and kidnappings, guidelines on how to build and use bombs, information on where to buy explosives, as well as handbooks on Al-Qaida's strategies.

In some cases, autonomous indoctrination by individuals using the internet has occurred. The Simon Wiesenthal Centre in Los Angeles found the number of extremist websites to have increased from 12 to 4,500 over the eight years to 2006. The Bavarian State Office of Criminal Investigation and the State Office for the Protection of the Constitution have employed experts on Islam to evaluate the content of radical sites and chat rooms, demonstrating from conversations in chat rooms, for instance, that young Muslims in Germany are increasingly open to recruitment for suicide missions.[12] Given the sheer amount of propaganda material on the web and the increasingly sophisticated know-how of those distributing the material, it has become virtually impossible to take effective counter-measures.

The role of the Mujahidaat[13]

The case of a Belgian woman (Muriel Degauque, the first Western female convert to Islam to carry out a suicide bombing) could also be an indicator of a new trend: namely, male-dominated terrorist groups increasingly recruiting Muslim women to join the global jihad. While women have carried out suicide missions in Palestine and Chechnya for some years, it was only recently that conservative and religiously motivated terrorist groups such as Al-Qaida began using them. However, Farhana Ali[14] argues that the 'liberal' door that now permits women to participate in operations will probably close once male jihadists attract new recruits and notch up a substantial number of successful attacks. The sudden increase in female bombers over the past years may be short-lived. In the short term, male fighters could encourage Muslim women to join their organisations, but there is no indication that these men would allow the *mujahidaat* to gain authority and replace images of the male folk-hero. There is also no evidence that Muslim female operatives have contact with senior male leaders, except to receive orders to carry out attacks.

Abdul Hameed Bakier, a counter-terrorism intelligence expert, writes that observers of jihadi cyber activities have noticed an increase in the number of websites dedicated to *mujahidaat*, linked either directly or ideologically to Al-Qaida.[15] It may not be the first time Muslim females have participated in high profile jihadi operations, yet Islamist websites have only recently posted female jihadi training documents. Bakier also argues that some of the postings are of a non-combatant nature, although interviews with female *mujahidaat* in Afghanistan, Palestine and elsewhere indicate that female Islamists are being trained for military operations as well. If Al-Qaida is able to increase the number of women engaged in the jihad, there are clear operational implications for counter-terrorism and security forces.

Suicide bombings and Islam

Robert A. Pape's study of every suicide bombing and attack around the globe between 1980 and 2003 found little evidence of a connection between suicide terrorism and Islamic fundamentalism. Rather, what nearly all suicide terrorist attacks have in common is a specific secular and strategic goal: to compel modern democracies to withdraw military forces from territories that the terrorists consider their homeland. Pape further argues that religion per se is rarely the root cause, although it is often used as a recruiting tool by terrorist organisations and serves broader strategic objectives.[16]

Radicalisation in prisons

State prisons in Europe have been identified as potential recruiting grounds for terrorists and there is indeed evidence of connections between former prisoners and terrorism. Yet, it is difficult to judge the extent to which radicalisation occurs in prison and to estimate the number of individuals currently in prison in pre-trial detention or sentenced and serving time for activities connected to jihadist terrorist activity.[17] The imam is not necessarily held in high regard by a prison's Muslim community and radicalisation may depend on a prisoner's cellmate. A report by the George Washington University Homeland Security Policy Institute on radicalisation in prisons concludes that radicalised prisoners are a potential pool of recruits for terrorist groups.[18] Jailed Islamist extremists take advantage of the few available Muslim chaplains and scarce religious monitoring programmes in US prisons to breed terrorists with violent interpretations of the Koran. There is also growing concern about violent radicalisation in European prisons. French officials report, for example, that radical Islamic views are being preached in a majority of French prisons.[19] Concerns over radicalisation in UK and Belgian prisons have also recently emerged, and there are also indications that Belgian citizens of Moroccan origin held in Moroccan prisons for drug smuggling are being recruited for terrorist activities.

If the issue of radicalisation and recruitment within prisons in the EU is a potential problem, the different penitentiary systems across the 27 countries make it difficult to define and implement common recommendations. Moreover, there is insufficient information about prisoner radicalisation to qualify the threat, though it seems clear that prevention will require analysis and response.

Radicalisation in mosques

The messages of religious leaders in European mosques, especially since 9/11, are under scrutiny following the discovery that certain mosques (the Finsbury Park and Baker Street Mosques in London and the al-Quds Mosque in Hamburg and radical mosques in France) had been used to spread extremist views and practices. Sheik Omar Bakri Muhammad, a Syrian-born cleric in London, urged young Muslim men to support the Iraq insurgency and has repeatedly referred to the terrorists who carried out the 9/11 attacks as 'the magnificent 19' in his sermons.[20] In the case of the Madrid attacks authorities also identified a connection between the terrorists and places of worship that advocated Wahhabi Islam. Keppel sums it up well: 'Without undergoing indoctrination or brainwashing or deprivation in an Afghan training camp they suddenly became activists bent on waging a jihad of terror, assisted by a few experienced militants who blended into the multivariate Spanish social landscape.'[21] Olivier Roy, research director at the Paris-based Centre National de la Recherche Scientifique, argues that the radicalisation of mosques is a result of the growing Salafist movement, which attracts young people who feel rejected by Western societies. The number of such radical mosques in France has increased significantly, according to a study by undercover police forces reported in Le Monde in February 2004, which revealed that there were 32 mosques largely under the control of Salafists – ten more than in the previous year.[22]

Salafists are not necessarily supporters of violence, however; they tend to prefer to stay out of the political process. Salafists advocate a pure interpretation of the Koran and the word 'Salafi' itself means fundamentalist in the sense of close adherence to the original texts of Islam. Salafists are primarily a manifestation of religious fundamentalism. This does not necessarily make them a security issue, though Jocelyne Cesari argues that even if Salafi doctrine bears no direct relation to terrorist activity, it provides a similar religious framework to that used by radical groups such as Al-Qaida and may contribute to the sense of familiarity or proximity that potential terrorists experience when they join radical groups. Moreover, while Salafi Islam is not the only interpretation of Islam in Europe, it has played a central role in determining how Muslims deal with their religious tradition in the West.[23]

Extremists increasingly withdraw from their local mosques because they are either under surveillance, are expelled because of their radical views, or leave voluntarily because they feel the imam is not teaching an appropriate (extremist) interpretation of Islam.[24] They move instead to private places to meet and pray, making their activities much harder to monitor. There is also concern that Islamic countries are seeking to exert control over the main Muslim institutions in Europe by, for example, financing major mosques. Saudi Arabia and Egypt regularly send delegations of Muslim scholars to Europe. These scholars often take a traditional approach to teaching that does not necessarily reflect the realities of life in European countries. In addition, for some years now, Riyadh has been offering an increasing number of free training courses in Saudi Arabia. The first students to benefit from this assistance have returned to Europe and many have since been championing a sectarian mode of life. By promoting a literal reading of the holy texts, they reject integration, oppose involvement in host societies and tend to regard Europe as a world naturally hostile to Islam, a world from which they must stand apart.[25] Yet, there are signs that this is changing. Second and third-generation Muslims have fewer ties with their countries of origin and an increasing number of Muslim organisations accept financial assistance only if it is given with no strings attached. More efforts have also been made across Europe to restrict the activities of radical imams who incite violence through militant sermons.

Dilemmas facing mosques and imams

Addressing the issue of mosques and imams in Europe is important for both social integration and for prevention of extremism, for their role is an important factor in the overall integration of Muslims in Europe. Again, there is a line between policies tending to 'oversecuritise' and those aiming to contribute to building a credible, integrated Muslim minority in Western society.

Many imams in Europe are inadequately trained to deal either with modern European culture or with problems that arise from the interaction between Muslims and Western societies. Moreover, many are not credible interlocutors for the younger generation. They were trained in their country of origin and are often unable to communicate with youngsters, not least because of language difficulties. This is a particular problem for Arabic-speaking imams, as the linguistic link with the country of origin remains stronger within the Turkish, Pakistani and Bengali communities.[26] This means that many young people do not identify with the discourse of traditional imams. They feel estranged from the religious services they provide, underlining the need for 'home-grown' imams.

One option is for European governments to establish programmes for training imams within the host country, thus ensuring provision of understanding for the values and the culture of the country in which they live and work. In the UK, for example, only around 30 imams have been educated in Britain, though arrivals from abroad number around a thousand, most of whom do not speak English. France has established institutes for some official religions such as Catholic, Protestant and Orthodox Christianity, but Islam is not recognised as such or funded. In Germany and Sweden, the training of imams is supported by institutes and universities. Islam has been recognised in Belgium since 1974, but imams do not receive state grants even though funds are provided for other religious officials. In addition, across Europe imams are very poorly paid, receiving an average monthly salary of just 500-1000 euros. They are thus heavily dependent on their mosque management committee. This can limit their freedom. One idea is to establish programmes to help create professional structures and to arrange the financing of mosques, thus improving the situation of imams in Europe.

Support networks and the diaspora

National assessment and analyses need to be shared if the identification and tracing process is to work and the activities of instigators of radicalisation are to be limited, whether they occur in prisons, schools or places of religious training and worship or through the internet. Recent acts of terrorism in Europe have involved multinational, transnationally operating terrorist cells, some directly linked to and others inspired by Al-Qaida. Several of the terrorists were allegedly affiliated with European support networks of Middle Eastern and North African jihadist movements, such as the Algerian GSPC.[27] In addition, organisations such as Jemaah Islamiyah, the Libyan Islamic Fighting Group and the Salafist Group for Call and Combat have shown willingness to support Al-Qaida's global operations.[28]

The diaspora is particularly important for the global Salafi jihad. Many young Muslims in Europe are not familiar enough with Islamic doctrine to filter out the radical messages they hear. Many who have become radicalised have little knowledge of either Arabic or Islam. What knowledge they do have has either come from 'recruiters' seeking to radicalise youngsters or from radical internet sites. There is no simple Islamist profile and it is difficult to understand what steps are involved in 'convincing' an individual who might already have radical views, actually to join a terrorist group.

Marc Sageman, an eminent scholar of terror networks, argues that a three-pronged process is at work: i) social affiliation with the jihad[29] accomplished through friendship, kinship, and discipleship; ii) progressive intensification of beliefs and faith leading to acceptance of the global Salafi jihad ideology; and iii) formal acceptance of the jihad through direct links to it. Relative deprivation, religious predisposition and ideological appeal are necessary but not sufficient conditions on their own to account for the decision to become a *mujaheed*. Social bonds are the critical element in the process. They precede ideological commitment to the cause.[30] Terrorist groups provide a sense of belonging which motivates individuals to join and a new belief system that defines terrorism as morally acceptable.

The Nixon Center Study of 373 *mujaheedin* in Western Europe and North America between 1993 and 2004 found that there were more than twice as many French as Saudis. And there were more Britons than Sudanese, Yemeni, Emiratis, Lebanese or Libyans. A quarter of the jihadists listed were from Western Europe.[31] One tentative conclusion might be that there is a growing preponderance of growth in the West as opposed to the external threat. Certainly, on balance there is an increasing threat from within western society. Whatever the origins, there are several groups operating across Europe which are cause for concern.

Examples of groups involved in the radicalisation process

The Salafist Group for Call and Combat

The Salafist Group for Call and Combat (GSPC) is a splinter faction of the Algerian-based Armed Islamic Group (GIA).[32] According to Italian investigators[33], the GSPC had taken over the GIA's external networks across Europe and North Africa by 2000 and was moving to establish an 'Islamic International' under the aegis of Osama bin Laden – clearly a cause for concern for Western authorities. They aimed to recruit new terrorists from among the ranks of the disenfranchised Algerian youth in Europe' s cities, especially in France. Many of these new supporters were involved in petty crimes such as car theft, credit-card fraud, and document forgery in their host and home countries, with their earnings now being channelled into financing terrorist operations. An 11 September 2006 video recording containing an interview with Ayman Al-Zawahiri, a high ranking figure in the Al-Qaida organization, contains a passage that makes reference to the Salafist Group for Call and Combat (GSPC). In this passage Al-Zawahiri states that the GSPC has joined the Al-Qaida organization. Statements were also made by the GSPC[34] appearing to formalise a movement of the GSPC from targeting primarily the near enemy (Algerian government) to including the far enemy (states that support the Algerian government). This approach would appear to bring the GSPC in line with the preferred strategy of Al-Qaida.

Hizb ut-Tahrir – the Party of Liberation

Hizb ut-Tahrir (HT, the Party of Liberation) is a transnational movement that has served as radical Sunni Islamism's ideological vanguard. Since 9/11, it has increasingly developed into a pan-European movement. Hizb ut-Tahrir has been banned in a number of countries in the Middle East, Central Asia, in Russia and more recently in Germany. The group advocates the re-establishment of the Islamic Caliphate and has an ambiguous relationship to the use of violence. Yet, seemingly, HT is not in itself a terrorist organisation, but rather a conveyor belt for terrorists. It indoctrinates individuals with radical ideology, priming them for recruitment by more extreme organisations where they can take part in violent operations. According to Baran, HT membership is estimated to number in the hundreds in European countries.[35] Analysts, of course, disagree on the amount of influence attributable to such groups. Some believe, for example, that HT plays a significant role in radicalising young people, while others believe that it will only have temporary influence among Muslim youth.

External factors

There are a series of external factors with direct influence on domestic sources and symptoms of terrorism. Fundamentalist charities, state failure, rogue states and economic interest are all of clear relevance to the search for causes within Europe (Von Hippel 2002:31). International events such as the Iranian Revolution of 1979, the Salman Rushdie affair after 1989, the rise of the Taliban, and the continuing Israeli-Palestinian conflict have heavily influenced perceptions of Islam in Europe. More recently, the wars in Afghanistan and Iraq have had a particular impact on European Muslim communities and on Western perceptions of them.

Declassified sections of the US National Intelligence Estimate from April 2006 conclude that despite serious damage to the leadership of Al-Qaida, the threat from Islamic extremists has spread both in numbers and in geographic reach. The report credits four factors with facilitating the spread of the jihadist movement: 1) 'entrenched grievances, such as corruption, injustice and fear of Western domination'; 2) the Iraq 'jihad'; 3) the slow pace of economic, social and political reforms in many Muslim majority nations; and 4) a 'pervasive anti-U.S. sentiment among most Muslims'. The unclassified sections of the document further state that the increased role of Iraqis in opposing Al-Qaida in Iraq might lead the terror group's veteran foreign fighters to refocus their efforts outside that country. Furthermore, the radicalisation process is occurring more quickly, more widely, and more anonymously in the internet age, raising the likelihood of surprise attacks by unknown groups whose members and supporters may be difficult to pinpoint.[36]

Research has shown that the war in Iraq and the Israeli-Palestinian conflict have had a strong impact on the thinking of young Muslims. This has not turned them into radicals, but it has led to frustration with the government and increased their sense of alienation. Yet, it would be misguided to believe that solving the Israeli-Palestinian conflict would lead to the end of militant Islam. Islamic militancy can hardly be reduced to any one problem. Jason Burke argues that the militants feel that the *umma*[37] is under attack and that in the militants' view, Israel is merely the West's most obvious outpost. If the Jewish state disappeared, the Islamists would still fight in Chechnya, Kashmir, Egypt, Uzbekistan, Indonesia, and Algeria. Their agenda is typically determined by local grievances, often with lengthy histories.[38] As Halliday puts it, 'the attacks on 11 September were, like the Madrid attacks and other events, the product of particular, identifiable, political factors – rooted in the recent history of the Middle East, of the cold war and its aftermath, or a combination of both. And it is the interplay of these factors in the years to come that will determine the future – whether there will be more dates codified as "9/11" or "3/11", whether the constellation of forces around Al-Qaida will be able to sustain their campaign, and whether this event will come to define and poison the broader pattern of relations between the west and the Muslim world.'[39]

The European Union's counter-terrorism agenda: guidelines and principles

Council strategy and guidelines

Just as the international dimension of terrorism has grown significantly, in particular as a consequence of globalisation, the increasing use of mass media, the spread of international banking systems and the cyber revolution, combating terrorism has become one of the EU' s greatest challenges. In the aftermath of September 11 and the Madrid and London bombings, new EU-wide anti-terrorism measures were adopted as other chapters describe. The European Council has regularly endorsed revised EU 'Plans of Action on Combating Terrorism', which regularly update and monitor implementation of the range of initiatives and measures identified and review progress. The measures involved increase cooperation in fields ranging from intelligence sharing to law enforcement and the control of financial assets, including the introduction of a European Arrest Warrant, efforts to strengthen the role of Europol, the appointment of an EU counter-terrorism coordinator and a broad EU Counter-Terrorism Strategy and Action Plan. These were adopted during the UK Presidency in December 2005. The purpose was to streamline agreed measures into a single framework, based on a four-pronged strategy: prevent, protect, pursue and respond.

A first step towards improving intelligence sharing was taken with the agreement to expand the Joint Situation Centre within the Council. Here, the objective was to help the Union develop an integrated analysis of the terrorist threat by bringing together experts from both the intelligence services and the security services and from both outside and inside the EU. In 2005 a European Border Agency was created in Warsaw to help border authorities in Europe cooperate more closely and share experience and best practice. Further priorities have included information sharing and law-enforcement cooperation; combating the financing of terrorism; civil protection and the protection of critical infrastructure; addressing the causes of radicalisation and the recruitment of Muslims by terrorist groups; and mainstreaming counter-terrorism activities in the EU' s external relations. Moreover, the European Security Strategy (ESS), drafted by the EU High Representative for Common Foreign and Security Policy Javier Solana and approved by the European Council on 12 December 2003, clearly identifies international terrorism as a key threat, stating that 'terrorism poses a growing strategic threat to the whole of Europe' and that 'Europe is both a target and a base for terrorism' (see Annex 3).

EU strategy to combat radicalisation and recruitment to terrorism

The specific issue of violent radicalisation was placed on the EU agenda at the December 2004 European Council, when heads of state and government agreed that the EU should conduct a study on radicalisation and terrorist recruitment, reiterating the conviction that long-term effectiveness requires an EU response to terrorism to address its root causes. This led to the adoption, in December 2005, of an EU 'Strategy for Combating Radicalisation and Recruitment to Terrorism', which builds on the European Commission's Communication on 'Terrorist Recruitment: addressing the factors contributing to violent radicalisation', published in September 2005 (see Annex 6). This strategy, in turn, is part of the broader EU Counter-Terrorism Strategy and Action Plan adopted in December 2005, based on the four pillars: prevention, protection, pursuit and response.

The strategy encompasses a strategic commitment to combat terrorism globally and make Europe safer, allowing its peoples to live in freedom, security and justice, within a framework that respects human rights. Under the theme of prevention, people are deterred from turning to terrorism by tackling the factors and root causes which can lead to radicalisation and recruitment, in Europe and internationally. The subjects of protection are citizens and infrastructure. This involves reducing vulnerability to attack, including through improved security of borders, transport and critical infrastructure. As to pursuit, the purpose is to pursue and investigate terrorists across borders and globally, to impede planning, to disrupt support networks, cut off funding and bring terrorists to justice. Finally, response implies preparedness to manage and minimise the consequences of a terrorist attack by improving capacity to deal with coordination of the response, the aftermath and the needs of victims.

In addressing the policy issues falling under the first pillar of the EU counter-terrorism strategy, the EU 'Strategy for Combating Radicalisation and Recruitment to Terrorism' outlines the range of measures for Member States to implement in order to address the problem of radicalisation. The Strategy is completed by an Action Plan for implementation. The Action Plan provides greater detail than the Strategy. Yet, in light of the ongoing effort better to understand radicalisation, more detail is required. The issue of radicalisation will need to be addressed primarily by individual Member States, as the EU does not have the competence to introduce the social, educational, and economic policies that can foster equality and inclusion within each society. But the Union can provide a framework for Member States to coordinate their policies and share information about best practice. The Council can also exercise peer pressure on Member States which are slow in implementing the agreed measures. But the Union' s competence stops there. In comparison to the previous Commission Communication, the Council Strategy goes further in addressing some of the issues raised by radicalisation and, on balance, puts more emphasis on the 'harder' aspects of security. However, the Strategy is fundamentally part of the 'soft' side of the EU' s counter-terrorism measures. As the Commission and the Council are aware of the sensitivities involved in addressing this issue, they avoid stigmatising a particular community. The Strategy therefore underlines that the majority of Europeans, irrespective of their beliefs, do not accept extremist ideologies.

EU projected measures to counter radicalisation and terrorist recruitment include the disruption of the activities of the networks and individuals who draw people into terrorism and ensuring that voices of mainstream opinion prevail over those of extremism and the promotion of security, justice, democracy and opportunity for all.[40] For its part, the Commission Communication of September 2005 on 'Terrorist recruitment: addressing the factors contributing to violent radicalisation' defines 'violent radicalisation' as the phenomenon of people embracing opinions, views and ideas which could lead to acts of terrorism as specified in Article 1 of the Framework Decision on Combating Terrorism.[41] The actions and recommendations presented in the Communication are a combination of 'soft' measures (for example, inter-cultural exchanges among young people) and 'less soft' measures (for example, the banning of satellite broadcasts inciting terrorism), and are complementary to current national efforts. The Commission argues that at European level, the EU – with its spectrum of policies in various areas that could be used to address violent radicalisation – is well placed to gather and spread the relevant expertise being acquired by Member States in addressing the problem. The core areas considered are: the broadcast media, the internet, education, youth engagement, employment, social exclusion and integration issues, equal opportunities, non-discrimination and inter-cultural dialogue.

The Commission Communication acknowledges the sensitivity and intricacy of this issue and takes a rather cautious approach, regarded as a first step in trying to understand the complex issue of radicalisation. The Commission has committed 450,000 euros for further studies, including on social science aspects of radicalisation. It has also set up a network of experts to guide the policy-making process. The following are some of the key points in the Commission Communication on 'Terrorist recruitment: addressing the factors contributing to violent radicalisation' :

1. *Broadcast media:* 'European law already prohibits incitement to hatred on grounds of race, sex, religion or nationality in broadcast media. Member States are responsible for its implementation.'
2. *The internet:* 'The use of the Internet to incite people into becoming violently radical, or as a vehicle for terrorist recruitment, is extremely worrying in view of its global reach, real-time nature and effectiveness. The objective of removing terrorist propaganda from the Internet can be taken into account in the e-Commerce Directive.[42] The Commission encourages Member States to make use of the enabling provisions in the Directive in the most effective way to address violent radicalisation in Europe. The Commission will gather best practices to examine the need of adopting a guidance document.'
3. *Education, youth engagement and active European citizenship:* 'The promotion of cultural diversity and tolerance can help to stem the development of violently radical mind-sets. The Commission supports several Youth and Culture Programmes and has recently launched a proposal to adopt a new programme "Citizens for Europe" to promote active European Citizenship.'
4. *Encouraging integration, inter-cultural dialogue and dialogue with religions:* 'The Commission is committed, under the framework of The Hague Programme, to taking action to promote more vigorous integration policies within Member States, based on the implementation of the Common Basic Principles on Integration adopted by the Justice, Liberty and Security Council in November 2004. The Commission will launch a proposal to establish 2008 as the Year of Intercultural Dialogue.'
5. *Law-enforcement authorities and security services:* 'Schemes should be considered which involve the police and law-enforcement authorities engaging more at the local level with young people. Those Member States which promote the recruitment of people from different backgrounds should also encourage other countries to do so by sharing their best practices. More preventive work in the area of counter-terrorism should be encouraged across the Member States, along with further cooperation between the operational, intelligence and policy levels. The Commission will gather and assess the Member States' best practices and consolidate them into periodic guidelines for all Member States.'

6. *Experts networks:* 'The Commission will allocate funds to establish a network of experts, which will submit a preliminary contribution in the beginning of 2006. The Commission will also launch a public tender for studies in this area.'

7. *External relations:* 'Dialogue and technical assistance to third countries and regional partners has to be an integral part of the approach to addressing violent radicalisation and terrorist recruitment. The EU Action Plans in the framework of the European Neighbourhood Policy (ENP) include a number of anti-radicalisation measures.'

Conclusion

Many of the issues underlying violent radicalisation are of a global and trans-boundary nature, necessitating a broad and transnational response, not least because of Europe' s large and open borders. The EU is in the early stages of addressing the issue of violent radicalisation and recruitment to terrorism, but could potentially play an important role in identifying best practices and monitoring the implementation of agreed measures. In addressing the issue of terrorist recruitment, enhanced coordination in security and intelligence cooperation is important. Difficulties in cooperation between intelligence and police services not only concern bilateral and multilateral cooperation between different member states, but also cooperation between the various agencies at national level. One of the difficulties in coordinating counter-terrorism efforts at the EU level is that there is no single body that deals with all matters related to terrorism.

This chapter has argued that it is crucial for governments, police and security services to work closely with local Muslim communities to improve the flow of information from them about suspected terrorist activities and to help identify those who promote radicalism and violence. Confidence of the Muslim community in policing is crucial. If individuals cannot trust the police, they are less likely to seek dialogue and cooperate with them. There is thus a clear need for greater efforts to recruit local police officers from different ethnic backgrounds.

Jihadists are constantly finding new recruiting tools to attract supporters – from the internet, online chat rooms and the distribution of 'recruitment' DVDs. The internet thus plays a key role in the recruitment process. It facilitates fast and anonymous flows of information and has given many disenfranchised individuals a sense of belonging to a global, virtual *umma*. However, given the quantity of propaganda material and the increasingly sophisticated know-how of those distributing it, it has become more difficult to implement effective counter-measures, yet vital to do so. In addition, there is considerable concern about the messages and ideologies advocated within mosques in Europe. Many young Muslims clearly regard the fight against terrorism, and especially the US 'global war on terror', as a 'war' on Islam. While places of worship are not necessarily a recruiting ground for terrorists, the known links between terrorists and radical mosques must engender growing pressure on local Islamic leaders to counter religious extremism and ensure that mosques do not remain or become recruitment or training camps.

Some European countries are undertaking efforts to clamp down on radical imams who incite violence. The hope must be that these efforts are undertaken in close partnership both with Muslim communities and partner countries. In the UK, for example, a national advisory council of imams now sets rules and educational standards to help create more 'home-grown' religious leaders. This should also help to prevent mosques being used by extremists and reduce their reliance on 'imported' religious ministers from abroad. Professional structures need to be established to arrange financing for mosques and improve the situation of imams in Europe. This could be one step in constructing a long-term strategy to tackle the root causes of terrorism, along with encouraging integration, addressing the issue of growing Islamophobia and identifying ways in which the nefarious role of external political factors might be countered.

Finally, close dialogue and partnership with Muslim communities and moderate Muslim representatives in Europe is crucial. Many immigrants in Europe still remain on the margins of society without real prospects of becoming part of it. A disproportionate number of Muslims are unemployed and fail to complete secondary school. Better access to jobs and education is thus necessary, as well as a focus on upward social mobility. Yet, while all these suggestions reflect commonplace views, they would clearly require considerable financial means. Terrorists come from all walks of life and there is no easy, one-size-fits-all solution to the problem of violent radicalisation. The kind of international terrorism inspired by Al-Qaida is likely to persist for years to come, even, as the head of the UK' s MI5 argued in November 2006, for a generation. Yet, Western society is still faced with a problem identified by von Hippel in 2002: 'currently many international organisations are trying to formulate development policy responses to terrorism based on an insufficient empirical database' (von Hippel, 2002: 28). As this chapter has shown, compiling an adequate database, given the multitude of identifiable potential causes of terrorism, is a task of Sisyphus-like proportions. Yet, neglecting the challenges and failing to counter the threats with common, coherent international approaches, between Muslims and non-Muslims, risks a self-fulfilling prophecy – a 'clash of civilisations' .

Bibliography

Von Hippel, Karin 'The Roots of Terrorism: probing the myths', in Freedman, L. (ed) 'Superterrorism: policy responses', *Political Quarterly*, 2002.

Appendix

Muslim communities in Europe

Muslim communities have grown rapidly in Europe in recent decades and Islam has emerged as the second religion in many European countries. Given continued immigration and high fertility rates among Muslim immigrants, the US National Intelligence Council projects that Europe's Muslim population will double by 2025. It is estimated at some 15 to 20 million in

2006, compared to only 800,000 in 1950. Yet, there are no precise figures for the number of Muslims living in Europe today, since there is no central registration of residents by religion in most countries.

The following statistics are based on estimates of the number of migrants from countries where Islam is the most important religion.[43]

Country	Total population	Muslims
Austria	8,102,600	300,000
Belgium	10,192,240	370,000
Denmark	5,330,020	150,000
France	56,000,000	4,000,000-5,000,000
Germany	82,000,000	3,040,000
Greece	10,000,000	370,000
Italy	56,778,031	700,000
Netherlands	15,760,225	695,600
Portugal	9,853,000	30,000-38,000
Spain	40,202,160	300,000 – 400,000
Sweden	8,876,611	250,000 – 300,000
UK	55,000,000	1,406,000

Endnotes:

1   CRS Report for Congress. *Muslims in Europe: Integration Policies in Selected Countries* (18 November 2005).
2   Militant Jihadism: Radicalization, Conversion, Recruitment, ITAC, Trends in terrorism Series,Volume 2006-4.
3   *Financial Times*, 25 March 2004.
4   Much of this chapter is based on a long term research project with interviews and visits to mosques and youth centres in several European countries, including Belgium, Germany, the UK and France.
5   Umma means 'community' and is used to describe the nation of the believers in Islam – in fact, on one reading, the whole Muslim World.
6   MI5 website: http://www.mi5.gov.uk/output/Page23.html
7   Peter Katzenstein. 'Same War – Different views: Germany, Japan, and Counterterrorism.' *International Organization*, vol.57, no.4, (2003).
8   http://www.icmresearch.co.uk/reviews/2004/guardian-muslims-march-2004.asp
9   Interviews ad research carried out between January 2004 and March 2006.
10 Gilles Kepel. *The War for Muslim Minds, Islam and the West*. (Belknap Press of Harvard University, 2004).
11 Olivier Roy. 'The Ideology of Terror.' *International Herald Tribune*, 23 July 2005.
12 Elmar Thevessen. *Terror Alarm, Deutschland und die islamistische Bedrohung*, (Berlin: Rowohlt, 2005): 104.
13 Muslim female fighters.
14 Farhana Ali. *Muslim Female Fighters: An Emerging Trend*. The Jamestown Foundation, http://www.jamestown.org/terrorism/news/article.php?articleid=2369824
15 Jihadis Provide Internet Training for Female Mujahideen, Abdul Hameed Bakier, Jamestown Foundation, Volume 3, Issue 40 (October 17, 2006).
16 Robert A. Pape. *'Dying to Win', The strategic logic of suicide Terrorism* (Random House, 2005).
17 Press reporting suggests that more than 2500 individuals are imprisoned or detained across the globe.

18   Out of the Shadows: Getting Ahead of Prisoner Radicalization, a Special Report by The George Washington University Homeland Security Policy Institute, September 2006.
19   Pascale Combelles Siegel, 'Radical Islam and the French Muslim Prison Population', *Terrorism Monitor*, Volume 4, Issue 15, July 2006.
20   Don Van Natta Jr. 'Militant Imams Under Scrutiny Across Europe.' *New York Times*, January 24, 2005.
21   Gilles Kepel. *The War for Muslim Minds, Islam and the West.* (Belknap Press of Harvard University, 2004).
22   'Les salafistes ont conquis de nouvelles mosquées en Ile-de-France', *Le Monde*, 22 February, 2004.
23   Jocelyne Cesari. *Ethnicity, Islam, and les banlieues: Confusing the Issues.* Social Science Research Council, www.riotsfrance.ssrc.org.
24   Research and interviews conducted from 2004 to 2006.
25   Tariq Ramadan. 'Home Countries or Host Countries in Control – Who speaks for Europe' s Muslims?' http://www.tariqramadan.org/document.asp?d=34&fichier =HomeCountries.
26   Research and interviews conducted from 2004 to 2006.
27   Petter Nesser, *Profiles of Jihadist Terrorists in Europe*, published in 'A Future for the Young, Options for helping Middle Eastern Youth Escape the Trap of Radicalization', Bernard 2006, RAND, Washington.
28   *Al Qaeda: The Many Faces of an Islamist Extremist Threat*, Report of the House Permanent Select Committee on Intelligence, June 2006.
29   Jihad connotes a wide range of meanings: anything from an inward spiritual struggle to attain perfect faith, to a political or militant struggle to defend or further Islam. Jihad is repeatedly used in the context of Holy War by Islamic militants. A person who engages in any form of jihad is called a mujaheed.
30   Marc Sageman. *Understanding Terror Networks.* (University of Pennsylvania Press, 2005).
31   Robert S. Leiken. 'Europe' s Angry Muslims.' *Foreign Affairs*, (July/August 2005).
32   On 24 January 2007, with the apparent blessing of Osama bin Laden, the GSPC changed its name to the Al-Qaida Organisation in the Islamic Maghreb.
33   Anthony Keats. 'In the Spotlight: The Salafist Group for Call and Combat (GSPC).' Center for Defence Information, Terrorism Project, 14 January, 2003
34   GSPC website released a statement dated 13 September 2006 swearing allegiance to Osama Bin Laden. The statement, entitled, *A Statement and Announcement and an Oath from the GSPC to Sheikh Abu Abdallah Osama Bin Laden*, was signed by the current head of the GSPC, Abdelmalek Droukdel.
35   Zeyno Baran. 'Fighting the War of Ideas.' *Foreign Affairs*, November/December 2005.
36   Declassified Key Judgements of the National Intelligence Estimate 'Trends in global Terrorism: Implications for the United States, dated April 2006. http://www.dni.gov/press_releases/press_releases.htm
37   Denotation for the community of Muslims, that is, the totality of all Muslims, considered to extend from Mauritania to Pakistan. The term comes from a word that simply means 'people'. In the Holy Koran, the word is used in several senses, but it always indicates a group of people that are a part of a divine plan and salvation.
38   Jason Burke, 'Al Qaeda', in *Foreign Policy*, May/June 2004.
39   Fred Halliday, *Terrorism in historical perspective*, 22.04.04, Open Democracy.
40   'The EU Strategy for Combating Radicalisation and Recruitment to Terrorism,' 14781/1/05 Rev. 1, www.eu.int .
41   Council Framework Decision 2002/475/JHA of 13 June 2002 on Combating Terrorism. Article 1 provides that: 'Each Member State shall take the necessary measures to ensure that the intentional acts referred to below... as defined as offences under national law, which given their nature and context, may seriously damage a country or an international organisation where committed with the aim of seriously intimidating a population, unduly compelling a Government or international organisation to perform or abstain from performing an act, or seriously destabilising or destroying the fundamental political, constitutional, economic or social structures of a country or an international organisation shall be deemed to be terrorist offences.'
42   Directive 2000/31/EC of the European Parliament and the Council of 8 June 2000.
43   These figures are taken from Frank J. Buijs and Jan Rath, Muslims in Europe: The State of Research, prepared for the Russell Sage Foundation, NYC 2002.

3. Judicial Cooperation in Europe against Terrorism

Hans Nilsson

Judicial cooperation in Europe against terrorism is not new. It may have gained a new dimension after the attacks in Madrid and London, but the fight against terrorism was one of the reasons why European judicial cooperation became a key theme in the mid-1970s when the so-called TREVI group was founded.[1] Terrorist groups such as the Baader-Meinhof Gang in Germany or the Red Brigades in Italy made it necessary to increase cooperation between law enforcement authorities. Given the nature of the criminal acts involved, the judiciary had to be involved early on in most cases, since coercive measures such as the interception of telecommunications, searches and seizures were necessary. Most Member States of the European Union require such procedural acts to be carried out with the authorisation of a judge. Yet, judicial cooperation against terrorism is no different from cooperation in general against criminal acts. It is not particularly specific to terrorism. It therefore follows that the general instruments regarding mutual legal assistance and extradition developed over the decades, first within the Council of Europe and then within the EU, also apply to judicial cooperation against terrorism. There are nonetheless, in particular in the field of the so-called political offence exception, some legal instruments specific to terrorism – as will be dealt with below.

Because of the seriousness of the criminal acts involved, judicial cooperation in Europe against terrorism is a field where the entire range of judicial instruments needs to be used. Problems arise, however, in that measures that infringe the privacy of the individual are often necessary. There is always tension between the protection of fundamental rights and the fight against terrorism. Yet, if one considers the fight against terrorism is carried out to protect those fundamental rights, there should not be a contradiction between the two. Nevertheless there is, and probably always will be, a discussion among governments, parliaments and civil society on the border line of tolerance for the infringement of individual liberties if the aim is to protect the lives of innocent persons that are targets of terrorist attacks. Thus, article 8, paragraph 1 of the European Convention of Human Rights provides that:

> Everyone has the right to respect for his private and family life, his home and his correspondence.

But paragraph 2 of that Article makes it possible to derogate from that right:

> except such as is in accordance with the law and is necessary in a democratic society in the interests of national security, public safety... for the prevention of disorder or crime... or for the protection of the rights and freedoms of others.

This chapter deals with instruments within the Council of Europe and the European Union that are particularly important in the fight against terrorism and relevant for judicial cooperation against terrorism. It is worth reiterating, however, that most of these instruments are not just relevant to the fight against terrorism and were not drafted specifically for that purpose, but in respect of other serious criminal offences. This chapter thus deals with a number of instruments of general application. It begins with the instruments that have been drawn up under the auspices of the Council of Europe, since these were the first on the international arena. Nevertheless it is fair to say that many instruments now relevant for judicial cooperation in Europe were drafted within the context of the European Union. Notwithstanding this, the Council of Europe instruments are also relevant to European Union Member States since they are considered an acquis of the Union and since all judicial cooperation of EU Member States with non-EU Member States is still carried out on the basis of Council of Europe instruments. The Council of Europe continues to work on terrorist offences, in particular within the so-called CODEXTER Committee and the Multidisciplinary Group against terrorism which performs excellent work within the context of the 46-nation Council of Europe. The chapter closes with a mention of some of the more important conventions that have been drafted within the context of the United Nations, not only because they are innovative but also because they have clear relevance for judicial cooperation among European countries.

Instruments of the Council of Europe

Cooperation within the Council of Europe in criminal law has existed since the 1950s. The European Committee on Crime Problems (CDPC) was set up in 1958 but, one year before, in 1957, under the auspices of the Parliamentary Assembly of the Council of Europe, an intergovernmental committee of the Committee of Ministers drafted an innovative convention, namely the **European Convention on Extradition**. This convention replaced several hundred bilateral treaties among the Member States of the Council of Europe. All Member States of the Council of Europe have ratified the convention and in addition Israel is a party to it. The significance of the convention cannot be underestimated. The contracting parties undertake to surrender to each other all persons against whom the competent authorities are proceeding for offences carrying a penalty of at least one year or who are wanted for execution of sentences or detention orders of at least four months. The period for the offences implies that minor offences cannot be subject to extradition. The annual number of extradition cases in Europe in the mid-1990s was between 750 and 1000 and all extradition cases were in principle carried out by the use of this convention, although regional arrangements such as the Benelux convention and the Nordic extradition arrangements have existed in parallel with the Extradition Convention.

One of the main weaknesses of the Extradition Convention was that there were a number of exceptions to the obligation to extradite. Some of these were due to the fact that extradition as it developed in the nineteenth century was considered to be between sovereigns that granted extradition to one another, mostly to ensure that political opponents were brought to 'justice' and even executed by the requesting sovereign who happened to be in power at the time. Extradition was, therefore, and still is, a very sensitive issue which, in today's more enlightened world encompasses the individual's fundamental freedoms. This was one of the reasons why extradition was not granted if the relevant offence was regarded by the requested state as a political offence or as an offence connected with a political offence. Exception was, however, later made in the 1977 Convention on the Suppression of Terrorism for certain offences in relation to this so-called political offence exception.

In the 1957 Convention, exception was also made for military offences, fiscal offences or offences that had been committed outside the territory of the requesting State. Extradition could also be refused if there were a pending proceeding for the same offences for reasons of so-called double jeopardy (*ne bis idem*). One of the most sensitive issues in Europe was the extradition of nationals. Many Member States´ constitutions in fact contained a definite prohibition of extradition of their own nationals, a feature also contained in the legal traditions of common law countries. It took the continental-law countries many years before even a discussion on the justification of extraditing nationals was considered appropriate. In fact, refusal of extradition of nationals can no longer be deemed appropriate in the context of the European Union, where internal borders have been abolished and an area of freedom, security and justice is being created, implying that concepts such as 'nationals' (for purposes at least of fighting crime and other related purposes) will become outdated.

There were also further bars to extradition in the old 1957 convention. Extradition was not possible if there had been a lapse in time of the prosecution of the offence or if there was a risk that capital punishment would follow. This latter issue became less and less relevant in the Member States of the Council of Europe with the drafting of the protocol to the European Convention on Human Rights.

As extradition was a procedure with its origin between sovereigns, and later between sovereign States, the procedure was also very heavy handed. Requests were made first through diplomatic channels and, as time passed, directly via Ministries of Justice. Requests had to be supported by a number of documents and description of the offences, so that the question of so-called double criminality (that the offence was punishable both in the requesting and the requested State) could be tried by the court. In many Member States the procedure was both judicial and political/administrative. The court was called upon to see that there was no obstacle against extradition caused by the many exceptions to the obligation to extradite, though the final decision often lay in the hands of the governments themselves. In addition, the requested person also had many forms of access to appeal the request for extradition, sometimes consecutively so that the periods of the entire procedure would tend to be very long. Even if the person did not contest his or her extradition, the translation requirements, the procedural requirements and the many different parts of the procedure meant that a non-contested extradition request would take about 6 months to process. In contested cases the period could often be 12 months or more. When a person had been arrested, the requesting State had 40 days from the arrest to submit the necessary documents – often simply for reasons of translation.

The additional Protocol of 15 October 1975 to the convention, specified that crimes against humanity, war crimes and the crime of genocide would not be considered political offences for purposes of extradition. The second additional Protocol of 17 March 1978 also sought to restrict the exceptions for fiscal offences and for judgements *in absentia*. The requested State could also refuse extradition if, in its opinion, the proceedings leading to the judgement did not satisfy the minimum rights of defence recognized as due to anyone charged with a criminal offence. However, extradition was granted if the requesting State gave an assurance considered sufficient to guarantee to the person claimed the right to a retrial.

In the specific field of terrorism a major convention was drafted one year before the second additional Protocol. On 27 January 1977, the **European Convention on the Suppression of Terrorism** was adopted. The convention specified in its Article 1 that for purposes of extradition between contracting states 'none of the following offences shall be regarded as a political offence or as an offence connected with a political offence or as an offence inspired by political motives':

a) an offence within the scope of the Convention for the Suppression of Unlawful Seizure of Aircraft, signed at The Hague on 16 December 1970;
b) an offence within the scope of the Convention for the Suppression of Unlawful Acts against the Safety of Civil Aviation, signed at Montréal on 23 September 1971;
c) a serious offence involving an attack against the life, physical integrity, or liberty of internationally protected persons, including diplomatic agents;
d) an offence involving kidnapping, the taking of a hostage or serious unlawful detention;
e) an offence involving the use of a bomb, grenade, rocket, automatic firearm or letter or parcel bomb if this use endangers persons;
f) an attempt to commit any of the foregoing offences or participation as an accomplice of a person who commits or intends to commit such an offence.

Article 2 specifies that a contracting State also may decide not to regard as a political offence serious offences involving an act of violence against the life, physical integrity or liberty of a person or serious offences involving an act against property if the act created a collective danger for persons.

Deciding that a certain specific offence cannot be regarded as a political offence is of course crucial. It means that extradition may follow in most cases where a terrorist has committed an offence, and that he or she would not be able to remain unpunished for their acts. Yet, the text did not constitute a solution to the problem discussed for decades, namely the definition of terrorism itself. It would be for the EU later to decide on this in its Framework Decision on terrorism – see below.

The 1977 convention also specified that there was no obligation to extradite if there were substantial grounds for believing that the request for extradition was made for purposes of prosecuting or punishing a person on account of his race, religion, nationality or political opinion, or that the person's position might be prejudiced for any of these reasons. The issue was one of great sensitivity. The Council of Europe thus had to make compromises, nullifying the force of the convention to a great extent. Article 13 provided for a State to reserve the right to refuse extradition, if it considered the relevant offence to be a political offence, an offence connected with a political offence or an offence inspired by political motives. States were obliged to undertake to give due consideration, when evaluating the character of the offence, as to whether the offence created a collective danger to the life, physical integrity or liberty of persons or whether it affected persons foreign to the motives behind it or cruel or vicious means were used in the commission of the offence. Over the years several States made such a reservation, and the convention thus became partly inapplicable – or at least its application was skewed. One of the reasons for this 'safeguard clause' was that the Constitutions of many Member States provided for the political offence exception. For instance, one Constitution provides for non-extradition of 'freedom fighters', though however that may be defined has long been a source of unresolved philosophical and operational inquiry.

This was one of the reasons why, in the context of the 9/11 bombings, the Council of Europe set out to draft a new convention that would seek to remove this right to formulate a reservation. **The Protocol amending the European Convention on Terrorism** was adopted on 15 May 2003. Paragraphs c-f of the Covention are replaced by the following paragraphs:

c) an offence within the scope of the Convention on the Prevention and Punishment of Crimes Against Internationally Protected Persons, Including Diplomatic Agents, adopted at New York on 14 December 1973;

d) an offence within the scope of the International Convention Against the Taking of Hostages, adopted at New York on 17 December 1979;

e) an offence within the scope of the Convention on the Physical Protection of Nuclear Material, adopted at Vienna on 3 March 1980;

f) an offence within the scope of the Protocol for the Suppression of Unlawful Acts of Violence at Airports Serving International Civil Aviation, done at Montreal on 24 February 1988;

In addition, the following conventions, that define specific offences relevant to terrorism are included in the list:

g) an offence within the scope of the Convention for the Suppression of Unlawful Acts Against the Safety of Maritime Navigation, done at Rome on 10 March 1988;

h) an offence within the scope of the Protocol for the Suppression of Unlawful Acts Against the Safety of Fixed Platforms Located on the Continental Shelf, done at Rome on 10 March 1988;

i) an offence within the scope of the International Convention for the Suppression of Terrorist Bombings, adopted at New York on 15 December 1997;

j) an offence within the scope of the International Convention for the Suppression of the Financing of Terrorism, adopted at New York on 9 December 1999.

This takes into account the development since 1977 of some of the UN conventions relevant in this area and thereby updates the scope of the political offence exception. The convention further updates the law as regards acts of complicity and spells out more clearly some further guarantees regarding torture and the death penalty. It further provides rules relating to the so-called *aut dedere, aut iudicare* rule, namely that if the State does not extradite a person it should prosecute itself. It also institutes a system of monitoring of the convention.

As this protocol only enters into force when all 46 Contracting States of the 1977 Convention have ratified the protocol, it is too early to judge its viability. The fact that 25 States have ratified the Protocol (as of May 2007) is encouraging, but there are still 21 that have not. In the meantime, the Council of Europe has drafted a further text on the prevention of terrorism. The **Convention on the Prevention of Terrorism** was adopted in Warsaw on 16 May 2005. It came into force on 1 June 2007 for the seven countries that had thus far ratified it (Albania, Bulgaria, Denmark, Romania, Russia, Slovakia and Ukraine). The Convention is the first international treaty to define as criminal infringements certain activities which may lead to the perpetration of attacks, such as incitement to terrorism, recruitment and training for terrorist purposes. Modifying the existing arrangements on extradition and legal cooperation, it also reinforces international cooperation in terrorism prevention.

The purpose of this convention is to prevent terrorism and its negative effects on the full enjoyment of human rights, both by measures taken at national level and through international cooperation. Interestingly, the convention provides that each party shall promote tolerance by encouraging inter-religious and cross-cultural dialogue involving NGOs and other elements of civil society with a view to preventing tensions that might contribute to the commission of terrorist offences. The parties also commit to promote public awareness regarding the existence, causes and gravity of the threat caused by terrorist offences and the offences contained in the convention.

The convention instigates for the first time an offence found in the anti-terrorist arsenal of some of the Member States, namely the so-called 'incitement to terrorism' offence. Public provocation to commit a terrorist offence is established as a criminal offence under the convention. Public provocation is defined as the distribution, or otherwise making available, of a message to the public, with intent to incite the commission of a terrorist offence, where such conduct (whether or not directly advocating terrorist offences), causes a danger that one or more terrorist offences may be committed. This definition of public provocation has been criticised by NGOs[2] for being too imprecise whereas in law enforcement circles it has been argued that the offence of 'incitement to terrorism' does not bring much added value to already existing offences on incitement to commit offences that generally exist in many Criminal Codes.

The convention also criminalises recruitment for terrorism as a criminal offence under domestic law. Recruitment for terrorism is defined as the attempt to solicit another person to commit or participate in the commission of a terrorist offence, or to join an association or group for the purpose of contributing to the commission of one or more terrorist offences by the association or the group. This definition has also been criticised by the same

NGOs for being too imprecise. Time will tell whether the recruitment offence or the public provocation offence will bring added value to the fight against terrorism.

The convention also establishes training for terrorism as a criminal offence under national law. Training for terrorism is defined as providing instruction in the making or use of explosives, firearms or other weapons or noxious substances, or in other specific methods or techniques for the purpose of carrying out or contributing to the commission of terrorist offences, knowing that the skills provided are intended to be used for this purpose. Significantly, under the provisions of the convention it is a requirement that a terrorist offence actually be committed for an act to constitute an offence.

The convention contains specific conditions and safeguards that are, on first sight, not a necessary part of the convention, as they would apply anyway. This is in particular true for the conditions and safeguards relating to upholding human rights obligations such as the right to freedom of expression, freedom of association and freedom of religion. Such obligations would in any case prevail over the convention as they are embodied in the European Convention for the Protection of Human Rights and Fundamental Freedoms. The convention also contains rules concerning the political offence exception, though the new convention contains provision for certain types of reservation. Finally, a specific reference is made to the principle of proportionality. Discussions are currently ongoing within the framework of the institutions of the European Union as to whether an initiative should be taken to adopt a Framework Decision compatible with the definition of the Council of Europe convention.

As regards mutual legal assistance, the Council of Europe adopted the **European Convention on Mutual Assistance in Criminal Matters** on 20 April 1959. This still serves as the basis for nearly all mutual assistance carried out within the European Union and the Member States of the Council of Europe, such as hearing of witnesses, searches and seizures and service of documents. It has been supplemented by rules in the 1990 Schengen Convention in so far as the European Union is concerned and by specific rules within the Benelux and Nordic Countries, but it is no exaggeration to state that the 1959 convention is still the major instrument concerning mutual legal assistance.

The 1959 convention has a very wide scope of application; it applies to 'the widest measure of mutual assistance in proceedings in respect of offences'. Very few grounds for refusal exist: political offences, offences connected with political offences, fiscal offences or if the requested State considers that execution of the request is likely to prejudice the sovereignty, security, *ordre public* or other essential interests (which of course gives considerable latitude to the requested State). Importantly, the convention does not foresee any requirement of double criminality but, under article 5 of the convention, the parties may reserve their right to make the execution of requests under the convention dependent on either extraditability (i.e. that extradition may follow for the offence), double criminality or consistency with the law of the requested State. Many Member States have made such declarations.

The convention also deals with service of writs and records of judicial proceedings and appearance of witnesses, experts and prosecuted persons and it includes provisions for the request of extracts from criminal records. In principle such requests should be transmitted between Ministries of Justice and returned through the same channel, but in urgent cases requests may also be transmitted directly via judicial authorities or by Interpol. The 1990 Schengen Convention made exception to these rules and provided that, as a rule, requests could be made directly between judicial authorities.

An additional protocol of 17 March 1978 makes certain procedures easier, for instance as regards fiscal offences. It specifies explicitly that service of documents concerning enforcement of sentences, payment of cost of proceedings as well as measures relating to suspension of pronouncement of sentences are included in the mutual legal assistance provisions. A second protocol has been adopted to the convention following to a large extent the European Union convention, for which see below.

A number of other instruments have also been adopted within the framework of the Council of Europe that are relevant to the fight against terrorism in general. However, as these instruments are also of a more general nature, it is only worth mentioning the 1990 Convention on Money Laundering, Search, Seizure and Confiscation of the Proceeds from Crime as particularly relevant. This convention, which has received 46 ratifications (all Council of Europe Member States), deals specifically with the offence of money laundering and procedures for tracing and identifying proceeds of crime. It has now been supplemented, and will in time be replaced by a new convention which specifically includes the financing of terrorism. This is the new **Convention on Money Laundering, Search, Seizure and Confiscation of the Proceeds from Crime and the Financing of Terrorism** which was adopted on 16 May 2005 in Warsaw. The convention will enter into force when it has been ratified by six countries; by 15 May 2007 it had been signed by 25 States but thus far ratified only by two. Under the convention, the Parties are obliged to ensure that they are able to search, trace, identify, freeze, seize and confiscate property of illicit origin, used or allocated to be used by any means, in all or in part, for the financing of terrorism or the proceeds of these offences, and to provide co-operation to this end to the widest possible extent.

The convention also deals with the management of confiscated property and the investigative powers and techniques available to law enforcement authorities. Among these investigative powers and techniques are the determination as to whether a natural or legal person is a holder or beneficial owner of a bank account, obtaining particulars of specific bank accounts and banking operations, monitoring of the banking operations that have been carried out through one or more identified accounts and ensuring that banks do not disclose to the bank customer concerned that information has been sought or obtained. The convention also deals with financial intelligence units (FIUs) and with measures to prevent money laundering in compliance with the recommendations adopted by the Financial Action Task Force on money laundering.

In conclusion, it may be said that cooperation among the 46 Council of Europe Member States is extensive and that a number of instruments have been adopted that will enable judicial cooperation to be efficient. An innovative approach has also been undertaken within the Council of Europe, for instance as regards the prevention of terrorism. The Council of Europe will clearly continue to play an important role as a standard setting authority on the international arena.

European Union judicial cooperation

It was only by the entry into force of the Treaty of Maastricht, on 1 November 1993, that judicial cooperation in criminal matters became a 'common interest'[3] of the Union, and it was only by the entry into force of the Treaty of Amsterdam, on 1 May 1999, that the Union actually acquired the legal instruments needed to draft effective and binding legal instruments. Before that, the Union worked with the very slow mechanisms of drafting, implementing and ratifying conventions, such as the 1995 and 1996 conventions on extradition, that have still not entered into force. It should also be underlined that, similarly to the instruments of the Council of Europe, most of the Union instruments are not directly geared to terrorism but rather to general cooperation within the framework of judicial cooperation in criminal matters. This is not well understood by critics of the Union, who accuse the Union of using the terrorist agenda to further wider goals and 'over-criminalise' certain types of behaviour or of adopting instruments that are not specifically 'terrorist relevant'. However, the fight against crime is usually best fought via these types of general instruments, such as the Convention on Mutual Legal Assistance in Criminal Matters, signed on 29 May 2000, which entered into force on 23 August 2005. Some instruments are nevertheless specifically geared to fighting terrorism and are mentioned below.

First, some general remarks about the work of the Union in setting up the Area of Freedom, Security and Justice. At Tampere, in Finland, the European Council met on 15 and 16 October 1999 to discuss specifically the creation of the area of freedom, security and justice. This was the first time that the European Council dealt exclusively with these issues. The so-called Tampere milestones set the agenda for crime-fighting in the European Union. The Tampere conclusions were extremely important, though they did not place great emphasis on the fight against terrorism, but were more concerned with organised crime. The Tampere programme did, however, mention terrorism in one respect, namely in the setting up of *joint investigative teams* (JITs)where trafficking in drugs and human beings as well as terrorism was concerned. Terrorism was also mentioned among the offences that needed 'approximation' (or harmonisation as some might prefer to call it, although the term 'approximation' is used by the Treaty on European Union).

At the time of the drafting of the Tampere conclusions the content of the 2000 **Mutual Legal Assistance Convention** was well known, and it was clear that a specific chapter in that convention would be devoted to the setting up of JITs. When, however, during the Portuguese Presidency in 2000 a specific Framework Decision was suggested, which would implement the principles of the 2000 convention, the Council did not act. It preferred to wait for the ratification of the 2000 convention. However, the 9/11 attacks led the Council to decide swiftly to draft a specific Framework Decision, implementing the convention with exactly the same contents. Framework

Decision 2002/465/JHA of 13 June 2002 on Joint Investigation Teams was thus capable of rapid adoption.

The Council thereafter adopted, on 8 May 2003, a Recommendation on a model agreement for setting up JITs though practice has since shown that it is difficult to set up these teams. Only one team so far exists on terrorism, that between Spain and France (there are six teams altogether). The Hague programme of November 2005 sought to boost the setting up of these teams by creating a network of specialists that meet within the framework of Eurojust (the European Judicial Cooperation Unit) and Europol (the European police body that, together with Eurojust, is based in The Hague).

The provisions of the 2000 convention are highly relevant to the fight against terrorism. Although most legal assistance requests were made until recently under the 1959 convention of the Council of Europe, it is likely that the provisions of the new convention of the EU will gradually assume greater importance. The convention includes provisions relating to spontaneous exchange of information, temporary transfer of persons held in custody for purposes of investigations, hearings by video conference, hearing of witnesses and experts by telephone conferences, undercover investigations and interceptions of telecommunications. It is clear that these measures, so-called special investigative techniques, are particularly relevant to terrorist investigations though they are, of course, relevant to investigations into other types of serious crime as well. The convention has so far been ratified by 20 Member States but will doubtless be ratified by all Member States in the coming years.

The Council has also adopted a number of other initiatives with a view to increasing the efficiency of mutual legal assistance in general within the Union, not only as regards terrorist cases but also in relation to other serious types of crime. Among these measures are a Joint Action of 1998 on best practices. Here the Council seeks to promote best practices so as to provide fluidity to mutual legal assistance requests among judicial authorities. Another Joint Action promoted the use of liaison magistrates among the Member States of the Union. One of the more important Joint Actions, drafted under the Maastricht regime, was the setting up of the European Judicial Network. This network, which had its first meeting in 1998, consists of approximately 200 magistrates/prosecutors across the Union, who meet in the Member States on a regular basis, usually in the country of the Presidency and also in Brussels. The magistrates/prosecutors, by meeting each other, get to know each other and have therefore higher trust and confidence in their respective work and, since they meet in the country of the Presidency, they also become better familiarised with other legal cultures, thereby gaining understanding for their respective problems and legal constraints. Between the meetings and in the margins of the meetings a good deal of mutual legal assistance issues are resolved. The network has now met 21 times and has created genuine added value for European judicial cooperation.

The Council also decided a Joint Action in 1997 on *mutual 'peer' evaluation* of measures in the fight against organised crime in particular. After evaluation in 1998/2001 of how mutual legal assistance operates, the Council, by a decision in 2003, set up a specific system of evaluation of terrorism, which has led to increased understanding of how terrorists can be fought through the exchange of best practices among Member States. This type of 'peer' evaluation is very thorough, teams being sent out to the various Member States with a requirement on Member States to answer questions on how they fight terrorism and how their internal structures operate. The team, consisting of experts from the member states, the European Commission, the general secretariat of the Council, Europol and Eurojust, then make recommendations which are discussed in the Multidisciplinary Group on organized crime and in the terrorism working group, where each Member State may comment upon the experts' report. Thus, the various legal systems and practices are being tested against one another and Member States' experts have structured means to further improve the fight against organised crime and terrorism.

One of the most important measures taken by the Council in the fight against terrorism is the setting up of *Eurojust*, the European Judicial Cooperation Unit of the European Union. The background to the creation of this unit was that mutual legal assistance was perceived as inefficient in the mid-1990s. Mutual legal assistance was operating on a bilateral basis between requested and requesting states. The emerging crime situation clearly needed increased multilateral cooperation, and the Tampere conclusions decided that the unit should be set up. Eurojust is composed of national members seconded by each Member State. They are either prosecutors, judges or police officers of equivalent competence. Most of them are prosecutors. The body, which has legal personality, is the first agency set up under the Third Pillar with a partly national, partly EU structure. Each national member and their assistants are paid for by the Member States, but the entire administration and functioning of Eurojust falls under the Community budget, at present around 13 million euros.

Eurojust national members have powers granted to them by their respective Member States, but some powers are specifically laid down in the Eurojust Decision. Member States' legislation must conform with that decision, which is binding under the Treaty. The national members have access to information contained in national criminal records or the many other registers of the Member States, in the same way as prosecutors, judges or police officers of equivalent competence. They are entitled to contact the competent authorities of the Member States directly. They may in addition have judicial powers granted to them by their Member State but will in that case have to make it known that they are exercising these judicial powers. As a national member of Eurojust they may act on their own towards their judicial authorities, or they may act as a College, deciding jointly and most often by simple majority. They may ask Member States to set up Joint Investigative Teams, for instance, and to undertake investigations and prosecutions. In certain cases they are entitled to have negative decisions by national authorities explained. National authorities are not inclined to deny a request made by Eurojust. In practice, therefore, it seems that cooperation is working smoothly.

Eurojust has set up a specific team of prosecutors working on terrorist cases within the unit. Its first coordination meeting in June 2001 in fact concerned Islamic terrorism. About 30 cases per year concerning terrorism have been coordinated by Eurojust. And it also organises strategic meetings concerning terrorism, where modus operandi, new trends and other issues of common interest are discussed, apart from general operational coordination matters. Although Eurojust is a relatively young body (it was set up formally on 28 February 2002), it has already provided clear added value in the fight against terrorism by organising coordination meetings through its headquarters in The Hague. Eurojust is clearly set to become an important tool for fighting terrorism in the EU, though mention must also be made of the Counter-Terrorism Task Force within Europol, which is specifically geared towards police cooperation and support for Europol in its anti-terrorism operations.

The extradition conventions, outlined above, of 1995 and 1996, have not yet entered into force. Practice has confirmed that the slow extradition system was not appropriate to the fight against terrorism and that new measures were needed. This was why one of the conclusions of the Tampere European Council was the need to review the issue of extradition. It was believed that, at least for cases where fugitives fleeing justice escaped to another country, the system of extradition was far too slow. In normal cases extradition often took one year or more and there were still cases dealt with under the old extradition system, where persons fleeing justice used the system of appeal to avoid prosecution in Member States of the European Union. The system was not satisfactory. The Commission was asked to examine the issue by the Tampere European Council. At the same time it was examining the drafting of a Framework Decision against terrorism. Having consulted the Member States, the Commission was ready to propose two draft Framework Decisions on a European Arrest Warrant and on terrorism. In fact the Commission would deposit its proposals with the Council on 19 September, only 8 days after 9/11, and could thus profit from the political momentum the new situation brought to the negotiations. Significantly, it had been thought when the European Commission originally drafted the Framework Decision on the European Arrest Warrant, that the negotiations might last for up to five years. However the European Council of 21 September decided that this Framework Decision, and the Framework Decision on fighting terrorism, should be approved by the meeting of the Justice and Home Affairs Council on 6 December. The European Council declared in its conclusions that it was necessary to 'define the modalities', so a specific system of negotiating the two Framework Decisions was created. The Council used the meetings of the Article 36 Committee (the senior level committee in the Council charged with preparation of Council meetings) and small working group meetings in the margins of that committee to negotiate the European Arrest Warrant. The process was aided by the fact that the 9/11 attacks were made during the Belgian Presidency and that the Belgian Prime Minister and his closest counsellor on Justice and Home Affairs, himself a previous JHA Counsellor of the Belgian Permanent Representation to the EU in Brussels, took a very close interest in these issues. The role of the European Council itself was also crucial. When the Ministers of Justice[4] cautiously suggested to 'downsize' the proposals of the Commission, the European Council in fact gave a new impetus to them.

The proposal of the Commission was extremely ambitious. It proposed the abolition of double criminality, i. e. that the offence must be punishable in both the requesting and the requested State which had been thus far, under the extradition system, the golden rule. The Commission proposed instead a so-called negative list,defining cases where double criminality would not be abolished. The subsequent negotiations showed that this was not appropriate but that it would be possible to develop a positive list.

It was only through successive meetings of the European Council that a wide range of offences was included on the list abolishing double criminality and that a penalty threshold of three years was set. The abolition of the double criminality requirement for the offences on the list was much criticised by NGOs and private lawyers, yet the salient issue was that it was offences *as defined by the national law of the issuing state* which were on the list. It was thus not the law of the executing State that decided on the offence or whether double criminality was at issue. It must be presumed that the investigating judge or the prosecutor in the State issuing the arrest warrant would be capable of correct classification of the offence under investigation, for some 98 or 99 percent of offences are committed in the issuing state, where the judge or the prosecutor is by definition well aware of the legal system in which he is operating. One should not therefore exaggerate the practical importance of the abolition of double criminality in the Framework Decision on the European Arrest Warrant. Moreover it is clearly the case that the creation of an area of freedom, security and justice, where borders are being abolished, requires fighting crime and terrorism to be undertaken in a comprehensive and coherent manner.

The system requires mutual faith that the respective legal systems are respectful of human rights and that, even if different results are sometimes achieved[5], those results and the method by which they are achieved, must be mutually agreeable. To a certain extent the principle of mutual recognition, which in the Tampere European Council was declared to be the corner stone of judicial cooperation, also means that States must provide for arrest of persons for crimes which are not recognised as crimes in a given country but which are crimes being investigated in the issuing State. This is, after all, a natural consequence of the principle of mutual recognition. However, the more national substantive criminal laws are harmonised, the less differences in the national systems are likely to cause problems in the execution of decisions from abroad.

Full faith and trust in other legal systems is thus key, for knowledge of the other legal system involved cannot be taken for granted. In fact, in the landmark case Gözutok/Brügge the European Court of Justice laid down the principle of mutual trust to be followed. The Court held that we must trust in each other's legal systems, even where we arrive at very different results and that the principle of *ne bis in idem* would be valid in such cases. In this case a Dutch coffee-shop owner had accepted a so-called 'transaction' for drugs offences and had agreed to pay approximately 1000 euros as part of an agreement signed with a prosecutor. He was subsequently prosecuted for the same offence in Germany and was sentenced to one year and 5 months imprisonment. The German Court of Appeal requested a preliminary ruling from the European Court of Justice which held that Article 54 of the Schengen implementation convention, which had become part of the Community legal order in 1999 through the incorporation of the Schengen Convention into the Treaty of Amsterdam, was applicable. Its provisions on double jeopardy would thus apply, and this despite the fact that the authors of the convention in 1990 did not in all likelihood consider that Article 54 should be applicable among the Member States of the Union. However, the Court noted that the provisions had to be interpreted in the light of the objective set by Article 29 TEU, which provides that a high level of safety should be created within an area of freedom, security and justice. It is thus worth underlining that the fight against terrorism is also mentioned in Article 29 of the TEU.

The Framework Decision on the European Arrest Warrant lays down certain procedural rules. These follow to some extent the extradition system, but the most important feature is that a specifically judicial system is created. The old system which implied political control has been abolished. The issuing and execution of an arrest warrant is now a purely judicial measure. The most important feature of the arrest warrant is that time limits are laid down. If the surrendered person consents, the surrender must take place within 10 days. If there is no consent the decision has to be taken in principle within 60 days, a limit which a judicial authority might prolong by a further 30 days. If the process has not been terminated within this 90 day time limit, a report must be filed with Eurojust and the latter will further examine the case. In 2005 Eurojust received 15 such reports, mostly related to the length of the procedures for appeal.

The European Arrest Warrant works well. Instead of a slow 9 to 12 month procedure, according to figures from the European Commission, the average time for surrender in contested cases is 43 days and in consented cases 14 days. The objective of the Council has thus been met, namely to reduce significantly the surrendering of persons within the European Union. Yet, it must be remembered that in most cases the crime has been committed in the issuing Member State and that the executing state is usually serving as a safe heaven for the fugitive. Since the procedure is completely judicial, one must note that it has become much safer and completely guided by the principle of the rule of law.

Why the arrest warrant has become so criticised is a moot point. Clearly the reluctance of Member States to put faith and trust in the legal systems cannot be underestimated. Criticism and mutual mistrust require other means than slow extradition procedures, which, in any case, usually end up with the person being extradited. Such measures include information about other legal systems, increased community financing of judicial training, and in particular the adoption of a Framework Decision on procedural rights which would set minimum standards for judicial procedure in Europe.

As noted above, at the same time as the Commission deposited its proposal for the European Arrest Warrant, it deposited its draft Framework Decision on combating terrorism. Given the context of the 9/11 attacks, and the preparatory work that had been undertaken by the Commission, it was relatively easy for the Council to agree on the Framework Decision: in fact the negotiations took some five weeks. It produced an instrument unique in the world; for the first time terrorist offences are defined in a binding legal instrument drafted within a multi-lateral forum. Despite this, however, the definition is to a certain extent a 'trompe-l'oeil' since reference to the pertinence of national law, as with the legal problems concerning terrorism and its definition, has been avoided. Nevertheless the Council has managed to define for the first time the so-called 'terrorist intention'. Article 1.1 of the

Framework Decision states:

> Each Member State shall take the necessary measures to ensure that the intentional acts referred to below in points (a) to (i), as defined as offences under national law, which, given their nature or context, may seriously damage a country or an international organisation were committed with the aim of:
> - seriously intimidating a population, or
> - unduly compelling a government or international organisation to perform or abstain from performing any act, or
> - seriously destabilising or destroying the fundamental political, constitutional, economic or social structures of a country or an international organisation, shall be deemed to be terrorist offences:
> (a)   attacks upon a person's life which may cause death;
> (b)   attacks upon the physical integrity of a person;
> (c)   kidnapping or hostage taking;
> (d)   causing extensive destruction to a government or public facility, a transport system, an infrastructure facility, including an information system, a fixed platform located on the continental shelf, a public place or private property likely to endanger human life or result in major economic loss;
> (e)   seizure of aircraft, ships or other means of public or goods transport;
> (f)   manufacture, possession, acquisition, transport, supply or use of weapons, explosives or of nuclear, biological or chemical weapons, as well as research into, and development of, biological and chemical weapons;
> (g)   release of dangerous substances, or causing fires, floods or explosions the effect of which is to endanger human life;
> (h)   interfering with or disrupting the supply of water, power or any other fundamental natural resource the effect of which is to endanger human life;
> (i)   threatening to commit any of the acts listed in (a) to (h).

The Framework Decision defines a terrorist group as a structured group of more than two persons, established over a period of time and acting in concert to commit terrorist offences. The structured group is deemed to mean a group that is not randomly formed for the immediate commission of an offence, but one without formally defined roles for members and continued membership.

The Framework Decision also defines certain offences which are linked to terrorist activities such as aggravated theft, extortion and drawing up of false administrative documents. The direction of a terrorist group implies a maximum penalty of 15 years and the other terrorist offences at least 8 years. The Framework Decision also deals with liability of legal persons and the jurisdiction and prosecution of terrorist offences. Certain provisions concerning protection of or assistance to victims of terrorist crimes are also included. Management of a terrorist group and participation in the activities of a terrorist group have been made criminal through the Framework Decision. 'Participation' includes the supplying of information or material resources, or the founding of group activities in any way, with knowledge of the fact that such participation will contribute to the criminal activities of the terrorist group.

A word is necessary on certain other instruments of the European Union relevant to the fight against terrorism, such as Council decision 2000/642/JHA of

17 October 2000, concerning arrangements for cooperation between financial intelligence units of the Member States in respect of exchanging information. The so-called FIUs are important in the context of fighting the financing of terrorism and the Financial Action Task Force on money laundering has now adopted nine special recommendations of particular importance to the fight against terrorism financing. Framework Decision 2003/577/JHA of 22 July 2003 on the execution in the EU of orders freezing properties or evidence, led to its entry into force on 2 August 2005. It provides that orders to freeze property or evidence should be executed within 24 hours of the issuing of the order in a Member State (see chapter 5).

In the context of radicalisation and recruitment of terrorists (see chapter 2), Joint Action 1996/443/JHA of 15 July 1996 concerning action to combat racism and xenophobia should also be mentioned. The European Commission has proposed a new Framework Decision, making the provisions of Amsterdam applicable to the Joint Action, but the negotiations have not yet been successful. Some Member States have blocked this Framework Decision on the grounds of its likely infringement of individual liberties. Other Framework Decisions of relevance in this context relate to combating money laundering and the identification, tracing, freezing, seizing and confiscation of the proceeds of crime (2001/500/JHA of 26 June 2001), and Framework Decision 2002/946/JHA of 28 November 2002 on the strengthening of the penal framework to prevent the facilitation of unauthorised entry, transit and residence.

Finally, mention must be made of Framework Decision 2001/220/JHA of 15 March 2001 on the standing of victims in criminal proceedings. This Framework Decision covers victims in criminal proceedings, when they are particularly vulnerable. It has already been the subject of a request for a preliminary ruling to the European Court of Justice in the so-called Pupino case (case C-105/03). The case is important because the Court declared that Framework Decisions, while not having direct effect, could have some form of direct applicability. The Court, using its standing case law concerning Directives, concluded that the principle of loyalty embodied in Article 10 of the Treaty was pertinent to the third pillar. The Court noted that there was an obligation on national judicial authorities to interpret national law in conformity with Framework Decisions adopted by the Council. Eleven governments had intervened in the case seeking to enjoin the Court to adopt the opposite approach. However the Court noted that any other interpretation would deprive Framework Decisions of their proper effect and, since they are binding on all the Member States, any other interpretation could not be reasonable – a rather sensational view, countering that of Ministries of Justice, which tend to hold that the Treaty of Amsterdam, along with the negotiations preceding it, did not envisage that Framework Decisions could produce such legal effects. It is possible that the Pupino case will make negotiations, already extremely difficult with 27 Member States, and the requirement of unanimity, even more difficult in the future.

Also of relevance are the judicial cooperation instruments adopted within the framework of the United Nations. These have a specific status within the European Union as the European Council in its declaration concerning terrorism has requested the Member States to ratify all these conventions as soon as possible. The most important conventions that can be mentioned in this context are the convention on the Financing of Terrorism and the so-called bombing convention.

A number of instruments currently being negotiated within the framework of the European Union should also be mentioned, since they are particularly relevant to the fight against terrorism. These include the Directive on data retention, the Framework Decision on simplifying the exchange of information between law enforcement authorities and the draft Framework Decision on the European Evidence Warrant. But, it is likely that none of these instruments will be on the statute books of the Member States within the next few years.

In conclusion however, the European Union has in a relatively short time, some six years, adopted an impressive *acquis* on judicial cooperation against terrorism. Counter-terrorism has become a top priority on the agenda of the European Union and it is likely to continue to remain there for many years to come.

Endnotes:

1   For background see Nilsson in chapter 6, Westlake and Galloway, *The Council of the European Union* (John Harper Publishing, London 2004).
2   Such as Human Rights Watch and Amnesty International.
3   As Article K 1 of the Treaty described it.
4   At their meeting in October in Luxembourg, in particular.
5   See the Gözutok/Brügge judgement of the ECJ, 187/01
6   The Directive has been adopted but it has been challenged by Ireland in a case before the Court of Justice

4. Managing Terrorism: Institutional Capacities and Counter-Terrorism Policy in the EU

Mark Rhinard, Arjen Boin and Magnus Ekengren

Introduction

The threat of modern terrorism poses a wide range of challenges to national governments and to the international organizations in which they cooperate. Terrorists operate in loose networks rather than in locally bound organizations (Sageman 2004). They possess ever more lethal tools, which range from hard-to-detect explosives to increasingly sophisticated biological agents. They can pick targets both 'hard' and 'soft', making it difficult for authorities to predict the next attack. Terrorists are able to mobilize like-minded agents across the globe (Laqueur 2003). No longer limited to local conflicts, modern terrorism demands a response from many governments and international organizations throughout the world.

Combating modern terrorism thus requires a host of resources, from policy tools and political leadership to general organizational capacity and coordination mechanisms. These resources must be directed not only at preventing and deterring attacks. They must also be employed during cases of 'failed security', to react quickly and effectively when an attack occurs. All of this translates into a bewildering array of challenges, to be met not only by defence and foreign ministries, but also by interior, environment, justice and public order authorities at local, national and supranational levels. Private actors, such as telecommunications and energy suppliers, also play a role in tackling the complex challenges wrought by modern terrorism (Boin and Smith 2006).

In Europe, national governments have increasingly turned to the European Union to help address these challenges. Cooperation ranges from the symbolic, such as joint declarations prioritizing the fight against terrorism on the European agenda, to the operational, including a wide range of common initiatives to further a coordinated response to terrorism. From one perspective, cooperation on terrorism issues is remarkable: EU governments are building common capacity in areas that were once the sole preserve of national governments. From another perspective, cooperation must be closely scrutinized: counter-terrorism is a 'high stakes game', where half-measures and political obstinacy may ultimately lead to lost lives.

This chapter takes an expanded view of what the EU can contribute to counterterrorism efforts by European states. As a benchmark for analysis, we assess what capacities the EU possesses to help prevent attacks, to prepare for a coordinated response, and to organize a quick recovery from an attack. After outlining and debating the merits of an international response to terrorism (section two), we survey the EU's counter-terrorism capacities at three levels of abstraction. The first level contains capacities explicitly engineered toward the 'fight against terrorism' (section three). The second level comprises capacities directed toward managing complex threats and natural disasters (section four). The third level includes those generic capacities found in the EU institutions that may help national organizations, of any type, respond to adverse events (section five). Following the empirical survey, we evaluate those capacities. We identify their contributions to counter-terrorism in Europe and document key shortcomings (section six). We conclude by summarizing the findings and suggesting areas for improvement.

Transboundary terrorism and the European Union

What makes terrorism – traditionally a concern for national states – a concern for the European Union? This section offers a two-fold answer. First, Europe has grown increasingly vulnerable to what were hitherto considered 'local' disturbances. The inter-coupled nature of the European continent demands a coordinated response to potential disturbances. Second, European states have imbued the EU with a growing number of responsibilities and 'core values' to protect – beyond economic concerns towards a renewed focus on the safety and security of citizens. We may say that the EU has opened, and subsequently widened, a policy space for European protection (Boin, Ekengren and Rhinard 2006). Let us explore these answers in somewhat more detail.

The successful integration of European economies has made the EU vulnerable to what not so long ago would have been isolated incidents. The lowering of internal borders, the increasing number of critical infrastructure connections, and growing proximity of populations have made it easier for local incidents to 'cascade' across geographical and functional boundaries (cf. Perrow 1999; OECD 2003). An economic problem in Italy can now become a monetary crisis for the entire eurozone. A glitch in the German electricity network sets off power outages across Europe. The threat of avian flu applies to all European countries. A terrorist attack in London or Madrid reverberates across the European security network. European states, we can argue, are now part of a single security calculus.

Member states recognize these realities. In recent years, EU governments have empowered supranational institutions with more responsibilities to address security related matters. This corresponds to a broadening definition of security – including what needs to be protected from which threat – which increasingly encompasses much of what the EU does as an international organization. As the EU has expanded in size and substance, so has the number of critical systems and core values that need to be protected.

A brief history puts this evolution into perspective. In the 1950s and 1960s, peaceful cooperation between states was a core value for the European Community. Dangers to cooperation itself thus became perceived as a threat to be addressed at both the national and supranational level. In the 1970s and

1980s, economic welfare and fiscal stability became perceived as prominent values to the countries involved in European integration; the EU responded to possible threats by working together to revitalize economies and stabilize monetary systems. In the 1990s, policy declarations and new initiatives revealed the emergence of a third value for the EU: peace and stability in the 'near abroad'. The European Security and Defence Policy (ESDP) can be seen as a key institutional response to protect this new value from impending threats.

A spate of terrorist attacks beginning with 11 September 2001 generated a reaction from EU governments that suggests a fourth value in the evolution of the EU: the protection of citizens against terrorist violence. The Solidarity Clause of the Constitutional Treaty (also agreed as a Solidarity Declaration by the Council in the wake of the Madrid bombings in 2004) pledges an all-for-one response to 'protect democratic institutions and the civilian population' not only from terrorist attack but also natural or man-made disasters (Art. I-43). This helps to explain the range of new instruments, practices, and policies evolving as part of the EU's emerging 'protection policy space' (Boin, Ekengren and Rhinard 2006).[1]

In short, the expansion of the acquis communautaire over the past half century took place alongside an evolution of what might be called 'EU values'. The list of threats to those values lengthened to include safety and security in the face of threats such as terrorism. In addition, the potential cross-border impact of terrorism made it a candidate for supranational coordination and drove the issue up the EU agenda.

Terrorism is not the only threat to European values, of course. Natural disasters such as floods, fires, and earthquakes can also compromise economic development, public safety, and territorial integrity. Technical accidents like explosions, or failures of critical infrastructure such as the internet, also fall into this category of threats. Indeed, even the most 'innocent' accidents may accelerate quickly in today's complex, interconnected world. As they accelerate, such events gain destructive potential (Boin 2004).

This might explain why the EU is increasingly taking an 'all hazards' approach to dealing with threats (European Commission 2004). Research by crisis scholars underscores this approach. It suggests that the fundamental issue at hand is not the type or nature of the threat that might strike, as the impact is rather similar. It also highlights the organizational capacity required of governments to respond to these critical events (Boin et al. 2005). This is not to downplay the specific threat of terrorism. Rather, such insights remind us of the array of capacities, some explicit and others implicit, that are relevant to dealing with all modern threats including terrorism.

Combating terrorism: challenges for government

The threat of modern terrorism and its impact on societies bears resemblance to other contemporary concerns. Flu pandemics, critical infrastructure breakdowns and so-called 'mega disasters' defy prediction, current preparedness efforts, and even collective imagination. All these threats compromise public safety, territorial integrity and the values a government purports to uphold.

With such commonalities in mind, the lessons learned from crisis management research prove useful. The 'crisis approach' directs us not towards the nature of the threat or the type of crisis that can strike a society, but the organisational capacity of a government to respond to those challenges. More specifically, it trains our attention on four types of activity that together comprise the 'crisis management' capacity of a society: preventing threats from materializing, preparing for potential crises, coping with them when they occur, and redressing the damages wrought by crises. The following discussion examines each of these activities in more detail, and considers them in the context of counter-terrorism.

Prevention

One would expect a government, in the first instance, to work to prevent known threats from materializing. This type of activity involves early warning: recognizing emerging threats and trying to 'nip them in the bud.' Prevention mechanisms typically include regulation and inspection regimes, which build on the precious lessons of previous mishaps. In doing so, governments must weigh the potential benefits of strong prevention policies against the price that excessive regulation may exert on social habits, economic activities, and civil liberties. Governments must also recognize that not all incidents and breakdowns can be prevented, as this would require a level of foresight and understanding that governments simply do not possess (Wilensky 1967; Turner 1978; Kam 1988).

Since 11 September 2001, governments worldwide have significantly stepped up their counter-terrorist programs. Much has been invested in reactive means: intelligence activities are aimed at identification and apprehension of potential terrorists. Western countries have approached the 'fight against terrorism' with great fervency, moulding their prevention efforts in line with a desire to fight root causes, to alleviate age-old conflicts, and to deter the radicalization of young men and women. Such efforts demand some form of international cooperation: when borders do not stop the movement of potential terrorists, national states will have to act in concert to detect and arrest them.

Preparation

Societies must prepare for the worst (Clarke 2006). Preparation is crucial because most type of threats cannot be completely prevented. Preparation involves the capacity to plan for unknown combinations of threats that may materialize at any time, anywhere: clearly a difficult task. The right policies, organizational structures and resources must be in place to deal with an emerging disturbance. Responders must be trained and facilities ready. A major obstacle for planning and training, however, is the unknown nature of the next contingency. It is one thing to prepare for routine incidents (a fire, a hostage situation, a major traffic incident), but it is much more difficult to plan for biological weapon attacks, long-term energy failures or extreme weather. The real challenge, as impossible as it sounds, is to prepare for the unknown (Weick and Sutcliffe 2002). The realization that terrorists can strike at any place or time, with potentially catastrophic, cross-border effects, evokes the question whether countries should coordinate their preparation efforts. After all, it may be too late to organize a concerted effort in the immediate wake of a catastrophic attack.

Response

When threats materialize, local and national government organizations must be ready and able to make critical decisions, to coordinate the actions of all those involved in the response operation, and to communicate to the public about the nature of the threat and the subsequent course of events. Administrative and governing elites must try to avert or contain the threat, minimize the damage, and prevent critical systems from breaking down. Several problems are sure to emerge.[2] There will be deep uncertainty as to the causes of the incident and the necessary response strategies. Communication between actors in the response network will be hampered by time pressure and the aforementioned uncertainty. Coordination will be a problem: it is never clear who amongst the many actors involved should make what decisions (Brecher 1979; Drabek 1985; Hermann and Hagan 1988; Janis 1989). After critical decisions are made, implementation hurdles pose yet another set of problems. All these challenges must be met under the glaring lights of an ever-present media.

All this becomes infinitely more complex when multiple nations and various functional systems come under attack. The occurrence of a transboundary crisis suggests the need for international coordination and cooperation. The international system has relatively few institutions and tools available for a coordinated crisis response. National states that wish to coordinate information flows and critical decision-making have little to fall back on and may therefore be forced to go-it-alone, seeking bilateral collaboration on an ad hoc basis.

Restoration and a return to normalcy

The aftermath of an energy-and emotion-consuming event is marked by the desire for a quick return to normalcy. The new order may be different from the old one, but without some sense of order the crisis cannot end. The process of restoration typically includes efforts to learn the right lessons and to render responsible actors accountable in public forums. Both learning and accountability processes tend to be heavily affected by the 'politics of crisis management' (Boin et al. 2005). Different stakeholders will seek to impose their definition of the situation upon the collective meaning-making process that takes place in the aftermath of any crisis. Political dynamics can prolong a crisis even after operational challenges have dissipated. If political-administrative elites fail to defend and explain their actions and intentions, the crisis aftermath can carry painful surprises for them.

Terrorism, in particular, complicates a return to normalcy. A terrorist attack challenges deeply held perceptions of religion, nationalities, history, states and authority. Different countries look upon terrorism in different ways, and public reaction to attacks can vary widely. Some citizenries impugn their own governments, while others rally around their leaders and support local governments. Different 'cognitive crisis maps' in different cultures can provide obstacles to international collaboration to terrorist attacks.

In short, effectively dealing with modern threats comprises a wide variety of activities, policies and mechanisms. The crucial question is what a supranational body such as the European Union can contribute to national capacities to manage transboundary threats such as 'catastrophic terrorism.' In the next sections, we take stock of EU capacities. We begin by considering the activities specifically initiated to enhance counter-terrorism efforts of the Member States.

EU counter-terrorism capacities: justice and home affairs

An obvious place to explore EU counter-terrorism capacities is within the field of Justice and Home Affairs (JHA). By this we mean the 'third pillar' issues included as part of the Maastricht Treaty (1992), along with the expanded competences associated with the goal of creating an 'Area of Freedom, Security and Justice' formalized in the Amsterdam Treaty (1997). Together, the competencies found in this pillar comprise what can be called the EU's explicit approach to managing the terrorist threat.[3]

Five areas of JHA activity stand out in relation to fighting terrorism. The first is police cooperation. The need to improve the interoperability of law enforcement agencies across Europe became clear in the mid-1990s. The development of the single market, along with the removal of frontier controls, led to a parallel commitment to ensuring a 'high level of safety' in the EU (Art. 29 of the Maastricht Treaty). The Tampere Council summit in October 1999 was a milestone in this respect. Frustrated by a lack of progress, EU leaders proposed a new cooperation forum – the EU Police Chiefs' Task Force – to better organize operational approaches to transnational crime problems. Moreover, leaders proposed joint investigation teams for the fight against drug trafficking, human trafficking, and terrorism (Fijnaut 2006). The attacks of 11 September 2001 had a focusing effect, redirecting the goals of existing activities towards the specific issue of terrorism. The 'EU Action Plan to Fight Terrorism', for instance, boosted the authority of Europol (the European Police Office) to develop a specialist anti-terrorist unit, to improve the sharing of police data and information, and to conclude operational agreements with countries such as the United States.

The second area of relevant JHA activity is judicial cooperation. Agreements here announce the creation of a European 'legal space' in regard to crime and terrorism. The establishment of Eurojust, the European Judicial Cooperation Unit, in 2002 signalled the intentions of Member States to enhance the effectiveness of national authorities when they must investigate and prosecute serious cross-border and organised crime. An operational responsibility of Eurojust is to facilitate mutual legal assistance and help implement extradition requests. Perhaps the highest profile agreement in recent years between EU leaders was the adoption of a European Arrest Warrant (EAW), by which each EU member state must recognize and respond to surrender requests from fellow states. The EAW was the first instrument of 'mutual recognition', a principle which is to serve as the backbone for further JHA cooperation (Dittrich 2005).

The third area is information exchange, which has two component parts. One is the sharing of information relevant for law enforcement and judicial tasks. The development of the Schengen Information System (SIS) is the most sophisticated instrument in this regard. Originally designed to ensure effective entry controls at external borders, the system has evolved into a general law enforcement instrument in the fight against cross-border crime (Monar 2006). The Hague Programme, agreed in November 2004, extends cooperation in JHA generally but also establishes the 'principle of availability'. This principle established that law enforcement officials in any state can request, and should receive, information necessary for crime fighting if that information is available (Dittrich 2005, 17). The other part of information exchange relates to more sensitive intelligence required for strategic analysis. Member States now cooperate with the Joint Situation Centre (SitCen) of the Council in order to provide EU Member States' leaders with analysis of threats such as terrorism. The SitCen helps to coordinate both external intelligence services and domestic security services responsible for terrorism in the Member States.

The fourth area of JHA activity with relevance for counter-terrorism is border control and immigration. Following the Madrid attacks in 2004, heads of state and government drew up an ambitious 'Declaration on Combating Terrorism'. Part of that declaration, and the subsequent revision of the 'Action Plan to Fight Terrorism', was a renewed focus on border control, asylum, and immigration issues. The EU has been criticized for mixing the issues of immigration and terrorism, but has nevertheless prioritized the need to 'ensure effective systems of border control' (Dittrich 2005, 16, 19). Renewed interest has also led to the creation of a European Border Agency (Frontex), operational in 2005, to coordinate border control operations, provide technical aid for deportations arranged by Member States, and monitor changes of border control technology.

The fifth area of JHA activity concerns the access of terrorists to financial resources. The EU now has a 'strategy' on the suppression of terrorist financing, including several instruments to allow for the freezing of assets and the tracking of monetary transfers across borders. Recently, the EU has focused on how to coordinate national financial intelligence units, and how to put an end to the financing of terrorism through non-traditional means. The Commission is expected to present proposals on how best to ensure that legitimate charitable organizations are not misused by terrorist financers.

Alongside these five thematic developments, the EU has embarked upon a number of institutional innovations. The March 2004 'Declaration on Combating Terrorism' endorsed the creation of a counter-terrorism coordinator to oversee European counter-terrorism activities. Although the first holder of that position, Gijs de Vries, was given limited formal authority, his role was to improve policy and institutional coherence in the EU fight against terrorism. The same Declaration also included integration of an intelligence structure on terrorism within the Council Secretariat, and reinforced the roles of the SitCen, Europol, Eurojust, and the Police Chiefs Task Force.

Considered in the light of the crisis management challenges outlined in the previous section, the EU's explicit approach to tackling terrorism consists largely of prevention efforts. JHA initiatives enhance national efforts to identify and apprehend terrorists, but they do little at present to boost national preparations or enhance the capacity to coordinate national crisis management operations.

Only in 2005, in the aftermath of the London train bombings, were the consequence management effects of terror attacks given a full airing. Under the leadership of the UK Presidency, the 'Action Plan to Fight Terrorism' was upgraded to an 'EU Counter-Terrorism Strategy'. This strategy emphasizes four dimensions to the fight against terrorism, including the need to prevent, protect, pursue, and respond to attacks when they take place. The EU, the new strategy argues, can add value to national efforts in all four areas by strengthening national capabilities, facilitating cooperation, developing collective capability, and promoting international partnership. It remains to be seen whether these objectives will be met in practice.

EU counter-terrorism capacities: cross pillar

Not all of the EU's counter-terrorism capacity resides in Pillar III. When we include the broader concerns associated with counter-terrorism – including the need to prepare for threats and respond effectively when they occur – other capacities within the EU's other pillars come to the fore.

Looking towards Pillar I, we find additional tools and systems designed to detect impending dangers. The EU health sector, for instance, contains a number of rapid alert systems connecting national health systems. In the event of an epidemic outbreak, the Commission's Directorate General for Health and Consumer Protection (DG Sanco) has the capacity to alert specialized bodies in the Member States. Common protocols instruct Member States how to respond to such outbreaks, and a venue for coordination – the Health Security Committee – can manage cross-border crises. Many of these capacities emerged in the aftermath of BSE ('mad cow' disease) and SARS, when the risks associated with a single market became clear. Yet after the US anthrax attacks in the fall of 2001, capacities were further expanded to include the creation of a bio-security threats division and new initiatives addressing the challenges of bioterrorism, chemical weapons, and vaccine supply.

Also in Pillar I, we find competences related to civil protection emergencies. Over the years, cooperation in the area of civil protection has grown to include two main components. The first component is training and preparation. The EU conducts joint exercises and training programmes for 'first responders', and funds efforts to harmonize the technologies used by civil protection teams across borders. The second component pertains to response and consequence management. The EU operates a collective database of personnel, supplies and equipment for deployment upon request by a stricken member state. EU teams can be deployed for disasters both inside and outside the EU, generally within 24 hours. Overseeing such efforts is the Commission's Monitoring and Information Centre (MIC), a round-the-clock hub that tracks potential problems, facilitates communication between EU states, and coordinates action when necessary. As a first pillar competence, civil protection cooperation takes place with considerable Commission involvement. Its traditional focus on natural disasters has expanded to include man-made disasters and terror attacks. To that end, a 'Solidarity Fund' was created to facilitate reconstruction in EU states affected by any type of disaster.

Another Pillar I competence that has been imbued with a security dimension is air transport. After 11 September 2001, Member States agreed to combine international safety regulations with European laws in a comprehensive approach that sets aviation security standards at all EU airports. To oversee implementation, an 'Aviation Security Regulatory Committee' of national representatives was created in 2002. Common EU standards exist on access to strategic sites, passenger screening, aircraft inspection, cargo procedures, staff training, and equipment. EU inspection teams carry out on-site evaluations on a regular basis. The foiled air terror plot in London in 2006 led to increased attention to passenger and baggage screening procedures, and resulted in a tightening of EU-wide rules.

A concerted effort to protect critical infrastructures is taking place across Pillar I policy areas. Following the Madrid train bombings in 2004, EU leaders asked the European Commission to prepare an overall strategy to protect the vital systems upon which European citizens depend. In response, the Commission outlined plans for a European Programme for Critical Infrastructure Protection (EPCIP), including initiatives in the areas of energy, transport, information systems and water supply (European Commission 2004, 2005). The perceived threats to critical systems in each area include terror attacks, along with natural disasters and technical accidents. Although major questions surround the idea of a European-wide approach to critical infrastructure, including the precise definition of a 'European' critical infrastructure, plans appear to be moving ahead (Fritzon et al. 2006).

The external dimension of counter-terrorism is addressed across the EU pillars. This was a central message of the 2003 'European Security Strategy' (ESS), which sought to construct a cohesive strategy for the EU's role in global security. The ESS argues that 'terrorism poses a growing strategic threat to the whole of Europe' and that 'Europe is both a target and a base for terrorism'. The key to addressing this threat, according to the ESS, is not only to manage the threat at home but also to tackle it abroad by addressing root causes. The 2004 revision of the 'EU Plan of Action to Combat Terrorism' takes a more operational approach. That revision pledges to use the full force of the EU's external authority (trade, diplomatic and aid) to take several key actions. One is to build counter-terrorism capacity in third countries. Another is to address the factors that contribute to the support for and recruitment of terrorists. Diplomatic efforts include the goal of deepening the international commitment to the fight against terrorism, and improving ties between the EU and other international organizations in counter-terrorism.

Pillar II, concerned with foreign policy and security activities, also broadly relates to counter-terrorism. The main instrument of the EU's external security policy, the ESDP, deals with 'crisis management' as it pertains to situations around the world requiring urgent intervention (peacekeeping or peacemaking). Military cooperation has been institutionalized only recently through the creation of working groups and diplomatic preparatory groups. The creation of an EU Military Committee and a permanent EU Military Staff in the Council's institutional apparatus marked a subtle but momentous event in the EU's history: the presence of uniformed officers within the EU institutions. The 'SitCen', described above, carries out threat assessments to enable EU working groups to develop counter-terrorism policies and monitors third country situations that might give rise to heightened security concerns.

A number of recent reforms internal to the EU institutions aim to improve political coordination of crises. The 'Emergency and Crisis Coordination Arrangements' set out procedures for convening a 'Crisis Group' in Brussels when necessary. The Crisis Group comprises relevant EU Commissioners, national diplomats, and Council officials, and has the authority to deploy available EU resources and to recommend actions for national officials (Council of Ministers 2006b). EU Member States have been encouraged to put in place the internal structures required to interact efficiently with 'Brussels' during a crisis (Council of Ministers 2006a). A new 'ARGUS' system of rapid alert aims to centralize the EU's various sector-based rapid alert systems (European Policy Centre 2006).

Finally, much of the EU's formal capacity to protect its citizens can be found in its agencies (Groenleer 2006). The creation of the European Food Safety Authority, for instance, signalled a growth in the EU's organizational capacity to deal with consumer protection issues. The European Centre for Disease Prevention and Control monitors potential pandemics and conducts risk assessments. Monitoring for cross-border weather effects, and impending natural and man-made disasters, takes place at the EU's Joint Research Centre and the EU Satellite Centre. Eurojust and Europol are used to increase information sharing, communication, and coordination on justice and police issues. The increased use of agencies marks growing issue specialization and an enhanced degree of independence that keeps these protection activities at arm's length from the political arena.

Broadening the inquiry: the EU's implicit capacities

Crisis researchers have long argued that complex threats demand organizational capacities of a generic fashion, in addition to specialized skills, policies and organizations that are designed to deal with very specific threats. Considering the difficulties associated with predicting which threats might emerge at any one time, from whom, and with what consequences, a number of generic capacities become relevant. Here we identify the EU's institutional and organizational features that reflect such capacities.

Monitoring policy domains. The EU's bureaucratic administration (consisting largely of the Commission DGs) has a well-developed capacity to monitor policy domains across Europe. The Commission has 'eyes and ears' that allow it to document and follow routine trends while noting sharp deviations that might raise warning flags. In the area of agriculture, for instance, the Commission closely tracks commodity output levels (Grant 1997), while in the area of consumer safety, the Commission attempts to pinpoint emerging food risks (Lezaun and Groenleer 2006). Not all such tracking efforts are geared explicitly towards risks and potential crises. The Commission's monitoring proficiency is largely directed at potential internal market problems and known risks to established policies. Nevertheless, EU authorities are well placed to track and monitor cross border trends within certain policy domains, which greatly benefits the EU's capacity of early warning and timely intervention once a transboundary threat materializes (see also Majone 1996).

Planning for the longer term. Critics are quick to deride EU decision making as slow and tortuous, requiring general consensus before arriving at decisions. The EU policy process has traditionally been dominated by technical experts and policy elites, at arm's length from 'political' interference (Christiansen 2001). For many years that formula worked, because even sensitive political questions could be broken down into their technical components and depoliticized. Although recent experience with the failed referendums on the Constitutional Treaty challenges the 'technocracy' approach, it still accurately describes EU policymaking in general. However, EU decision structures can be very effective for delivering long-term, goal-oriented framework policies. This quality sets the EU apart from national governments, which find their capacity to address long-term goals burdened by the highly politicized nature of the policymaking process.

Regulatory capacity. The prevention of certain types of crises would benefit from well-formulated rules and regulation. The European Union is a regulatory regime par excellence (Majone 1996). This stems from the original goal of the Treaty of Rome to dismantle barriers between the national economies of Member States (Young and Wallace 2000). Supranational regulations were seen as the vehicle through which to pursue the 'market making' effort that could improve competitiveness. The EU displays several features that make it a proficient regulator: the strength of the European legal process, the expertise and machinery needed to promote technical cooperation, and a distance from national influence so that technical, rather than political, approaches characterize problem solving.

Coordinating capacities. The EU has a robust set of institutions and mechanisms for cooperation in place. The Member States interact regularly within them and keep sizable diplomatic delegations permanently stationed in Brussels. Member states have a stake in the system, participating intensely on a daily basis and working to reform and shape that system during treaty revisions (Wallace 2005). In short, the EU has become a known and trusted venue for cooperation. Even in areas in which no formal EU competences exist, states sometimes display a 'coordination reflex' (Tonra 2003). That is, they seek out the views and opinions of European partners through Brussels institutions before defining national positions. Brussels has become a familiar and tested site of cooperation in a wide array of areas. This capacity to coordinate complex activities of multiple Member States enhances the EU's potential to manage transboundary crises.

Marshalling Expertise. During a crisis, policymakers often need experts to advise on technical issues (Rosenthal and 't Hart 1991). The EU institutions routinely generate, and then call upon, broad networks of competent experts (Pedler and Schaefer 1996; Rhinard 2002). On any given work day, hundreds of advisory groups are meeting in Brussels, bringing together thousands of consultants, civil servants and scholars to focus on narrow policy questions. The Commission must formulate high-quality policy standards that accommodate the interests of twenty-five different countries. This suggests the EU institutions have a developed capacity to quickly assemble and access expert networks – something many national governments find hard to do during a crisis.

Analysis and assessment: the EU's added value to national counter-terrorism

Thus far, the chapter has taken a 'bird's eye' approach to EU activities relevant to fighting global terrorism. It has shown a rapid evolution of supranational capacity to further a coordinated approach of Member States. An assessment of this capacity is not easy, given the notable absence of events with a true cross-border impact in Europe. It is hard to predict how the EU can and will employ the tools explicitly designed for counterterrorist purposes; it is impossible to foresee if and how the Union will employ its generic tools that were originally designed for other purposes.

Nevertheless, it is worth evaluating the potential constraints in the use of these explicit and implicit tools, since the EU's counter-terrorism activities do not take place against an institutional blank-slate. There are a number of institutional and political divides that can constrain (and at other times enable) the EU's role in counter-terrorism. We offer a brief overview of some critical variables that need to be taken into account when assessing the EU's counter-terrorism capacity.

The inter-pillar divide

One factor relates to the division between the EU's different pillars. As made clear above, the EU's counter-terrorism capacities reside in all three pillars, along with the various new European agencies. Policies in each pillar are made by different procedures, prioritize different constellations of actors, and are driven by different political dynamics. Member states strictly control the pace of policy-making in Pillars II and III, while the Commission plays a stronger agenda setting role in Pillar I. The Commission can also take autonomous action, using its own resources, in Pillar I policy areas, while individual Member States are less likely to exercise a veto. As a result, the pace of policy-making can be much quicker in some pillars than others. When Member States want to move forward unanimously in Pillar III, policy-making takes place swiftly. When one member state objects, however, it can slow dramatically. The average time for reaching a decision in Pillar III can take up to four months (Dittrich 2005, 13). The Commission can speed the policy process and preserve continuity through its direct role in policy management in Pillar I. When its own services disagree, or when a majority of Member States object, that process can slow down as well.

Institutional fissures create competition and confusion, as well. Actors in the different pillar structures prioritize different threats and bring different resources to bear on the problem. Indeed, some parts of the Commission and Council are focused on prevention and deterrence, for instance, while others direct their energies towards consequence management (Boin and Rhinard 2005). If well coordinated, such differentiation does not present an inherent problem. If the various components are not cooperating, however, dangerous gaps can arise. One notable example is the difficulty of coordinating the civil protection tasks of Pillar II with the civil protection mechanism in Pillar I. The respective policy officials view one another with scepticism, because of different institutional and political allegiances, despite a declared willingness to work together.

It is not entirely clear who is 'responsible' for the management of terrorism in the EU. Leadership is diffused across the EU institutions, which presents problems for both policy management and democratic accountability. Different counter-terrorism related policies are progressing at different speeds, and in an ad hoc fashion. Internal and external observers alike have a difficult time identifying the main political actors. Moreover, no single actor can be held accountable for policy problems. At national levels, familiar forms of democratic legitimacy underpin efforts to hold security actors accountable. At the supranational level, since competences are shared between national and European authorities, accountability suffers (Höreth 1999). Overseeing decisions regarding security, which often collide with civil liberty concerns, can be problematic. Holding officials responsible in the aftermath of a disaster or attack can present a similar challenge. Recent constitutional referendums in France and The Netherlands suggest dissatisfaction with the EU's technical, depoliticized style of operation. In the crisis management field, such defects can become magnified, potentially threatening the long-term legitimacy of the EU.

The national – supranational divide

The national-supranational divide presents one of the more fundamental constraints on the Commission's role in counter-terrorism. The vertical relationship, between supranational institutions and national governments, has evolved into a rather sophisticated one, but it is not without tensions. Since the 'major leaps' toward integration embodied by the Single European Act (in force from 1987) and the Maastricht Treaty (in force from 1993), Member States have become more critical of the Commission and its accumulated powers. In a variety of areas, there have even been demands for 'decentralisation' – 'often little disguised attempts at repatriation of Commission powers back to national administrations' (Christiansen 2001, 103). The national divide manifests itself both in the EU's inputs and in response to its outputs. EU governments are increasingly cautious about what competences they choose to delegate to 'Brussels'. New institutional structures give Member States more control over the EU policy process than hitherto and Member States have proved reluctant to comply with policies that emerge from the supranational policy process (Steunenberg 2006).

Any efforts to organize counter-terrorism at the supranational level thus meet with a primary constraint: despite ownership of the mechanisms, the Commission's crisis management capacity depends on member state resources. Whether it is critical information about the situation at hand or the ability to carry out operational tasks (securing public order, fixing system breakdowns, providing medical care, etc.), the Commission must rely on Member States. The capacities of individual Member States may not always be robust, nor are they always used to manage crises effectively, but they seemingly remain the central focus of governments' efforts to protect their citizens. The development of a supranational counter-terrorism role in Europe is thus heavily constrained by this member state-centred reality.

Furthermore, implementation problems stem from the supranational-national divide. While most EU Member States initially addressed issues related to counter-terrorism with great urgency, many have yet to implement commitments made on paper. Overall progress has been made on a range of measures, but the overall process of implementation is too slow and there are not enough checks on implementation (Dittrich 2005, 12-13).

Part of the problem is explained by the central driver behind EU counter-terrorism efforts: actual terror attacks. The immediate aftermath of an attack brings public attention, political will and policy ideas. Yet with the passage of time, enthusiasm slows not only at the European level but also at the national level. Policies agreed under Pillar II and Pillar III, moreover, come with no oversight mechanism to ensure compliance.

The internal – external divide

Although the European Security Strategy declares that the internal and external aspects of modern threats are 'indissolubly linked', the institutional and political divisions described above militate against an operational approach with the same spirit. Not only is coherence between the EU's external policies (trade, aid, development, diplomatic, and ESDP) difficult to draw together, but linking the internal with the external has become a lofty challenge. The reasons for such difficulties are clear: institutional and political loyalties come into play, along with the more generic challenges of trying to combine 'security-political' issues with 'aid-development' operations (Ekengren, this volume).

This is an unfortunate development, since the EU's potential strength as a counter-terrorism player, and as a crisis manager more generally, will depend on its willingness to draw together the full range of capacities, tools and instruments that it has acquired over the years. In many respects, the EU is well-suited (arguably even more so than national governments) to dissolve the boundary between external and internal security matters. In the 1950s, the European Union was able to transcend that divide for its Member States by generating cooperation and community through transnational networking. Fifty years later, it might dissolve the boundary between external and internal EU security by expanding its internal safety, police and defence cooperation to neighbouring areas and linking it to the EU's contribution to international security.

In this respect, both the ESS and the 'Solidarity Clause' in the Constitutional Treaty (and adopted later as an independent Council declaration) offer the prospect of conceptual guidance. The ESS essentially defines security as a cross-border issue, and identifies an expansive number of 'referent objects' requiring transnational protection. The Solidarity Clause suggests that Member States shall come to one another's assistance in the face of any threat, intentional or unintentional. Together, the documents provide a new framework for cooperation and signal a new chapter in the history of European integration. The remaining question is whether existing forms of cooperation, previously associated with economic rather than security cooperation, are still sufficient for this new beginning (Ekengren, 2006).

Conclusion

This chapter builds on an encompassing definition of what governments need to combat modern terrorism. We used that definition to categorize EU capacities across its institutional landscape and policy spectrum. We found that explicit counter-terrorism agreements, instruments and policies present only part of the picture. The EU features additional, albeit more general, capacities relevant for fighting different threats – intentional and unintentional – and houses a number of generic capacities useful for dealing with adverse events.

Our findings reveal more EU capacity in this area than commonly understood. The EU's responsibilities have certainly grown in recent years, but
there is a general lack of awareness of this role. Supranational efforts tend to
'fly under the radar' for several reasons. One is the incremental nature of the
EU's development. Another is that efforts can be highly technical, related to
specific guidelines for pandemic diseases, for instance, or to sensitive intelligence-sharing parameters. Further still, national politicians have shied away
from informing their publics of the EU's contribution to security. Recent failed
referendums on the Constitutional Treaty for Europe revealed the sensitivities
that some national publics have towards the EU. It may be time to forge a new
consensus on the precise role of the EU, and the future shape of cooperation,
in this qualitatively new area of European cooperation.

More immediately, the three divisions outlined above – between pillars,
between governance levels, and between the external and the internal –
promise to shape the EU's role in counter-terrorism. Major questions need
to be resolved, such as the precise objective of supranational cooperation,
the balance of power between EU states and EU institutions, and the extent
of the threat to be addressed before carrying on. The ESS and the Solidarity
Clause represent important conceptual moves in this direction, but more
specific answers will be necessary in the years ahead.

Endnotes

1   An unresolved question for the EU is whether a fifth core value is emerging. Increasingly,
the EU seems to be taking part in military and civilian missions far away from its own borders.
EU efforts in Africa, the Middle East, and South East Asia exemplify this trend and suggest the
EU is carving out a new security role and new values. A threat to this value may implicate not
only European citizens, European states, and European neighbors but also citizens of the world
threatened, for instance, with human rights violations. The 2003 European Security Strategy
(ESS) articulates such values and threats.
2   A voluminous literature exists on patterns and pitfalls of crisis management. For an
overview, see Comfort (1988); Rosenthal, Charles and 't Hart (1989); Boin (2004); Rodriquez,
Quarantelli and Dynes (2006).
3   We note that several issues discussed here straddle both pillar three and pillar one. For
instance, immigration, terrorist financing, and critical infrastructure protection requires tools
and means found in both pillars and demands considerable cooperation between actors associated with each pillar. For the sake of clarity, however, we group these issues together. See
Nilsson (this volume) for a more detailed essay on the EU's role in JHA issues.

References

Boin, R. A. (2004) 'Lessons from Crisis Research', *International Studies Review*, 6
(1): 165-174.

Boin, R. A. and Rhinard, M. (2005) 'Shocks Without Frontiers: transnational
breakdowns and critical incidents, what role for the EU?' Issue Paper no. 42,
European Policy Centre, Brussels, November 2005.

Boin, R. A. and Smith, D. (2006) 'Terrorism and critical infrastructures:
Implications for public-private crisis management', *Public Money and Management*,
volume 26, number 5, November, pp. 295-304.

Boin, R. A., 't Hart, P., Stern, E. and Sundelius, B. (2005) *The Politics of Crisis*

Management: Understanding Public Leadership When it Matters Most, Cambridge: Cambridge University Press.

Boin, R. A., Ekengren, M. and Rhinard, M. (2006) 'Protecting the Union: Analyzing an Emerging Policy Space', *Journal of European Integration*, vol. 28, no. 5, pp. 405-421.

Brecher, M. (1979) *Studies in Crisis Behavior*, New Brunswick: Transaction.

Christiansen, T. (2001) 'The European Commission: Administration in Turbulent Times' in J. Richardson (ed) *European Union: Power and Policy-Making*, London: Routledge.

Clarke, L. (2006) *Worst Cases: Terror and Catastrophe in the Popular Imagination*, Chicago: Chicago University Press.

Comfort, L.K. (ed) (1988) *Managing Disaster: Strategies and Policy Perspectives*, Durham: Duke University Press.

Council of Ministers (2006a) 'Reinforcing the European Union's Emergency and Crisis Response Capacities', Document No. 9552/2/06. Brussels, Council of the European Union, 15 July 2006.

Council of Ministers (2006b) 'Manual on Emergency and Crisis Coordination', Document No. 9552/2/06', Brussels, Council of the European Union, 27 July 2006.

Dittrich, M. (2005) 'Facing the Global Terrorist Threat: A European Response', Working Paper no. 14, European Policy Centre, Brussels, January 2005.

Drabek, T.E. (1985) 'Managing the Emergency Response', *Public Administration Review*. 45: 85-92.

Ekengren, M. (2006) 'New Security Challenges and the Need for New Forms of EU Cooperation' *European Security*, vol. 15, no. 1, pp. 89-111.

European Commission (2004) 'Critical Infrastructure Protection in the Fight Against Terrorism', COM(2004) 702 final, 20 October 2004.

European Commission (2005) 'Green Paper on a European Programme for Critical Infrastructure Protection', COM(2005)576, 17 November 2005.

European Policy Centre (2006) Progress Report from the Task Force on 'Managing Emergencies: The EU's Role in Security and Safety', Brussels, December 2006.

Fijnaut, C. (2006) 'Police Cooperation and the Area of Freedom, Security and Justice', in N. Walker (ed) *Europe's Area of Freedom, Security and Justice*, Oxford: Oxford University Press.

Fritzon, Å., Ljungkvist, K., Boin, R. A. and Rhinard, M. (2006) 'Protecting Europe's Critical Infrastructure: Problems and Prospects' *Journal of Contingencies and Crisis Management*, vol. 17, no. 1, pp.30-41.

Grant, W. (1997) *The Common Agricultural Policy*, London: Macmillan.

Groenleer, M. (2006) 'The European Commission and Agencies' in D. Spence (ed) *The European Commission*, London: John Harper, pp.156-172.

Hermann, M.G. and Hagan, J. (1988) 'International Decision Making: Leadership Matters', *Foreign Policy*, 110: 124-137.

Höreth, M. (1999) 'No way out for the beast? The unsolved legitimacy problem of European governance', *Journal of European Public Policy*, vol. 6, no. 2, pp. 249-268.

Janis, I.L. (1989) *Crucial Decisions: Leadership in Policymaking and Crisis Management*, New York: The Free Press.

Kam, E. (1988) *Surprise Attack*, Cambridge: Harvard University Press.

Laqueur, W. (2003) *No End to War: Terrorism in the Twenty-first Century*, New York: Continuum.

Lezaun, J. and Groenleer, M. (2006) 'Food Control Emergencies and the

Territorialisation of the European Union', *Journal of European Integration*, vol. 28, no. 5, pp. 437-455.

Majone, G. (1996) *Regulating Europe*, London: Routledge.

Monar, J. (2006) 'Cooperation in the Justice and Home Affairs Domain: Characteristics, Constraints, and Progress', *Journal of European Integration*, vol. 28, no. 5, pp. 495-501.

OECD (2003) *Emerging Risks in the 21st Century: An agenda for action*, Paris: OECD.

Pedler, R. and Schaefer, G (eds) (1996) *Shaping European Law and Policy: The Role of Committees and Comitology in the Political Process*, Maastricht: European Institute of Public Administration.

Perrow, C. (1999) *Normal Accidents: Living with high-risk technologies*, Princeton: Princeton University Press.

Rhinard, M. (2002) 'The Democratic Legitimacy of the European Union Committee System', *Governance*, vol. 15, no. 2, pp. 185-210.

Rodriguez, H., Quarantelli, E.L. and Dynes R.R. (eds) (2006) *Handbook of Disaster Research*, New York: Springer.

Rosenthal, U. and 't Hart, P. (1991) 'Experts and Decision Makers in Crisis Situations' in *Knowledge, Diffusion, Utilization* 12(4): 350-372.

Rosenthal, U., Charles, M.T. and 't Hart, P. (eds) (1989) *Coping with Crises: The management of disasters, riots and terrorism*, Springfield: Charles C Thomas Publishers.

Sageman, M. (2004) *Understanding Terror Networks*, Philadelphia: University of Pennsylvania Press.

Steunenberg, B. (2006) 'Turning swift policy-making into deadlock and delay: National policy coordination and the transposition of EU directives', *European Union Politics*, vol. 7, no. 3, pp. 293-319.

Tonra, B. (2003) 'Constructing the Common Foreign and Security Policy: The Utility of a Cognitive Approach', *Journal of Common Market Studies*, vol. 41, no. 4, pp. 731-756.

Turner, B.A. (1978) *Man-made Disasters*, London: Wykeham.

Wallace, W. (2005) 'Post-sovereign Governance' in H. Wallace, W. Wallace, and M. Pollack (eds) *Policy-Making in the European Union*, Oxford: Oxford University Press.

Weick, K.E. and Sutcliffe, K.M. (2002) *Managing the Unexpected: Assuring High Performance in an Age of Complexity*, San Francisco: Jossey-Bass.

Wilensky, H.L. (1967) *Organizational Intelligence: Knowledge and Policy in Government and Industry*, New York: The Free Press.

Young, A. and Wallace, H. (2000) 'The Single Market' in H. Wallace and W. Wallace (eds) *Policy-making in the European Union*, Oxford: Oxford University Press.

5.   The EU, Terrorism and Effective Multilateralism

Kim Eling

Introduction: Counter-terrorism, the EU and the United Nations – the birth of an unexpected alliance

Until 11 September 2001, the United Nations and other international organizations did not feature at the top of a counter-terrorism practitioner's shortlist list of significant players in the fight against international terrorism. Counter-terrorism covered, first and foremost, national law enforcement and legislation. As Spence points out in the introduction to this book, to the extent that counter-terrorism had an international angle, it implied bilateral cooperation. This is not to say that the UN and other multilateral fora were not engaged in efforts to prevent terrorism. Within the UN, work had been under way for several years on a comprehensive convention on terrorism, as had efforts to promote the ratification of the UN's (at the time) twelve sectoral counter-terrorism conventions. Yet, notwithstanding the UN Security Council's targeted sanctions against Al-Qaida and the Taliban, the multilateral system was scarcely geared up for an operational contribution to the fight against terrorism.

9/11 changed this. In the wider multilateral system, as in the EU, 9/11 prompted a burst of activity. Some of the initiatives were purely declamatory. Others – in particular a small number of decisions by the Security Council – put the UN at the centre of international efforts to prevent a repetition of the attacks on the US, while taking the Security Council into new territory, as it sought to coax States into adopting effective domestic policies against terrorism, thereby prompting the EU into going further and faster in the development of key counter-terrorism instruments. Moreover, the interaction between the EU and the UN Security Council, which was also reflected in fora such as the G8, triggered an unprecedented effort on the part of the EU to present and explain its policies in a multilateral context.

As counter-terrorism moved to the top of the foreign policy agenda in European capitals, national policy was clearly reflected in the work of the EU institutions after 9/11. But the key factors influencing EU policies were to be found in the interaction that developed rapidly from late 2001 between the EU and international organizations – particularly the UN. The EU went to great lengths to implement and support counter-terrorism policies designed in the UN framework. This followed from and simultaneously enhanced its 'innate' commitment to 'effective multilateralism'.[1] Two specific elements of the European response to terrorism must be considered in this context: first, the European contribution to the fight against terrorist financing, which was driven almost entirely by the agenda set in multilateral fora; and second, the emergence of terrorism prevention as a factor in programming EC development assistance. In both cases, the existence of clear UN standards and policies enabled the EU to go beyond what it might have been able to achieve alone in adopting new policy tools. The initiatives launched in the UN context by the UN Security Council, acting under Chapter VII of the UN Charter, were of crucial importance. They enabled the EU to bypass lengthy internal processes, themselves impregnated with concerns about the desirability and feasibility of integration in an area as sensitive as counter-terrorism. Laborious discussion on these issues might otherwise have constrained the EU's ability to act decisively. The immediate post-9/11 political context undoubtedly presented a window of opportunity for enhanced European integration. Yet, just as significantly – if more discreetly, and with less obvious results to date – the EU's interaction with multilateral fora allowed a distinctly European perspective to be brought into play in discussions on counter-terrorism in UN fora. This obtained in particular with regard to the safeguarding of individual rights in the context of the 'war on terror', and specifically the rights of individuals subject to UN targeted sanctions on account of their suspected links with the Taliban or Al-Qaida.

1.   Putting the UN on the agenda: the jolt of 9/11

Terrorism had been on the agenda of the United Nations before 11 September 2001. The 12 international conventions on international terrorism, concluded under the auspices of the UN or of specialized agencies such as the International Civil Aviation Organization or the International Maritime Organization, sought to prescribe basic standards to states on subjects such as the criminalization of specific terrorist offences, action on terrorist financing or the prevention of hijacking.[2] In addition, negotiations on a comprehensive convention on the prevention of terrorism had been under way since 1996. A small Terrorism Prevention Branch (TPB) of the UN Office on Drugs and Crime in Vienna provided technical assistance to UN Member States for the implementation of the conventions. However, discussions on terrorism were neither central to the agenda of any major UN body nor were they imbued with any particular sense of urgency. Negotiations on the draft comprehensive convention had become deadlocked over the definition of terrorism, and the process of ratification of the sectoral UN conventions on terrorism was not subject to any particular urgency.[3]

9/11 changed this virtually overnight. The universal revulsion at the attacks on the US, and the near-universal desire to be seen to be acting to prevent a repetition of the attacks, led to a flurry of activity at the UN. This centred on the Security Council which became the hub of UN action on terrorism. On 28 September 2001, the Council adopted a resolution that at one stroke went further than any previous multilateral instrument for the prevention of terrorism, and arguably took the Security Council further than with any previous resolution beyond foreign policy and into the domain of domestic legislation. Security Council Resolution 1373, adopted under Chapter VII of the UN Charter (and thus set squarely in the context of a threat to international peace and security), was binding on all States. It prescribed an unprecedented range of measures to be taken by governments to prevent a repetition of 9/11.

Resolution 1373 focussed on the financing of terrorism, with provisions requiring all States to criminalize the financing of terrorism, to freeze the funds of individuals and organizations involved in terrorist acts and to prevent funds being made available to terrorists or terrorist organizations. It also laid down in broad terms a requirement that States refrain from providing support or 'safe haven' to terrorists, suppress the recruitment of terrorists, eliminate the supply of weapons to terrorists and prevent the movement of terrorists across borders by means inter alia of effective border controls and measures to prevent the counterfeiting of identity documents. It also required States to establish terrorist acts as serious criminal offences in domestic law. The resolution was intended in a sense as a 'fast-forwarded' version of the UN's sectoral counter-terrorism conventions: by adopting a Chapter VII resolution, the Security Council circumvented the vagaries of national ratification procedures and the protracted negotiations on the comprehensive convention, and distilled crucial elements from individual conventions into a single, binding text that packed all the more punch for its concision.

The resolution further set up a committee of the Security Council to scrutinize implementation of the resolution – the Counter-Terrorism Committee (CTC). In itself, this was nothing unusual – UN Security Council sanctions resolutions routinely establish sanctions committees to monitor implementation of specific sanctions regimes imposed by the Council. However, the vast scope of 1373 and its unusual reach into many areas of domestic security policy, as well as the political urgency with which the Security Council addressed the aftermath of 11 September 2001, made it unlikely that the CTC would be a paper-pushing exercise. Moreover, the high political priority given to counter-terrorism within the Security Council after 9/11 was reflected in the level of representation of Security Council members on the CTC, with Permanent Representatives and, for some UNSC members, senior counter-terrorism officials from capitals participating in its meetings.

2.   Resolution 1373 and the EU: the UN as a catalyst for policy innovation in Brussels

Within the EU, the adoption of 1373 prompted a number of discrete but interlinked processes. At a general political level, the Council adopted a Common Position[4] expressing its commitment to the implementation of the resolution, and indeed integrating the objectives of 1373 into the Common Foreign and Security Policy (CFSP). While this was essentially a statement of political intent, it underlined that 1373 would be one of the cornerstones of the EU's external counter-terrorism policy. At the same time, the EU (both individual Member States and, within the Commission, the External Relations Directorate-General) conducted a 'screening' of UNSCR 1373 in its entirety. The purpose was to establish which provisions were covered by EU policies or legislation, and which elements would require new policy measures.

1373 and terrorist financing

Without any doubt the most important element of 1373 for the EU was the requirement (in paragraph 1 of the resolution) to 'Freeze without delay funds and other financial assets or economic resources of persons who commit, or attempt to commit, terrorist acts or participate in or facilitate the commission of terrorist acts', and the related provisions aimed at preventing terrorists from raising funds. With this, the Security Council obliged States to freeze the assets of suspected terrorists as a preventive measure; and while it did not specify the precise legal means to do so, it was clear that action taken by individual States would be subject to scrutiny by the CTC.[5] Significantly, with this provision the Security Council required governments to go beyond its own existing financial sanctions against Al-Qaida and Taliban suspects, which had been in place since the adoption of Security Council Resolution 1267 in 1999 (imposing freezing measures and other sanctions, such as a travel ban, against individuals listed by the Security Council). Resolution 1373 was not limited in its scope to any particular terrorist grouping. It required action against terrorism, not just against the perpetrators of the 11 September attacks. This added to its potency, while ensuring its political viability within the Security Council.

For the EU, there were two reasons for taking the prescription from the Security Council seriously. Most importantly, the EU had for several years practised a consistent policy of transcribing UNSC sanctions resolutions into EU (and, for economic sanctions, EC) instruments – both as an expression of its principled commitment to aligning EU foreign policy on binding decisions of the UN, and (where economic sanctions are concerned) as a logical concomitant of its common commercial policy, as inscribed in the EC Treaty. The second reason was that in the absence of legal instruments at the European level to implement the provisions, some Member States would have had difficulty adopting national instruments to implement the requirement, because original primary legislation would have been necessary. EU legislation would facilitate the process of national implementation. This made it all the more urgent for the EU to act swiftly.

The EU had, of course, long since implemented the Taliban/Al-Qaida sanctions imposed by UNSCR 1267 and its successor resolutions (1333 and 1390). Now, however, 1373 required action to prevent the funding of *all* terrorists and those aiding and abetting them – not just of Taliban/Al-Qaida suspects, who in any case fell into the ambit of the 1267 procedures. Crucially, and in a major departure from the EU's past practice of simply implementing the lists issued by a Committee of the UN Security Council under the 1267 sanctions regime, this would require an autonomous identification by the EU of terrorist suspects and organizations.

The Council and Commission thus set about establishing from scratch, and with no obvious precedent, a system for designating individuals and organizations not covered by the existing 1267 system. The latter provides for the EU simply to take over wholesale the lists established on a binding basis by the Security Council and to ensure that their assets are effectively frozen. In spite of the complexity of the challenge (and of the institutional questions raised by the exercise), the Council adopted the relevant instruments within a relatively short period of time: on 27 December 2001, it adopted Council Common Position 2001/931/CFSP and Council Regulation 2580/2001, which, taken together, create for the first time an autonomous EU system for designating individuals and groups suspected of involvement in terrorist activities, and (for those linked to terrorist groups from outside the EU) for the freezing of their assets, and for corresponding judicial cooperation between Member States for all the individuals and groups listed.

The significance of this new mechanism can hardly be exaggerated. On the one hand, it took the EU into the territory of identifying individual terrorists and terrorist organizations. This was a huge leap forward considering that the EU's efforts to prevent terrorism had until then focused on the more traditional instrument of adopting framework legislation to be applied by Member States. On the other, this transition from 'merely' setting standards for the legal fight against terrorism to something approaching enforcement undoubtedly enhanced the EU's credibility abroad as an actor in the fight against international terrorism. The list of designated persons and entities in 2006 comprised 45 individuals and 48 'entities'[6,] with a diverse line-up of organizations ranging from intra-European groups such as ETA, the Real IRA and the UVF, to foreign organizations such as the LTTE, Shining Path, Hamas and Kach.

The process by which organizations and individuals are added to or subtracted from the list is confidential, although the criteria for inclusion are stated clearly in the Common Position. The requirement that any change be adopted by unanimity is also clearly enunciated in Regulation 2580/2001. The confidential nature of the process has not prevented governments outside the EU from commenting freely on the process and the list (and on occasion criticizing the process for not being sufficiently flexible in accommodating new entries). Nor has it prevented some non-European governments from lobbying actively for the inclusion of particular groups on the list (with a very public lobbying effort, for example, to persuade the EU to list Hezbollah[7]). Conversely, it also in one case led one of the EU's partners to make an exception to its otherwise consistent practice of aligning itself on EU sanctions measures: Norway, which had previously taken the lead from the EU's listing decisions, declared in early 2006 that it would henceforth no longer implement automatically the EU's listing decisions in its own legislation, since it felt the EU's decision to list certain organizations would affect its role in certain peace processes.[8] Ironically, it is perhaps these debates surrounding individual listing decisions, and the extent to which they have provoked interest on the part of non-EU governments, which underscore more strongly than anything else the real significance of the new instruments, and their centrality in the EU's counter-terrorism arsenal.

1373 and technical assistance

The second area in which 1373 impacted significantly on counter-terrorism policy at the European level was technical assistance. Only a few weeks into its existence, the Counter-Terrorism Committee set out, in its first work programme[9], its intention to work with States and relevant international organizations to address possible needs for technical assistance in the implementation of the resolution. Drawing on the text of the resolution, the CTC identified seven specific areas in which assistance was sought: drafting of counter-terrorism legislation; financial law and practice; customs law and practice; immigration law and practice; extradition law and practice; police and law enforcement work; illegal arms trafficking; and other assistance related to implementation of the resolution. In devising this follow-up mechanism, the Security Council was able to draw to some extent on the follow-up to resolution 1267, which imposed financial sanctions on Al-Qaida and the Taliban. In that context, too, the Security Council had already established in July 2001 (thus even before 9/11) a monitoring mechanism comprising not only a Monitoring Group but also a sanctions enforcement support team to assist States.

Within the EU, the primary responsibility for dealing with the question of technical assistance fell to the Commission. Just as the provisions of the resolution on the financing of terrorism had prompted a review of existing EU practice against the provisions set out by the Security Council, the CTC's call for technical assistance prompted a review of the EC's existing external assistance programmes. Until 9/11, the EU had not been consciously a prominent actor in the delivery of counter-terrorism assistance to third countries. One of the few assistance actions designed specifically with a counter-terrorism objective was the EU's assistance programme for the forensic and investigative capacity of the Palestinian police, delivered as a Joint Action in the framework of the CFSP. The Commission, for its part, and as part of its development policy and regional assistance programmes in e.g. the CIS countries, was implementing a wide range of programmes and projects with direct relevance for the obligations set out in 1373. Some of these activities, conceived as governance programmes rather than counter-terrorism assistance, dealt with issues such as the strengthening of border controls, training for the judiciary, the fight against money laundering, or capacity-building for national police services (which in some cases, in the then accession countries, included specific counter-terrorism training). As such, these activities directly supported specific requirements of 1373, though they were not labelled 'counter-terrorism assistance'.

The adoption of 1373, and the pro-active outreach by the CTC to potential providers of assistance[10], put the prevention of terrorism prominently on the agenda for EC development assistance for the first time. In order to determine the extent to which existing assistance programmes were contributing to the effective implementation of 1373, in October 2001 the External Relations Directorate-General of the Commission launched a review of ongoing EC assistance, covering the European Development Fund, geographical instruments for Asia and Latin America and the specific instruments for what would subsequently become the 'new neighbours' of the EU (TACIS, CARDS and MEDA). The results of this initial screening were summarized in a Commission Staff Working Paper[11], shared with Member States and submitted to the CTC in February 2002. The paper – subsequently integrated into the CTC's on-line database of sources of technical assistance – set out assistance falling under the different categories set out by the CTC, and noted that there was 'scope for further assistance to facilitate the implementation of the Resolution in the framework of the main assistance programmes and programming documents'.

This initial inventory constituted only a first step towards more substantial policy innovation. As a next step, the Commission's DG Relex reviewed options for launching projects with a more explicit counter-terrorism focus to support the CTC's efforts. Re-opening assistance programmes for individual countries and regions quickly proved a less than promising avenue, given that national and regional indicative strategies are programmed multi-annually in agreement with the recipient government. They are thus not easily adjusted to new priorities emerging at short notice. However, the Commission was able to draw on the Rapid Reaction Mechanism (RRM), a financing instrument created specifically to enable the EU to intervene rapidly in crisis situations and to kick-start conflict prevention activities. Proceeding in close consultation with the Presidency and the Council's COTER working group, the Commission set about identifying countries that would most benefit from assistance. Taking into account suggestions provided by the CTC itself, seven countries were identified for enhanced assistance with the RRM used to kick-start pilot projects focussing on some of the areas set out by the CTC as requiring particular attention. The Philippines, Indonesia and Pakistan were the first to receive assessment missions in preparation for targeted technical assistance.

At a later stage, in March 2004, the creation of a Counter-Terrorism Committee Executive Directorate (CTED) as a more permanent secretariat to the CTC gave further focus to the Security Council's efforts at coordinating technical assistance. It also reinforced its ability to identify assistance needs proactively, rather than merely (as the CTC had done in its early stages) taking at face-value requests sent in by States. Indeed, the CTED has carried out joint assessment missions with representatives of the EU and of other international organizations.[12]

3.   Interaction between the EU and the UN on counter-terrorism

The adoption of UNSCR 1373 not only triggered significant policy processes within the EU; it also prompted the EU to make an unusually cohesive effort to present its implementation of the resolution and its counter-terrorism action more generally at the UN. UNSCR 1373, like more conventional UN sanctions resolutions, contained a reporting requirement whereby States were required to submit a report on their national implementation within a fixed timeframe to the CTC. The CTS's role was modelled in this regard on that of a conventional Security Council sanctions committee.[13] As if to underline the unusual impetus that attached to efforts within the EU institutions to implement 1373, and the sense that 1373 was in no way a conventional resolution, the EU decided to prepare a common report. This contrasts with reporting to UN sanctions committees on the implementation of 'conventional' sanctions resolutions, which remains to this day essentially a national process, even if UN sanctions are in many cases implemented by binding European legislation.

The first EU report on the implementation of UNSCR 1373 was drafted jointly by the Commission and the Council. It was finalized in the Council's relevant CFSP working groups, COTER and the Relex Counsellors working group. It was formally endorsed by the Council at Ministerial level on 20 December 2001 and submitted by the Presidency to the Chairman of the CTC on 24 December 2001.[14] National reports were submitted in parallel by all Member States. The EU report provided a broad overview of legislative and other action taken both before and after the adoption of 1373 which corresponded to particular provisions of the resolution. Perhaps fortuitously, political agreement on the adoption of the Framework Decision on Combatting Terrorism and the European Arrest Warrant had been reached just before the submission of the EU report. This enabled the EU to point in the report to the strides taken in the area of judicial harmonization and cooperation – and to highlight tangible joint action on two of the requirements set out in the resolution, namely the criminalization of terrorist offences and mutual assistance in the investigation and prosecution of terrorist acts. In addition, the report covered measures in areas as diverse as money-laundering and European legislation to curb illicit possession and trafficking of firearms. As such, it also served two important internal functions. It drove home to policy-makers within the EU the message that a wide range of policy instruments, managed under different pillars and by different EU institutions, were relevant to the EU response to 9/11. And it underlined the fact that effective EU action in accordance with 1373 was not only (and perhaps not even primarily) a matter of high-level political declarations. It depended on technical instruments that could be used by law enforcement authorities at the operational level.

In order to maintain the pressure for effective implementation of 1373, the CTC decided after the first round of reports to assess these and, where necessary (and this applied to almost all States that submitted reports) to request clarification or further information from the States concerned. In the early days of the CTC, as noted earlier, the possibility of some form of enforcement action by the Security Council aiming at those States that did not implement crucial provisions of the resolution did not seem entirely far-fetched. In fact the subsequent development of CTC practice conformed more to the usual practice of UN Sanctions Committees with regard to weaknesses in sanctions implementation by individual States. Nevertheless, the initial sense of urgency surrounding 1373 lent itself to follow-up questions from the CTC being taken seriously. In the case of the EU report, the CTC addressed a request for clarification on some of the issues covered to the EU Presidency on 1 August 2002.[15] A second report was then prepared, in much the same way as the first one, responding to specific questions from the CTC and providing information on policy developments subsequent to the first report, such as the formal adoption of the Framework Decision on Terrorism and the European Arrest Warrant. The second report was formally adopted by the Council on 26 July and submitted to the CTC by the Presidency on 8 August 2002.[16] While the reports submitted by some States to the CTC were followed up in several iterations (with some States making five submissions to the CTC in succession), for the EU the reporting process ended after the second report – perhaps reflecting the fact that, in the UN context, the distinction between States and the EU as a sui generis organization remains fundamental, even if a substantial part of the legislative function required to implement resolutions such as 1373 has in fact shifted to the EU.

The reports undoubtedly initiated a more consistent dialogue with the CTC. In April 2002, the EU (represented by the then Spanish Presidency and the Commission) was thus invited to appear before the CTC for the first time, for a briefing on the main EU actions pursuant to 1373. Since then, EU representatives have frequently appeared before the CTC and the Security Council to present updates on EU action against terrorism – and with the appointment of Gijs de Vries as EU Counter-Terrorism Coordinator in March 2004, the EU acquired a single 'face' in the presentation of its policies to the outside world, including not least the UN. With the adoption, on 28 April 2004, of Security Council Resolution 1540, aimed at addressing nuclear proliferation with a particular focus on preventing the access of terrorists to nuclear materials and technology, the 1373 'model' was to a certain extent replicated, both in the way the Security Council dealt with follow-up to the resolution, and in the EU's approach to implementation. As with 1373, an EU report on implementation was thus prepared and submitted to the 1540 Committee on 28 October 2004.[17]

Of course, the dialogue with the UN on implementation of 1373 was, by definition, an asymmetrical one. The resolution was adopted under Chapter VII of the UN Charter, and – as for conventional UN sanctions resolutions – the understanding among EU policy-makers has always been that implementing action by the EU is not an optional luxury, but a necessity in those areas in which legislative and regulatory responsibility rests with the EU (and more specifically, in which EC legislation is required). To this extent, the relation between the UN and the EU has been one of global standard-setter to (regional) implementing entity – and this is entirely consistent with the EU's adherence to the basic principles of international law and its much-repeated support for effective global governance. Nevertheless, there have been specific areas, however limited, where the EU has also begun to shape policy and have an impact on the global approach to counter-terrorism. One such example, outside the 1373 framework, is the implementation of the UN sanctions regime targeting Al-Qaida and the Taliban.

1267, 1390 and all that: the EU, targeted sanctions and individual rights

Security Council Resolution 1373, as we saw earlier, prompted the EU to put in place its own system of targeted financial sanctions against suspected terrorists or terrorist organizations. Yet before this the EU had been implementing the targeted sanctions regime against the Taliban and Al-Qaida put in place by the UN in the late 1990s, as a reaction notably to the US embassy bombings in East Africa of 1998. Security Council Resolution 1267 (1999) – modified notably by resolutions 1333 (2001), 1390 (2002) and 1617 (2005) – established (amongst other measures, such as an arms embargo) a system for the listing of individuals and organizations part of or associated with the Taliban or Al-Qaida, instructing all states to freeze the funds and other assets and economic resources of individuals and groups on the list, and (in a subsequent tightening of the measures) to 'prevent the entry into or the transit through their territories' of individuals on the list. The listing process, as with other targeted sanctions measures, consists of a designation procedure within the 1267 Committee (composed of the 15 members of the Security Council), acting upon a proposal from any UN Member State. If no member of the Committee objects within a set period, the proposal for a new listing is adopted and a public notice issued by the 1267 Committee – following which, in principle, all States are obliged (given that 1390 is a Chapter VII resolution) to adopt national implementing measures to ensure that individuals and organizations listed are not able to access any of the types of economic resources covered in the resolution, and to deny them access to their territory. It is worth noting in this context the sustained political support for the 1267/1390 process on the part of the United States, which has ensured a consistent degree of pressure on the part of the Security Council for effective implementation of the measures.

For the EU, effective implementation of UN Security Council resolutions imposing restrictive measures is an article of faith, predating 9/11 and, indeed, independent of whether a resolution targets terrorist suspects or, say, individuals impeding the peace process in Côte d'Ivoire.[18] Implementation of 1267 and its successor resolutions, in this context, implies several steps: first of all, adoption (as for any sanctions measure implying both a political framework decision in the CFSP and legally binding implementing measures in the EC framework) of a Council Common Position and of a Council Regulation;[19] and subsequently, whenever the 1267 Committee adds new individuals or entities to the list, the adoption by the Commission of Commission Regulations implementing the changes to the list in Community law (and thus immediately binding throughout all Member States). Since the adoption of 1267, the changes to the list have been frequent – by the end of 2006, the Commission had adopted no fewer than 73 Regulations amending the list.

As it would subsequently do for resolution 1373, in July 2001 the Security Council established a mechanism for monitoring implementation of 1267 – specifically by creating a Monitoring Group, reporting to the 1267 Committee and tasked with assessing overall implementation of the targeted sanctions by individual states. To date, the Monitoring Group has released five reports. To a greater degree than for more conventional sanctions resolutions, these have also touched on implementation by the EU. One of the questions taken up by the Group relates to implementation of the travel ban within the EU – and specifically, what the Monitoring Group has seen as the issues posed for full implementation by the absence of regular border controls between the Schengen countries, an issue on which a genuine dialogue has developed between the Monitoring Team and EU representatives, which is reflected in some detail in the Team's reports.[20]

Thus far, implementation of 1390 is analogous to that of any other sanctions resolution. However, quite apart from its important role in the UN's counter-terrorist arsenal, and indeed from the EU's role in implementing the resolution at the (in UN terms) 'regional' level, implementation of 1390 is of interest here because it touches on the wider issue of the balance between security and individual rights, discussed in the introductory chapter and chapter 7 of this book. Two issues, in particular, merit closer attention here. Both, it should be stressed, are common to all of the targeted sanctions measures that have emerged in recent years as the instrument of choice not only of the Security Council, but also of the EU in its autonomous sanctions regimes; but both have been thrown into most prominent relief in the context of implementation of resolution 1390.

The first issue relates to the impact of financial freezing measures on the ability of the individuals targeted to satisfy their basic needs: by definition, a freezing measure in essence both blocks the accounts belonging to the individual in question and prevents any new funds or resources being made available to them. However, this raises the question of how the individuals whose funds are frozen are to make the payments necessary to meet even the most basic of needs (such as rent or foodstuffs). Resolution 1267 was relatively elliptic in this regard, allowing only exemptions specifically authorized on a case-by-case basis by the Security Council, without specifying the general circumstances in which such exemptions might be justified.

For the EU, ensuring that adequate 'humanitarian exemptions' are foreseen in all targeted sanctions measures has for several years been a basic principle of its sanctions policy. Indeed, the principle is 'codified' in the EU Sanctions Guidelines agreed under the Italian Presidency in 2003.[21] And while the possibilities for the EU to weigh on the deliberations of the Security Council, in which it is not represented as such, are by definition heavily circumscribed, its concerns did have an impact. On 20 December 2002, the Security Council adopted Resolution 1452 (2002), which specifically provided for humanitarian exemptions in a range of circumstances – and which adapted the procedure applying to the authorization of exemptions, such that exemptions in most cases now only had to be notified to the Sanctions Committee, and were deemed to have been authorized unless the Committee specifically objected. The wording of the provisions in the resolution coincidentally mirrored the exemptions language used in autonomous EU sanctions measures. The change was explicitly welcomed by the EU. The Presidency thus noted in a statement to the Security Council on 29 July 2003: 'Respect for human rights, fundamental freedoms and the rule of law is essential in all efforts to combat terrorism. In this respect, the European Union deeply shares the approach followed by the Security Council with the adoption of resolution 1452 of 20 December 2002 aimed at defining criteria for the granting of such exemptions, in specific cases, based on grounds of humanitarian needs.' It is worth noting that the issue of humanitarian exemptions has also been followed closely by the European Parliament – which, given the legal bases used for certain Council Regulations implementing targeted freezing measures, has the right to be consulted on proposed Regulations. It does not, however, and this must be stressed, have the right to co-decide, although it has consistently proposed amendments to the texts of regulations implementing targeted sanctions proposed by the Commission.

A second aspect of 1390 implementation on which the EU has consistently called for individual rights to be taken adequately into account in the application of the targeted sanctions measures – and arguably a far more delicate one even than the issue of humanitarian exemptions – concerns the process by which individuals and groups are designated by the 1267 Committee. The Committee designates new additions to the list by silence procedure on the basis of information provided by a Member State of the

UN. The information in question is not rendered public. Perhaps more importantly, there is no individual right of appeal against a listing: only States can approach the Committee with requests to reconsider listing decisions. This, it could be said, is a necessary concomitant of the philosophy underlying the targeted sanctions – which holds that the Security Council is not, and can never be, a judicial organ, and that the sanctions are part of the Security Council's efforts to safeguard international peace and security, rather than *judicial* decisions.[22]

Again, and without questioning the need for the measures (or indeed their universally binding status), the EU has been concerned in this context to ensure that basic standards of due process and human rights are upheld in the implementation of the UN's targeted sanctions. In the July 2003 statement to the Security Council mentioned above, the EU thus went on to note that 'the European Union remains convinced that every effort must be made in order to promote due process in the proceedings of the Committee. (...) Sanctions must be implemented on the basis of transparent, technical criteria in order to create maximum legal certainty in the matter. The European Union stands ready to work in order to further improve the Committee's guidelines as appropriate.' It is worth noting at least in passing that, at the time of writing, a number of legal cases were pending before European courts relating to both the 'autonomous' sanctions and the implementation of the 1267 sanctions regime in the EU. The fact that EC sanctions measures are subject to the jurisdiction of the European Court of Justice means the balance between security and individual rights is anything but an academic issue in the area of targeted sanctions.

The issue of due process clearly remains a preoccupation for the EU. Contacts between the EU and the 1267 Committee – such as on the occasion of a seminar on sanctions organized in March 2005 by the then Luxembourg Presidency in New York, or a visit by the Chair of the 1267 Committee to the EU institutions in Brussels in May 2005 – have served mainly to discuss EU implementation of the targeted sanctions. Yet they have also provided a platform for the EU to stress, however obliquely, its concern for adequate listing and de-listing procedures. In June 2005, the EU's then Counter-Terrorism Coordinator, Gijs de Vries, thus noted in a statement to the 1267 Committee that the EU 'attaches great importance to the respect for fundamental rights in the context of listings, including due process considerations (...) It is important that we get this list right. States will only add to it if they are confident that it is consistent with basic human rights.' On the one hand, the EU thus continues to implement whatever listing decisions the Security Council arrives at, consistent with their binding nature under the UN Charter. On the other, the issue of due process in the listing – and perhaps more important, in the de-listing – of individuals targeted by 1390 remains an issue in the implementation of 1390, and is also now explicitly under consideration by the 1267 Committee itself, which has progressively amended its own internal guidelines to take account of some of the concerns expressed.[24] It is also a notable case of the EU not only being true to its principled commitment to rigorous implementation of Security Council measures, but seeking at the same time to influence the UN's agenda in favour of more general principles of human rights and due process.

UN action beyond the Security Council: the UN conventions

This chapter has focussed on the EU's interaction with the United Nations, for the UN emerged as the central locus for multilateral policy discussions and standard-setting to prevent terrorism after 9/11. More specifically, it has focussed on the Security Council, again because within the UN, the Security Council has been at the centre of action against terrorism, both with the 1267 (and later 1390) process, and, after 9/11, with 1373, the CTC and CTED.

Of course, other parts of the UN system, and indeed organizations outside the UN system, have equally played a part in fashioning a multilateral response to terrorism, and the EU has contributed, to varying degrees, to their work. Without attempting to be exhaustive (and leaving aside operational cooperation between law enforcement agencies, which would be beyond the scope of this chapter), this section briefly reviews the most important of these, focussing on those which have impinged most directly on tangible policy measures at the EU level.

Within the UN system, until the adoption of 1373, the only comprehensive normative framework establishing legal and judicial standards for preventing and combating terrorism took the form of the twelve international conventions on terrorism, referred to earlier in this chapter (to which a 13th convention was added on 13 April 2005 with the conclusion of the International Convention for the Suppression of Acts of Nuclear Terrorism). In addition, work has been under way since 1996 on a comprehensive convention on international terrorism, on the basis of a draft initially proposed by India – an ambitious undertaking that would inter alia define terrorism and require the criminalization of terrorist offences. After 9/11, there was some hope that the negotiations on the comprehensive convention – which continue in an ad-hoc committee of the General Assembly in New York – would be accelerated and brought to a rapid conclusion. Similarly, it was hoped that universal ratification of the 12 (and now 13) existing conventions – and most important, on the international convention on the financing of terrorism – would be achieved rapidly. For the EU, conclusion of negotiations on the comprehensive convention was enshrined as an important policy objective in the EU counter-terrorism roadmap, and ratification of the conventions became a regular feature on the agenda of the COTER working group in Brussels, with periodic updates on the state of ratification and, concomitantly, a gentle sense of 'peer pressure' brought to bear on Member States to ratify any outstanding conventions.

Some six years on, these hopes have been met only in part. 9/11 undoubtedly brought a sense of urgency to the negotiations on the draft comprehensive convention. However, discussions have faltered on the question of the scope of the draft convention, and on the activities to be excluded from its definition of terrorism. In addition, serious differences of approach remain between Islamic and Western states. As to the ratification of the thirteen conventions, significant progress was made by EU Member States in the wake of 9/11. However, in late 2006, barely a third of UN Member States had ratified all Conventions, and a very small number of ratifications were still outstanding even among EU Member States (see annex to this chapter). In short, there has been useful activity on counter-terrorism in the UN beyond the confines of the Security Council and the work of the Vienna-based Terrorism Prevention Branch of the UN Office on Drugs and Crime, which has been focussed on ratification and implementation of the UN conventions. Yet there is no doubt that the initiative and the centre of gravity itself, as regards impact on EU policies, has lain since 9/11 with the Security Council.

4.   Beyond the United Nations: FATF and G8

Outside the UN system, two international organizations merit particular attention for the impact they have had on EU counter-terrorism policy. The first, the Financial Action Taskforce (FATF), was established in 1989 at the initiative of the G7.[25] It deals with money-laundering, rather than terrorist financing per se. However, it emerged after 9/11 as an increasingly important forum for discussing issues linked to the use of the financial system by terrorist organizations, and for de facto standard-setting by means of 'recommendations' and a rigorous system of peer review. The EU is present in FATF both through the membership of the European Commission and through the individual membership of 15 of its Member States (that is, the 15 'pre-enlargement' Member States). The focus of interaction between the Commission and FATF has been not so much on the financial freezing measures that have been at the core of the EU's implementation of UN counter-terrorism policy, but rather on money-laundering legislation in the form of the three EC money-laundering directives, the most recent of which was adopted in 2005. References to the earlier legislation were included in the EU's reports to the CTC on implementation of resolution 1373. The lead on FATF within the Commission lies not with the External Relations Directorate-General (as for freezing measures and terrorist financing more generally), but with the Internal Market Directorate-General, which is responsible for drafting and oversight of Community legislation on money-laundering. While a detailed discussion of anti-money laundering legislation is beyond the scope of this chapter, the role of FATF as an impetus for legislative action – notably by dint of the 'peer pressure' among members which it mobilizes – has been significant, including for the EU.[26]

A second grouping that merits a mention in this context is the G8 – which, while not a formal multilateral institution, has served as an important forum for preparing discussions in the UN context. Within the G8, counter-terrorism work has been the domain more specifically of the Lyon/Rome group (resulting from the merger of the Rome and Lyon expert groups – the former bringing together the external counter-terrorism experts of G8 members, usually from foreign ministries; the latter composed of their counterparts in interior ministries) and of the more recent Counter-Terrorism Action Group (CTAG), which deals more specifically with technical assistance. EU representation in these fora is more diffuse than in formal (e.g. UN) settings – only four Member States and the Commission participate, with the EU counter-terrorism coordinator also participating in G8 meetings, since the creation of that position. There is no formal EU coordination for G8 business, though European G8 members brief the Council's COTER working group on G8 deliberations and decisions. Nevertheless, to the extent that discussions in the G8 focussed on issues that were also at the heart of UN action against terrorism – notably terrorist financing and capacity-building for the prevention of terrorism – the EU's various voices have clearly mattered in shaping the G8's collective response to 9/11. However, it is worth stressing the extent to which the G8's agenda on counter-terrorism was shaped (perhaps somewhat counter-intuitively, given popular misperceptions of the G8 as a global *'directoire'*) by developments at the UN, and more specifically in the Security Council.[27]

Conclusion: assessing the EU's contribution to the multilateral effort

This chapter noted that the impact of 9/11 in the United Nations was in many ways comparable to the jolt it induced in the EU. Overnight, terrorism moved to the top of the agenda; and both the UN – more specifically, the Security Council – and the EU felt compelled to move beyond discrete (and often discreet) sectoral activities, however useful, to adopt all-encompassing horizontal measures. Moreover, as a review of the financial freezing measures adopted by the Council of the EU in December 2001 and the initiatives on technical assistance to third countries in areas relevant to counter-terrorism demonstrates, the decisions adopted by the Security Council, notably resolution 1373 (2001), reinforced and canalised the impetus to European policy-makers. In the case of the autonomous EU targeted sanctions adopted under Common Position 931/2001 and Council Regulation 2580/2001 it is doubtful whether European policy-makers, acting in a CFSP context and with unanimity, would ever have agreed on the politically ground-breaking step constituted by the creation of an EU 'terrorist list', had it not been for the impetus (and indeed obligation) that issued from 1373. As regards technical assistance to third countries in areas relevant to the prevention of terrorism, similarly, it is arguable that encouragement from the UN (and more specifically, the Counter-Terrorism Committee) served as the catalyst for the introduction of an explicit focus on terrorism prevention in EC assistance programmes. This would otherwise have been difficult to attain. As for the UN's Taliban and Al-Qaida sanctions regime, which predated 9/11, the EU's general commitment to unfailing implementation of Security Council sanctions measures coincided in this case with the particular sense of urgency which the Security Council has imparted to resolutions 1267 and 1390.

In short, the EU has undeniably sought to be an exemplary 'implementer' for the prescriptions issued by the Security Council after 9/11. Conversely, the question whether it has also had a role beyond that of 'implementer', in actively shaping the counter-terrorism agenda of the UN (or of the multilateral system more generally) is more difficult to answer. At one level, the EU institutions have not missed an opportunity to communicate the EU's approach to combating terrorism to various UN bodies, notably the Security Council and its various committees dealing with counter-terrorism issues. Moreover, the EU has acted in this context with a degree of consistency (and cross-pillar cooperation) that is probably without precedent in a policy area touching so closely on Member States' national security concerns. At another level, the decisive normative work on counter-terrorism in the multilateral system has been carried out in a forum – the Security Council – in which the EU is not represented, in which there is no EU coordination, and in which Member States (or rather, those Member States that also happen to be Security Council members) are traditionally keen to maintain their national prerogatives. For this simple reason alone, it is difficult to identify a tangible EU influence on the main counter-terrorism instruments adopted in the multilateral context, which, with some degree of simplification, this chapter has determined to be Security Council Resolutions 1373 and 1267/1390. Indeed, the question is perhaps a moot one to the extent that the EU shares the overall approach embodied in the resolutions in question. There is, however, one significant nuance to this: in the area of targeted sanctions, and specifically the Taliban/Al-Qaida sanctions established by resolutions 1267 and 1390, the EU's concern for fundamental rights has undoubtedly had an impact on the terms of the debate in New York, both with regard to 'humanitarian exemptions' and with regard to the listing and de-listing process. It is probably too early to assess the full extent of this impact. But these concerns do suggest that there is a distinctive EU 'approach' to combating terrorism, which, without being at odds with that of its partners, places a particular emphasis on safeguarding individual rights. Where the EU conveys this approach persistently and consistently, its voice has increasingly been heard and its visibility and importance in the fight against international terrorism have been correspondingly enhanced.

Annex: Overview of participation by EU Member States in multilateral instruments on terrorism (ratification, accession or succession) – status as at 18 December 2006

Convention 1 (see list below)	2	3	4	5	6	7	8	9	10	11	12	13
AU	X	X	X	X	X	X	X	X	X	X	X	X
BE	X	X	X			X	X	X	X	X	X	X	
BG	X	X	X			X	X	X	X	X	X	X	X
CYP	X	X	X			X	X	X	X	X	X	X	X
CZ	X	X	X	X	X	X	X	X	X	X	X	X	X
DK	X	X	X			X	X	X	X	X	X	X	X
EST	X	X	X			X	X	X	X	X	X	X	X
FI	X	X	X			X	X	X	X	X	X	X	X
FR	X	X	X			X	X	X	X	X	X	X	X
DE	X	X	X			X	X	X	X	X	X	X	X
GR	X	X	X			X	X	X	X	X	X	X	X
HU	X	X	X			X	X	X	X	X	X	X	X
IE	X	X	X			X	X	X	X	X	X	X	X
IT	X	X	X			X	X	X	X	X	X	X	X
LV	X	X	X	X	X	X	X	X	X	X	X	X	X
LT	X	X	X			X	X	X	X	X	X	X	X
LU	X	X	X			X	X	X	X	X			X
MT	X	X	X			X	X	X	X	X	X	X	X
NL	X	X	X			X	X	X	X	X	X	X	X
PL	X	X	X			X	X	X	X	X	X	X	X
PT	X	X	X			X	X	X	X	X	X	X	X
RO	X	X	X			X	X	X	X	X	X	X	X
SK	X	X	X	X	X	X	X	X	X	X	X	X	X
SI	X	X	X			X	X	X	X	X	X	X	X
ES	X	X	X			X	X	X	X	X	X	X	X
SV	X	X	X			X	X	X	X	X	X	X	
UK	X	X	X			X	X	X	X	X	X	X	X

Deposited with the UN:

1. Convention on the Prevention and Punishment of Crimes against Internationally Protected Persons, including Diplomatic Agents, adopted by the General Assembly of the United Nations on 14 December 1973.

2. International Convention against the Taking of Hostages, adopted by the General Assembly of the United Nations on 17 December 1979

3. International Convention for the Suppression of Terrorist Bombings, adopted by the General Assembly of the United Nations on 15 December 1997

4. International Convention for the Suppression of the Financing of Terrorism, adopted by the General Assembly of the United Nations on 9 December 1999

5. International Convention for the Suppression of Acts of Nuclear Terrorism

New York, 13 April 2005

Deposited with other organizations or governments:

6. Convention on Offences and Certain Other Acts Committed on Board Aircraft, signed at Tokyo on 14 September 1963 (Deposited with the Secretary-General of the International Civil Aviation Organization)

7. Convention for the Suppression of Unlawful Seizure of Aircraft, signed at the Hague on 16 December 1970 (Deposited with the Governments of the Russian Federation, the United Kingdom and the United States of America)

8. Convention for the Suppression of Unlawful Acts against the Safety of Civil Aviation, signed at Montreal on 23 September 1971 (Deposited with the Governments of the Russian Federation, the United Kingdom and the United States of America)

9. Convention on the Physical Protection of Nuclear Material, signed at Vienna on 3 March 1980 (Deposited with the Director-General of the International Atomic Energy Agency)

10. Protocol on the Suppression of Unlawful Acts of Violence at Airports Serving International Civil Aviation, supplementary to the Convention for the Suppression of Unlawful Acts against the Safety of Civil Aviation, signed at Montreal on 24 February 1988 (Deposited with the Governments of the Russian Federation, the United Kingdom and the United States of America and with the Secretary-General of the International Civil Aviation Organization)

11. Convention for the Suppression of Unlawful Acts against the Safety of Maritime Navigation, done at Rome on 10 March 1988 (Deposited with the Secretary-General of the International Maritime Organization)

12. Protocol for the Suppression of Unlawful Acts against the Safety of Fixed Platforms Located on the Continental Shelf, done at Rome on 10 March 1988 (Deposited with the Secretary-General of the International Maritime Organization)

13. Convention on the Marking of Plastic Explosives for the Purpose of Detection, signed at Montreal on 1 March 1991. (Deposited with the Secretary-General of the International Civil Aviation Organization)

Endnotes:

1 See, for example, the Commission Communication 'The European Union and the United Nations: The choice of multilateralism', COM (2003) 526 final, 10 September 2003; the European Security Strategy of 12 December 2003; or the European Council Conclusions of 12 December 2003.

2 With the conclusion of the convention on nuclear terrorism in 2005, the number of UN counter-terrorism conventions rose to 13. These are complemented by a number of UN protocols, and by regional conventions concluded under the auspices, for example, of the Council of Europe, the Arab League, the OAS or the CIS.

3 See the annex to this chapter for an overview of the UN's 13 terrorism conventions.

4 Council Common Position 2001/930/CFSP of 27 December 2001.

5 In the early days of the CTC, the question of possible 'enforcement' by the Security Council, going beyond mere 'monitoring', was frequently evoked in corridor discussions at the UN. Yet discussions did not yield concrete results, not least since the universally shared sense of urgency for action against terrorism in the wake of 9/11 was somewhat displaced in 2003 by the launch of the Iraq war, which became the single issue dominating the work of the Security Council.

6 As at 29 May 2006, when the most recent amending Common Position (2006/380/CFSP) was adopted.

7 US officials have on numerous occasions called for Hezbollah to be added to the EU terrorist list, and in March 2005 the US House of Representatives passed a resolution (H. Res. 101) urging the EU to add Hezbollah to the list.

8 See for example ' Norway drops EU terror list' , Aftenposten, 4 January 2006.

9 Security Council document S/2001/986 of 19 October 2001.

10 In the case of the EU, this took the form not only of formal notices from the CTC, but also of

informal contacts between senior representatives of the CTC – chaired at the time by the UK Permanent Representative to the UN, Sir Jeremy Greenstock – and Commission officials.

11 Commission Staff Working Paper SEC 2002 (231) of 25 February 2002 (http://ec.europa.eu/comm/external_relations/un/docs/sec02_231.pdf)

12 By February 2006, EU representatives had thus participated in CTED missions to Morocco, Kenya and Albania.

13 Paragraph 6 of the Resolution, which establishes the CTC, also 'calls upon all States to report to the Committee, no later than 90 days from the date of adoption of this resolution and thereafter according to a timetable to be proposed by the Committee, on the steps they have taken to implement this resolution'.

14 The report, made available as document S/2001/1297, is accessible on the CTC website at http://www.un.org/Docs/sc/committees/1373/other_submissions.htm

15 See Security Council document S/2002/821 of 1 August 2002.

16 Security Council document S/2002/928 of 16 August 2002.

17 Security Council document S/AC.44/2004/(02)/48 of 15 November 2004.

18 See the EU 'Basic principles on the use of restrictive measures (sanctions)', Council document 10198/1/04 REV 1.

19 Common Position 2002/402/CFSP, as amended by Common Position 2003/140/CFSP, and Council Regulation (EC) No 881/2002, as most recently amended by Council Regulation (EC) No 1823/2006.

20 See notably the second report of the Monitoring Team, Security Council document S/2005/83 of 15 February 2005, and the third report of the Monitoring Team, Security Council document S/2005/572 of 9 September 2005.

21 'Guidelines on implementation and evaluation of restrictive measures (sanctions) in the framework of the EU Common Foreign and Security Policy', Council document 15114/05 of 2 December 2005 (a previous version of the Guidelines was adopted by the Council on 8 December 2003, Council document 15579/03).

22 For a more extensive discussion of the issues surrounding listing and delisting procedures, see, for example, *Strengthening Targeted Sanctions Through Fair And Clear Procedures*, White Paper of the Watson Institute Targeted Sanctions Project, Brown University, 30 March 2006; or the most recent report of the UNSC's 1267 Monitoring Team,

23 Address by Gijs de Vries to the 1267 Committee, 24 June 2005, http://www.consilium.europa.eu/uedocs/cmsUpload/06_24_final_1267.pdf

24 See, for example, the fifth report of the 1267 Monitoring Team, Security Council document S/2006/750 of 20 September 2006.

25 For a more extensive discussion of FATF's role with regard to terrorist financing, see e.g. Navias, Martin S., 'Finance Warfare as a Response to International Terrorism', Political Quarterly 73 (s1), 57-79, August 2002

26 The most recent Money Laundering Directive has thus updated EU provisions in accordance with FATF recommendations, and extended existing legislation to cover terrorist financing, and the EU has undertaken a sustained effort to transpose FATF's nine Special Recommendations on Terrorist Financing into EU legislation.

27 See, for example, the 'backgrounder' on G8 counter-terrorism cooperation issued at the 2002 Kananaskis G8 summit, which places implementation of 1373 (and technical assistance for implementation of 1373) at the heart of the G8's counter-terrorism strategy: http://www.g8.gc.ca/2002Kananaskis/counterterrorism-en.asp.

6.   Transatlantic Relations and Terrorism

Fraser Cameron

Introduction

Just as the fall of the Berlin Wall in November 1989 was a defining moment for Europe, the September 2001 attacks on New York and Washington were to change the US in a fundamental way. Americans experienced a real sense of their own vulnerability for the first time since Pearl Harbor. There was an immediate and genuine outpouring of sympathy all over the world. In Europe this was symbolized by the famous *Le Monde* headline 'We are all Americans Now'. Europeans offered to invoke article V of the NATO Treaty and supported the US military efforts to overthrow the Taliban regime in Afghanistan. However, the US turned down these offers, leaving a sour taste in European mouths. President Bush declared a 'war on terrorism' and spoke of a threat to the very foundations of Western civilization. The global war on terrorism swiftly became the central organizing principle of US national security, comparable to the Cold War containment strategy. 9/11 did not have the same impact on Europe, given its decades-long experience with terrorism. Even the 2004 Madrid and 2005 London attacks, while leading to closer cooperation in the fight against terrorism, did not fundamentally alter the perception of most Europeans that there were no swift or easy solutions in tackling global terrorism.

The terminology used to describe the response to the terrorist threat highlights the difference in approach by the EU and US. While Americans speak of a 'war on terror', Europeans talk about the 'fight against terrorism'. The European attitude was perhaps best articulated by Professor Michael Howard shortly after 9/11 when he wrote:

> By conceiving of the struggle against international terrorism as a war, loudly proclaiming it as such, and waging it as one, we have given our enemies the battle they aimed to provoke but could not get unless the United States gave it to them. To declare that one is at war also tends to create a war psychosis that may be totally counterproductive for the objective being sought. It arouses an immediate expectation, and demand, for spectacular military action against some easily identifiable adversary, preferably a hostile state. It also helps create the perception that terror-

ism is an evil that can be eradicated rather than a more complex phenomenon with different aspects to be considered.[1]

Most European governments also distanced themselves from other Bush rhetoric like the 'axis of evil' speech, his calls for pre-emptive strikes and his demand that allies follow the US – 'you are either with us or against us' Europeans also do not believe that terrorism can be fought primarily with military means. According to Gijs de Vries, the EU's counter-terrorism coordinator, speaking at an EPC meeting on 23 September 2004, the US and Europe had cooperated very effectively in many ways, especially in criminal investigations, but the US had unnecessarily alienated many of its allies by relying too heavily on a military response and had consistently undervalued the political dimension. Europeans, he argued, place more emphasis on long-term, painstaking police and intelligence cooperation, on dealing with the fundamental reasons that allow terrorists fertile ground and above all, they do not accept that breaching human rights (as in Guantánamo Bay and Abu Ghraib) or rendition can be part of any counter-terrorist policy.

There are also differences on root causes. The December 2004 European Council reiterated 'its conviction that in order to be effective in the long run the Union's response to terrorism must address the root causes of terrorism. Radicalisation and terrorist recruitment can be closely connected. The European Council called on the Council to establish a long-term strategy and action plan on both issues by June 2005.'[2]

But whatever the differences over tactics and rhetoric, the US decision to go to war against Iraq on the flimsiest of intelligence alleging links between Saddam Hussein, weapons of mass destruction (WMD) and Al-Qaida was the most damaging blow to transatlantic relations to date. Senior US politicians seemed to take delight in pouring oil on troubled waters with references to 'old and new Europe.'[3] Since 2003, differences over Iraq have lessened but most Europeans doubt whether the US ever had an effective strategy to deal with the insurgency in Iraq. There is also considerable concern that the Iraq invasion has led to an upsurge in terrorism in Europe, particularly in those countries that supported the US-led war to oust Saddam Hussein. British Prime Minister, Tony Blair, was at pains to deny such a link but most analysts, and Pentagon experts, agree that the Iraq invasion did lead to an upsurge in terrorism.[4]

Most Americans reject European concerns about how the US is tackling terrorism and many have been ready to criticize Europe for being 'soft on terrorism'. Senator Schumer, speaking to a group of members of the European Parliament on 12 September 2001 was very clear on US expectations: 'We have to let our European allies know that the finger is not just pointed at us, but at them. And this idea that for temporary economic advantage they can continue to have strong trading relations with countries that help, abet and harbour terrorists must go out the window.'[5] According to a policy brief by the Heritage Foundation, published in the aftermath of the July 2005 London bombings, only the UK could really be relied on in the war on terror. The paper argued that the UK should denounce European conventions that 'shackled its efforts' to tackle terrorism.[6]

Publics on both sides of the Atlantic agree on the high priority to be accorded to the threat of terrorism. A survey conducted by the German

Marshall Fund in September 2004 shows that while Americans and Europeans have similar threat perceptions, they differ markedly on how best to deal with these threats and under what aegis. For example, while 71% of Europeans and 76% of Americans consider international terrorism one of the most important international threats, 54% of Americans agree that the best way to ensure peace is through military strength, compared with only 28% of Europeans.

Despite these differences, the EU and US continue to cooperate closely in many areas relating to terrorism. As terrorism has turned into a global phenomenon both sides recognize that they have to work together to understand each other's policies and to develop a multifaceted response that reflects the dimension of the threat. Yet the official desire to cooperate is circumscribed by European public concerns about the rectitude of US tactics and strategy.

From 9/11 to Iraq

Americans responded to the 9/11 attacks with a mixture of fear, determination for revenge, and an outpouring of patriotism. The author recalls visiting Washington suburbs a week after the attacks and finding almost every house displaying the Stars and Stripes. Speaking to Congress on 20 September 2001, President Bush stressed that the US, in responding to the attacks, would make no distinction between the terrorists who committed these acts of war and those who harbour them. He promised a 'crusade' against terrorism. The use of the terms 'war' and 'crusade' was perhaps unfortunate. The President said that there would be a lengthy campaign to defeat terrorism that could include dramatic strikes, covert operations, starving terrorists of funding and pursuing nations that provide aid or safe haven to terrorists. Although the initial American reaction to the attacks involved calls for revenge, the administration swiftly recognized that there were no quick or easy solutions to dealing with the terrorist issue. At a press briefing on 25 September, Defence Secretary Donald Rumsfeld remarked that 'terrorism is by its very nature something that cannot be dealt with by some form of massive attack or invasion. It is a much more subtle, nuanced, difficult, shadowy set of problems.' The President himself commented the following day, 'what is the point of sending two million dollar missiles to hit a ten dollar tent that's empty?' These statements sit oddly with the later decision to invade Iraq.

In the weeks following the attacks, the US assembled an international coalition to support the war on terrorism and sought to maintain that there was an identity of interests between the US and the international community in preventing terrorism. The UN, NATO, the EU, the Organization of American States (OAS) and the Organization of the Islamic Conference were quick to condemn the attacks and offer the US support. Russia, China, Pakistan and India were also brought on board as were some strange bedfellows, particularly the authoritarian regimes of Central Asia and the Arab world. Bush, who stated that there were 'interesting opportunities' for diplomatic exchanges, apparently was working on the old Cold War maxim 'my enemy's enemy is my friend.'

For the neoconservatives who were so influential in the first Bush administration, 9/11 gave the opportunity to push for regime change in Iraq. Led by Vice President Dick Cheney, they sought to make the case that Saddam Hussein was stockpiling weapons of mass destruction either to use himself against the US, or to provide terrorists with WMD material.[7] In his address to Congress on 20 September 2001, Bush stated that the US 'will make no distinction between the terrorists who committed these acts ands those who harbour them'. He continued:

> We will pursue nations that provide aid or safe haven to terrorists. Every nation, in every region, now has a decision to make. Either you are with us, or you are with the terrorists. From this day forward, any nation that continues to harbour or support terrorism will be regarded by the US as a hostile regime.

The President also went on to outline his vision for a strong American leadership in the world, a leadership that would project America's power and influence.

> The advance of human freedom now depends on us. Our nation – this generation – will lift a dark threat of violence from our people and our future. We will rally the world to this cause by our efforts, by our courage. We will not tire, we will not falter, and we will not fail.

In his state of the union address in January 2002 Bush introduced the idea of an 'axis of evil' that included Iraq, Iran and North Korea, and signalled that the US was prepared to act pre-emptively to deal with such nations. To the neocons this was a green light to start war preparations against Iraq. During the summer of 2002 Bush hardened his position against states that support terrorism and in a speech in June stated that the US must be ready for 'pre-emptive action' when necessary to defend the US. It is clear from leaked documents that the decision to invade Iraq was taken in the summer of 2002. The following nine months were thus a diplomatic charade as the US and UK sought and failed to muster a majority of votes in the UNSC to support military action.

After the swift military campaign and occupation of Iraq, in May 2003 the US established Paul Bremer, a senior State Department official, as head of the Coalition Provisional Authority, a sort of pro-consul for Iraq. One of his first decisions, to disband the Iraqi army, proved hugely controversial. According to many critics, it turned the US instantly from an army of liberation to an army of occupation and helped fuel the insurgency. As American casualties mounted, the US arranged to hand over political responsibility in May 2004 to an Iraqi interim government. US forces were still very much responsible for the security situation which showed little improvement even after the return of 'sovereignty' to the interim government in January 2005. American prestige suffered a huge blow with the publication of photographs showing American service men and women torturing Iraqi captives in the notorious Abu Ghraib prison. There were also revelations of similar torture at Guantánamo Bay where America kept several hundred 'enemy combatants' without recourse to the Geneva Conventions. By the summer of 2005, America had suffered almost two thousand deaths in Iraq; no one knew exactly how many Iraqis had died and estimates varied very widely.

The US, despite talk of an international coalition, provided 90% of all the forces in Iraq – at an annual cost to the American taxpayer of $50 billion.

The war in Iraq was initially supported by huge majorities in Congress, the media and public opinion. But as the campaign began to turn sour so was there a backlash in the US that fed into the 2004 election campaign. Senator John Kerry, although voting for the war, charged the President with taking the US into 'the wrong war, at the wrong time, in the wrong place'. Perhaps the most damaging critique came from Richard Clarke, the long-time head of the anti-terror campaign under both Democrat and Republican administrations. In his book (*Against All Enemies*) published in the spring of 2004 he charged the Bush team with 'taking their eye off the ball' in pursuing Saddam Hussein. The Iraqi leader may have been evil but he had nothing to do with 9/11 or supporting international terrorism. He described the war in Iraq 'an avaricious, premeditated, unprovoked war against a foe who posed no immediate threat but whose defeat did offer economic advantages. For Osama bin Laden, the American invasion and occupation of Iraq was like a Christmas present – and would be a magnet for anti-US terrorists'.

Why do the terrorists hate us?

Few Americans seem able to comprehend why anyone should hate them and even fewer seem willing to understand the extent and depth of resentment toward the US in some parts of the world, especially in Europe and the Middle East. A *Newsweek* journalist, noted that 'today, you cannot find a single political group in the Middle East that is pro-America. Anti-Americanism has poisoned the political culture. People are suspicious of US interests, goals and even its culture. Although the US dominates the world it does so in a way that inevitably arouses anger or opposition.[8] After the initial and understandable calls for revenge, there were some Americans who began to question why the US aroused so much hatred that could lead to the devastating terrorist attacks of September 2001. Retired air force general, Chuck Boyd, the staff director of the Hart-Rudman Commission (the US Commission on National Security/21st Century), told the author that during his visits to more than twenty-eight countries with the Commission, one of the principal recurring themes was the resentment felt toward the US. He considered that there were several reasons for this resentment: first, a lingering hatred in some parts of the world as a result of anti-American propaganda during the Cold War; second, US support for corrupt and/or anti-democratic regimes; third, the leading American role in international institutions that 'dominated the globalised world' such as the IMF, WTO, and World Bank; fourth, antipathy to the global influence of American culture. Boyd noted a dichotomy between elite hostility to US values and culture in Europe, and the popular embrace of them.

In the wake of the September attacks, a number of Europeans called on the US to change its policy on the Middle East. Some influential American experts also called for the US to review its policies. According to two former national security advisers, Brent Scowcroft and Zbigniew Brzezinski, the US needed to re-examine its policies in the Middle East and the Gulf. Scowcroft suggested the US need to be more even-handed in its approach towards the Arab world while Brzezinski saw no justification 'for Israel's indefinite suppression of the Palestinians.' Brzezinski further questioned the uncritical US support for a Saudi regime 'that had grown increasingly corrupt and become the object of resentment in the region'.[9] Another commentator, equally critical of US support for the Saudi and Egyptian regimes, argued that 'the region won't be stable, the oil fields won't be secure, and America won't be free of the fear of terrorism, unless we identify with the aspirations of the Arab people to live under legitimate governments.'[10]

Despite acknowledging that these factors may have played a role in fuelling anti-American resentment, neither Bush nor Powell showed any inclination to change US policy in the months after 9/11 beyond lukewarm efforts to kick-start the Middle East peace process. It was another four years before his successor, Condoleezza Rice, stood up before an audience in Cairo and conceded the failure of sixty years of American foreign policy in the Middle East.[11] Henceforth, the US priority would be promoting democracy rather than propping up authoritarian regimes. The American flagship policy to promote democracy was the Broader Middle East Initiative. It was not clear whether the US would have the staying power to achieve change or whether it would accept unpalatable election results The US did, however, step up its efforts in the public relations war with the terrorists. For a country with the biggest marketing industry in the world, the US has made a surprisingly poor job of managing its own image abroad. President Bush acknowledged at a press conference that 'we are not doing a very good job at getting our message across to the Arab and Muslim worlds.' This was a major understatement. One problem was that the US message focused more on appealing to Arab leaders rather than to the average citizen. According to Richard Holbrooke, Osama bin Laden, speaking from a cave and portraying himself as an underdog, was able to communicate much more effectively with the wider Arab population.[12] In November 2004 a Pentagon study came to a similar conclusion. It stated that 'America's image in world opinion and diminished ability to persuade are consequences of factors other than the failure to implement communications strategies'. The report also criticised the administration for casting the new threat of Islamic terrorism in a way that offends a large part of those living in the Muslim world.[13] In summer 2005 President Bush appointed one of his closest aides, Karen Hughes, to oversee US public diplomacy towards the Arab world.

These concerns about US foreign policy made it difficult for even the most pro-American European politicians to ignore. Indeed a number of European politicians, including Chancellor Schröder, were able to mobilise anti-American sentiment for electoral purposes. This in turn had a negative effect on the Bush administration's perception of Europe. The powerful anti-Bush feeling in Europe as well as the resentment towards Washington in the wider Middle East also made it difficult for EU leaders to be seen to be lining up behind America's new democracy project for the region.

Policy dilemmas

One of the consequences of terrorism moving to the top of the political agenda in the US is that the State Department is mandated by Congress to report annually on patterns of global terrorism. Its 2004 report aroused considerable controversy as it contained many errors and was considered to have been released for political purposes, i.e. to demonstrate that the Bush administration was winning the war on terrorism. In actual fact the true figures revealed a substantial increase in the number of 'significant terrorist incidents', up from 124 to 175 in twelve months. It is important, however, to see things in perspective. In 2004, a total of 625 people – including 25 Americans – were killed in international terrorist incidents worldwide. Meanwhile, over 43,000 people died from automobile accidents in the US alone, and 3 million people died of AIDS around the world. But such deaths do not have the same resonance as those dying from terrorist attacks.

What are the policy dilemmas in tackling terrorism? Essentially US counter-terrorist policy is based on four tenets;

– bring terrorists to justice for their crimes
– pressure on state sponsors of terrorism
– no concessions to terrorists and no deals
– seek support and assist allies in fighting terrorism.

The first three of these tenets reflect a confrontational approach that is very much in the mainstream of American thinking. Not all principles, however, have been applied evenly. The fourth tenet recognizes the international dimension of terrorism and that most progress in the fight against terrorism ultimately depends on the perspectives and behaviour of foreign governments, groups, publics and individuals. But it begs a number of important questions. How much does a state have to cooperate with the US to be deemed a partner? What if that state is engaged in suppressing its own citizens?

In its fight against terrorism, the US, like European governments confronted with the problem, often faces conflicting goals and courses of action. In the past, some governments, for example Spain with regard to the Basque terrorist group ETA, have preferred to handle terrorism as a national problem without outside interference. Some governments have also been wary of getting involved in others' battles and possibly attracting additional terrorism in the form of reprisals.[14] Others have been reluctant to join in sanctions if their own trade interests might be damaged or if they sympathized with the perpetrators' cause. Finally, there is the persistent problem of extraditing terrorists without abandoning the long-held principle of asylum for persons fleeing persecution for legitimate political or other activity. To the consternation of the British government, for many years the US authorities turned a blind eye to American financial contributions to IRA front organizations. It was also a very slow and difficult process to extradite suspected Irish terrorists from the US to the UK.

One obvious dilemma is providing security from terrorist acts, i.e. limiting the freedom of individual terrorists, terrorist groups, and support networks to operate unimpeded in a relatively unregulated environment versus maximizing individual freedoms, democracy, and human rights.[15] Efforts to combat terrorism are complicated by a global trend toward deregulation, open borders, and expanded commerce. The September 2001 attacks provide a good example of how the Al-Qaida network took advantage of globalization. Before hijacking the planes, the terrorists studied in Hamburg, took flying lessons in Florida, used cellular phones and e-mail to communicate with each other and accessed the internet to make hotel and plane reservations.

Another dilemma for policymakers is the need to identify the perpetrators of particular terrorist acts and those who train, fund, or otherwise support or sponsor them. The majority of those involved in the September 2001 attacks were Saudi citizens but the US struck back at Afghanistan not Saudi Arabia. A further complicating factor is that many terrorists seem to be individuals who do not work for any state and who may have no or only loose links to a known terrorist organization. The worldwide threat of such individual terrorism, or spontaneous terrorist activity is likely to increase. This will pose problems for the US which has traditionally sought to pin responsibility for terrorism on states. A desire to punish a state for supporting international terrorism may also be subject to conflicting foreign policy objectives. Another problem in the wake of the number of incidents associated with Islamic fundamentalist groups is how to condemn and combat such terrorist activity, and the extreme and violent ideology of specific radical groups, without appearing to be anti-Islamic in general. President Bush seemed to recognize this dilemma as one of his first acts after 11 September was to visit a mosque in an attempt to reassure the four million Muslims living in the US that they were not tarred with the brush of the terrorists. Similarly Tony Blair invited representatives from Britain's Muslim community to meet with him in the immediate aftermath of the July 2005 London attacks.

Policy options

The US has employed a range of options to combat international terrorism, from diplomacy and international cooperation to economic sanctions, covert action, protective security measures and military force. The two prime examples of the use of force are the military campaign against the Taliban regime and the Al-Qaida network in Afghanistan in 2001 and the 2003 invasion of Iraq. The swift military victory over the Taliban, accomplished with the Afghan Northern Alliance, was unforeseen and gave rise to a new confident spirit in the Pentagon and White House. Military force, especially the precision bombing and the use of special units, was seen to have played a crucial role in bringing about a change of government in Afghanistan. Many argued that it should be employed for similar purposes elsewhere, particularly an attack on Iraq. Yet the military was also criticised for failing to capture Osama bin Laden in the Afghanistan campaign.

Although the war on terrorism was being fought by bankers, police, customs agents and IT specialists, it was the military that captured the headlines. Washington made it abundantly clear that it was not only ready to use force in retaliation for terrorist acts but that it had the best military capabilities in the world for such tasks. The administration also hoped that proof of US military success and its willingness to act overseas might deter other groups or states harbouring terrorist groups. Not everyone was pleased at the emphasis on a military response. Strobe Talbott, the Deputy Secretary of State during the Clinton administration, held that 'encouraging stable political development is the key to reducing our greatest security threat. We have no option but to get back into the nation-building business.'[16] Apart from the President's commitment to assist in the reconstruction of Afghanistan, there was little sign of the US wishing to become more engaged in dealing with 'failed states.' This could be a short-sighted attitude as sooner or later, the US is invariably

drawn into the problems resulting from 'failed states' as witness the involvement in Haiti, Somalia, Kosovo, and now Iraq.

There have been calls to attack 'the root causes of terrorism' but there is
no agreement on what are the root causes. There is little evidence, for
example, that poverty plays a role in motivating the Al-Qaida network.
Osama bin Laden has stated that his wish to destroy America is based on the
poisonous nature of its flagrantly secular and sexualised popular culture
which is contrary to Islamic morals. There is no doubt that Al-Qaida wishes
to impose an Islamic theocracy wherever possible. Under these conditions it
is difficult to imagine any compromise solution. Neither the Madrid train
bombers nor the Muslim assassin of Dutch film-maker van Gogh showed
any remorse for their murderous actions.

There were some who hoped that the US opposition to the International
Criminal Court (ICC) would mellow following the 11 September attacks.
The US opposition to the new court was all the more difficult to fathom in
the light of its potential to deal with war criminals and terrorists such as
Slobodan Milosevic. But the administration and Congress continued to
assert that the US would not join if it meant that American soldiers could be
arraigned before the ICC. To many, this was a case of one law for the rest of
the world – another for the US.

Homeland defence

The US response to 11 September was felt in many policy areas, including
the provision of more resources for 'homeland defence', law enforcement
agencies and national security policy. On the domestic front, there was a thorough reorganization of homeland defence. The chain of command on anti-terrorism planning runs from the President through the NSC and involves
several parts of the administration including the State, Justice, Treasury and
Commerce departments. To try and impose some overall coordination, Bush
established a new cabinet level post for Homeland Defence, and named
Governor Tom Ridge as the first occupant of the office. The massive new
bureaucracy, however, struggled to impose itself against the vested interests
of the traditional federal departments of government.

In the wake of the September 2001 terrorist attacks, Congress rapidly
passed the 2001 USA Patriot Act that gave the government significant new
powers in dealing with the terrorist threat. Building on anti-terrorist laws
passed after the 1995 Oklahoma City bombing, the new act gave the federal
government increased powers for wire-tapping, seizing telephone and
email records, medical, banking, educational and business files, and even
secret searches of suspects' homes. Defending the bill, John Ashcroft, the
attorney general, stated 'we are at war and we have to do things differently'.
Civil rights groups were concerned that some of these powers, particularly
relating to domestic surveillance by law enforcement agencies, could
infringe basic rights to privacy. Also controversial was the proposal to
establish military courts to try foreigners residing in the US for terrorist acts.
Former Secretary of Defence, William Cohen, drew attention to the conflict
between individual privacy and protection from terrorism in a lecture on 2
October 2001: 'I believe that we as a democratic society have yet to come to
grips with the tension that exists between our constitutional protection of

the right to privacy and the demand that we make to protect us.'[17] Congress reacted to these concerns by insisting on 'sunset clauses' for many provisions in the Patriot Act.

European responses

European responses to terrorism have generally followed major incidents and could be described, unkindly, as knee-jerk reactions to assure public opinion that governments were 'doing something'. The basic problem, however, has been that there does not exist an overall EU competence for tackling terrorism. The highly complex EU institutional structure for dealing with terrorism is constantly changing and there are many sensitivities between the EU member states, let alone between the EU and US. These hinder effective action against terrorism.[18] For example, in July 2005 Germany's highest court ruled that a German citizen of Syrian origin, Mamoun Darkazanli, could not be extradited to Spain, where a prosecutor wanted to try him as an 'interlocutor and assistant' of Osama bin Laden and his network. The reason given was that the federal government had not correctly transposed the EU arrest warrant into German law. Within the EU, the main focus has been trying to achieve agreement on a number of practical issues relating to a common arrest warrant, data sharing and restricting the financing opportunities for terrorist groups. The military role has been downplayed with the war in Afghanistan being seen as something of an exception. The European Security and Defence Policy (ESDP) is generally regarded as complementary and supportive of other policy instruments.[19]

Europeans, more than Americans, also accept that terrorism is primarily driven by domestic grievances rather than a global Islamic mastermind. The European Security Strategy gives high prominence to terrorism but emphasizes the importance of tackling the root causes at the global, regional and local level.[20]

The 9/11 attacks did not catch the EU unprepared in terms of proposals for closer cooperation to fight terrorism. A list of proposals had been tabled at the 1999 Tampere European Council but no follow-up action had been taken. 9/11 therefore provided an environment for speeding up the implementation of adopted measures and shifting the priority of security policy towards the fight against terrorism. In retrospect, it could be argued that the EU then did not fully take advantage of the situation in which the population was ready to accept many security reforms and measures, which are usually difficult to adopt. This lack of major terrorism-linked changes within the EU was often perceived as a lack of threat perception by the EU Member States, even though some experts on terrorism warned that Europe could become a more tempting target for the terrorists as it is less well protected than the United States. The involvement of Europe in the fight against terrorism in Afghanistan and especially in Iraq, together with its geographical position and its growing Muslim population, are only some of the characteristics that make Europe an obvious target. The Madrid and London terrorist attacks underlined the EU's vulnerability.

Immediately after 9/11 there was a special European Council meeting that adopted an Action Plan for combating terrorism, which was followed a month later by a detailed description of concrete measures in a 'roadmap' for the fight against terrorism.

At the same meeting the European Council emphasized that the fight against terrorism required greater Union involvement in preventing and stabilizing regional conflicts, especially in the Middle East. The Action Plan concerned all three pillars and involved mostly the Council structures (General Affairs Council, ECOFIN, JHA Council), in cooperation with Member States and the Commission. Some existing institutions were to be strengthened (Europol), some were newly created (Eurojust), and some specialised task forces were established within existing structures (Counter-terrorism task force in Europol).[21]

Immediately after the Madrid attacks, the EU agreed to revise the 2001 Plan of Action on Terrorism and agree an Implementation Plan that would then identify key tasks and specific achievable targets and the EU bodies responsible for delivery. The EU also agreed to establish a security coordinator, who would be responsible for the enhancement of cooperation between EU bodies and third countries concerning the fight against terrorism. The proposal of the Belgian prime minister, Guy Verhofstadt, to create a European CIA, which had been submitted to the JHA Council in February by the Austrian Minister of Interior, was however rejected by most other member states, notably France and Germany.[22] The EU was clearly not ready for such a step and most EU officials still stress the importance of improving the functioning of the existing institutions before creating new structures.

The European Commission has found it difficult to establish itself as a leader in this policy area. But it has used its right of initiative to present timely communications on combating terrorism, and it is also not afraid to remind member states of their failure to implement agreed policies such as the European search and arrest warrant. As noted above, the fight against terrorism is one of the priorities of the European Security Strategy, which clearly states the need to address the terrorist threat by better cooperation between the external action and Justice and Home Affairs policies, which is complicated because of the EU's pillar construction. In March 2004 the EU adopted a Declaration on Combating Terrorism which underlines the priorities and objectives of the EU's anti-terrorist efforts.

As the Commission's communication of September 2006 illustrates, some two-thirds of the Action Plan proposals have been translated into political decisions, including EU-wide agreements to bring in passports with two biometric identifiers (facial scans and fingerprints) and to play a bigger part in the international drive against illegal money transfers. The 'situation centre' or Sitcen in the Council in Brussels, where EU members share intelligence assessments, has begun looking at domestic as well as external threats. Following the London attacks, the European Commission proposed more measures to tackle money laundering, make explosives more easily traceable and restrict sales of farm fertiliser.

The EU's embryonic law-enforcement institutions – the Europol police agency, and Eurojust, through which prosecutors co-operate – are heavily engaged in anti-terrorism work, building relations with their much bigger brothers in America. Important decisions came in the autumn of 2005, such as making personal data more easily available to investigators while also introducing an EU-wide system of data protection. The Commission produced a paper on 'radicalisation' with the focus on discontent among young Muslims that prompts a few to become terrorists. But this described the problem; it did not prescribe solutions – only national governments could do that. The US has also established a Centre of Excellence at the University of Maryland to study similar issues.

This climate left the EU's top counter-terrorism official, Gijs de Vries of the Netherlands, in the role of persuader rather than enforcer. Clearly, individual acts of co-operation between European countries are one thing. Longer-term efforts to turn counter-terrorism into a pan-European activity are something else. And, as the Darkazanli case shows, that is a much harder task. Moreover, the problems are not just legal and technical, but political and ethical. In all European countries, hard questions have been posed by the twin challenges of terrorism and Muslim disaffection. One is how far civil liberty should be sacrificed for security. Another is how to balance help for ethnic and religious minorities with a harder-nosed insistence that all citizens obey the law. Whatever the answers, they are not likely to be imposed from Brussels.

Transatlantic cooperation

The attacks of 11 September 2001 had a major impact on transatlantic relations generally, but also on specific mechanisms for managing US/EU relations. Both the Justice Dialogue, which pre-dated September 2001, and the Policy Dialogue on Borders and Transport Security (PDBTS), have become central to US/EU cooperation on counter-terrorism. The Justice Dialogue began in 1998 on the heels of the New Transatlantic Agenda (NTA), but has always had quasi-autonomous status. The dialogue brings together representatives of the US Department of Justice (DOJ) with EU colleagues in DG Justice and Home Affairs. The DOJ has long had relationships with the interior ministries and law enforcement agencies of EU member states, primarily as a result of extradition issues and cross-border prosecutions. As the EU began to extend its competence in JHA, the informal Justice dialogue was established as a means of ensuring that the US had information and access in this rapidly growing area of policy. It has found discussions at the European level to be of increasing importance, as the EU develops a more common set of judicial procedures and institutions (including Europol and Eurojust), and as the EU enlarges to include new members which, in the absence of strong national judiciaries and police forces, rely more on Brussels for guidance. The Justice Dialogue has usually been convened twice per EU Council presidency, initially at the staff level, and since 2002 at ministerial level.

Despite the fact that meetings can be crowded, with US delegations generally numbering 20-30, the Dialogue as a whole is viewed as very productive. First, most of the individuals involved have deep experience in judicial or law enforcement matters. They are familiar with the technical questions and, particularly at the staff level, are able to relate to each other as law enforcement professionals. Second (and in part because of the first), the use of talking points is relatively rare. This allows the discussion to be much more free form than is commonly experienced in strictly diplomatic discussions and to address specific problems in a practical way. The Justice Dialogue has been a central forum for developing agreements on mutual legal assistance and extradition and on liaison with Europol and potentially Eurojust. A recent Justice Dialogue meeting had the following issues on its agenda: terrorist financing; the use of classified information in courts of law; trafficking in people, drugs, and other illicit substances; and strategies for fighting organized crime.

The issue of data protection and how it is handled in criminal investigations has been a subject of discussion. It has become even more important as the EU attempts to harmonize member state procedures in this area. The Justice Dialogue also succeeded (at least occasionally) in identifying potential areas of disagreement and finding ways to work toward a solution before a dispute arises. It contributed to an enhanced level of interaction more generally between principal policy-makers. In the first George W. Bush administration, Attorney General John Ashcroft regularly saw European justice ministers when they came through Washington, either in meetings or in less formal social situations. Attorney General Alberto Gonzales continued this practice, having met with the Luxembourg Justice Minister during his first day in office.

Following September 2001, but prior to the establishment of the Department of Homeland Security (DHS), the agenda of the Justice dialogue became increasingly dominated by questions concerning the security of US borders. This discussion began to intersect with an existing transatlantic attempt to establish customs cooperation, as represented by the signature in 1997 of a formal EU/US Customs Cooperation Agreement. Beginning in early 2002, the US government undertook a series of measures designed to increase the security of US borders, including the Container Security Initiative (CSI), new requirements on Passenger Name Records (PNR), and a Congressionally mandated requirement that foreigners entering the United States hold biometric passports. With these and other initiatives, the DHS and the renamed Customs and Border Protection (CBP) Bureau sought to 'extend our zone of security outward so that American borders are the last line of defence, not the first'. In doing so, however, the US imposed on its EU and other partners a series of onerous requirements.

The extra-territorial implications of US homeland security policies agreed in the aftermath of 9/11 both caused huge problems for the EU and seemed to have been subject to little reflection on the part of US legislators and regulators as they were formulated.

Announced in January 2002, the CSI sought to identify and examine maritime containers that posed a risk of terrorism while they were still in foreign ports before being shipped to the United States. The US began negotiating bilateral agreements with individual countries, including a number of European countries, that would allow the stationing of US customs agents at those foreign ports. The European Commission immediately objected and began infringement proceedings (later suspended) against a number of EU member states, while seeking the authority to negotiate an EU-wide agreement with the US. That agreement, signed in April 2004 established standards for extending CSI to other EU ports; set minimum standards for port security; established the 24-hour rule (requiring the provision of 24 hours' advance notice of the contents of any maritime container bound for US ports); revitalized the standing Joint Customs Cooperation Committee (JCCC) from the 1997 agreement; and created new working groups on security standards and trade facilitation. Participants credit the agreement with having removed a significant obstacle to improving transatlantic relations.[23] The number of ports participating in the Container Security Initiative has continued to grow and now includes 20 EU ports in 9 countries accounting for over 80% of US-bound containers from the EU.

In early 2003, CBP required airlines to provide, within 15 minutes of departure, electronic access to the Personal Name Records of all passengers on flights entering the United States. Failure to comply would result in substantial fines for the airlines and enhanced security screenings for passengers. This requirement created particular problems for European airlines, which faced possible prosecution under the terms of the EU's Data Privacy Directive. The Commission agreed to allow airlines to forward the information to the US on a temporary basis, while negotiating a bilateral agreement with the United States. This agreement, concluded in early 2004 after often difficult negotiations, saw the US agree to limit the number of data fields it would collect, the length of time it would hold them, and the uses of the data. The Commission obtained a decision recognising the adequacy of US measures under the terms of the Data Protection Directive. The US and the EU also adopted a bilateral agreement authorizing the continuing transfer of PNR data by European airlines to the United States. The agreement was criticized by many consumer groups and the European Parliament for providing inadequate data protection, and the EP challenged these arrangements before the European Court of Justice. The issue of data protection thus remains a difficult area. Both sides stress that they want to balance anti-terrorism measures with the protection of individual rights but there are different emphases according to political demands.

Another sensitive issue is passport data. In 2002 the US Congress established new requirements for biometric passports featuring digital photos and other biometric information such as fingerprints and iris scans. It further required that travellers without such passports would require a visa to enter the United States after October 2004, even if currently from a visa waiver country (as are 15 EU member states). Alarmed by the prospect of all European travellers having to go through the cumbersome process of obtaining a US visa, EU officials objected, noting that while the Union had begun the process of introducing biometric passports, no EU member state, nor indeed the United States itself, would be in a position to meet the October 2004 deadline. The US government requested a two-year extension from Congress, but Congress agreed to postpone the deadline only for one year, until October 2005. EU and US officials worked closely on this issue, with US officials supporting another extension of the deadline as well as an effort within the International Civil Aviation Organization (ICAO) to establish global standards for biometric passports.

Although the State Department and Customs had taken the lead roles in negotiating solutions to these conflicts with the EU, it was clear that the new DHS would find US/EU relations a challenging area. Then, over the 2003 Christmas holidays, the US government cancelled several flights from Europe to the United States on security grounds with little notice to the European governments (or the passengers). For those managing the US/EU relationship in the State Department, this very public disruption of transatlantic travel was a disaster. Moreover, they were aware that the number of issues that needed to be addressed, in what was now a very conflictual and tense atmosphere, was piling up. What had previously been a relatively prosaic (and primarily economic) process of bilateral customs cooperation had become heavily securitised and politicised. It was clear that instead of simply engaging in *reactive* regulatory cooperation aimed at managing conflicts, there was a real need for customs cooperation and mutual assistance in customs matters to include cooperation on container security and related matters.

The institutional solution was the creation of a new, specialised forum for US-EU exchange, the Policy Dialogue on Borders and Transport Security (PDBTS), in early 2004. The need for proactive cooperation led to the creation of a US/EU dialogue dedicated specifically to border and transportation issues. Labelled the PDBTS, it was launched in April 2004 at a meeting chaired by US Under-Secretary for Transport and Border Security Asa Hutchinson and EU Director-General for Justice and Home Affairs Jonathan Faull. EU anti-terrorism coordinator Gijs de Vries also attended as did relevant officials from the Departments of State and Justice. A second meeting was held in November 2004 and further meetings took place in 2005 and 2006. On the US side, they involved officials from the Departments of Homeland Security (DHS), Justice and State (usually chaired by DHS) and on the European side, from the Commission, Council, and Presidency. Although the Dialogue is new, the PDBTS has garnered a reputation as a success, both among those who manage the NTA process as well as among officials directly responsible for the issues involved.

Participants credit the PDBTS with getting the right people in the room to deal with common border security issues, and with averting future crises through ongoing consultation. Throughout 2003, DHS had developed some contacts in Europe as it dealt with PNR and other issues, but the new Dialogue allowed for more regular, predictable interaction. Participants noted that they were in frequent touch between dialogue sessions with their transatlantic counterparts by telephone and other methods, and were even able to provide advance warning of delicate matters. The dialogue sessions have been described as much less formal than senior level group (SLG) sessions by one participant. It is striking that none of the senior DHS officials had any exposure to the EU prior to their involvement in PDBTS (one described the Union as 'incomprehensible').[24]

Success in the PDBTS has spilled over to even higher levels, with Secretary of Homeland Security Tom Ridge having increasingly frequent interaction with his EU counterparts. In a speech in November 2004 at the EPC, he noted that one of his few regrets as Secretary had been his late appreciation of the benefits of US/EU coordination: 'What I have discovered is that when we sit down, make our case, discuss, negotiate finding a common solution of mutual benefit, we have made a lot of progress. Part of me wishes we had started that a little bit earlier, but there were other things that it seemed at the time were higher priorities.'

The EU/US agenda in transport and border security is still a potential source of major conflict. Yet, participants in PDBTS point in particular to three factors that made the dialogue initially successful:

– it brought together experts in a somewhat informal setting. Both sides
  started with a conviction that solutions had to be found. Discussions
  focused on finding ways to satisfy security needs, rather than about
  whether they existed;
– the dialogue forced both sides to get their respective houses in order.
  DHS in particular was a new department that had brought together
  many disparate agencies with competing cultures and agendas. Few
  officials had any significant international experience and the Dialogue
  required DHS to think about the international impact of a particular
  measure and pressured the various agencies and bureaus to develop
  one position. Similarly, in the EU, the Commission was a relatively
  new actor in this area, and although its (then) JHA Directorate was
  most often in the lead, many other DGs were implicated (CSI was a
  customs issue, for example). In addition, the new Coordinator for
  Counter-terrorism at the Council of Ministers also had to establish his
  role.

Finally, both US and EU participants in the PDBTS were able to use the
discussions to reinforce their position within their own bureaucracies.
Taking a lead with the US reinforced the Commission's competence in this
area, while DHS participation did the same for a relatively new Cabinet
department. The PDBTS has reversed the fear that issues concerning borders and transportation would become a minefield for US/EU relations.
Instead, these matters are now widely considered an area of US/EU success.

Cooperation on terrorism has also been blessed at the highest levels. The
March 2004 Declaration was a useful backdrop to the EU-US summit in
Ireland in June that year when the two sides issued a declaration on
Combating Terrorism. This marked a significant increase in the willingness
of both sides to cooperate in tackling terrorism. The action points in the
Declaration cover a wide range of areas, in particular intelligence, law
enforcement, judicial cooperation, the prevention of access by terrorists to
financial resources and transport security. In addition the US announced
that a senior official from the US Department of Homeland Security would
be posted to the US Mission to the EU. This new appointment would be in
addition to representatives from the FBI, Justice Department and Customs.
The US also sent a liaison offer to Europol. Plans for the EU and the US to
hold an annual summit on Justice and Home Affairs issues at the ministerial
level were also announced as well as the creation of a High Level Policy
Dialogue on Border and Transport Security.

Many other EU-US agreements have been signed to tackle terrorism. In
April 2004, an agreement on container security within the scope of the existing EU/US customs co-operation agreement was signed. In June 2003, the
mutual legal assistance and extradition agreements (MLAT) were signed.
Both agreements provide important new tools for combating terrorism and
fighting transnational crime. The extradition agreement, among other
things, reduces delays in the handling of requests, improves channels of
transmission for extradition requests, in particular in urgent cases concerning provisional arrest, and facilitates direct contacts between central authorities. It allows Member States to make extradition contingent upon the
condition that the death penalty will not be imposed. The mutual legal

assistance will give US law enforcement authorities access to bank accounts throughout the EU (and vice versa) in the context of investigations into serious crimes, including terrorism, improve practical co-operation by reducing delays in mutual legal assistance and also allow for the creation of Joint Investigative Teams and the possibility of video conferencing. However, to move these treaties forward, a number of bilateral instruments needed to be signed so as to bring the bilateral relationships into conformity with the EU-US MLAT treaties.

In June 2005, the EU and US reviewed their cooperation at their annual summit in Washington. The US, in a declaration at the summit, noted several UN actions and UNSC resolutions that were aimed at combating terrorism. For example there were resolutions aimed at strengthening sanctions against Al-Qaida; and UNSCR 1535 establishing the Counter-terrorism Executive Directorate. The US also provided funding to the Terrorism Prevention Branch (TPB) of the UN Office on Drugs and Crime (UNODC) which has helped provide legislative drafting assistance to almost 100 countries. Both the EU and US had worked together in the Counter Terrorism Action Group (CTAG) to facilitate universal adherence to the international counter-terrorism conventions and protocols.

The EU and US have also deepened cooperation on measures to curtail the financing of terrorists and meet regularly in the troika format to review cooperation on technical assistance issues. The two sides have started outreach seminars to countries as diverse as Tanzania and Bahrain. US-EU efforts to enhance cyber security include providing technical assistance for drafting improved substantive and procedural cyber crime laws, promoting the G8 Critical Information Infrastructure Principles and G8 24/7 Computer Crime Network, building support for the Cybercrime Convention of the Council of Europe, and providing law enforcement officials with capacity-building training on investigations involving computer and electronic evidence. US laws require internet service providers to preserve, upon request, specified log files, electronic mail, and other records for a limited period of time, and to make available that information upon court order or through statutory processes to investigators and prosecutors for use in criminal and/or terrorist cases.

In March 2005, the US and Europol reviewed their agreement and issued a report finding that their provisions, including those relating to personal data, were working well. The volume of information shared has continued to increase while the US hopes to gain access to Europol's analytical case files, and is optimistic that the Europol Convention will soon be amended to allow this. The US has begun discussions with Eurojust on a formal arrangement to govern its interaction with US law enforcement authorities. The US has completed negotiations on bilateral instruments to implement the Agreements on extradition and Mutual Legal Assistance (MLA) with nearly all of the original fifteen EU member states. It has made substantial progress towards completion with the ten new member states as well.

Both the EU and US have held seminars to allow officials from each side to understand their respective structures and procedures for tackling terrorism. The US has established contacts with the EU Chiefs of Police, the new Police College Centre (UK), with OLAF, the EU's anti-corruption arm and with the new EU border agency in Warsaw.

Another transatlantic forum where terrorism has been discussed is NATO. The US has supported discussions between NATO and the EU on four crisis management items: non-binding guidelines and minimum standards for protection of civilian populations against chemical/biological/-radiological/nuclear risks; a framework agreement on the facilitation of vital cross border transport; creation of a common data base of national points of contact; and cross participation as observers in consequence management exercises. There is also an ongoing dialogue on terrorist recruitment and related issues in the biannual meetings with the Committee on Terrorism (COTER) troika.

Problem areas in EU-US cooperation

Despite the increase in cooperation between the EU and US there are many problem areas. The issues of the weight to give to a military response, human rights and data protection have been touched on above. Another very sensitive issue relates to the problem of rendition. The decision of an Italian judge in June 2005 to order the arrest of 13 people linked to the CIA on charges of kidnapping a terrorist suspect was interpreted as a sign of a growing rift between European and American counter-terrorism officials. European officials had pursued a policy of building criminal cases against terrorist suspects through surveillance, wiretaps, detective work and the criminal justice system The US has increasingly used other means, including renditions – abducting terror suspects from foreign countries and transporting them to third countries – some of which are known to use torture. The case that aroused Italian anger concerned Abu Omar, an Egyptian radical cleric based in Milan. Italian and American authorities were cooperating in preparing a dossier on Abu Omar when he disappeared on 17 February 2003. When the Italians began investigating they were surprised to find that some of the CIA officers who had been helping them on the case were involved in his abduction to Egypt.

Other European services have made similar complaints about US rendition, and also criticise the US for failing to allow them access to terrorist suspects held by the US. According to one Italian official, 'the American system is of little use to us. It's a one way street. We give them what we have, but we are given no useful information that can help us prosecute people'. Milan's deputy chief prosecutor, Armando Spataro, also went public in his criticism of the US, stating that he thought people in Washington may not understand that in Italy a prosecutor does not choose what to investigate. He has a legal obligation to investigate any crime. He added: 'I feel the international community must struggle against terrorism and international terrorist groups in accordance with international laws and the rights of the defendant. Otherwise we are giving victory to the terrorists'.[25]

Sharing intelligence and access are further sore points. Both sides complain about lack of timely intelligence exchange but there is little prospect of significantly increased sharing given the sensitivities in this field. German officials were highly critical of US failure to provide evidence in the case of Mounir el-Motassadeq, a suspected associate of several 9/11 hijackers. He was convicted in Germany on charges related to the attacks of 2001 – the only conviction so far – but the case collapsed on appeal. He was released in

April 2004 with German officials blaming US officials for this occurrence. The Bush administration also refused to allow Spanish officials to interview Ramzi bin al-Shibh, a central Al-Qaida suspect, in their case against two men on trial in Madrid on charges of helping to plan the 2001 attacks.

Conclusion

Despite some public and official misgivings, both the US and the EU have steadily increased their cooperation on counter-terrorism. The terrorist attacks on 11 September 2001 were a defining moment for the US. The terrorist attacks on Madrid and London were a salutary reminder that Europe is also a main target for terrorist groups. The America that emerged from the attacks was a different country, more united, yet more fearful of the future. President Bush sought to reassure Americans that the war would be fought largely outside the US and he envisaged the military playing the major role. European leaders found it more difficult to define a role for the EU, partly because of lack of unity on key issues (such as Iraq) and partly because of the domestic consequences of their foreign policy actions.

It is by no means clear, however, whether terrorism will become a lasting or ephemeral preoccupation for the US. Contrary to the fighting words of the President, this is not a war for existence or for the survival of western civilization. The terrorists are largely a rag-bag of misfits who could not even seize control in their own countries. It is also not clear whether it will mean a new emphasis on getting to the political roots of the problem. Will it lead, as Condoleezza Rice suggested in Cairo and many European governments hope, to a new approach toward the Middle East? Much will depend on whether there are further terrorist outrages against the US. But in the short term one can safely predict that terrorism will remain the top priority for the US and that it will continue to seek allies to fight against terrorism wherever it can find them.

At the same time, by undertaking an open-ended war on terrorism, the US has undoubtedly made itself a continued target for terrorists and criticism and made it difficult to implement the President's 'non-negotiable demands' on values such as respect for human rights, the rule of law, religious freedom and equality for women. These values are not shared in practice by many of America's allies, including many that host US bases. The EU should, arguably, be more supportive of these American goals but for internal reasons it will find it difficult to express openly such support during the lifetime of the Bush administration.[26] Nonetheless, as the war in Iraq became a 'cause célèbre' for Islamic extremists in 2005 – 2006, it clearly bred deep resentment of the United States (and its main ally in Europe, the UK), while lending credence to the view that the EU could in fact provide an alternative. This view was strengthened in the autumn of 2006 by a report at odds with President Bush's argument that the world was growing safer as a result of US action.[27] It argued that the threat from Islamic extremists had spread both in numbers and in geographic reach and that: 'The confluence of shared purpose and dispersed actors will make it harder to find and undermine jihadist groups.' By the end of 2006, therefore, there was little dissension from the view that the underlying factors emphasized in chapter 2 of this book (entrenched grievances, the slow pace of reform in Muslim countries, rising anti-US sentiment and the Iraq war) were clearly fuelling the spread of Muslim extremism and the EU and its member states were increasingly ranked high on US lists of actors that can bring something to the table in counter-terrorism.

Both Tom Ridge, in his farewell tour in Europe, and Michael Cherthoff, in his introductory tour, publicly emphasised the importance of the EU in combating terrorism. In the longer term the US is too powerful compared to the rest of the world not to return to some degree of complacency, albeit not to the same extent as prevailed before 11 September 2001. But the EU has no such luxury and is hence likely to be *demandeur* for US support in the future, while pursuing a gad-fly role insisting, as Javier Solana and the Austrian Chancellor Wolfgang Schüssel did at the EU-US summit in June 2006, that the fight against terrorism should not be allowed to compromise human rights, and that there are other priorities than terrorism – in the Balkans, at the WTO or in the Middle East.[28] Indeed, in the aftermath of the war in Lebanon, with the US bogged down in Iraq and Afghanistan and obsessed with Iran, the main potential contribution by Europe to EU-US relations would be to strengthen its own, different, role in these issues and thus strengthen transatlantic relations in the long term.

Endnotes:

1   *Foreign Affairs*, January/February 2002
2   Presidency Conclusions, Brussels European Council, 16/17 December 2004 (Doc 16238/1/04 Rev 1)
3   See Cameron F, *US Foreign Policy since the Cold War* (2005) Routledge
4   Blair press conference, 22 July and Chatham House study, July 2005; 'Trends in Global Terrorism: Implications for the United States,' National Intelligence Estimate, 2006. A June 2006 poll by the Pew Research Center found that America's image in 15 nations dropped sharply in 2006. Moreover, US Undersecretary of State Karen Hughes said the Iraq war 'is the latest excuse' for anti-American grievance in the Muslim world.
5   The author was present at this meeting on Capitol Hill
6   Heritage Foundation Backgrounder 1871 of 21 July 2005
7   Bob Woodward, *Plan of Attack*, 2004
8   Fareed Zakaria, *Newsweek*, 15 October 2001
9   *National Journal*, 22 September 2001
10 Beatty 2001
11 Rice speech in Cairo, 22 June 2005
12 *Financial Times*, 23 July 2005
13 *International Herald Tribune*, 25 November 2004.
14 A number of EU ambassadors told the author of the reluctance of their governments to train Iraqi security forces for fear of terrorist reprisals.
15 See the reports of Amnesty International for criticism of over-reacting to the terrorist threat
16 *Foreign Policy in Focus*, November/December 2001
17 *Washington Post*, 3 October 2001
18 for an overview of European response wee Mirjam Dittrich, EPC Working Paper no 14 *Facing the global terrorist threat; a European response*
19 The main areas of action of the ESDP contribution to counterterrorism are identified as follows: prevention, protection, response/consequence management and support to third countries. See: *Conceptual Framework on the ESDP dimension of the fight against terrorism*. Council of the European Union, DG E VIII/EUMS, 14797/04, 18 November 2004
20 European Security Strategy adopted by December 2003 European Council.
21 The complexity of EU institutional arrangements for tackling terrorism is well documented

in Lada Parizkova 'The EU Institutional Framework for Fighting Terrorism', EUISS occasional paper.
22 Moller, Marie-Luise, 'EU backs Away from New Anti-terror Organizations', Reuters, 16 March 2004
23 Agreement between the European Community and the United States of America on customs cooperation and mutual assistance in customs matters, *Official Journal* L 222 of 12/08/1997, pp. 17-24
24 Private conversations
25 *International Herald Tribune* 27 June 2005
26 Rik Coolsaet, *Between al-Andalus and a failing integration – Europe's pursuit of a long-term counterterrorism strategy in the post-al-Qaeda era*, Egmont Paper no 5
27 'Trends in Global Terrorism: Implications for the United States,' National Intelligence Estimate, 2006
28 Other transatlantic interests are described by Commissioner Benita Ferrero-Waldner: 'The Transatlantic Partnership: a balance sheet' Speech to the American Business Forum on Europe and the US Council for International Business, New York, 20 September 2006.

7.   Human Rights, Intelligence Cooperation and the EU Counter-Terrorism strategy

Florian Geyer[1]

Introduction

'All our action in the fight against terrorism is based on the absolute primacy of the rule of law. We fight terrorism by the law and within the law. Fighting terrorism is about preserving our most fundamental and cherished human rights (...)'[2]

Many observers and citizens alike will gratefully take notice of such clear and unambiguous words written in the preface to this volume by Commissioner Frattini, responsible for the European Area of Freedom, Security and Justice. It is reassuring to identify that the starting point and overall end of the Commission's counter-terrorism agenda is the rule of law and the preservation of fundamental rights. Yet, based on recent revelations that foreign and European intelligence services may actually have been complicit in extraordinary renditions and unlawful detentions, one might wonder whether Commissioner Frattini is not describing an ideal – still to be achieved by all involved actors – rather than an every-day reality. In fact, investigations pursued by Dick Marty for the Council of Europe[3] and Claudio Fava for the European Parliament[4], together with a number of inquiries carried out at member state level, have exposed how far the EU may actually be – or at least may have been – from this ideal.

Concern for the state of human rights, civil liberties and the rule of law is not only justified, with regard to these secret but clear violations of fundamental principles. 'Open' counter-terrorism measures agreed at national, supranational and international level after 9/11 have also often ended up being quashed in the courts.[5] The appointment of a 'Special Rapporteur on the promotion and protection of human rights while countering terrorism' by the UN Human Rights Commission in April 2005[6] highlights that excessive, unlawful counter-terrorism activity poses a real and tangible threat to liberal democracies. Dick Marty, the Council of Europe Rapporteur, in his second report of June 2007, put it like this:

We have said it before and others have said it much more forcefully, but we must repeat it here: having recourse to abuse and illegal acts actually amounts to a resounding failure of our system and plays right into the hands of the criminals who seek to destroy our societies through terror. Moreover, in the process, we give these criminals a degree of legitimacy – that of fighting an unfair system – and also generate sympathy for their cause, which cannot but serve as an encouragement to them and their supporters.[7]

This chapter looks at some of the issues at stake in this respect. It does not and cannot provide a comprehensive account and evaluation of all the questions involved. Instead, building on findings until mid-2007, this chapter addresses EU member states' indirect, second-hand use of situations and 'possibilities' created by extraordinary renditions and unlawful detentions, as opposed to their direct complicity or silent consent in secret US intelligence activities.[8] It therefore deals with how EU member states could not resist the temptation of taking advantage of extraordinary renditions and unlawful detentions and how they still profit from such practice. Recent examples of this are provided, together with an assessment of their legality. The second part of the chapter addresses the issue from an EU perspective and evaluates various related implications of and for EU counter-terrorism policies, in particular the question of these policies being tainted by the questionable counter-terrorism behaviour of member states, and what possible solutions exist to prevent or at least lessen such entanglement. To this end a concrete set of policy recommendations is proposed in the last part.

In the context of this chapter 'rendition' is understood as a situation in which one state obtains custody over a person suspected of involvement in a serious crime in the territory of another state, with the aim of transferring such a person to custody in the first state's territory (or a place subject to its jurisdiction) or to a third state. A rendition is considered 'extraordinary' when it is not executed in accordance with the law applying in the state where the person was situated at the time of seizure.[9] 'Unlawful detention' is understood as a deprivation of personal liberty characterised by a violation of indispensable defence rights, e.g. access to judicial review and professional legal advice[10]; in short: a detention, which places the detained person de facto outside the protection of law.[11]

1.   Taking advantage of extraordinary rendition and unlawful detention

At least two variations of how European 'security professionals'[12] profited or tried to profit from extraordinary renditions and unlawful detentions have come to light in recent months.

1.1   Variation No. 1 – Interrogations at Guantánamo Bay and other detention centres

The EP resolution on the alleged use of European countries by the CIA for the transportation and illegal detention of prisoners states that at least two member states and one candidate country have sent security professionals to Guantánamo Bay and detention centres in Pakistan and Syria. The duty of these officials has not been to provide assistance to their detained citizens or long-term residents, but to interrogate and gain information from them. The countries named in the EP resolution are the UK,[13] Germany[14] and Turkey.[15] Media coverage suggests that other countries might have done the same, e.g. France, which according to these sources sent French intelligence agents to question six French citizens inside the Guantánamo camp in 2002.[16] In addition, certain countries have adopted the practice of not sending their own officials for the interrogations on these sites, but supplying instead questions to foreign interrogators, making it practically impossible to control the methods of interrogation.[17]

In Germany, at least[18], the federal government has not denied having sent its officials abroad. The practice came under scrutiny early in 2006 by the Parlamentarische Kontrollgremium. This parliamentary control panel of the German Bundestag has the statutory mandate to observe and hold accountable the activities of the German intelligence service. In its report for the panel, the German government conceded that officials had been interrogating detainees abroad and held that such activities were an indispensable part of intelligence information gathering. The government stressed that the information obtained was destined only to serve intelligence purposes and not as evidence in criminal court proceedings. The German government guaranteed that 'in future', officials of criminal investigation services will no longer be part of interrogation teams, but this guarantee in itself demonstrated that, in the past, the distinction between intelligence and criminal investigations had not been observed. The government report further noted that interrogations abroad only took place – and will continue to do so – with the free consent of the person interrogated. In addition, no interrogation will commence or continue – according to the government – when there are signs that the person has been subjected to torture.[19] With the majority of its members in the parliamentary control panel, the government coalition of Christian Democrats (CDU) and Social Democrats (SPD) largely accepted the government's statements, cleared its activities and acknowledged the promises to draw a clearer line between intelligence and criminal investigation in the future.[20] However, this rather lenient outcome met with well-pronounced dissent from the members of the opposition in the panel.[21]

1.2 Variation No. 2 – Information exchange with foreign services and the use of such information

The second variation of profiting from extraordinary renditions and unlawful detention is somewhat more sophisticated: officials themselves are not obliged to travel around and be confronted with the difficult question of whether a detainee has 'voluntarily' given consent to the interrogation. The 'neutral' information itself makes its way from detention centres abroad to databases and files in Europe. The – valuable – information is offered by foreign services, and the question of whether these services have used torture or other inhuman or degrading treatment in order to obtain the information remains unclear. The German government's report to the parliamentary control panel, mentioned above, makes this clear:

> Interrogation output – also from the American side – has been occasionally offered in the past to the German government, insofar as foreign authorities considered it

relevant for German authorities. This interrogation output contains statements that the interrogated persons have made in relation to specific issues. However, it does not contain any information on the whereabouts of the detainees nor of their rendition to other countries. The interrogation protocols neither contain information on the circumstances of the interrogation nor the personal condition of the detainees.[22]

Concerning the use of information obtained in this way, a telling example is provided by recent proceedings in the UK. Unlike the German government, which according to its February 2006 report does not intend to use such information in court proceedings, the UK government strongly propagated the view that information obtained through torture abroad (hereafter 'foreign torture information') must be admissible as evidence in court as long as there is no direct participation of British officials during the torture itself.[23] It may come as a surprise that not only the Special Immigration Appeals Commission (SIAC) – no less than a superior court – but also the Court of Appeal for England and Wales[24] approved this 'innovative' interpretation. It eventually required the Law Lords in the House of Lords to remind the executive and the lower courts of the common law tradition, as well as European and international law obligations, prohibiting the use of torture. The House of Lords rejected this 'new' understanding in no uncertain terms. To cite Lord Bingham of Cornhill:

> But the English common law has regarded torture and its fruits with abhorrence for over 500 years, and that abhorrence is now shared by over 140 countries which have acceded to the Torture Convention. I am startled, even a little dismayed, at the suggestion (and the acceptance by the Court of Appeal majority) that this deeply-rooted tradition and an international obligation solemnly and explicitly undertaken can be overridden by a statute and a procedural rule which make no mention of torture at all.[25]

As clear as this position seems to be, there still remain unresolved questions. One of them is of a procedural – but no less important – nature and concerns the burden of proof: who should prove that evidence presented by the prosecutors is in fact a fruit of torture: the accused or the prosecutor? The majority in the House of Lords has shifted this burden ultimately to the accused, yet not without facing heavy criticism from some of their peers. Again, Lord Bingham of Cornhill:

> (…) it is inconsistent with the rudimentary notions of fairness to blindfold a man and then impose a standard which only the sighted could hope to meet.[26]

Lord Bingham of Cornhill's criticism can be deemed justified, as the majority of the Law Lords in fact imposed too high a standard on the burden of proof. As a consequence, the Law Lords' test has provoked the UN Special Rapporteur of the Commission on Human Rights on torture and other cruel, inhuman or degrading treatment or punishment, Manfred Nowak, to submit an interim report to the UN General Assembly analysing the Law Lords' decision. In this report he recalls that according to the individual complaints procedures before the UN Committee against torture, it is established that the applicant is only required to demonstrate that his or her allegations of torture are well-founded. The ultimate burden of proof thereafter shifts to the state.[27]

The second remaining open question in the House of Lords' judgment – as the Lords did not have to rule on it – is whether there is a difference between foreign torture information used in courts and such information used by executive bodies. While the Lords ruled out the first, their *obiter dicta* suggest that they accept the latter. The issue is dealt with in detail below.

1.3 Contradictory combinations of these two variations

The account of these two variations of profiting from extraordinary renditions and unlawful detention serves as an interim conclusion before this chapter moves on to a legal assessment and discusses EU implications. At this stage it is important to note that in practice neither variation stands separately from the other. They are complementary or even overlap. But, complementarity might have adverse effects: responsible behaviour of security officials in questionable situations might be frustrated by the fact that the information these officials were originally supposed to obtain, but refused to do so, nevertheless finds its way to interested parties at a later stage. In November 2006, German media reported the case of 74-year old Abdel-Halim Khafagy, a long-term German resident of Egyptian nationality reported to have been captured in 2001 in Bosnia-Herzegovina, maltreated and brought to a US military base in Tuzla, named 'Eagle base.'[28] Two officials from the Bundeskriminalamt, the German federal criminal police office and one interpreter from the Bundesnachrichtendienst, the German secret service, were apparently sent to interrogate Khafagy. Since they formed the impression that detainees in Eagle base were subject to inhuman, torture-like treatment, they refused to interrogate, travelled back to Germany and reported the situation to their offices. Cited by Süddeutsche Zeitung, one of the officials said: 'Serbs found themselves before the UN criminal tribunal in The Hague for what the Americans did in Tuzla.'[29] After three weeks Khafagy was supposedly brought to Egypt and then back to Germany. He later applied for German citizenship. During the administrative naturalisation proceedings pursued by the local Munich administration, Khafagy – in 2004 – was suddenly confronted with information he was said to have given at Eagle Base in 2001, insinuating links with a terrorism suspect. In essence this means that although German officials declined to take advantage of the situation in 2001, information obtained in Eagle Base nevertheless made its way to Germany, was saved, stored, and subsequently provided to local administrations and then used in naturalisation proceedings. If proven correct, these findings suggest that inter-service exchange of information might well override efforts of individual officials to comply with legal and moral standards in counter-terrorism activities.

2. Legal assessment

In general there is no dissent on the legal principles regarding the use of torture and inhuman or degrading treatment. However, the consequences derived from these principles are extensive and open to dispute.

2.1 The foundations

To put it bluntly: torture is outlawed and criminalised. 'The torturer has become, like the pirate and the slave trader before him, *hostis humani generis*, an enemy of all mankind.'[30] The prohibition of the use of torture and other inhuman or degrading treatment is enshrined in many human rights treaties of international law[31], the most prominent being the UN Convention against Torture and other Cruel, Inhuman or Degrading Treatment or Punishment of 10 December 1984 (CAT).[32] In many national criminal laws, torture is explicitly formulated as an offence, in accordance with Article 4 CAT.[33] The Convention also goes beyond the traditional understanding of territorial and national jurisdiction and establishes – with the aim of avoiding safe havens for torturers – the principle of universal jurisdiction: all states are entitled and obliged to investigate and prosecute torture allegations, no matter if they have been committed on their territory or by one of their citizens or residents.[34] Article 14 of the UN Convention provides an enforceable right for the victims of torture to fair and adequate compensation.[35]

In addition, 'because of the importance of the values it protects this principle has evolved into a peremptory norm or *jus cogens*, that is, a norm that enjoys a higher rank in the international hierarchy than treaty law and even "ordinary" customary rules.'[36] This means that states cannot derogate from the prohibition of torture through international treaties or local custom.[37] In addition, the classification as *jus cogens* imposes direct obligations on individuals that transcend national obligations imposed by individual states. Even if a state were to authorise the use of torture, each individual official – although authorised and thus legitimised by his state – would nevertheless be bound to comply with the principle. This personal criminal liability is furthermore enhanced by the entitlement of every other state to prosecute and punish any torturer present in its jurisdiction, as stated above.[38]

Concerning the scope of obligations put on states by this principle, the International Criminal Tribunal for the Former Yugoslavia has ruled:

> States are obliged not only to prohibit and punish torture, but also to forestall its occurrence: it is insufficient merely to intervene after the infliction of torture, when the physical or moral integrity of human beings has already been irremediably harmed. Consequently, States are bound to put in place all those measures that may pre-empt the perpetration of torture. As was authoritatively held by the European Court of Human Rights in Soering, international law intends to bar not only actual breaches but also potential breaches of the prohibition against torture (as well as any inhuman and degrading treatment). It follows that international rules prohibit not only torture but also (i) the failure to adopt the national measures necessary for implementing the prohibition and (ii) the maintenance in force or passage of laws which are contrary to the prohibition.[39]

Due attention must furthermore be paid to the following legal bedrocks:

a) Article 1 of the UN Torture Convention asks for more than just abstention from the use of torture but also explicitly outlaws consent and acquiescence of a public official or other person acting in an official capacity.

b) Article 3 ECHR, prohibiting torture or any other inhuman or degrading treatment or punishment enshrines one of the most fundamental values of democratic society and requires states inter alia to take positive action to prevent individuals within their jurisdiction from falling subject to torture or inhuman or degrading treatment, according to the European Court of Human Rights (ECtHR).[40]

c) Finally, and most importantly: states cannot abandon their human rights obligations simply by acting outside their territorial jurisdiction. This has not only been held by the International Court of Justice (ICJ) and the ECtHR, but lately also reaffirmed in another important ruling by the UK House of Lords.[41]

With regard to the legal assessment of 'extraordinary renditions', the EU Network of Independent Experts on Fundamental Rights stated the following in its opinion no. 3-2006 of 25 May 2006:

> 'Extraordinary renditions' infringe on various national and international laws, like the Convention on International and Civil Aviation of 7 December 1944 (Chicago Convention) and other bilateral aviation agreements, the principle of sovereignty and domestic laws regulating the legality of activities of foreign agents on the host State's territory, and, most importantly, a number of human rights provisions, including the right to personal liberty, freedom of movement and the prohibition of arbitrary expulsion, the right to a fair trial and, finally, the right not to be subjected to torture or other forms of cruel, inhuman or degrading treatment or to be brought to a country where there are substantial grounds for believing that the personal risk to be tortured is high (principle of nonrefoulement).[42]

As a consequence of the fact that actions labelled 'extraordinary renditions' also amount to criminal offences, as do deprivation of liberty and battery[43], public prosecutors and judges in several EU member states, e.g. Italy and Germany, have issued arrest warrants against individuals suspected of having committed these offences.[44] Although prosecutors in Italy have faced considerable difficulties (e.g. being themselves accused of revealing state secrets), the first trial eventually opened in June 2007.[45] At the same time in the United States, the American Civil Liberties Union (ACLU) has filed a federal lawsuit against Jeppesen Dataplan, Inc., a subsidiary of Boeing Company, on behalf of three victims of the United States government's extraordinary rendition program. The civil suit is brought under the Alien Tort Claims Act that provides that US government agencies and corporations can be held responsible for human rights abuses against foreigners resulting from activities in a foreign country. ACLU claims that Jeppesen knowingly provided direct flight services to the CIA that enabled the secret transportation of the three victims to overseas detention centres where they were subjected to torture and other forms of cruel, inhuman and degrading treatment.[46]

2.2   The participation of agents in interrogations abroad

What follows from this for the assessment of the first variation of member states' profiting? The interrogation by agents of European intelligence or law enforcement services of an individual kept in unlawful detention or having been subject to extraordinary rendition appears not only to be highly hypocritical from a political point of view, given the fact that in June 2006 EU leaders urged President Bush to close the Guantánamo camp,[47] but – in view of the legal foundations outlined above – would also appear to be legally borderline, and most probably beyond what is legal.

A joint report by five UN Special Rapporteurs was submitted to the UN Human Rights Commission on the 'Situation of detainees at Guantánamo Bay' in February 2006. The report highlights severe violations of human rights obligations by the US administration, inter alia article 9 ICCPR[48] (prohibition of arbitrary detention) and article 14 (right to fair trial). The interrogation methods applied were said to amount to degrading treatment in violation of article 7 ICCPR and article 16 CAT.[49] The general conditions, and in particular the uncertainty about the length of detention and prolonged isolation confinement, were considered to represent inhuman treatment and to be in violation of the obligation to treat detainees with humanity and respect for the inherent dignity of the human person, article 10 ICCPR.[50] An analysis applying the obligations deriving from the ECHR would reach different conclusions, as highlighted by the Venice Commission's opinion on the international legal obligations of Council of Europe member states in respect of secret detention facilities and inter-state transport of prisoners. This opinion also supports the argument that prolonged unlawful detention as such – independent of the question of torture being applied – may constitute inhuman or degrading treatment – prohibited by article 3 ECHR – not to mention the violation of the right to a fair trial as enshrined in article 6 ECHR.[51] In July 2006 the Spanish Tribunal Supremo – Sala de lo Penal, the highest Spanish court in criminal matters, ruled that detention in Guantánamo Bay was unlawful and beyond justification.[52] In May 2006 the EU Network of Independent Experts on Fundamental Rights concluded that EU member states are under an obligation to prohibit the removal of persons under their jurisdiction to Guantánamo Bay or any other location where such persons risk being subject to torture or to forms of treatment which are considered cruel, inhuman or degrading under international law, and that member states are furthermore obliged to start criminal proceedings and investigate substantiated allegations of torture and unlawful detentions.[53] The findings of the Venice Commission in relation to Council of Europe member states have been no different in this regard.

In conclusion, member states' practice of taking advantage of extraordinary renditions and unlawful detention by sending their agents to these sites hardly seems legal or justifiable. If member states are under an obligation to protect their citizens and residents from such treatment and to start criminal investigations against the abductors, the only acceptable reasons for their officials to visit sites where individuals are unlawfully detained or subject to inhuman treatment must be to provide assistance to the detainees or to gather evidence against the persons responsible for the rendition or detention. The categorical misunderstanding that seems to cloud official discourse so far, however, is illustrated by the German government's report of 23 February 2006. While the government seeks to emphasise the legality of interrogations abroad by establishing that these will only take place with the free consent of the person interrogated and that no interrogation will commence or continue when there are signs that the person has been subject to torture, it – intentionally or not – ignores the fact that entanglement and complicity is still there, even if the person has not been subject to torture. Indeed the 'simple' fact of illegal rendition and detention is already a violation of human rights and a breach of law severe enough to prohibit member states from taking any advantage of it. Indeed, there is another dimension to this issue that may have been neglected so far: member states not only bear responsibility for their detained citizens or residents, but also for their agents. As argued above, one of the consequences of the *jus cogens* nature of torture prohibition is that every person who finds himself in breach of this principle will be held individually responsible and will not be allowed to justify himself by referring to higher orders or state legitimisation. Member state governments are thus constrained to be aware of the duty of care for their officials and not expose them to the risk of criminal charges by sending them to questionable sites.

2.3   The use of information obtained through torture

The second question that needs to be addressed relates to the use of 'foreign torture information' obtained by intelligence services or law enforcement agencies. As outlined above, the official discourse discerns two possible uses of such information: a) the use of foreign torture information as evidence in courts and b) the use of foreign torture information for executive purposes, e.g. intelligence activities, prevention of imminent dangers, etc.

In relation to the ECHR, the Court in Strasbourg has ruled that the use of evidence in criminal proceedings obtained through methods of coercion or oppression in defiance of the will of the accused has to be assessed by the right not to incriminate oneself; a right that is considered part of the fair trial provision of article 6 ECHR.[54] With regard to the UN Convention against Torture and other Cruel, Inhuman or Degrading Treatment or Punishment its article 15 stipulates:

> Each State Party shall ensure that any statement which is established to have been made as a result of torture shall not be invoked as evidence in any proceedings, except against a person accused of torture as evidence that the statement was made.

As was clearly demonstrated in the House of Lords judgment of December 2005,[55] the underlying rationale of this provision is that evidence under torture is most often proven to be unreliable and that investigators should therefore be discouraged from applying torture.[56] In addition, the admissibility of evidence obtained through torture would shock the judicial conscience, degrade the proceedings and involve the state in moral defilement.[57] Consequently, the House of Lords unanimously rejected the UK government's notion that only 'homemade' torture evidence would be barred from serving as evidence in courts. This judgment should be considered as a leading case and serve as persuasive authority for similar proceedings in other member states' courts. However, as mentioned earlier, the Lords did not have to rule on the question of foreign torture information being admissible for usages outside the court room. They nevertheless addressed the issue and took a rather different approach. Lord Nicholls of Birkenhead's opinion serves as an illustration of this:

67. Torture attracts universal condemnation, as amply demonstrated by my noble and learned friend Lord Bingham of Cornhill. No civilised society condones its use. Unhappily, condemnatory words are not always matched by conduct. Information derived from sources where torture is still practised gives rise to the present problem. The context is cross-border terrorism. Countering international terrorism calls for a flow of information between the security services of many countries. Fragments of information, acquired from various sources, can be pieced together to form a valuable picture, enabling governments of threatened countries to take preventive steps. What should the security services and the police and other executive agencies of this country do if they know or suspect information received by them from overseas is the product of torture? Should they discard this information as 'tainted', and decline to use it lest its use by them be regarded as condoning the horrific means by which the information was obtained?

68. The intuitive response to these questions is that if use of such information might save lives it would be absurd to reject it. If the police were to learn of the whereabouts of a ticking bomb it would be ludicrous for them to disregard this information if it had been procured by torture. No one suggests the police should act in this way. Similarly, if tainted information points a finger of suspicion at a particular individual: depending on the circumstances, this information is a matter the police may properly take into account when considering, for example, whether to make an arrest.

69. In both these instances the executive arm of the state is open to the charge that it is condoning the use of torture. So, in a sense, it is. The government is using information obtained by torture. But in cases such as these the government cannot be expected to close its eyes to this information at the price of endangering the lives of its own citizens. Moral repugnance to torture does not require this.[58]

Lord Nicholls' statement that it would be 'absurd' and 'ludicrous' to reject torture information that might help prevent imminent danger to the lives of citizens is representative of this discussion so far. Likewise, the German government stated that the principles of rule of law do not prevent the government from accepting interrogation-output from foreign services. Although it concedes that there is no guarantee that this information might not have been gained by unlawful means, the government held that in order to protect public security it is obliged to pursue any hints that might help to prevent imminent acts of violence.[59] In an interview with a German newspaper, the federal minister of the interior, Wolfgang Schäuble was cited: 'If we were to say that under no circumstances would we use information where we cannot be certain it was obtained under completely constitutional conditions that would be totally irresponsible. We must use such information.'[60] He repeated this assessment during the Transatlantic Forum of the German Marshall Fund and the Bertelsmann Foundation in 2007 in Brussels.[61] Similarly, in 2004 the UK Home Secretary David Blunkett commented on the favourable decision of the Court of Appeal.[62]

The fact that even those Law Lords who so vigorously rejected the government's attempt to rewrite the history of torture prohibition have been willing to accept that in certain circumstances foreign torture information may be used by executive agencies, cannot be easily dismissed.[63] On the other hand there can be no doubt that such use of torture information undermines the absolute prohibition of torture and also runs counter to one of the underlying reasons of article 15 CAT: the discouragement of security professionals from resorting to torture or inhuman or degrading treatment. In addition, there remains a question mark over why the other reasons underlying the exclusion of torture evidence in court proceedings shall not pertain to executive decisions. Is there no 'degrading of proceedings'? No 'state involvement in moral defilement'? The Australian scholar Ben Saul has put it like this: 'there is a certain moral hypocrisy about the House of Lords judgment which finds that torture evidence can never be allowed to contaminate the purity of judicial process, while holding that governments have a duty to get their hands dirty precisely this way.'[64]

This dilemma has also been addressed in an inquiry into the UN Convention against torture, conducted by the House of Lords and House of Commons Joint Committee on Human Rights. The approach taken by the members of the Committee acknowledges the underlying difficulties but refuses to give a 'carte blanche' to the executive; this seems a good basis for further discussions and needs citing in more detail:

55. We accept that UNCAT and other provisions of human rights law do not prohibit the use of information from foreign intelligence sources, which may have been obtained under torture, to avert imminent loss of life by searches, arrests or other similar measures. We cannot accept the absolutist position on this subject advanced by some NGOs when human life, possibly many hundreds of lives, may be at stake. (...) However great care must be taken to ensure that use of such information is only made in cases of imminent threat to life. Care must also be taken to ensure that the use of information in this way, and in particular any repeated or regular use of such information, especially from the same source or sources, does not render the UK authorities complicit in torture by lending tacit support or agreement to the use of torture or inhuman treatment as a means of obtaining information which might be useful to the UK in preventing terrorist attacks. Ways need to be found to reduce and, we would hope, eliminate dependence on such information. (...).

56. In our view, the fundamental importance of the obligations on the UK concerning torture makes it incumbent on the intelligence services to move beyond the essentially passive stance towards the methods and techniques of foreign intelligence agencies (...). In Canada, the Canadian Security and Intelligence Service ('CSIS') is under a statutory obligation to notify the Government of any arrangements for sharing information with any foreign intelligence agencies. Those liaison arrangements are also subjected to independent scrutiny by the Canadian Security and Intelligence Review Committee, a statutory body external to the intelligence agencies and at arms length from the Government. We do not necessarily suggest this as a model, but we do draw attention to the greater degree of formality in the making of arrangements between domestic and foreign intelligence services and to the fact that such arrangements are subjected to independent scrutiny. **In our view, the need to use information which has or may have been obtained by torture could be significantly reduced if the UK intelligence services took a more proactive approach when establishing the framework arrangements for intelligence sharing with other intelligence agencies, by making clear the minimum stan-**

dards which it expects to be observed and monitoring for compliance with those standards, and if there were some opportunity for independent scrutiny of those arrangements.[65] [emphasis in the original].

Several aspects of this statement are important:

1) As a rule, the use of foreign torture information is inadmissible. Only in exceptional circumstances, i.e. to avert imminent threats to life, might it be acceptable.
2) Security services must under all circumstances avoid making themselves complicit in torture, let alone become directly involved. They are barred from granting tacit support or agreement to the use of torture or inhuman or degrading treatment.
3) Security services are not allowed to be passive consumers of foreign torture information but are under an obligation to reduce the need to use such information and must establish minimum standards for the exchange of information with foreign services.
4) A certain degree of formality in the making of liaison arrangements with foreign services and the independent scrutiny of these arrangements are both deemed crucial.

3.   Implications of and for EU counter-terrorism policies and actions

What is the European Union's part in all this? So far it appears as if the EU has found itself – justifiably or not – quite well-positioned in investigations surrounding CIA flights, detention centres on European territory and the complicity of European security agencies. Public outrage and the sincere concern of civil society and the media has so far focused mainly on the member states and essentially spared the EU level. The recent resolution on CIA activities in Europe by one of its ever more important institutions, the European Parliament, has hugely contributed to this position and has largely helped to keep the EU out of the line of fire.[66]

In addition, EU counter-terrorism activities, including one of its early measures after 9/11: the framework decision on the European arrest warrant,[67] but also Europol,[68] Eurojust[69] and other mechanisms, networks and bodies established under the EU's second and third pillar,[70] could even help to bring to trial the suspects allegedly involved in extraordinary renditions, such as the CIA agents sought by Italy and Germany. That EU counter-terrorism measures might serve as a useful tool in the investigation and prosecution of other counter-terrorism activities, only at first sight appears to be a contradiction undermining the 'global war on terror'. On closer inspection, however, such measures are not only consequential but crucial, given that countering terrorism by illegal means, such as extraordinary renditions and secret detention (measures that undermine rule of law and respect for fundamental rights) eventually serve the terrorist's cause, i.e. the destruction of the liberal and democratic state, the overturning of its basic legal principles and guiding moral values.[71] A token that brings us back to the beginning of this chapter and to Dick Marty's statement; an insight that proves Commissioner Frattini right to anchor all counter-terrorism efforts tightly to the rule of law and the preservation of fundamental rights as we know them, rejecting calls by others[72] to rewrite human rights and to 'modernise the law'.

In spite of these beneficial elements of EU action, policy-makers and institutional actors at EU level run the risk that the entanglement of member states' intelligence services or law enforcement agencies might easily rebound on their efforts under the 'European Union counter-terrorism strategy'.[73] One of the inherent risks for the EU in illegal activities by member states exists on a practical level, namely profiting from unlawful renditions and detentions: the use of foreign torture information. Yet, there can be no question that the *jus cogens* obligations in relation to the prohibition of torture – including personal criminal responsibility – as outlined above – bind both institutional and individual actors at EU level. Further, that the EU as such is not a signatory to any of the international human rights treaties does not exempt the Union from the requirement to respect fundamental rights based on the rule of law, as per article 6 of the Treaty on European Union (TEU).[74] Furthermore, the EU and its member states constantly repeat their commitment to the protection of human rights and the rule of law, most recently in the so called 'Berlin Declaration' of 25 March 2007.[75]

At the heart of the EU counter-terrorism strategy stands the strengthening of information exchange and the enhancement of cooperation among all relevant security services, including intelligence, law enforcement and judicial authorities.[76] The EU's own security actors, namely (but not exclusively) Europol and its Counter-Terrorism Taskforce, Eurojust, the external border agency Frontex[77] as well as the EU Joint Situation Centre within the Council Secretariat (Sitcen)[78] rely on information provided by member states in order to perform their intelligence-driven tasks.[79] In addition, the EU financial sanctions system directed against certain persons and entities with a view to combating terrorism,[80] commonly known as 'terror lists'[81] also depend on member states' information (or names provided by the UN Security Council[82]); information that is then transformed into EU acts. But who guarantees that information thus processed is not the fruit of torture abroad? As far as can be seen there is no mechanism in force at EU level that would allow a control over the information provided and subsequently processed by member states to establish whether it is tainted by torture or other inhuman or degrading treatment. Moreover, it seems as if awareness of the problem is lacking in the first place.[83]

A recent landmark decision by the Court of First Instance (CFI) in Luxembourg dealing with the Council's 'terror lists' illustrates this lack of control over the exchange and use of information: requested by the Court to give a coherent answer on the question of which national decision was the basis for the placing of an alleged terror group on the 'terror list', neither the Council nor the UK government involved were able to provide this answer and identify the underlying national measure.[84] Attention must furthermore be given to the fact that the European Area of Freedom, Security and Justice (AFSJ) aims at the free availability of relevant security information.[85] Until now, however, there has been no common framework in place that would regulate the conditions determining how such information enters the AFSJ. As a result, even if some member states and their services should strive to come closer to the spirit and intention of the UN Torture Convention and human right obligations by establishing clear agreements of cooperation and intelligence sharing with foreign services (centred on the refusal to collaborate in or take advantage of torture or other unlawful treatment),[86] these efforts would eventually be undermined by the fact that other member states might cooperate less carefully with foreign services. Tainted information would therefore nevertheless make its way to the AFSJ and hence be shared and processed; this is a scenario that resembles the German Khafagy case as illustrated earlier.

Finally, in the vast majority of cases, information processed at EU level does not serve to avoid '*imminent* threats to life' but rather mid – and long-term objectives, like the freezing of financial means or – as in the case of Europol, Frontex and Sitcen – the creation of risk or crime analysis and strategic reports, e.g. threat assessments.[87] Relevant questions touch on whether the argument at national level to justify the use of foreign torture information, i.e. a state's duty to prevent imminent threat to life, is applicable at EU level, and which consequences need to be drawn from the answer to this question. This is a question which requires urgent address, not only for the simple reason of respecting international obligations and human rights law, but also in order to avoid (very likely) court proceedings. With regard to the 'terror lists' and the obscure manner in which these lists are drawn up[88], the Council – after some years of a period of grace – has eventually come under well-pronounced criticism by the European Courts in Luxembourg. In the decision of 12 December 2006, the Court of First Instance ruled that in relation to one listed group the Council act had infringed the right to a fair hearing, the obligation to state reasons and the right to effective judicial protection.[89] Contrary to the Court's ruling, however, the Council has only reluctantly and half-heartedly begun a process of altering its 'terror list' procedures.[90] In another most important decision of 27 February 2007, the Court of Justice of the European Communities (ECJ), in a complicated procedural context, opened up the possibility for national courts to ask the ECJ for a preliminary ruling in matters referring to third pillar fields of police and judicial cooperation in criminal matters, including 'terror list' issues.[91]

These developments highlight the fact that there is growing concern about the EU's counter-terrorism activities as currently discussed by the Council of Ministers; concern not only among European and national parliamentarians, but also among European judges. An irresponsible and careless use of foreign torture information will only serve to nurture this justified concern.

Conclusions and policy recommendations at EU level

Recent investigations and inquiries on various levels have shed light on the illegal practice of extraordinary renditions and unlawful detention by foreign services on European territory. However, the fact has also been revealed that many European states and their security agencies cannot easily wash their hands of these incidents. Many indications suggest that the line between cooperation and complicity is only too often blurred. Apart from direct participation in extraordinary renditions or a reproachable 'aversion of the eyes' to the facts, some member states have made indirect use of situations and 'possibilities' created by extraordinary renditions and unlawful detentions. This use essentially manifested itself in two variations: 1) interrogations carried out by member states' agents in Guantánamo and other sites and 2) exchange and use of foreign torture information.

This chapter has argued that for various reasons member states should refrain from sending their agents to places where persons are unlawfully detained or made subject to extraordinary renditions, provided these interrogations do not serve to offer assistance to the detainees or aim to gather evidence against the abductors. On the use of foreign torture information, this chapter concurs with the House of Lords judgment that such information may under no circumstances serve as admissible evidence in court. Yet, it differs from the judgment in so far as it poses a question mark over the Law Lords' *obiter dicta* (and other official statements) that foreign torture information may be used without restrictions by governments and their services for executive activities.

The implications of and for EU counter-terrorism activities were reviewed in the second part of this chapter. It was contended that while European institutions, namely the EP and recently the Court in Luxembourg, play a creditable role in trying to keep the EU on a lawful and legitimate track, there is no reason to relax these efforts. The EU's counter-terrorism activities centre on the exchange and processing of information. Since *jus cogens* obligations in the context of torture prohibition, fundamental rights and the rule of law do bind EU institutional and individual actors, measures must be discussed and instigated to guarantee that the EU does not become entangled in unlawful behaviour by using and processing foreign torture information provided by member states' security services.

Building on these findings the following policy recommendations seem relevant:

1. EU governments and their national authorities should work together and make all possible use of the existing EU counter-terrorism tools and cross-border cooperation mechanisms to support the ongoing investigations or trials in some member states against those suspected of being involved in extraordinary renditions.

2. EU governments within the Council should address the issue of European involvement in the interrogation of detainees who have been abducted and/or unlawfully detained. A code of conduct outlawing such interrogations should be drawn up. Visits of officials should only offer assistance to the detainees or to gather evidence against the abductors.

3. In the context of the follow-up discussions on the European Parliament resolution of 14 February 2007 concerning CIA activities on European territory[92], the most likely eventuality – that foreign torture information was exchanged, stored and processed on EU level and that such information might serve as a basis for the adoption of EU acts and executive decisions – must be addressed.

4. A second round of peer-evaluation of national arrangements in the fight against terrorism[93] should be instigated. This second round should not, however, as did the first, focus on the objective of making information exchange between law enforcement agencies within the EU more effective, but address instead the existing arrangements with non-EU intelligence and law enforcement services and the

question of how these arrangements provide for compliance with international law, human rights obligations and the rule of law.[94]

5. The aim of this peer-evaluation should be the adoption of a common, EU-wide accord on the conditions of cooperation and intelligence sharing with foreign services, centring on the refusal to collaborate in or take advantage of torture or other unlawful treatment. As far as general principles of this common accord are concerned (rather than operational modes), the European Parliament must be involved in the debates.[95]

6. In addition, a mechanism should be established to monitor the compliance with this common accord. This mechanism could take the form of a 'yellow card, red card' system: the transmission of tainted information in breach of the common accord will be followed by a warning ('yellow card') and in case of a repeated offence eventually by exclusion ('red card') of the information sharing network.[96]

7. Democratic oversight and accountability of security services' activities must be ensured.[97] As both the national and EU level are concerned, a proposal that has already been made for the scrutiny of Europol's work, appears to be the appropriate solution in this context: a joint committee composed of representatives from national parliaments or other bodies that control national intelligence services and the European Parliament.[98] In addition, the European Data Protection Supervisor could assist the work of the Committee and provide his opinion.[99]

8. Regarding the EU financial sanction system, based on the so-called terror lists, the Council should enhance its efforts to revise and alter the procedures in order to comply with the judgment of the Court of First Instance.[100] Revision should include that in future every national decision to place an individual or group on the list must be traceable. In addition, there should be an obligation to disclose – at least within the Council – the source that has provided the information upon which the suspicion against the individual or the entity is based.

Endnotes

1   This chapter is the updated and amended version of an earlier paper, published under the title *Fruit of the Poisonous Tree – Member States' indirect use of extraordinary rendition and the EU Counter-Terrorism Strategy* as CEPS Working Document No. 263/April 2007 by the Centre for European Policy Studies in Brussels. It falls within the scope of the CHALLENGE project – *the Changing Landscape of European Liberty and Security*, funded by the Sixth EU Framework Programme of DG Research, European Commission, see www.libertysecurity.org. The author would like to thank Elspeth Guild, Daniel Gros, Peter Hobbing and Sergio Carrera for their valuable comments.
2   F. Frattini in the preface to this volume.
3   Dick Marty, Committee on Legal Affairs and Human Rights, Council of Europe Parliamentary Assembly, *Secret detentions and illegal transfers of detainees involving Council of Europe member states: second report*, Doc. AS/Jur (2007) 36, 7.6.2007; Dick Marty, Committee on Legal Affairs and Human Rights, Council of Europe Parliamentary Assembly, *Alleged secret detentions and unlawful inter-state transfers of detainees involving CoE member States*, Doc. 10957, 12.06.2006; cf. also 'CIA rejects secret jail report', BBC News, 8.6.2007, retrieved 11.6.2007 from www.news.bbc.co.uk.

4   European Parliament, *Resolution on the alleged use of European countries by the CIA for the transportation and illegal detention of prisoners* (2006/2200(INI)), P6_TA-PROV(2007)0032, 14.2.2007; see also EP Temporary Committee on the alleged use of European countries by the CIA for the transport and illegal detention of prisoners, *Working document* No. 9, 26.2.2007.
5   Cf. also, Valery Grebennikov, Committee on Legal Affairs and Human Rights, Council of Europe Parliamentary Assembly, *Respect for human rights in the fight against terrorism*, Doc. AS/Jur (2006) 29, 12.12.2006.
6   UN Commission of Human Rights, *Protection of human rights and fundamental freedoms while countering terrorism*, Human Rights Resolution 2005/80, 21.4.2005; the office is currently held by Prof. Martin Scheinin, Finland.
7   Dick Marty, Committee on Legal Affairs and Human Rights, Council of Europe Parliamentary Assembly, *Secret detentions and illegal transfers of detainees involving Council of Europe member states: second report*, Doc. AS/Jur (2007) 36, 7.6.2007, para. 15.
8   For a perspective from beyond European borders see the case of Maher Arar and the entanglement of Canadian authorities, Commission of Inquiry into the actions of Canadian officials in relation to Maher Arar, *Report of the events relating to Maher Arar – analysis and recommendations*, 2006, retrieved 30.3.2007 from www.ararcommission.ca; see also Government of Canada, Office of the *Prime Minister, Prime Minster releases letter of apology to Maher Arar and his family and announces completion of mediation process*, 26.1.2007, retrieved 30.3.2007 from http://news.gc.ca.
9   Cf. also E.U. Network of Independent Experts on Fundamental Rights (CFR-CDF), *Opinion no 3-2006: The human rights responsibilities of the EU member states in the context of the C.I.A. activities in Europe ('extraordinary renditions')*, 25.5.2006, p. 6.
10 Cf. European Commission for Democracy through Law (Venice Commission), *Opinion no 363/2005 on the international legal obligations of Council of Europe member states in respect of secret detention facilities and inter-state transport of prisoners*, adopted by the Venice Commission at its 66th plenary session (Venice, 17-18 March 2006), CDL-AD(2006)009, 17.3.2006, para. 121.
11 Cf. Art. 2 International Convention for the protection of all persons from enforced disappearances as adopted by the UN General Assembly on 20 December 2006.
12 See for this term: D. Bigo, 'Globalized (in)security: the Field and the Ban-opticon', in D. Bigo & A. Tsoukala (eds), *Illiberal Practices of Liberal Regimes: the (In)Security Games*, L'Harmattan: Paris, 2006, pp. 5-49.
13 European Parliament, *Resolution on the alleged use of European countries by the CIA for the transportation and illegal detention of prisoners* (2006/2200(INI)), P6_TA-PROV(2007)0032, 14.2.2007, para. 76, 77.
14 European Parliament, *Resolution on the alleged use of European countries by the CIA for the transportation and illegal detention of prisoners* (2006/2200(INI)), P6_TA-PROV(2007)0032, 14.2.2007, para. 87, 93.
15 European Parliament, *Resolution on the alleged use of European countries by the CIA for the transportation and illegal detention of prisoners* (2006/2200(INI)), P6_TA-PROV(2007)0032, 14.2.2007, para. 135.
16 Cf. 'French agents questioned detainees in Guantanamo', *The Independent*, 6.7.2006, retrieved 27.3.2007 from www.independent.co.uk.
17 Cf. House of Lords/House of Commons, Joint Committee on Human Rights, *The UN Convention against Torture* (UNCAT), Nineteenth report of session 2005-06, Volume I – Report and formal minutes, 18 May 2006, p. 22, relying on a court statement by the Director General of the Security Services, Dame Eliza Manningham-Buller.
18 For the UK see also House of Lords/House of Commons, Joint Committee on Human Rights, *The UN Convention against Torture* (UNCAT), Nineteenth report of session 2005-06, Volume I – Report and formal minutes, 18 May 2006, para. 57.
19 Bericht der Bundesregierung (Offene Fassung) gemäß Anforderung des Parlamentarischen Kontrollgremiums vom 25. Januar 2006 zu *Vorgängen im Zusammenhang mit dem Irakkrieg und der Bekämpfung des Internationalen Terrorismus*, Berlin, 23.2.2006, pp. 82-87, retrieved 24.11.2006 from http://www.bundestag.de. On the debate in Germany see also W. Hetzer, *Verschleppung und Folter: Staatsraison oder Regierungskriminalität?*, Rechtspolitisches Forum Nr. 34, Institut für Rechtspolitik: Trier, 2006, 36 pp.
20 Deutscher Bundestag, Parlamentarisches Kontrollgremium, *Bewertung des Parlamentarischen Kontrollgremiums (PKGr) zum Bericht der Bundesregierung zu den Vorgängen im Zusammenhang mit dem Irak-Krieg und der Bekämpfung des internationalen Terrorismus*, 22.2.2006, pp. 35-39, retrieved 24.11.2006 from http://www.bundestag.de.
21 Cf. Abweichende Bewertung des Abg. Dr. Max Stadler (FDP), 22. Februar 2006, retrieved

24.11.2006 from under http://www.bundestag.de ; Abweichende Bewertung des Abg. Wolfgang Neskovic (Die Linke), no date, retrieved 24.11.2006 from http://www.bundestag.de, Abweichende Bewertung des Mitglieds des Parlamentarischen Kontrollgremiums Hans-Christian Ströbele (Bündnis 90/Die Grünen), 23.2.2006, retrieved 24.11.2006 from http://www.bundestag.de.

22 Bericht der Bundesregierung (Offene Fassung) gemäß Anforderung des Parlamentarischen Kontrollgremiums vom 25. Januar 2006 zu *Vorgängen im Zusammenhang mit dem Irakkrieg und der Bekämpfung des Internationalen Terrorismus*, Berlin, 23.2.2006, p. 80 (translation by the author).

23 See European Parliament, *Resolution on the alleged use of European countries by the CIA for the transportation and illegal detention of prisoners* (2006/2200(INI)), P6_TA-PROV(2007)0032, 14.2.2007, para. 79.

24 England and Wales Court of Appeal (Civil Division), 1123. judgment of 11.8.2004.

25 House of Lords, Opinions of the Lords of Appeal for judgment in the cause A (FC) and others (FC) v. Secretary of State for the Home Department, [2005] UKHL 71, 8.12.2005, para. 51.

26 House of Lords, Opinions of the Lords of Appeal for judgment in the cause A (FC) and others (FC) v. Secretary of State for the Home Department, [2005] UKHL 71, 8.12.2005, para. 59.

27 Report of the Special Rapporteur on torture and other cruel, inhuman or degrading treatment or punishment, United Nations General Assembly Doc. A/61/259, 14.8.2006, p. 17.

28 'Behörden nutzten Informationen von Misshandelten', *tagesschau.de*, 24.11.2006, retrieved 24.11.2006 from www.tagesschau.de; 'Unbequeme Fragen im Untersuchungsausschuss', *Süddeutsche Zeitung*, 25./26.11.2006, p. 7.

29 'In der Rolle eines lästigen Bittstellers', *Süddeutsche Zeitung*, 1.3.2007, p. 6 (translation by the author).

30 US Court of Appeals for the Second Circuit, 30.6.1980, Filartiga v. Peña-Irala, 630 F.2d 876.

31 Cf. Article 7 International Covenant on Civil and Political Rights (ICCPR); Article 5 Universal Declaration of Human Rights (non-binding, but persuasive authority); Article 3 Convention for the Protection of Human Rights and Fundamental Freedoms (ECHR); Article 4 Charter of Fundamental Rights of the European Union (non binding, but persuasive authority).

32 UN Treaty Series, Vol. 1465, p. 85. The Convention entered into force on 26.6.1987 and has currently (June 2007) 144 parties.

33 See for a detailed survey on EU member states compliance with article 4 CAT: EU Network of Independent Experts on Fundamental Rights (CFR-CDF), *Opinion no 3-2006: The human rights responsibilities of the EU member states in the context of the C.I.A. activities in Europe ('extraordinary renditions')*, 25.5.2006, pp. 18-20.

34 On the reluctance of making use of this principle see, United Nations Special Rapporteur on torture and other cruel, inhuman or degrading treatment or punishment, Manfred Nowak, Report, United Nations General Assembly Doc. A/HRC/4/33, 15.1.2007, pp. 11-15.

35 United Nations Special Rapporteur on torture and other cruel, inhuman or degrading treatment or punishment, Manfred Nowak, Report, United Nations General Assembly Doc. A/HRC/4/33, 15.1.2007, pp. 20-21; see also 'Torturers 'must pay victims' – UN', BBC News, 27.3.2007, retrieved 28.3.2007 from www.news.bbc.co.uk.

36 International Criminal Tribunal for the Former Yugoslavia, Prosecutor v. Anto Furundzija [1998] ICTY 3, 10 December 1998, para. 153.

37 Cf. also Council of Europe, *Guidelines on human rights and the fight against terrorism*, adopted by the Committee of Ministers on 11 July 2002 at the 804th meeting of the Ministers' Deputies, p. 12.

38 Cf. International Criminal Tribunal for the Former Yugoslavia, Prosecutor v. Anto Furundzija [1998] ICTY 3, 10.12.1998, para. 155, 156.

39 International Criminal Tribunal for the Former Yugoslavia, Prosecutor v. Anto Furundzija [1998] ICTY 3, 10.12.1998, para. 148.

40 ECtHR, Z. and others v. U.K., application no. 29392/05, 10.5.2001, para. 69-75.

41 International Court of Justice (ICJ), Advisory opinion on legal consequences of the construction of a wall in the occupied Palestinian territory, 9.7.2004, para. 109; ECtHR, Öcalan v. Turkey, application no. 46221/99, 12.5.2005, para. 91; ECtHR, Issa and others v. Turkey, application no. 31821/96, 16.11.2004, para. 66-71; ECtHR, Ilascu and others v. Moldova and Russia, application no. 48787/99, 8.7.2004, para. 310-319; House of Lords, Opinions of the Lords of Appeal for judgment in the cause Al-Skeini and others v. Secretary of State for Defence, [2007] UKHL 26, 13.6.2007; see also E. Guild, *Security and European Human Rights: protecting individual rights in times of exception and military action*, Wolf Legal Publishers: Nijmegen, 2007, pp. 17-21.

42 EU Network of Independent Experts on Fundamental Rights (CFR-CDF), *Opinion no 3-2006: The human rights responsibilities of the EU member states in the context of the C.I.A. activities in*

Europe ('extraordinary renditions'), 25.5.2006, p. 25; Cf. also Committee on International Human Rights of the Association of the Bar of the City of New York and the Center for Human Rights and Global Justice, New York University School of Law, Torture by Proxy: international and domestic law applicable to 'extraordinary renditions', 2004, modified June 2006.

43 For some scholars even war crimes, see 'Post-9/11 renditions: An extra-ordinary violation of international law', *International Consortium of Investigative Journalists*, 22.5.2007, retrieved 5.6.2007 from www.publicintegrity.org.

44 Cf. Pressemitteilung der Staatsanwaltschaft München I in Sachen El Masri, 31.1.2007, retrieved 22.3.2007 from http://www4.justiz.bayern.de; 'The CIA in the dock', *Spiegel online*, 10.1.2007 retrieved 22.3.2007 from http://www.spiegel.de.

45 'Italy prosecutes CIA agents in kidnapping', *International Herald Tribune*, 9.6.2007, retrieved 11.6.2007 from www.iht.com; 'First CIA rendition trial opens', BBC News, 8.6.2007, retrieved 11.6.2007 from www.news.bbc.co.uk.

46 'Boeing unit to face suit in CIA seizures', *International Herald Tribune*, 29.5.2007, retrieved 30.5.2007 from www.iht.com; 'ACLU suit alleges firm is profiting from torture', Los Angeles Times, 31.5.2007, retrieved, 31.5.2007 from www.latimes.com.

47 'EU to press for Guantánamo closure', *Financial Times*, 12.6.2006, retrieved 12.3.2007 from www.ft.com; 'Guantanamo clouds EU-US meeting', BBC News, 21.6.2006, retrieved 12.3.2007 from http://news.bbc.co.uk. Cf. also: 'The right to a fair trial is another basic human right. With respect to secret or incommunicado detention centres, the EU's position is clear. As Javier Solana has said, any such centres, in Europe or elsewhere, would violate international human rights and humanitarian law', G. de Vries, *The fight against terrorism – five years after 9/11*, Presentation by Gijs de Vries, EU Counter-Terrorism Coordinator, Annual European Foreign Policy Conference, London School of Economics & King's College London, 30.6.2006, p. 8 retrieved 24.3.2007 from http://consilium.europa.eu.

48 See footnote 27.

49 For documentation on the so called 'torture memos' of the US administration, see K.J. Greenberg & J.L. Dratel, *The Torture Papers – the Road to Abu Ghraib*, Cambridge University Press: Cambridge, 2005.

50 UN Economic and Social Council, Commission on Human Rights, *Situation of detainees at Guantánamo Bay*, UN Doc. E/CN.4/2006/120, 15.2.2006, pp. 36-40.

51 European Commission for Democracy through Law (Venice Commission), *Opinion no 363/2005 on the international legal obligations of Council of Europe member states in respect of secret detention facilities and inter-state transport of prisoners*, adopted by the Venice Commission at its 66th plenary session (Venice, 17-18 March 2006), CDL-AD(2006)009, 17.3.2006, para. 121.

52 Tribunal Supremo, Sala de lo Penal, Sentencia No. 829/2006, 20.7.2006; see also 'Sentence of the Spanish Supreme Court about a Muslim Spanish Citizen', CHALLENGE Observatory, 26.7.2006, retrieved 24.5.2007 from www.libertysecurity.org.

53 EU Network of Independent Experts on Fundamental Rights (CFR-CDF), *Opinion no 3-2006: The human rights responsibilities of the EU member states in the context of the C.I.A. activities in Europe ('extraordinary renditions')*, 25 May 2006, p. 28.

54 ECtHR, Saunders v. UK, application no. 43/1994/490/572, 17 December 1996, para. 68, 69; ECtHR, Funke v. France, application no. 10828/84, 25 February 1993, para. 44.

55 Cf. e.g. T. Thienel, 'The admissibility of evidence obtained by torture under international law', *European Journal of International Law*, vol. 17 no. 2, 2006, pp. 349-367; N. Rasiah, 'A v Secretary of State for the Home Department (No 2): Occupying the moral high ground?', Modern Law Review, Vol. 69, No. 6, 2006, pp. 995-1005.

56 Cf. J.H. Burgers & H. Danelius, *The United Nations Convention against Torture: Handbook on the Convention against Torture*, Dordrecht et al: Martinus Nijhoff Publishers, 1988, p. 148; see also T. Bruha & C. J. Tams, 'Folter und Völkerrecht', *Aus Politik und Zeitgeschichte*, no. 36, September 2006, pp. 16-22; Report of the Special Rapporteur on torture and other cruel, inhuman or degrading treatment or punishment, United Nations General Assembly Doc. A/61/259, 14.8.2006, p. 10.

57 House of Lords, Opinions of the Lords of Appeal for judgment in the cause A (FC) and others (FC) v. Secretary of State for the Home Department, [2005] UKHL 71, 8.12.2005, para. 39.

58 House of Lords, Opinions of the Lords of Appeal for judgment in the cause A (FC) and others (FC) v. Secretary of State for the Home Department, [2005] UKHL 71, 8.12.2005, para. 67-69.

59 Bericht der Bundesregierung (Offene Fassung) gemäß Anforderung des Parlamentarischen Kontrollgremiums vom 25. Januar 2006 zu *Vorgängen im Zusammenhang mit dem Irakkrieg und*

der Bekämpfung des Internationalen Terrorismus, Berlin, 23.2.2006, pp. 80, retrieved 24.11.2006 from http://www.bundestag.de.

60 Cited after EP Temporary Committee on the alleged use of European countries by the CIA for the transport and illegal detention of prisoners, Working document No. 9, 26.2.2007, p. 16 (translation by the author).

61 'Schäuble will erfolterte Informationen für Terrorabwehr nutzen', ORF, 30.4.2007, retrieved 30.4.2007 from www.orf.at.

62 Cf. Human Rights Watch, *Dangerous Ambivalence: UK Policy on Torture since 9/11*, November 2006, p.14; on the U.K.'s counter-terrorism policy in general see also R. Parkes & A. Maurer, *Britische Anti-Terror-Politik und die Internationalisierung der inneren Sicherheit- Zur Balance zwischen Freiheit, Sicherheit und Demokratie*, SWP Studie S 3, Berlin, January 2007.

63 On the difficulties of the debate in general see e.g. M. Ignatieff, 'If torture works...', Prospect, issue 121, April 2006, retrieved 24.3.2007 from http://www.prospect-magazine.co.uk/ vis_index.php?select_issue=519; yet the debate is nothing new as recalled not least by W. Hetzer, *Verschleppung und Folter: Staatsraison oder Regierungskriminalität?*, Rechtspolitisches Forum Nr. 34, Institut für Rechtspolitik: Trier, 2006, p. 32, when he states: 'The question of emergency-torture has been discussed since the 18th century when Jeremy Bentham supported and Immanuel Kant opposed it' (translation by the author).

64 B. Saul, *'The Torture Debate: International Law and the Age of Terrorism'*, Australian Red Cross: NSW International Humanitarian Law Program Lecture Series, NSW Law Week, 28.3.2006, p. 10, retrieved 12.3.2007 from http://www.gtcentre.unsw.edu.au/publications/ docs/pubs/tortureSpeech_Mar06.pdf.

65 House of Lords/House of Commons, Joint Committee on Human Rights, *The UN Convention against Torture (UNCAT)*, Nineteenth report of session 2005-06, Volume I – Report and formal minutes, 18 May 2006, pp. 20-21.

66 Although the way political and national considerations of some MEPs threatened to water down the Temporary Committee's effort at the last minute was a rather disillusioning and startling incident, in view of the gravity of the issues at stake, cf. D. Oosting, 'Responsibility vanishes like CIA flights', *European Voice*, 8-14 February 2007, p. 9.

67 Council framework decision of 13 June 2002 on the European arrest warrant and the surrender procedures between Member States, OJ L 190, 18.7.2002, pp. 1-18; in May 2007, the European Court of Justice issued the long awaited judgment on the European Arrest warrant, cf. ECJ, C-303/05 (Advocaten voor de Wereld VZW), 3.5.2007.

68 Convention based on Article K.3 of the Treaty on European Union, on the establishment of a European Police Office, OJ C 316, 27.11.1995, pp.2-32; See also Proposal for a Council decision establishing the European Police Office (Europol), presented by the Commission, COM(2006) 817 final of 20.12.2006.

69 Council decision of 28 February 2002 setting up Eurojust with a view to reinforcing the fight against serious crime (2002/187/JHA), OJ L 36 of 6.3.2002, pp.1-13.

70 For overview and analysis see the dossier 'Mapping the field of European Security' on the website of the CHALLENGE project, http://www.libertysecurity.org/mot96. html?var_recherche=mapping; see also H. Nilsson, 'Judicial cooperation in Europe against terrorism', chapter 3 of this volume.

71 On the requirements of an EU counter-terrorism strategy that is centered on the dimensions of freedom and justice, see T. Balzacq & S. Carrera, *The EU's fight against international terrorism – security problems, insecure solutions*, CEPS Policy Brief No. 80, July 2005; cf. also T. Balzacq & S. Carrera, 'The Development of JHA: Policy Recommendations', in T. Balzacq & S. Carrera (eds), *Security versus Freedom? – A Challenge for Europe's Future*, Aldershot: Ashgate, 2006, pp. 291-295; D. Bigo, S. Carrera, E. Guild, R.B.J. Walker, T*he Changing Landscape of European Liberty and Security: Mid-term Report on the Results of the CHALLENGE Project*, CHALLENGE Research Paper No. 4, February 2007, p. 15.

72 See e.g. a recent speech by UK Home Secretary John Reid, 'Reid urges human rights shake up', BBC News, 12.5.2007, retrieved 13.5.2007 from www.news.bbc.co.uk.

73 Council of the European Union, *The European Union counter-terrorism strategy: prevent, protect, pursue, respond – The European Union's strategic commitment to combat terrorism globally while respecting human rights, and make Europe safer, allowing its citizens to live in an area of freedom, security and justice*, Council doc. 14469/4/05, 30.11.2005.

74 Cf. only K. Lenaerts & P. van Nuffel, *Constitutional Law of the European Union*, 2nd edition, Sweet & Maxwell: London, 2005, para. 17-073 pp.

75 '(...) for us, the individual is paramount. His dignity is inviolable. His rights are inalienable (...). We are striving for peace and freedom, for democracy and the rule of law, for mutual

respect and shared responsibility, for prosperity and security, for tolerance and participation, for justice and solidarity', *Declaration on the occasion of the fiftieth anniversary of the signature of the Treaties of Rome*, 25.3.2007, retrieved 26.3.2007 from www.eu2007.de.

76 Cf. Council of the European Union, *The European Union counter-terrorism strategy: prevent, protect, pursue, respond – The European Union's strategic commitment to combat terrorism globally while respecting human rights, and make Europe safer, allowing its citizens to live in an area of freedom, security and justice*, Council doc. 14469/4/05, 30.11.2005, p. 12; EU Council Secretariat, Factsheet – The European Union and the fight against terrorism, 16.2.2007, p. 3. See also Council decision 2005/671/JHA of 20 September 2005 on the exchange of information and cooperation concerning terrorist offences, OJ L 253, 29.9.2005, pp. 22-24, recitals 2 and 3.

77 For an assessment of Frontex activities see S. Carrera, T*he EU Border Management Strategy – Frontex and the challenges of irregular immigration in the Canary Islands*, CEPS Working Document No. 261, March 2007; for an institutional overview see H. Jorry, *Construction of a European model for managing operational cooperation at the EU's external borders: is the Frontex agency a decisive step forward?*, CHALLENGE Research Paper No. 6, March 2007.

78 The 'new' Sitcen, operational since 2005, now comprises not only the external. 2nd EU pillar intelligence dimensions but in addition also the internal 3rd pillar intelligence dimensions. Sitcen is located within the Council Secretariat and composed of analysts from member states' external and internal security services. Their task is to assess the terrorist threat as it develops both inside Europe and outside. Cf. Interview with G. de Vries, EU Counter-Terrorism Coordinator, *Terrorism, Islam and democracy*, 4.3.2005, retrieved 27.3.2007 from www.EurActiv.com; G. de Vries, 'The European Union's role in the fight against terrorism', *Irish Studies in International Affairs*, vol. 16 (2005), pp. 3-9; cf. also Council Conclusions, *Terrorism – Follow-up to the European Council Declaration*, 8.6.2004, point 1, Council of the European Union, Press Release 2588th Council meeting, Justice and Home Affairs, Luxembourg 8 June 2004, Council doc. 9782/04 (Presse 173), p. 9. See also Statewatch, EU: *'Anti-terrorism' legitimizes sweeping new 'internal security' complex*, Statewatch bulletin, Vol. 14, No. 5, August-October 2004, retrieved 27.3.2007 from www.statewatch.org; on Sitcen and alternative EU intelligence structures cf. D. Spence, 'Introduction: International terrorism – the quest for a coherent EU response', p. 16-17 of this volume.

79 Cf. 'Intelligence … not shared is useless and sometimes dangerous', Max-Peter Ratzel, Director of Europol, *Working together to fight terrorism and crime*, 12.9.2005, retrieved 24.3.2007 from www.epc.eu.

80 Cf. Council common position of 27 December 2001 on the application of specific measures to combat terrorism, OJ L 344, 28.12.2001, pp. 93-96; Council regulation (EC) No 2580/2001 of 27 December 2001 on specific restrictive measures directed against certain persons and entities with a view to combating terrorism, OJ 344, 28.12.2001, pp. 70-75; Council common position of 27 May 2002 concerning restrictive measures against Usama bin Laden, members of the Al-Qaida organization and the Taliban and other individuals, groups, undertakings, and entities associated with them (…), OJ L 139, 29.5.2002, pp. 4-5; Council regulation (EC) No 881/2002 of 27 May 2002 imposing certain restrictive measures directed against certain persons and entities associated with Usama bin Laden, the Al-Qaida network and the Taliban (…), OJ L 139, 29.5.2002, pp. 9-22.

81 Cf. only 'EU's terror list is hard to escape', *European Voice*, 8-14 March 2007, p. 7; on 'targeted sanctions' see also, K. Eling, 'The EU, terrorism and effective multilateralism', in this volume.

82 See article 1(4) Council common position of 27 December 2001 on the application of specific measures to combat terrorism, OJ L 344, 28.12.2001, pp. 93-96.

83 Cf. Council of the European Union, *Final Report on the evaluation of national anti-terrorist arrangements: improving national machinery and capability for the fight against terrorism*, Council doc. 12168/05, 26.9.2005, recommendations 5 and 6, p. 9.

84 CFI, T-228/02, Organisation des Modjahedin du peuple d'Iran v. Council of the European Union, 12.12.2006, para. 171.

85 Council of the European Union, *The Hague Programme: strengthening freedom security and justice in the European Union*, OJ C 53, 3.3.2005, pp. 1-14, point 2.1; See also Council decision 2005/671/JHA of 20 September 2005 on the exchange of information and cooperation concerning terrorist offences, OJ L 253, 29.9.2005, pp. 22-24; concerning the exchange of data held by law enforcement agencies see Commission of the European Communities, *Proposal for a Council framework decision on the exchange of information under the principle of availability*, COM(2005) 490 final, 12.10.2005; cf. also D. Bigo, W. Bruggeman, P. Burgess, V. Mitsilegas, *The principle of information availability*, 1.3.2007, retrieved 24.3.2007 from http://www.libertysecurity.org

/article1376.html; concerning European Justice and Home Affairs databases see Commission of the European Communities, *Communication on improved effectiveness, enhanced interoperability and synergies among European databases in the area of justice and home affairs*, COM(2005) 597 final, 24.11.2005; cf. also P. Hobbing, *An Analysis of the Commission Communication (Com(2005) 597 Final of 24.11.2005) on Improved Effectiveness, Enhanced Interoperability and Synergies among European Databases in the Area of Justice And Home Affairs*, 31.1.2006, retrieved 24.3.2007 from http://www.libertysecurity.org/article1182.html.

86   See the House of Lords and House of Commons Joint Committee on Human Rights recommendations cited earlier.

87   See Council of the European Union, *EU Action Plan on combating terrorism*, Council Doc. 5771/1/06 Rev 1, 13.2.2006, p. 7, point 2.1.

88   Cf. 'EU's secretive counter-terror group to face scrutiny', euobserver, 13.6.2007, retrieved 14.6.2007 from www.euobserver.com. For details on the procedure see K. Eling in this volume.

89   CFI, T-228/02, Organisation des Modjahedin du peuple d'Iran v. Council of the European Union, 12.12.2006.

90   Cf. 'EU's terror list is hard to escape', *European Voice*, 8-14 March 2007, p. 7; 'EU backing down on terror list secrecy', euobserver, 16.1.2007; see also EU Council Secretariat, *Factsheet – Judgment by the Court of First Instance in the OMPI case T-228/02*, no date. A revised procedure was adopted by the General Affairs and External Relations Council on 23.-24.4.2007, cf. Council of the European Union, Press Release, Council Doc. 8425/07 (Presse 80), pp. 34-35.

91   ECJ, C-354/04 P, Gestoras Pro-Amnistía, Juan Mari Olano and Julen Zenarain Enarrasti v. Council of the European Union, 27.2.2007.

92   With regard to the fact that neither the Council nor EU governments have so far officially reacted to this resolution, the EP civil liberties committee's (LIBE) recent proposal to keep the topic on the agenda and to set up regular hearings on the progress during each Council presidency is an adequate step that deserves unconditional approval, see also 'MEPs keep pressure on EU over CIA flights', theparliament.com, 21.3.2007. The Commission's response has been made available in June 2007 on the Statewatch website, http://www.statewatch.org/news/2007/jun/ep-com-rendition.pdf.

93   For the first round see G. de Vries, 'The European Union's role in the fight against terrorism', *Irish Studies in International Affairs*, Vol. 16 (2005), pp. 3-9; Council decision of 28 November 2002 establishing a mechanism for evaluating the legal systems and their implementation at national level in the fight against terrorism, OJ L 349, 24.12.2002, pp. 1-3; Council of the European Union, *Final report on the evaluation of national anti-terrorism arrangements: Improving national machinery and capability for the fight against terrorism*, Council doc. 12168/05, 26.9.2005.

94   In the broader context cf. also EP Policy Department External Policies, *The implementation of the EU guidelines on torture or other inhuman or degrading treatment or punishment*, EP/Expol/B/2006/12, April 2007.

95   This common approach will eventually not only strengthen the position of EU intelligence and law enforcement services in the world but would – and this is even more important – reinforce the absolute prohibition of torture and other inhuman and degrading treatment. See also D. Bigo, Intelligence services, police and democratic control: the European and transatlantic collaboration, Briefing Paper, 13.7.2006, p. 13, retrieved 27.3.2007 form www.liberty security.org.

96   See D. Bigo, Intelligence services, police and democratic control: the European and transatlantic collaboration, Briefing Paper, 13.7.2006, p. 13, retrieved 27.3.2007 from www.libertysecurity.org.

97   See F. Frattini, *Accountability of the intelligence and security agencies and human rights*, Speech/07/378, 7.6.2007; cf. also European Commission for Democracy through Law (Venice Commission), *Report on the democratic oversight of the security services*, adopted by the Venice Commission at its 71st plenary session (Venice, 1-2 June 2007), CDL-AD(2007)016, 11.6.2007; H. Born & I. Leigh, *Making intelligence accountable: Legal standards and best practices for oversight of intelligence agencies*, Publishing House of the Parliament of Norway: Oslo, 2005; T. Wetzling, *The democratic control of intergovernmental intelligence cooperation*, DCAF Working Paper No. 165, Geneva Centre for the Democratic Control of Armed Forces (DCAF): Geneva 2006. Cf. also the discussion in Canada as a consequence of the secret service's entanglement in unlawful behaviour, Commission of Inquiry into the actions of Canadian officials in relation to Maher Arar, *A new review mechanism for the RCMP's national security activities*, 2006, retrieved 30.3.2007 from www.ararcommission.ca.

98   Cf. with further references, B. Müller-Wille, *SSR and European intelligence cooperation impli-*

cations of the new security challenges and enlargement (both EU and NATO) for structuring European intelligence cooperation, as an important aspect of SSR, Conference paper, Geneva Centre for the Democratic Control of Armed Forces (DCAF), Geneva June 2003, p. 5, retrieved 27.3.2007 from www.dcaf.ch.

99 The bi-annual High Level Political Dialogue on Counter-Terrorism between the Council, the Commission, and the European Parliament Council of the European Union is a positive element, but does not remedy the need for proper democratic oversight over EU wide intelligence and law enforcement cooperation with non-EU services. On this High Level Dialogue see, The European Union counter-terrorism strategy: prevent, protect, pursue, respond – *The European Union's strategic commitment to combat terrorism globally while respecting human rights, and make Europe safer, allowing its citizens to live in an area of freedom, security and justice*, Council doc. 14469/4/05, 30.11.2005, p. 17.

100 CFI, T-228/02, Organisation des Modjahedin du peuple d'Iran v. Council of the European Union, 12.12.2006.

Conclusion: the Continuing Quest for Coherence: Sovereignty, Human Rights and EU Coordination

David Spence

This book has cantered through EU policies related to international terrorism while arguing that its response since 2001 has brought a new dynamic to EU domestic and foreign policy making and thus to the process of European integration itself. Meeting the political and organisational challenges posed by the intricate interlinkage between internal and external security has obliged decision-makers to recognise that the EU framework is indispensable to effective national action. However, the EU's right to articulate and manage policy on behalf of twenty-seven sovereign European nation states remains contested. National responses and preparedness are crucial, but the global nature of the terrorist threat requires a European response. A hurdle to further integration is the fact that EU citizens still look to their national governments for immediate protection. And they regard the nation state as the natural home of security policy.

The security threat posed by terrorism is not set to abate. Globally, the number of attacks and casualties has surged according to the State Department, though attacks in Iraq and Afghanistan are a major element in the figures.[1] As to terrorism in Europe, in 2006 Europol listed 498 attacks in 11 of the 27 member states of the Union. 424 were the work of separatist movements (mainly Corsican and Basque). Extreme left or anarchist movements perpetrated 55. In most cases, the purpose of the attacks was not to create victims, though terrorism with a link to Islam (the remaining nineteen cases) was a notable exception. The failed attacks against planes taking off from London and the attempted booby-trapped suitcase attacks in Germany in 2006, and the defused car bombs in London's West End and the attempt to cause havoc at Glasgow airport in June 2007 demonstrate clearly that Islamist terrorism simply targets a maximum number of victims, with no specific links to states, let alone their security structures. Half of the 706 terrorists arrested in 2006 in 15 member states of the EU were of Islamic origin. Their arrests followed allegations ranging from distributing propaganda to recruitment, terrorist financing and kidnapping. Investigations by member states focused on 59 different terrorist groups, one third of which had already carried out attacks outside the EU.[2]

So, challenges remain. They are in part due to economic stagnation and high unemployment in Islamic countries, social exclusion in European countries and the disaffection of Muslims from the values of their adopted European homes. These are clear, if not justified, motivations for terrorism. There are likely to be more Al-Qaida-type terrorist groups and they are likely one day to use modern technology successfully to achieve their goals. They are also likely to develop their links further with organised crime in order to obtain weapons, forged documents and assistance with the transfer of their agents and equipment. These are all activities where purely national responses are demonstrably insufficient, and where EU competence is consequently growing. But European integration has never been smooth and steady. Arguably, moments of great crisis and popular emotion offer an opportunity to vault hurdles to the progress of European integration, and 9/11 may prove to have been one such moment. Yet, the inherent political difficulty of achieving new surrenders of national competence to deal with security threats will likely continue to be compounded by deep-seated official reluctance. The creation, for example, of an authoritative centre for coordinating and managing the overall fight against terrorism with more sophisticated counter-terrorism measures is likely to remain elusive.

EU action abroad in response to terrorism is composed of a wide panoply of measures. The threat of a nuclear confrontation between super-powers in Europe may seem gone for the foreseeable future. And the threat of massive conventional war that characterised the twentieth century may well be relegated to the dustbin of history. But, contributory factors to international terrorism – WMD proliferation, state fragility and failure, poverty, abuse of human rights, environmental degradation, international crime and irrational fundamentalism – are all on the increase. The EU is making strenuous practical attempts to address these major issues through its development policies, its security sector reform policies, its advocacy of effective multilateralism and good governance, as well as its emerging capability to use force as a last resort.[3] The EU has decided that it cannot abdicate responsibility. It may not be to blame for the ills of the world, but in the eyes of the suffering, worldwide, and in the eyes of its own citizens, it has a duty of presence and active support in the search for remedies.[4] Indeed, an important lesson emerging from the chapters of this book is the need to improve the EU's capacity to diagnose the danger signs and prevent the slide from poverty and conflict towards threat, crisis and violence.

Could Europe disband its armed forces and its security/intelligence teams? Could it concentrate on butter, not guns? Hardly. Europe has not only inherited the responsibilities and challenges of yesteryear's great powers, but also an expectation at home and abroad of active involvement in continuing bitter disputes, whether over Palestine and Kashmir, arbitrary borders throughout the Middle East and Africa or all the root causes of terrorism. These issues not only remain unresolved; they are seemingly beyond resolution. Yet, collective European commitment to the resolution of at least those international conflicts, which arguably result from the hubris of historical European policies, might help; not only because European nations played a role in creating some of these conflicts, not only because European states have security interests in stability there, but because an ethical stance by the world's rich countries demands continued involvement and carries continued implications for foreign policy, trade policy, development aid and humanitarian action. The catch, of course, is that greater international involvement raises visibility and exposes those involved to the risk of becoming a terrorist target. Significantly, also, assuming historical responsibility is one potential precursor to intervention, so however welcome Europe's positive contribution to international relations is to some, its aims continue to be doubted by others.[5]

It is a commonplace to assert that since its inception, the EU has had a range of competences and applicable resources that are wider than those of any other international organisation, capable of covering all the currently recognised dimensions of security and soon even collective military defence. It is obvious that its regulatory, indeed legalistic, character gives it unique potential to address all dimensions of threat and to mobilise for positive ends both states outside and sub-state actors. Its border-free internal market both allows and obliges it to find and exploit transnational remedies for security threats. Its tradition of common external negotiating positions allows it, in principle, to make coherent, often influential collective inputs to global-level discussion, whether in the UN or elsewhere. So, the EU has the means and can afford to be proactive. Its capacities are growing, even if they remain inadequate to the task of playing the lead role within the UN framework to which some EU politicians aspire. The EU struggles, for example, to harmonise its policies on nuclear and chemical weapons and on conventional arms. It boosts continually its assistance to states in need of guidance in the fight against all the ills, not least terrorism and its root causes. But its practical action, however extensive the ambition, seems a drop in the ocean of needs. Nonetheless, Europe is contributing to the cause of outlawing terrorism in the way two centuries ago it was brought to outlaw piracy and slavery. But rhetoric alone does not provide the political and administrative wherewithal for effective policy implementation. Soft power brings the power of leverage, but if there is a job to be done, it is not the political structures and the political potential but political will that counts.

As public support for American action declines and it is recognised that the 'war on terror' has made little progress, its effects in Europe are significant. There may not have been any further attacks within the United States, but terror attacks have increased dramatically abroad, as the figures quoted above demonstrate. And anti-American feeling has clearly helped provide fertile ground for Al-Qaida. 'Enhanced interrogation' and the Guantánamo Bay facility have been counterproductive and Europeans have regrettably been found guilty by association. They knew the 'war on terror' was not initially devised as a coherent strategic plan, but that it emerged as the product of a series of seemingly random policy choices by US politicians and officials. They suspected it was driven by some largely unexamined and initially unchallenged assumptions about the scope and nature of the threat. One such assumption was that the new 'mass terrorism' meant a 'paradigm shift', implying in turn that the United States and its allies would suffer an escalating series of mass-casualty attacks, ultimately including atomic, biological or chemical attacks, unless preventive action was undertaken in the form of powerful shared policies on WMD – not least in Iraq. Another was the assumption that Al-Qaida must be an exceptionally powerful organisation. It had obviously received support from the Taliban government in Afghanistan, but it was also assumed that other 'rogue states', such as Iraq, Iran and North Korea, might have provided, or would consider providing, training, sanctuary or financial support. It actually seems likely now that the war on terror has made Al-Qaida more powerful than ever it was, not least as an ideological force able to mobilise Muslim discontents. Most of the US assumptions now appear critically flawed, but Europe is associated with their consequences; like it or not.

'Terrorists' may represent an irrational new enemy, as the introduction to this book surmised. Indeed, it is certainly unlike the West's former enemy, the Soviet Union – a rational state actor, which responded in fairly predictable ways to traditional Western diplomacy and statecraft. Al-Qaida's disciples lack political or economic interest, and they are willing to launch suicide attacks, even if they are no match, as an enemy, for a large well-endowed state. But the significant point is that 'terror' is a condition and a method; it is not an adversary. Describing the conflict specifically as a 'war' was politically shrewd in one sense, since it helped galvanise political support for the US administration's military and security responses to September 11, but it clearly backfired as the public began to analyse what the term actually meant – and entailed. The price of rhetoric was high for the US image abroad, for anti-American feeling has risen sharply, particularly in the Muslim world, but also in Europe – notwithstanding the fair assumption that the roots of much of the negative sentiment predated the Bush administration. Indeed it most probably predated the administration of the first President Bush. One thing is certain, however: US policies appear to have entrenched and deepened anti-American views. A Pew report in June 2007 concluded that 'global distrust of American leadership is reflected in increasing disapproval of the cornerstones of U.S. foreign policy'.[6]

With hindsight it actually seems there was little threat of domestic Islamic terrorism in the US. The 9/11 attacks were seemingly an isolated incident that exploited a particular vulnerability – unlocked aircraft flight crew cabins. And it is now clear (after years of debate about Guantánamo Bay) that constitutional judicial processes (as opposed to extra-territorial and extra-legal action) might be a boon to counter-terror efforts, rather than a hindrance. If it is possible to prosecute terrorists under existing criminal justice systems, the argument for more robust and specific counter-terrorism action may lose sway. Indeed, treating terrorists humanely, in contrast to the brutality of their actions, might well significantly undermine support for their cause. Many argue the contrary case, of course; that only forceful methods produce effective operational results. But, the original rationale for treating terrorist detainees harshly – tough interrogations might help extract vital intelligence that could save lives – now appears flawed in practice and no longer merely morally questionable. A study by America's National Defense Intelligence College has demonstrated that there is no scientific evidence that enhanced interrogation techniques improve the quality of intelligence gleaned from terror suspects.[7] So, US responses to September 11 might well not only have been predicated on dubious assumptions, but the alternative, cautious (Venus-like?) policies of the EU are arguably a more sensible strategic approach. Certainly, the emphasis in the EU on addressing root causes and terrorist motives seems sound in hindsight, and not a softy's cop-out – Venus-like 'appeasement'. European governments (especially those in countries where terrorist attacks occurred) of course warned their publics to be vigilant in the face of the perceived threat. But the risk was that by turning a vague terror threat in a low probability environment into high drama and then turning a blind eye to subsequent abuses, governments would inevitably grant terrorists a 'victory', even if there were no successful attacks. Effective counter-terrorism involves quiet intelligence work, not public scaremongering, and the EU has admittedly been slow to organise a coherent response at this level.

Yet, overall EU policy today seems coherent and comprehensive. Enhanced effectiveness in the fight against terrorism, the security of its citizens, critical infrastructure protection and a tight legal framework shared by 27 states are surely to be welcomed, and will doubtless become increasingly important. If the EU accepts to play a role in these same areas outside the EU, the importance of a coordinated policy reflex in such widely diverse areas as international development cooperation, money-laundering, arms control and disarmament will increase apace.[8] All these policy areas have far-reaching relevance for overall security, as the European Security Strategy and various other policy documents argue. There is as much self-interest as altruistic concern in finding European outcomes with such a richly endowed toolbox. Yet how far the European Union's institutions can mobilise and create policy based on the dauntingly wide range of possibilities and resources it commands; how far it can even keep track and control of the narrower range of instruments directed against terrorism as such, remain open questions. There are simply not the human resources in the EU institutions to meet the challenges or even adequately to administer the resources already in existence, if politicians' ambitions are to be met.

But meeting these ambitions in practice runs up against the fact that 'international terrorism' is a moving target and thus a moving source of threat. The presumed objectives of weak and rogue states still set much of the agenda of international relations. Their potential threat to international stability are arguably of equivalent importance to the threat of terrorism itself. Despite progress in critical infrastructure protection, Europe continues to be congenitally unprepared for the next crisis. True, methods improve with each new terrorism attack and each new call on the EU to assist with the results of crises abroad. Yet, behind the successes, such as the prevention of the plans of a handful of extremists from becoming reality, lies the potential for other, untraceable madcaps to succeed. Behind the big successes, such as the return to the fold of the international community by Libya, lay the revelation that a Pakistani scientist, Abdul Qadeer Khan, had been running a network for disseminating the components of WMD programmes. Equally, however, behind the tragedies of European impotence in the Balkans or Africa, when security threats turned into genocidal action, lay new incentives to enhance efficiency, lay holy cows to rest and engage the process of European integration for international ethical purpose.

However, such successes should not mask the realisation that the world of fundamentalism, whether at home or abroad, whether Christian or Muslim, hides practical threat. The threat from proliferation remains real and omnipresent. And there is a seemingly unending string of suicide and other bomb attacks outside Europe, which demonstrate that the international community is far from mastering the menace posed by terrorism. That the same methods could be used in Europe (indeed, were used successfully in London and Madrid) remains a very real threat. The inescapable fact is that while the EU 27 can be congratulated for its commitment to human security at home and abroad, and for visible strides towards effective supranational governance, there is still suboptimal cohesion, which arguably affects ability to rise to the challenge of coming crises. Lack of coherence may not spell complacency, but the operational result is the same.

Finally, and most importantly, there is the risk of abdicating responsibility for the protection of human rights in the name of heightened security against terrorism. Compromising human rights risks proving the counterpart to increasing human security, a suspicion from which the EU has been keen to distance itself. Yet, responding to the increased threat and operationalising lessons learned has disguised the erosion of civil liberties, the rule of law and human rights. This, too, is a complicated issue, stretching far beyond the rights and wrongs of the simplistic plea for time-limited compromise to human rights in the name of a greater security good. Human rights infringements, deplorable in themselves, have been a key reason for growing public disaffection with the policies of counter-terrorism. The unlimited periods of detention in Guantánamo Bay, in Iraq and elsewhere have doubtless caused lasting disaffection, as has the alleged use of torture by proxy, emergency legislation escaping meaningful judicial control and Western association with some of the world's most authoritarian regimes. They have all taken a toll in terms of western public diplomacy, though it is increasingly the case that the argument of military security or safety of oil supplies has not duped a growingly sensitive and sceptical public. The EU's political debates on these issues show as much concern about the stakes for liberal democracy as debates in the US. So, it is worth recalling that the EU and the US subscribed to a joint declaration at their summit on 21 June 2006, where they stated that:

> Consistent with our common values, we will ensure that measures taken to combat terrorism comply fully with our international obligations, including human rights law, refugee law and international humanitarian law. We attach great importance to our ongoing in-depth dialogue on our common fight against terrorism and our respective domestic and international legal obligations.

Indeed, this commitment was reinforced by the G8 summit in Heiligendamm in June 2007, the G8 states declaring that:

> We reconfirm that international cooperation to fight terrorism must be conducted in conformity with international law, including the UN Charter and relevant international conventions and protocols. States must ensure that any measures taken to combat terrorism comply with their obligations under international law, in particular human rights law, refugee law and international humanitarian law.[9]

Fine words, but within the EU there were continued doubts. Policy on border controls was seemingly confusing concerns about terrorist infiltration with the issue of illegal migration and there was a growing risk of xenophobia. Amnesty International has long criticised the EU's lax definition of terrorism in its 2002 Framework Decision on Combating Terrorism (see Annex 2) and its apparent disregard for human rights in the European Arrest Warrant (Annex 1). Is extradition allowed on the basis of evidence acquired while the prisoner was under duress? Such is the growing strength of the non-governmental lobby that the European Commission is now proposing a framework decision on common minimum standards for the rights of defendants and suspects, though even here Amnesty has expressed fears that terrorism and organised crime offences might be exempted from the decision, just as it argued the Commission's draft directive on asylum procedures was seemingly silent on the issue of extradition orders applied while asylum hearings are pending. It is not surprising that criticism is levelled at the EU for failing to ensure that the response to security dilemmas posed by terrorism does not create loopholes in existing rules to protect human rights. But the momentum to close them clearly reflects a positive side of liberal democracy.

In February 2007, the European Parliament (EP) criticised fourteen member states for allegedly colluding with US officials on counter-terrorism at the cost of human rights breaches. A report claimed the CIA was directly responsible for illegal operations on European soil against terrorist suspects and accused particularly the United Kingdom, Germany and Italy, of turning a blind eye to CIA flights carrying alleged terrorists to secret prisons outside the United States.[10] The European Parliament thus became the most vociferous European institutional advocate of caution against throwing the human rights baby out with the anti-terrorist bathwater. In addition to its substantial criticisms, the EP report also accused several European countries of unwillingness to cooperate with its enquiry, condemning the 'omissions' of the EU High Representative for CFSP Javier Solana, the lack of cooperation from the anti-terrorist coordinator Gijs de Vries (who announced his resignation days before the Report was formally published) and the refusal of NATO Secretary General Jaap de Hoop Scheffer to be interviewed by the parliamentary committee's team. Though the Council and the Commission restated their attachment to the protection of fundamental rights in combating terrorism, parliamentarians criticised them for leaving responsibility to member states to carry out their own investigations on the allegedly illegal activities of US secret services on their soil rather than opting for a European level investigation. European Commissioner Franco Frattini argued that member states alone had the responsibility to 'reveal the truth, although it may be upsetting', but he added that he could do little, since the Commission's legal competence does not extend to legislation on the secret services. He nevertheless stated that the Commission would 'draw conclusions and formulate proposals' including 'political reflection on the role of the intelligence services'.[11] There will inevitably be further focus on the shortcomings in intelligence sharing and counter-terrorism leadership described in the introduction to this book.[12]

The EP's criticisms added to those of Council of Europe Parliamentary Assembly investigator Dick Marty, who had rebuked the UN Security Council for the 'flagrant injustice' of blacklisting individuals suspected of having links to terrorism without evidence of wrong-doing. The process of listing – in which individuals have their assets frozen and are banned from travelling – is decided, as Eling describes in chapter 5, by the UN '1267 committee'. Those listed are not informed or given a chance to be heard, and there has been no right of appeal. Marty has also announced that he would be extending his investigation to the similar and interlinked system of lists run by the European Union.[13] But, human rights appear to be under threat not only by the actions of governments against individuals. The discovery, through EU monitoring of the international banking arrangement 'Swift' (Society for Worldwide Interbank Financial Telecommunications) in November 2006, that it had flouted EU data protection rules by providing US intelligence agencies with details of millions of financial transactions was but one example of the intricacy and inherent risks of the modern capitalist state.[14] Thus, heightened vigilance has allegedly been accompanied by heightened disregard for human rights. But is effective counter terrorism increasingly incompatible with human rights conventions and the principles of liberal democracy themselves, as the Schlesinger Report highlighted in its review of blame in the US military for the acts committed at Abu Ghraib?[15]

Hopefully, however, this book has shown that the achievements of the EU have not been negligible. In terms of the EU's own institutional development the threat of international 'hyper-terrorism' has reinforced awareness of the political impotence of the three-pillar policy-making structure of the Maastricht Treaty. The EU's potential for rising above its internal incoherence thus seems greater than ever before. But, it is political will not potential that counts. The question 'where does the EU stand?' is not rhetorical. The EU response to 9/11 focused heavily on improving collaboration between EU member states and between the EU and its main partners, commendably within the UN framework. If the important practical measure of creating a European centre for counter-terrorism excellence with a powerful European counter-terrorism coordinator has not been achieved, this is not because the issue of human rights has stymied progress. It is because supporters of national sovereignty have proved unready for such an important integrative step. Yet the threat of international terrorism persists. It has clearly had a catalytic effect on European integration so far, and the transnational nature of the issue, the political challenge of safeguarding human rights and the practical challenge of effective coordination are clearly set to structure the EU's next steps.

Endnotes

1 State Department Country Reports on Terrorism, 2006.
2 EU Terrorism and Situation Report, Europol, 2007.
3 See D. Spence and P. Fluri, *The EU and Security Sector Reform*, John Harper, forthcoming.
4 For a critical view of how far the EUI successfully assumes this duty see G. Evans *The Unfinished Responsibility to Protect Agenda: Europe's Role*, Presentation to EPC/IPPR/Oxfam Policy Dialogue on Europe's Responsibility to Protect: What Role for the EU?, Brussels, 5 July 2007.
5 See Sjursen, H, 2006, Special issue of the *Journal of European Public Policy* Volume 13, no 2. 'What Kind of Power? European Foreign Policy in Perspective'.
6 Pew Research Center Global Attitudes Survey, June, 2007
7 R. Coulam, *Approaches to Interrogation in the Struggle Against Terrorism in Educing Information: interrogation, science and art.* National Defense Intelligence College, 2006.
8 See D. Spence 'EU diplomacy and global governance' in A. Cooper, B. Hocking and W. Maley (eds), *Worlds Apart: Exploring the Interface between Governance and Diplomacy*, Tokyo, United Nations University Press.
9 Report on G8 Support to the United Nations' Counter-Terrorism Efforts, G8, Heiligendamm.
10 MEPs approved the report by a committee of inquiry on CIA activities in Europe by a majority of 382 for, 256 against and 76 abstentions. MEPs accused European countries of ceding

control over their airspace and their airports and turning a blind eye to flights operated by the CIA for the illegal transfer of prisoners to detention centres where they were tortured.

11 Agence Europe 15 February 2007

12 The issue will reach a broader public with a Motion Picture Production Incorporated documentary film in 2007 on the basis of the book 'Torture Taxi: On the Trail of the CIA's Rendition Flights,' which shows how plane spotters' groups helped European media track the story.

13 See: Dick Marty 'UN Security Council Blacklists'. Council of Europe Committee on Legal Affairs and Human Rights, 2007 and Proceedings of The Security Council Committee established pursuant to resolution 1267 (1999) (also known as 'the Al-Qaida and Taliban Sanctions Committee').

14 *International Herald Tribune*, Nov 23rd 2006. EU agency finds Swift flouted law.

15 Final Report of the Independent Panel to Review DoD Detention Operations, August, 2004. www.defenselink.mil/news/Aug2004/d20040824finalreport.pdf. See also J. Apap and S. Carrera *Maintaining Security within borders: towards a permanent state of emergency in the EU?'* CEPS policy brief no 41, November 2003, and Baldaccini, A. and Guild, E. (2006) *Terrorism and the Foreigner: a decade of tension around the rule of law in Europe*, Martinus Nijhoff.

Annex 1

COUNCIL FRAMEWORK DECISION

of 13 June 2002

on the European arrest warrant and the surrender procedures between Member States

(2002/584/JHA)

THE COUNCIL OF THE EUROPEAN UNION,

Having regard to the Treaty on European Union, and in particular Article 31(a) and (b) and Article 34(2)(b) thereof,

Having regard to the proposal from the Commission[1],

Having regard to the opinion of the European Parliament[2],

Whereas:

(1)   According to the Conclusions of the Tampere European Council of 15 and 16 October 1999, and in particular point 35 thereof, the formal extradition procedure should be abolished among the Member States in respect of persons who are fleeing from justice after having been finally sentenced and extradition procedures should be speeded up in respect of persons suspected of having committed an offence.

(2)   The programme of measures to implement the principle of mutual recognition of criminal decisions envisaged in point 37 of the Tampere European Council Conclusions and adopted by the Council on 30 November 2000[3], addresses the matter of mutual enforcement of arrest warrants.

(3)   All or some Member States are parties to a number of conventions in the field of extradition, including the European Convention on extradition of 13 December 1957 and the European Convention on the suppression of terrorism of 27 January 1977. The Nordic States have extradition laws with identical wording.

(4)   In addition, the following three Conventions dealing in whole or in part with extradition have been agreed upon among Member States and form part of the Union acquis: the Convention of 19 June 1990 implementing the Schengen Agreement of 14 June 1985 on the gradual abolition of checks at their common borders[4] (regarding relations between the Member States which are parties to that Convention), the Convention of 10 March 1995 on simplified extradition procedure between the Member States of the European Union[5] and the Convention of 27 September 1996 relating to extradition between the Member States of the European Union[6].

(5)   The objective set for the Union to become an area of freedom, security and justice

leads to abolishing extradition between Member States and replacing it by a system of surrender between judicial authorities. Further, the introduction of a new simplified system of surrender of sentenced or suspected persons for the purposes of execution or prosecution of criminal sentences makes it possible to remove the complexity and potential for delay inherent in the present extradition procedures. Traditional cooperation relations which have prevailed up till now between Member States should be replaced by a system of free movement of judicial decisions in criminal matters, covering both pre-sentence and final decisions, within an area of freedom, security and justice.

(6)   The European arrest warrant provided for in this Framework Decision is the first concrete measure in the field of criminal law implementing the principle of mutual recognition which the European Council referred to as the "cornerstone" of judicial cooperation.

(7)   Since the aim of replacing the system of multilateral extradition built upon the European Convention on Extradition of 13 December 1957 cannot be sufficiently achieved by the Member States acting unilaterally and can therefore, by reason of its scale and effects, be better achieved at Union level, the Council may adopt measures in accordance with the principle of subsidiarity as referred to in Article 2 of the Treaty on European Union and Article 5 of the Treaty establishing the European Community. In accordance with the principle of proportionality, as set out in the latter Article, this Framework Decision does not go beyond what is necessary in order to achieve that objective.

(8)   Decisions on the execution of the European arrest warrant must be subject to sufficient controls, which means that a judicial authority of the Member State where the requested person has been arrested will have to take the decision on his or her surrender.

(9)   The role of central authorities in the execution of a European arrest warrant must be limited to practical and administrative assistance.

(10)   The mechanism of the European arrest warrant is based on a high level of confidence between Member States. Its implementation may be suspended only in the event of a serious and persistent breach by one of the Member States of the principles set out in Article 6(1) of the Treaty on European Union, determined by the Council pursuant to Article 7(1) of the said Treaty with the consequences set out in Article 7(2) thereof.

(11)   In relations between Member States, the European arrest warrant should replace all the previous instruments concerning extradition, including the provisions of Title III of the Convention implementing the Schengen Agreement which concern extradition.

(12)   This Framework Decision respects fundamental rights and observes the principles recognised by Article 6 of the Treaty on European Union and reflected in the Charter of Fundamental Rights of the European Union[7], in particular Chapter VI thereof. Nothing in this Framework Decision may be interpreted as prohibiting refusal to surrender a person for whom a European arrest warrant has been issued when there are reasons to believe, on the basis of objective elements, that the said arrest warrant has been issued for the purpose of prosecuting or punishing a person on the grounds of his or her sex, race, religion, ethnic origin, nationality, language, political opinions or sexual orientation, or that that person's position may be prejudiced for any of these reasons. This Framework Decision does not prevent a Member State from applying its constitutional rules relating to due process, freedom of association, freedom of the press and freedom of expression in other media.

(13)   No person should be removed, expelled or extradited to a State where there is a serious risk that he or she would be subjected to the death penalty, torture or other inhuman or degrading treatment or punishment.

(14)   Since all Member States have ratified the Council of Europe Convention of 28 January 1981 for the protection of individuals with regard to automatic processing of personal data, the personal data processed in the context of the implementation of this Framework Decision should be protected in accordance with the principles of the said Convention,

HAS ADOPTED THIS FRAMEWORK DECISION:

CHAPTER 1

GENERAL PRINCIPLES

Article 1

Definition of the European arrest warrant and obligation to execute it

1.   The European arrest warrant is a judicial decision issued by a Member State with a view to the arrest and surrender by another Member State of a requested person, for the purposes of conducting a criminal prosecution or executing a custodial sentence or detention order.

2.   Member States shall execute any European arrest warrant on the basis of the principle of mutual recognition and in accordance with the provisions of this Framework Decision.

3.   This Framework Decision shall not have the effect of modifying the obligation to respect fundamental rights and fundamental legal principles as enshrined in Article 6 of the Treaty on European Union.

Article 2

Scope of the European arrest warrant

1.   A European arrest warrant may be issued for acts punishable by the law of the issuing Member State by a custodial sentence or a detention order for a maximum period of at least 12 months or, where a sentence has been passed or a detention order has been made, for sentences of at least four months.

2.   The following offences, if they are punishable in the issuing Member State by a custodial sentence or a detention order for a maximum period of at least three years and as they are defined by the law of the issuing Member State, shall, under the terms of this Framework Decision and without verification of the double criminality of the act, give rise to surrender pursuant to a European arrest warrant:

-       participation in a criminal organisation,
-       terrorism,
-       trafficking in human beings,
-       sexual exploitation of children and child pornography,
-       illicit trafficking in narcotic drugs and psychotropic substances,
-       illicit trafficking in weapons, munitions and explosives,
-       corruption,
-       fraud, including that affecting the financial interests of the European Communities within the meaning of the Convention of 26 July 1995 on the protection of the European Communities' financial interests,

–   laundering of the proceeds of crime,
–   counterfeiting currency, including of the euro,
–   computer-related crime,
–   environmental crime, including illicit trafficking in endangered animal species and in endangered plant species and varieties,
–   facilitation of unauthorised entry and residence,
–   murder, grievous bodily injury,
–   illicit trade in human organs and tissue,
–   kidnapping, illegal restraint and hostage-taking,
–   racism and xenophobia,
–   organised or armed robbery,
–   illicit trafficking in cultural goods, including antiques and works of art,
–   swindling,
–   racketeering and extortion,
–   counterfeiting and piracy of products,
–   forgery of administrative documents and trafficking therein,
–   forgery of means of payment,
–   illicit trafficking in hormonal substances and other growth promoters,
–   illicit trafficking in nuclear or radioactive materials,
–   trafficking in stolen vehicles,
–   rape,
–   arson,
–   crimes within the jurisdiction of the International Criminal Court,
–   unlawful seizure of aircraft/ships,
–   sabotage.

3.   The Council may decide at any time, acting unanimously after consultation of the European Parliament under the conditions laid down in Article 39(1) of the Treaty on European Union (TEU), to add other categories of offence to the list contained in paragraph 2. The Council shall examine, in the light of the report submitted by the Commission pursuant to Article 34(3), whether the list should be extended or amended.

4.   For offences other than those covered by paragraph 2, surrender may be subject to the condition that the acts for which the European arrest warrant has been issued constitute an offence under the law of the executing Member State, whatever the constituent elements or however it is described.

Article 3

Grounds for mandatory non-execution of the European arrest warrant

The judicial authority of the Member State of execution (hereinafter "executing judicial authority") shall refuse to execute the European arrest warrant in the following cases:

1.   if the offence on which the arrest warrant is based is covered by amnesty in the executing Member State, where that State had jurisdiction to prosecute the offence under its own criminal law;

2.   if the executing judicial authority is informed that the requested person has been finally judged by a Member State in respect of the same acts provided that, where there has been sentence, the sentence has been served or is currently being served or may no longer be executed under the law of the sentencing Member State;

3.   if the person who is the subject of the European arrest warrant may not, owing to his age, be held criminally responsible for the acts on which the arrest warrant is based under the law of the executing State.

Article 4

Grounds for optional non-execution of the European arrest warrant

The executing judicial authority may refuse to execute the European arrest warrant:

1. if, in one of the cases referred to in Article 2(4), the act on which the European arrest warrant is based does not constitute an offence under the law of the executing Member State; however, in relation to taxes or duties, customs and exchange, execution of the European arrest warrant shall not be refused on the ground that the law of the executing Member State does not impose the same kind of tax or duty or does not contain the same type of rules as regards taxes, duties and customs and exchange regulations as the law of the issuing Member State;

2. where the person who is the subject of the European arrest warrant is being prosecuted in the executing Member State for the same act as that on which the European arrest warrant is based;

3. where the judicial authorities of the executing Member State have decided either not to prosecute for the offence on which the European arrest warrant is based or to halt proceedings, or where a final judgment has been passed upon the requested person in a Member State, in respect of the same acts, which prevents further proceedings;

4. where the criminal prosecution or punishment of the requested person is statute-barred according to the law of the executing Member State and the acts fall within the jurisdiction of that Member State under its own criminal law;

5. if the executing judicial authority is informed that the requested person has been finally judged by a third State in respect of the same acts provided that, where there has been sentence, the sentence has been served or is currently being served or may no longer be executed under the law of the sentencing country;

6. if the European arrest warrant has been issued for the purposes of execution of a custodial sentence or detention order, where the requested person is staying in, or is a national or a resident of the executing Member State and that State undertakes to execute the sentence or detention order in accordance with its domestic law;

7. where the European arrest warrant relates to offences which:

    (a) are regarded by the law of the executing Member State as having been committed in whole or in part in the territory of the executing Member State or in a place treated as such; or
    (b) have been committed outside the territory of the issuing Member State and the law of the executing Member State does not allow prosecution for the same offences when committed outside its territory.

Article 5

Guarantees to be given by the issuing Member State in particular cases

The execution of the European arrest warrant by the executing judicial authority may, by the law of the executing Member State, be subject to the following conditions:

1. where the European arrest warrant has been issued for the purposes of executing a sentence or a detention order imposed by a decision rendered in absentia and if the person concerned has not been summoned in person or otherwise informed of the date and place of the hearing which led to the decision rendered in absentia, sur-

render may be subject to the condition that the issuing judicial authority gives an assurance deemed adequate to guarantee the person who is the subject of the European arrest warrant that he or she will have an opportunity to apply for a retrial of the case in the issuing Member State and to be present at the judgment;

2.   if the offence on the basis of which the European arrest warrant has been issued is punishable by custodial life sentence or life-time detention order, the execution of the said arrest warrant may be subject to the condition that the issuing Member State has provisions in its legal system for a review of the penalty or measure imposed, on request or at the latest after 20 years, or for the application of measures of clemency to which the person is entitled to apply for under the law or practice of the issuing Member State, aiming at a non-execution of such penalty or measure;

3.   where a person who is the subject of a European arrest warrant for the purposes of prosecution is a national or resident of the executing Member State, surrender may be subject to the condition that the person, after being heard, is returned to the executing Member State in order to serve there the custodial sentence or detention order passed against him in the issuing Member State.

Article 6

Determination of the competent judicial authorities

1.   The issuing judicial authority shall be the judicial authority of the issuing Member State which is competent to issue a European arrest warrant by virtue of the law of that State.

2.   The executing judicial authority shall be the judicial authority of the executing Member State which is competent to execute the European arrest warrant by virtue of the law of that State.

3.   Each Member State shall inform the General Secretariat of the Council of the competent judicial authority under its law.

Article 7

Recourse to the central authority

1.   Each Member State may designate a central authority or, when its legal system so provides, more than one central authority to assist the competent judicial authorities.

2.   A Member State may, if it is necessary as a result of the organisation of its internal judicial system, make its central authority(ies) responsible for the administrative transmission and reception of European arrest warrants as well as for all other official correspondence relating thereto. A Member State wishing to make use of the possibilities referred to in this Article shall communicate to the General Secretariat of the Council information relating to the designated central authority or central authorities. These indications shall be binding upon all the authorities of the issuing Member State.

Article 8

Content and form of the European arrest warrant

1.   The European arrest warrant shall contain the following information set out in accordance with the form contained in the Annex:

        (a)   the identity and nationality of the requested person;

(b) the name, address, telephone and fax numbers and e-mail address of the issuing judicial authority;

(c) evidence of an enforceable judgment, an arrest warrant or any other enforceable judicial decision having the same effect, coming within the scope of Articles 1 and 2;

(d) the nature and legal classification of the offence, particularly in respect of Article 2;

(e) a description of the circumstances in which the offence was committed, including the time, place and degree of participation in the offence by the requested person;

(f) the penalty imposed, if there is a final judgment, or the prescribed scale of penalties for the offence under the law of the issuing Member State;

(g) if possible, other consequences of the offence.

2. The European arrest warrant must be translated into the official language or one of the official languages of the executing Member State. Any Member State may, when this Framework Decision is adopted or at a later date, state in a declaration deposited with the General Secretariat of the Council that it will accept a translation in one or more other official languages of the Institutions of the European Communities.

CHAPTER 2

SURRENDER PROCEDURE

Article 9

Transmission of a European arrest warrant

1. When the location of the requested person is known, the issuing judicial authority may transmit the European arrest warrant directly to the executing judicial authority.

2. The issuing judicial authority may, in any event, decide to issue an alert for the requested person in the Schengen Information System (SIS).

3. Such an alert shall be effected in accordance with the provisions of Article 95 of the Convention of 19 June 1990 implementing the Schengen Agreement of 14 June 1985 on the gradual abolition of controls at common borders. An alert in the Schengen Information System shall be equivalent to a European arrest warrant accompanied by the information set out in Article 8(1).

For a transitional period, until the SIS is capable of transmitting all the information described in Article 8, the alert shall be equivalent to a European arrest warrant pending the receipt of the original in due and proper form by the executing judicial authority.

Article 10

Detailed procedures for transmitting a European arrest warrant

1. If the issuing judicial authority does not know the competent executing judicial authority, it shall make the requisite enquiries, including through the contact points of the European Judicial Network[8], in order to obtain that information from the executing Member State.

2. If the issuing judicial authority so wishes, transmission may be effected via the secure telecommunications system of the European Judicial Network.

3.   If it is not possible to call on the services of the SIS, the issuing judicial authority may call on Interpol to transmit a European arrest warrant.

4.   The issuing judicial authority may forward the European arrest warrant by any secure means capable of producing written records under conditions allowing the executing Member State to establish its authenticity.

5.   All difficulties concerning the transmission or the authenticity of any document needed for the execution of the European arrest warrant shall be dealt with by direct contacts between the judicial authorities involved, or, where appropriate, with the involvement of the central authorities of the Member States.

6.   If the authority which receives a European arrest warrant is not competent to act upon it, it shall automatically forward the European arrest warrant to the competent authority in its Member State and shall inform the issuing judicial authority accordingly.

Article 11

Rights of a requested person

1.   When a requested person is arrested, the executing competent judicial authority shall, in accordance with its national law, inform that person of the European arrest warrant and of its contents, and also of the possibility of consenting to surrender to the issuing judicial authority.

2.   A requested person who is arrested for the purpose of the execution of a European arrest warrant shall have a right to be assisted by a legal counsel and by an interpreter in accordance with the national law of the executing Member State.

Article 12

Keeping the person in detention

When a person is arrested on the basis of a European arrest warrant, the executing judicial authority shall take a decision on whether the requested person should remain in detention, in accordance with the law of the executing Member State. The person may be released provisionally at any time in conformity with the domestic law of the executing Member State, provided that the competent authority of the said Member State takes all the measures it deems necessary to prevent the person absconding.

Article 13

Consent to surrender

1.   If the arrested person indicates that he or she consents to surrender, that consent and, if appropriate, express renunciation of entitlement to the "speciality rule", referred to in Article 27(2), shall be given before the executing judicial authority, in accordance with the domestic law of the executing Member State.

2.   Each Member State shall adopt the measures necessary to ensure that consent and, where appropriate, renunciation, as referred to in paragraph 1, are established in such a way as to show that the person concerned has expressed them voluntarily and in full awareness of the consequences. To that end, the requested person shall have the right to legal counsel.

3.   The consent and, where appropriate, renunciation, as referred to in paragraph 1, shall be formally recorded in accordance with the procedure laid down by the domestic law of the executing Member State.

4.   In principle, consent may not be revoked. Each Member State may provide that consent and, if appropriate, renunciation may be revoked, in accordance with the rules applicable under its domestic law. In this case, the period between the date of consent and that of its revocation shall not be taken into consideration in establishing the time limits laid down in Article 17. A Member State which wishes to have recourse to this possibility shall inform the General Secretariat of the Council accordingly when this Framework Decision is adopted and shall specify the procedures whereby revocation of consent shall be possible and any amendment to them.

Article 14

Hearing of the requested person

Where the arrested person does not consent to his or her surrender as referred to in Article 13, he or she shall be entitled to be heard by the executing judicial authority, in accordance with the law of the executing Member State.

Article 15

Surrender decision

1.   The executing judicial authority shall decide, within the time-limits and under the conditions defined in this Framework Decision, whether the person is to be surrendered.

2.   If the executing judicial authority finds the information communicated by the issuing Member State to be insufficient to allow it to decide on surrender, it shall request that the necessary supplementary information, in particular with respect to Articles 3 to 5 and Article 8, be furnished as a matter of urgency and may fix a time limit for the receipt thereof, taking into account the need to observe the time limits set in Article 17.

3.   The issuing judicial authority may at any time forward any additional useful information to the executing judicial authority.

Article 16

Decision in the event of multiple requests

1.   If two or more Member States have issued European arrest warrants for the same person, the decision on which of the European arrest warrants shall be executed shall be taken by the executing judicial authority with due consideration of all the circumstances and especially the relative seriousness and place of the offences, the respective dates of the European arrest warrants and whether the warrant has been issued for the purposes of prosecution or for execution of a custodial sentence or detention order.

2.   The executing judicial authority may seek the advice of Eurojust[9] when making the choice referred to in paragraph 1.

3.   In the event of a conflict between a European arrest warrant and a request for extradition presented by a third country, the decision on whether the European arrest warrant or the extradition request takes precedence shall be taken by the competent authority of the executing Member State with due consideration of all the circumstances, in particular those referred to in paragraph 1 and those mentioned in the applicable convention.

4.   This Article shall be without prejudice to Member States' obligations under the
        Statute of the International Criminal Court.

Article 17

Time limits and procedures for the decision to execute the European arrest warrant

1.   A European arrest warrant shall be dealt with and executed as a matter of urgency.

2.   In cases where the requested person consents to his surrender, the final decision on
        the execution of the European arrest warrant should be taken within a period of 10
        days after consent has been given.

3.   In other cases, the final decision on the execution of the European arrest warrant
        should be taken within a period of 60 days after the arrest of the requested person.

4.   Where in specific cases the European arrest warrant cannot be executed within the
        time limits laid down in paragraphs 2 or 3, the executing judicial authority shall
        immediately inform the issuing judicial authority thereof, giving the reasons for the
        delay. In such case, the time limits may be extended by a further 30 days.

5.   As long as the executing judicial authority has not taken a final decision on the
        European arrest warrant, it shall ensure that the material conditions necessary for
        effective surrender of the person remain fulfilled.

6.   Reasons must be given for any refusal to execute a European arrest warrant.

7.   Where in exceptional circumstances a Member State cannot observe the time limits
        provided for in this Article, it shall inform Eurojust, giving the reasons for the delay.
        In addition, a Member State which has experienced repeated delays on the part of
        another Member State in the execution of European arrest warrants shall inform the
        Council with a view to evaluating the implementation of this Framework Decision
        at Member State level.

Article 18

Situation pending the decision

1.   Where the European arrest warrant has been issued for the purpose of conducting
        a criminal prosecution, the executing judicial authority must:

        (a)   either agree that the requested person should be heard according to Article 19;
        (b)   or agree to the temporary transfer of the requested person.

2.   The conditions and the duration of the temporary transfer shall be determined by
        mutual agreement between the issuing and executing judicial authorities.

3.   In the case of temporary transfer, the person must be able to return to the executing
        Member State to attend hearings concerning him or her as part of the surrender pro-
        cedure.

Article 19

Hearing the person pending the decision

1.   The requested person shall be heard by a judicial authority, assisted by another person
        designated in accordance with the law of the Member State of the requesting court.

2.   The requested person shall be heard in accordance with the law of the executing Member State and with the conditions determined by mutual agreement between the issuing and executing judicial authorities.

3.   The competent executing judicial authority may assign another judicial authority of its Member State to take part in the hearing of the requested person in order to ensure the proper application of this Article and of the conditions laid down.

Article 20

Privileges and immunities

1.   Where the requested person enjoys a privilege or immunity regarding jurisdiction or execution in the executing Member State, the time limits referred to in Article 17 shall not start running unless, and counting from the day when, the executing judicial authority is informed of the fact that the privilege or immunity has been waived.

      The executing Member State shall ensure that the material conditions necessary for effective surrender are fulfilled when the person no longer enjoys such privilege or immunity.

2.   Where power to waive the privilege or immunity lies with an authority of the executing Member State, the executing judicial authority shall request it to exercise that power forthwith. Where power to waive the privilege or immunity lies with an authority of another State or international organisation, it shall be for the issuing judicial authority to request it to exercise that power.

Article 21

Competing international obligations

This Framework Decision shall not prejudice the obligations of the executing Member State where the requested person has been extradited to that Member State from a third State and where that person is protected by provisions of the arrangement under which he or she was extradited concerning speciality. The executing Member State shall take all necessary measures for requesting forthwith the consent of the State from which the requested person was extradited so that he or she can be surrendered to the Member State which issued the European arrest warrant. The time limits referred to in Article 17 shall not start running until the day on which these speciality rules cease to apply. Pending the decision of the State from which the requested person was extradited, the executing Member State will ensure that the material conditions necessary for effective surrender remain fulfilled.

Article 22

Notification of the decision

The executing judicial authority shall notify the issuing judicial authority immediately of the decision on the action to be taken on the European arrest warrant.

Article 23

Time limits for surrender of the person

1.   The person requested shall be surrendered as soon as possible on a date agreed between the authorities concerned.

2.   He or she shall be surrendered no later than 10 days after the final decision on the execution of the European arrest warrant.

3.   If the surrender of the requested person within the period laid down in paragraph 2 is prevented by circumstances beyond the control of any of the Member States, the executing and issuing judicial authorities shall immediately contact each other and agree on a new surrender date. In that event, the surrender shall take place within 10 days of the new date thus agreed.

4.   The surrender may exceptionally be temporarily postponed for serious humanitarian reasons, for example if there are substantial grounds for believing that it would manifestly endanger the requested person's life or health. The execution of the European arrest warrant shall take place as soon as these grounds have ceased to exist. The executing judicial authority shall immediately inform the issuing judicial authority and agree on a new surrender date. In that event, the surrender shall take place within 10 days of the new date thus agreed.

5.   Upon expiry of the time limits referred to in paragraphs 2 to 4, if the person is still being held in custody he shall be released.

Article 24

Postponed or conditional surrender

1.   The executing judicial authority may, after deciding to execute the European arrest warrant, postpone the surrender of the requested person so that he or she may be prosecuted in the executing Member State or, if he or she has already been sentenced, so that he or she may serve, in its territory, a sentence passed for an act other than that referred to in the European arrest warrant.

2.   Instead of postponing the surrender, the executing judicial authority may temporarily surrender the requested person to the issuing Member State under conditions to be determined by mutual agreement between the executing and the issuing judicial authorities. The agreement shall be made in writing and the conditions shall be binding on all the authorities in the issuing Member State.

Article 25

Transit

1.   Each Member State shall, except when it avails itself of the possibility of refusal when the transit of a national or a resident is requested for the purpose of the execution of a custodial sentence or detention order, permit the transit through its territory of a requested person who is being surrendered provided that it has been given information on:

   (a)   the identity and nationality of the person subject to the European arrest warrant;
   (b)   the existence of a European arrest warrant;
   (c)   the nature and legal classification of the offence;
   (d)   the description of the circumstances of the offence, including the date and place.

   Where a person who is the subject of a European arrest warrant for the purposes of prosecution is a national or resident of the Member State of transit, transit may be subject to the condition that the person, after being heard, is returned to the transit Member State to serve the custodial sentence or detention order passed against him in the issuing Member State.

2.   Each Member State shall designate an authority responsible for receiving transit requests and the necessary documents, as well as any other official correspondence

relating to transit requests. Member States shall communicate this designation to the General Secretariat of the Council.

3.   The transit request and the information set out in paragraph 1 may be addressed to the authority designated pursuant to paragraph 2 by any means capable of producing a written record. The Member State of transit shall notify its decision by the same procedure.

4.   This Framework Decision does not apply in the case of transport by air without a scheduled stopover. However, if an unscheduled landing occurs, the issuing Member State shall provide the authority designated pursuant to paragraph 2 with the information provided for in paragraph 1.

5.   Where a transit concerns a person who is to be extradited from a third State to a Member State this Article will apply mutatis mutandis. In particular the expression "European arrest warrant" shall be deemed to be replaced by "extradition request".

CHAPTER 3

EFFECTS OF THE SURRENDER

Article 26

Deduction of the period of detention served in the executing Member State

1.   The issuing Member State shall deduct all periods of detention arising from the execution of a European arrest warrant from the total period of detention to be served in the issuing Member State as a result of a custodial sentence or detention order being passed.

2.   To that end, all information concerning the duration of the detention of the requested person on the basis of the European arrest warrant shall be transmitted by the executing judicial authority or the central authority designated under Article 7 to the issuing judicial authority at the time of the surrender.

Article 27

Possible prosecution for other offences

1.   Each Member State may notify the General Secretariat of the Council that, in its relations with other Member States that have given the same notification, consent is presumed to have been given for the prosecution, sentencing or detention with a view to the carrying out of a custodial sentence or detention order for an offence committed prior to his or her surrender, other than that for which he or she was surrendered, unless in a particular case the executing judicial authority states otherwise in its decision on surrender.

2.   Except in the cases referred to in paragraphs 1 and 3, a person surrendered may not be prosecuted, sentenced or otherwise deprived of his or her liberty for an offence committed prior to his or her surrender other than that for which he or she was surrendered.

3.   Paragraph 2 does not apply in the following cases:

(a)   when the person having had an opportunity to leave the territory of the Member State to which he or she has been surrendered has not done so within 45 days of his or her final discharge, or has returned to that territory after leaving it;

(b)   the offence is not punishable by a custodial sentence or detention order;

(c) the criminal proceedings do not give rise to the application of a measure restricting personal liberty;

(d) when the person could be liable to a penalty or a measure not involving the deprivation of liberty, in particular a financial penalty or a measure in lieu thereof, even if the penalty or measure may give rise to a restriction of his or her personal liberty;

(e) when the person consented to be surrendered, where appropriate at the same time as he or she renounced the speciality rule, in accordance with Article 13;

(f) when the person, after his/her surrender, has expressly renounced entitlement to the speciality rule with regard to specific offences preceding his/her surrender. Renunciation shall be given before the competent judicial authorities of the issuing Member State and shall be recorded in accordance with that State's domestic law. The renunciation shall be drawn up in such a way as to make clear that the person has given it voluntarily and in full awareness of the consequences. To that end, the person shall have the right to legal counsel;

(g) where the executing judicial authority which surrendered the person gives its consent in accordance with paragraph 4.

4.   A request for consent shall be submitted to the executing judicial authority, accompanied by the information mentioned in Article 8(1) and a translation as referred to in Article 8(2). Consent shall be given when the offence for which it is requested is itself subject to surrender in accordance with the provisions of this Framework Decision. Consent shall be refused on the grounds referred to in Article 3 and otherwise may be refused only on the grounds referred to in Article 4. The decision shall be taken no later than 30 days after receipt of the request.

For the situations mentioned in Article 5 the issuing Member State must give the guarantees provided for therein.

Article 28

Surrender or subsequent extradition

1.   Each Member State may notify the General Secretariat of the Council that, in its relations with other Member States which have given the same notification, the consent for the surrender of a person to a Member State other than the executing Member State pursuant to a European arrest warrant issued for an offence committed prior to his or her surrender is presumed to have been given, unless in a particular case the executing judicial authority states otherwise in its decision on surrender.

2.   In any case, a person who has been surrendered to the issuing Member State pursuant to a European arrest warrant may, without the consent of the executing Member State, be surrendered to a Member State other than the executing Member State pursuant to a European arrest warrant issued for any offence committed prior to his or her surrender in the following cases:

(a) where the requested person, having had an opportunity to leave the territory of the Member State to which he or she has been surrendered, has not done so within 45 days of his final discharge, or has returned to that territory after leaving it;

(b) where the requested person consents to be surrendered to a Member State other than the executing Member State pursuant to a European arrest warrant. Consent shall be given before the competent judicial authorities of the issuing Member State and shall be recorded in accordance with that State's national law. It shall be drawn up in such a way as to make clear that the person concerned has given it voluntarily and in full awareness of the consequences. To that end, the requested person shall have the right to legal counsel;

(c)   where the requested person is not subject to the speciality rule, in accordance with Article 27(3)(a), (e), (f) and (g).

3.   The executing judicial authority consents to the surrender to another Member State according to the following rules:

(a)   the request for consent shall be submitted in accordance with Article 9, accompanied by the information mentioned in Article 8(1) and a translation as stated in Article 8(2);
(b)   consent shall be given when the offence for which it is requested is itself subject to surrender in accordance with the provisions of this Framework Decision;
(c)   the decision shall be taken no later than 30 days after receipt of the request;
(d)   consent shall be refused on the grounds referred to in Article 3 and otherwise may be refused only on the grounds referred to in Article 4.

For the situations referred to in Article 5, the issuing Member State must give the guarantees provided for therein.

4.   Notwithstanding paragraph 1, a person who has been surrendered pursuant to a European arrest warrant shall not be extradited to a third State without the consent of the competent authority of the Member State which surrendered the person. Such consent shall be given in accordance with the Conventions by which that Member State is bound, as well as with its domestic law.

Article 29

Handing over of property

1.   At the request of the issuing judicial authority or on its own initiative, the executing judicial authority shall, in accordance with its national law, seize and hand over property which:

(a)   may be required as evidence, or
(b)   has been acquired by the requested person as a result of the offence.

2.   The property referred to in paragraph 1 shall be handed over even if the European arrest warrant cannot be carried out owing to the death or escape of the requested person.

3.   If the property referred to in paragraph 1 is liable to seizure or confiscation in the territory of the executing Member State, the latter may, if the property is needed in connection with pending criminal proceedings, temporarily retain it or hand it over to the issuing Member State, on condition that it is returned.

4.   Any rights which the executing Member State or third parties may have acquired in the property referred to in paragraph 1 shall be preserved. Where such rights exist, the issuing Member State shall return the property without charge to the executing Member State as soon as the criminal proceedings have been terminated.

Article 30

Expenses

1.   Expenses incurred in the territory of the executing Member State for the execution of a European arrest warrant shall be borne by that Member State.

2.   All other expenses shall be borne by the issuing Member State.

CHAPTER 4

GENERAL AND FINAL PROVISIONS

Article 31

Relation to other legal instruments

1.   Without prejudice to their application in relations between Member States and third States, this Framework Decision shall, from 1 January 2004, replace the corresponding provisions of the following conventions applicable in the field of extradition in relations between the Member States:

    (a)   the European Convention on Extradition of 13 December 1957, its additional protocol of 15 October 1975, its second additional protocol of 17 March 1978, and the European Convention on the suppression of terrorism of 27 January 1977 as far as extradition is concerned;

    (b)   the Agreement between the 12 Member States of the European Communities on the simplification and modernisation of methods of transmitting extradition requests of 26 May 1989;

    (c)   the Convention of 10 March 1995 on simplified extradition procedure between the Member States of the European Union;

    (d)   the Convention of 27 September 1996 relating to extradition between the Member States of the European Union;

    (e)   Title III, Chapter 4 of the Convention of 19 June 1990 implementing the Schengen Agreement of 14 June 1985 on the gradual abolition of checks at common borders.

2.   Member States may continue to apply bilateral or multilateral agreements or arrangements in force when this Framework Decision is adopted in so far as such agreements or arrangements allow the objectives of this Framework Decision to be extended or enlarged and help to simplify or facilitate further the procedures for surrender of persons who are the subject of European arrest warrants.

Member States may conclude bilateral or multilateral agreements or arrangements after this Framework Decision has come into force in so far as such agreements or arrangements allow the prescriptions of this Framework Decision to be extended or enlarged and help to simplify or facilitate further the procedures for surrender of persons who are the subject of European arrest warrants, in particular by fixing time limits shorter than those fixed in Article 17, by extending the list of offences laid down in Article 2(2), by further limiting the grounds for refusal set out in Articles 3 and 4, or by lowering the threshold provided for in Article 2(1) or (2).

The agreements and arrangements referred to in the second subparagraph may in no case affect relations with Member States which are not parties to them.

Member States shall, within three months from the entry into force of this Framework Decision, notify the Council and the Commission of the existing agreements and arrangements referred to in the first subparagraph which they wish to continue applying.

Member States shall also notify the Council and the Commission of any new agreement or arrangement as referred to in the second subparagraph, within three months of signing it.

3.   Where the conventions or agreements referred to in paragraph 1 apply to the territories of Member States or to territories for whose external relations a Member State is responsible to which this Framework Decision does not apply, these instruments

shall continue to govern the relations existing between those territories and the other Members States.

Article 32

Transitional provision

1. Extradition requests received before 1 January 2004 will continue to be governed by existing instruments relating to extradition. Requests received after that date will be governed by the rules adopted by Member States pursuant to this Framework Decision. However, any Member State may, at the time of the adoption of this Framework Decision by the Council, make a statement indicating that as executing Member State it will continue to deal with requests relating to acts committed before a date which it specifies in accordance with the extradition system applicable before 1 January 2004. The date in question may not be later than 7 August 2002. The said statement will be published in the Official Journal of the European Communities. It may be withdrawn at any time.

Article 33

Provisions concerning Austria and Gibraltar

1. As long as Austria has not modified Article 12(1) of the "Auslieferungs- und Rechtshilfegesetz" and, at the latest, until 31 December 2008, it may allow its executing judicial authorities to refuse the enforcement of a European arrest warrant if the requested person is an Austrian citizen and if the act for which the European arrest warrant has been issued is not punishable under Austrian law.

2. This Framework Decision shall apply to Gibraltar.

Article 34

Implementation

1. Member States shall take the necessary measures to comply with the provisions of this Framework Decision by 31 December 2003.

2. Member States shall transmit to the General Secretariat of the Council and to the Commission the text of the provisions transposing into their national law the obligations imposed on them under this Framework Decision. When doing so, each Member State may indicate that it will apply immediately this Framework Decision in its relations with those Member States which have given the same notification. The General Secretariat of the Council shall communicate to the Member States and to the Commission the information received pursuant to Article 7(2), Article 8(2), Article 13(4) and Article 25(2). It shall also have the information published in the Official Journal of the European Communities.

3. On the basis of the information communicated by the General Secretariat of the Council, the Commission shall, by 31 December 2004 at the latest, submit a report to the European Parliament and to the Council on the operation of this Framework Decision, accompanied, where necessary, by legislative proposals.

4. The Council shall in the second half of 2003 conduct a review, in particular of the practical application, of the provisions of this Framework Decision by the Member States as well as the functioning of the Schengen Information System.

Article 35

Entry into force

This Framework Decision shall enter into force on the twentieth day following that of its publication in the Official Journal of the European Communities.

Done at Luxembourg, 13 June 2002.

For the Council

The President

M. Rajoy Brey

(1)   OJ C 332 E, 27.11.2001, p. 305.
(2)   Opinion delivered on 9 January 2002 (not yet published in the Official Journal).
(3)   OJ C 12 E, 15.1.2001, p. 10.
(4)   OJ L 239, 22.9.2000, p. 19.
(5)   OJ C 78, 30.3.1995, p. 2.
(6)   OJ C 313, 13.10.1996, p. 12.
(7)   OJ C 364, 18.12.2000, p. 1.
(8)   Council Joint Action 98/428/JHA of 29 June 1998 on the creation of a European Judicial Network (OJ L 191, 7.7.1998, p. 4).
(9)   Council Decision 2002/187/JHA of 28 February 2002 setting up Eurojust with a view to reinforcing the fight against serious crime (OJ L 63, 6.3.2002, p. 1).

ANNEX

Note: the detailed format of the arrest warrant is attached to the Framework Decision as an annex) (not reproduced here).

Statements made by certain Member States on the adoption of the Framework Decision

Statements provided for in Article 32

Statement by France:

Pursuant to Article 32 of the framework decision on the European arrest warrant and the surrender procedures between Member States, France states that as executing Member State it will continue to deal with requests relating to acts committed before 1 November 1993, the date of entry into force of the Treaty on European Union signed in Maastricht on 7 February 1992, in accordance with the extradition system applicable before 1 January 2004.

Statement by Italy:

Italy will continue to deal in accordance with the extradition rules in force with all requests relating to acts committed before the date of entry into force of the framework decision on the European arrest warrant, as provided for in Article 32 thereof.

Statement by Austria:

Pursuant to Article 32 of the framework decision on the European arrest warrant and the surrender procedures between Member States, Austria states that as executing Member State it will continue to deal with requests relating to punishable acts committed before the date of entry into force of the framework decision in accordance with the extradition system applicable before that date.

Statements provided for in Article 13(4)

Statement by Belgium:

The consent of the person concerned to his or her surrender may be revoked until the time of surrender.

Statement by Denmark:

Consent to surrender and express renunciation of entitlement to the speciality rule may be revoked in accordance with the relevant rules applicable at any time under Danish law.

Statement by Ireland:

In Ireland, consent to surrender and, where appropriate, express renunciation of the entitlement to the "specialty" rule referred to in Article 27(2) may be revoked. Consent may be revoked in accordance with domestic law until surrender has been executed.

Statement by Finland:

In Finland, consent to surrender and, where appropriate, express renunciation of entitlement to the "speciality rule" referred to in Article 27(2) may be revoked. Consent may be revoked in accordance with domestic law until surrender has been executed.

Statement by Sweden:

Consent or renunciation within the meaning of Article 13(1) may be revoked by the party whose surrender has been requested. Revocation must take place before the decision on surrender is executed.

Annex 2

(Acts adopted pursuant to Title VI of the Treaty on European Union)

COUNCIL FRAMEWORK DECISION

of 13 June 2002

on combating terrorism

(2002/475/JHA)

THE COUNCIL OF THE EUROPEAN UNION,

Having regard to the Treaty establishing the European Union, and in particular Article 29, Article 31(e) and Article 34(2)(b) thereof,

Having regard to the proposal from the Commission[1],

Having regard to the opinion of the European Parliament[2],

Whereas:

(1)   The European Union is founded on the universal values of human dignity, liberty, equality and solidarity, respect for human rights and fundamental freedoms. It is based on the principle of democracy and the principle of the rule of law, principles which are common to the Member States.

(2)   Terrorism constitutes one of the most serious violations of those principles. The La Gomera Declaration adopted at the informal Council meeting on 14 October 1995 affirmed that terrorism constitutes a threat to democracy, to the free exercise of human rights and to economic and social development.

(3)   All or some Member States are party to a number of conventions relating to terrorism. The Council of Europe Convention of 27 January 1977 on the Suppression of Terrorism does not regard terrorist offences as political offences or as offences connected with political offences or as offences inspired by political motives. The United Nations has adopted the Convention for the suppression of terrorist bombings of 15 December 1997 and the Convention for the suppression of financing terrorism of 9 December 1999. A draft global Convention against terrorism is currently being negotiated within the United Nations.

(4)   At European Union level, on 3 December 1998 the Council adopted the Action Plan of the Council and the Commission on how best to implement the provisions of the Treaty of Amsterdam on an area of freedom, security and justice[3]. Account should also be taken of the Council Conclusions of 20 September 2001 and of the Extraordinary European Council plan of action to combat terrorism of 21 September 2001. Terrorism was referred to in the conclusions of the Tampere European Council of 15 and 16 October 1999, and of the Santa María da Feira

European Council of 19 and 20 June 2000. It was also mentioned in the Commission communication to the Council and the European Parliament on the biannual update of the scoreboard to review progress on the creation of an area of 'freedom, security and justice' in the European Union (second half of 2000). Furthermore, on 5 September 2001 the European Parliament adopted a recommendation on the role of the European Union in combating terrorism. It should, moreover, be recalled that on 30 July 1996 twenty-five measures to fight against terrorism were advocated by the leading industrialised countries (G7) and Russia meeting in Paris.

(5)   The European Union has adopted numerous specific measures having an impact on terrorism and organised crime, such as the Council Decision of 3 December 1998 instructing Europol to deal with crimes committed or likely to be committed in the course of terrorist activities against life, limb, personal freedom or property[4]; Council Joint Action 96/610/JHA of 15 October 1996 concerning the creation and maintenance of a Directory of specialised counter-terrorist competences, skills and expertise to facilitate counter-terrorism cooperation between the Member States of the European Union[5]; Council JointAct ion 98/428/JHA of 29 June 1998 on the creation of a European Judicial Network[6], with responsibilities in terrorist offences, in particular Article 2; Council Joint Action 98/733/JHA of 21 December 1998 on making it a criminal offence to participate in a criminal organisation in the Member States of the European Union[7]; and the Council Recommendation of 9 December 1999 on cooperation in combating the financing of terrorist groups[8].

(6)   The definition of terrorist offences should be approximated in all Member States, including those offences relating to terrorist groups. Furthermore, penalties and sanctions should be provided for natural and legal persons having committed or being liable for such offences, which reflect the seriousness of such offences.

(7)   Jurisdictional rules should be established to ensure that the terrorist offence may be effectively prosecuted.

(8)   Victims of terrorist offences are vulnerable, and therefore specific measures are necessary with regard to them.

(9)   Given that the objectives of the proposed action cannot be sufficiently achieved by the Member States unilaterally, and can therefore, because of the need for reciprocity, be better achieved at the level of the Union, the Union may adopt measures, in accordance with the principle of subsidiarity. In accordance with the principle of proportionality, this Framework Decision does not go beyond what is necessary in order to achieve those objectives.

(10)   This Framework Decision respects fundamental rights as guaranteed by the European Convention for the Protection of Human Rights and Fundamental Freedoms and as they emerge from the constitutional traditions common to the Member States as principles of Community law. The Union observes the principles recognised by Article 6(2) of the Treaty on European Union and reflected in the Charter of Fundamental Rights of the European Union, notably Chapter VI thereof. Nothing in this Framework Decision may be interpreted as being intended to reduce or restrict fundamental rights or freedoms such as the right to strike, freedom of assembly, of association or of expression, including the right of everyone to form and to join trade unions with others for the protection of his or her interests and the related right to demonstrate.

(11)   Actions by armed forces during periods of armed conflict, which are governed by international humanitarian law within the meaning of these terms under that law, and, inasmuch as they are governed by other rules of international law, actions by

the armed forces of a State in the exercise of their official duties are not governed by this Framework Decision,

HAS ADOPTED THIS FRAMEWORK DECISION:

Article 1

Terrorist offences and fundamental rights and principles

1. Each Member State shall take the necessary measures to ensure that the intentional acts referred to below in points (a) to (i), as defined as offences under national law, which, given their nature or context, may seriously damage a country or an international organisation where committed with the aim of:

— seriously intimidating a population, or

— unduly compelling a Government or international organisation to perform or abstain from performing any act, or

— seriously destabilising or destroying the fundamental political, constitutional, economic or social structures of a country or an international organisation,

shall be deemed to be terrorist offences:

(a)   attacks upon a person's life which may cause death;

(b)   attacks upon the physical integrity of a person;

(c)   kidnapping or hostage taking;

(d)   causing extensive destruction to a Government or public facility, a transport system, an infrastructure facility, including an information system, a fixed platform located on the continental shelf, a public place or private property likely to endanger human life or result in major economic loss;

(e)   seizure of aircraft, ships or other means of public or goods transport;

(f)   manufacture, possession, acquisition, transport, supply or use of weapons, explosives or of nuclear, biological or chemical weapons, as well as research into, and development of, biological and chemical weapons;

(g)   release of dangerous substances, or causing fires, floods or explosions the effect of which is to endanger human life;

(h)   interfering with or disrupting the supply of water, power or any other fundamental natural resource the effectof which is to endanger human life;

(i)   threatening to commit any of the acts listed in (a) to (h).

2. This Framework Decision shall not have the effect of altering the obligation to respect fundamental rights and fundamental legal principles as enshrined in Article 6 of the Treaty on European Union.

Article 2

Offences relatingto a terrorist group

1. For the purposes of this Framework Decision, 'terrorist group' shall mean: a structured group of more than two persons, established over a period of time and acting in concert to commit terrorist offences. 'Structured group' shall mean a group that is not randomly formed for the immediate commission of an offence and that does not need to have formally defined roles for its members, continuity of its membership or a developed structure.

2. Each Member State shall take the necessary measures to ensure that the following intentional acts are punishable:

(a)   directing a terrorist group;

(b)   participating in the activities of a terrorist group, including by supplying infor-
        mation or material resources, or by funding its activities in any way, with knowl-
        edge of the fact that such participation will contribute to the criminal activities of
        the terrorist group.

Article 3

Offences linked to terrorist activities

Each Member State shall take the necessary measures to ensure that terrorist-linked offences include the following acts:

(a)   aggravated theft with a view to committing one of the acts listed in Article 1(1);

(b)   extortion with a view to the perpetration of one of the acts listed in Article 1(1);

(c)   drawing up false administrative documents with a view to committing one of the
        acts listed in Article 1(1)(a) to (h) and Article 2(2)(b).

Article 4

Inciting, aiding or abetting, and attempting

1. Each Member State shall take the necessary measures to ensure that inciting or aiding or abetting an offence referred to in Article 1(1), Articles 2 or 3 is made punishable.

2. Each Member State shall take the necessary measures to ensure that attempting to commit an offence referred to in Article 1(1) and Article 3, with the exception of possession as provided for in Article 1(1)(f) and the offence referred to in Article 1(1)(i), is made punishable.

Article 5

Penalties

1. Each Member State shall take the necessary measures to ensure that the offences referred to in Articles 1 to 4 are punishable by effective, proportionate and dissuasive criminal penalties, which may entail extradition.

2. Each Member State shall take the necessary measures to ensure that the terrorist offences referred to in Article 1(1) and offences referred to in Article 4, inasmuch as they relate to terrorist offences, are punishable by custodial sentences heavier than those imposable under national law for such offences in the absence of the special intent required pursuant to Article 1(1), save where the sentences imposable are already the maximum possible sentences under national law.

3. Each Member State shall take the necessary measures to ensure that offences listed in Article 2 are punishable by custodial sentences, with a maximum sentence of not less than fifteen years for the offence referred to in Article 2(2)(a), and for the offences listed in Article 2(2)(b) a maximum sentence of not less than eight years. In so far as the offence referred to in Article 2(2)(a) refers only to the act in Article 1(1)(i), the maximum sentence shall not be less than eight years.

Article 6

Particular circumstances

Each Member State may take the necessary measures to ensure that the penalties referred to in Article 5 may be reduced if the offender:

(a)   renounces terrorist activity, and

(b)   provides the administrative or judicial authorities with information which they would not otherwise have been able to obtain, helping them to:

(i)   prevent or mitigate the effects of the offence;

(ii)   identify or bring to justice the other offenders;

(iii)   find evidence; or

(iv)   prevent further offences referred to in Articles 1 to 4.

Article 7

Liability of legal persons

1. Each Member State shall take the necessary measures to ensure that legal persons can be held liable for any of the offences referred to in Articles 1 to 4 committed for their benefit by any person, acting either individually or as part of an organ of the legal person, who has a leading position within the legal person, based on one of the following:

(a)   a power of representation of the legal person;

(b)   an authority to take decisions on behalf of the legal person;

(c)   an authority to exercise control within the legal person.

2. Apart from the cases provided for in paragraph 1, each Member State shall take the necessary measures to ensure that legal persons can be held liable where the lack of supervision or control by a person referred to in paragraph 1 has made possible the commission of any of the offences referred to in Articles 1 to 4 for the benefit of that legal person by a person under its authority.

3. Liability of legal persons under paragraphs 1 and 2 shall not exclude criminal proceedings against natural persons who are perpetrators, instigators or accessories in any of the offences referred to in Articles 1 to 4.

Article 8

Penalties for legal persons

Each Member State shall take the necessary measures to ensure that a legal person held liable pursuant to Article 7 is punishable by effective, proportionate and dissuasive penalties, which shall include criminal or non-criminal fines and may include other penalties, such as:

(a)   exclusion from entitlement to public benefits or aid;

(b)   temporary or permanent disqualification from the practice of commercial activities;

(c)   placing under judicial supervision;

(d)   a judicial winding-up order;

(e)   temporary or permanent closure of establishments which have been used for committing the offence.

Article 9

Jurisdiction and prosecution

1. Each Member State shall take the necessary measures to establish its jurisdiction over the offences referred to in Articles 1 to 4 where:

(a)   the offence is committed in whole or in part in its territory. Each Member State may extend its jurisdiction if the offence is committed in the territory of a Member State;

(b)   the offence is committed on board a vessel flying its flag or an aircraft registered there;

(c)   the offender is one of its nationals or residents;

(d)   the offence is committed for the benefit of a legal person established in its territory;

(e)   the offence is committed against the institutions or people of the Member State in question or against an institution of the European Union or a body set up in accordance with the Treaty establishing the European Community or the Treaty on European Union and based in that Member State.

2. When an offence falls within the jurisdiction of more than one Member State and when any of the States concerned can validly prosecute on the basis of the same facts, the Member States concerned shall cooperate in order to decide which of them will prosecute the offenders with the aim, if possible, of centralising proceedings in a single Member State. To this end, the Member States may have recourse to any body or mechanism established within the European Union in order to facilitate cooperation between their judicial authorities and the coordination of their action. Sequential account shall be taken of the following factors:

— the Member State shall be that in the territory of which the acts were committed,

— the Member State shall be that of which the perpetrator is a national or resident,

— the Member State shall be the Member State of origin of the victims,

— the Member State shall be that in the territory of which the perpetrator was found.

3. Each Member State shall take the necessary measures also to establish its jurisdiction over the offences referred to in Articles 1 to 4 in cases where it refuses to hand over or extradite a person suspected or convicted of such an offence to another Member State or to a third country.

4. Each Member State shall ensure that its jurisdiction covers cases in which any of the offences referred to in Articles 2 and 4 has been committed in whole or in part within its territory, wherever the terrorist group is based or pursues its criminal activities.

5. This Article shall not exclude the exercise of jurisdiction in criminal matters as laid down by a Member State in accordance with its national legislation.

Article 10

Protection of, and assistance to, victims

1. Member States shall ensure that investigations into, or prosecution of, offences covered by this Framework Decision are notdependent on a report or accusation made by a person subjected to the offence, at least if the acts were committed on the territory of the Member State.

2. In addition to the measures laid down in the Council Framework Decision 2001/220/JHA of 15 March 2001 on the standing of victims in criminal proceedings[9], each Member State shall, if necessary, take all measures possible to ensure appropriate assistance for victims' families.

Article 11

Implementation and reports

1. Member States shall take the necessary measures to comply with this Framework Decision by 31 December 2002.

2. By 31 December 2002, Member States shall forward to the General Secretariat of the Council and to the Commission the text of the provisions transposing into their national law the obligations imposed on them under this Framework Decision. On the basis of a report drawn up from that information and a report from the Commission, the Council shall assess, by 31 December 2003, whether Member States have taken the necessary measures to comply with this Framework Decision.

3. The Commission report shall specify, in particular, transposition into the criminal law of the Member States of the obligation referred to in Article 5(2).

Article 12

Territorial application

This Framework Decision shall apply to Gibraltar.

Article 13

Entry into force

This Framework Decision shall enter into force on the day of its publication in the Official Journal.

Endnotes:

(1) OJ C 332 E, 27.11.2001, p. 300.
(2) Opinion delivered on 6 February 2002 (notyet published in the Official Journal).
(3) OJ C 19, 23.1.1999, p. 1.
(4) OJ C 26, 30.1.1999, p. 22.
(5) OJ L 273, 25.10.1996, p. 1.
(6) OJ L 191, 7.7.1998, p. 4.
(7) OJ L 351, 29.12.1998, p. 1.
(8) OJ C 373, 23.12.1999, p. 1.
(9) OJ L 82, 22.3.2001, p. 1.

Annex 3

A SECURE EUROPE IN A BETTER WORLD

EUROPEAN SECURITY STRATEGY

Brussels, 12 December 2003

Introduction

Europe has never been so prosperous, so secure nor so free. The violence of the first half of the 20th Century has given way to a period of peace and stability unprecedented in European history.

The creation of the European Union has been central to this development. It has transformed the relations between our states, and the lives of our citizens. European countries are committed to dealing peacefully with disputes and to co-operating through common institutions. Over this period, the progressive spread of the rule of law and democracy has seen authoritarian regimes change into secure, stable and dynamic democracies. Successive enlargements are making a reality of the vision of a united and peaceful continent.

No single country is able to tackle today's complex problems on its own

The United States has played a critical role in European integration and European security, in particular through NATO. The end of the Cold War has left the United States in a dominant position as a military actor. However, no single country is able to tackle today's complex problems on its own.

Europe still faces security threats and challenges. The outbreak of conflict in the Balkans was a reminder that war has not disappeared from our continent. Over the last decade, no region of the world has been untouched by armed conflict. Most of these conflicts have been within rather than between states, and most of the victims have been civilians.

As a union of 25 states with over 450 million people producing a quarter of the world's Gross National Product (GNP), and with a wide range of instruments at its disposal, the European Union is inevitably a global player. In the last decade European forces have been deployed abroad to places as distant as Afghanistan, East Timor and the DRC. The increasing convergence of European interests and the strengthening of mutual solidarity of the EU makes us a more credible and effective actor. Europe should be ready to share in the responsibility for global security and in building a better world.

As a union of 25 states with over 450 million people producing a quarter of the world's Gross National Product (GNP), the European Union is inevitably a global player... it should be ready to share in the responsibility for global security and in building a better world.

I. THE SECURITY ENVIRONMENT: GLOBAL CHALLENGES AND KEY THREATS

Global Challenges

The post Cold War environment is one of increasingly open borders in which the internal and external aspects of security are indissolubly linked. Flows of trade and investment, the development of technology and the spread of democracy have brought freedom and prosperity to many people.

Others have perceived globalisation as a cause of frustration and injustice. These developments have also increased the scope for non-state groups to play a part in international affairs. And they have increased European dependence – and so vulnerability – on an interconnected infrastructure in transport, energy, information and other fields.

Since 1990, almost 4 million people have died in wars, 90% of them civilians. Over 18 million people world-wide have left their homes as a result of conflict.

In much of the developing world, poverty and disease cause untold suffering and give rise to pressing security concerns. Almost 3 billion people, half the world's population, live on less than 2 Euros a day. 45 million die every year of hunger and malnutrition. AIDS is now one of the most devastating pandemics in human history and contributes to the breakdown of societies. New diseases can spread rapidly and become global threats. Sub-Saharan Africa is poorer now than it was 10 years ago. In many cases, economic failure is linked to political problems and violent conflict.

> *45 million people die every year of hunger and malnutrition... Aids contributes to the breakdown of societies... Security is a precondition of development*

Security is a precondition of development. Conflict not only destroys infrastructure, including social infrastructure; it also encourages criminality, deters investment and makes normal economic activity impossible. A number of countries and regions are caught in a cycle of conflict, insecurity and poverty.

Competition for natural resources - notably water - which will be aggravated by global warming over the next decades, is likely to create further turbulence and migratory movements in various regions.

Energy dependence is a special concern for Europe. Europe is the world's largest importer of oil and gas. Imports account for about 50% of energy consumption today. This will rise to 70% in 2030. Most energy imports come from the Gulf, Russia and North Africa.

Key Threats

Large-scale aggression against any Member State is now improbable. Instead, Europe faces new threats which are more diverse, less visible and less predictable.

Terrorism: Terrorism puts lives at risk; it imposes large costs; it seeks to undermine the openness and tolerance of our societies, and it poses a growing strategic threat to the whole of Europe. Increasingly, terrorist movements are well-resourced, connected by electronic networks, and are willing to use unlimited violence to cause massive casualties.

The most recent wave of terrorism is global in its scope and is linked to violent religious extremism. It arises out of complex causes. These include the pressures of modernisation, cultural, social and political crises, and the alienation of young people living in foreign societies. This phenomenon is also a part of our own society.

Europe is both a target and a base for such terrorism: European countries are targets and have been attacked. Logistical bases for Al Qaeda cells have been uncovered in the UK, Italy, Germany, Spain and Belgium. Concerted European action is indispensable. Proliferation of Weapons of Mass Destruction is potentially the greatest threat to our security. The international treaty regimes and export control arrangements have slowed the spread of WMD and delivery systems. We are now, however, entering a new and dangerous period that raises the possibility of a WMD arms race, especially

> *The last use of WMD was by the Aum terrorist sect in the Tokyo underground in 1995, using sarin gas. 12 people were killed and several thousand injured. Two years earlier, Aum had sprayed anthrax spores on a Tokyo street.*

in the Middle East. Advances in the biological sciences may increase the potency of biological weapons in the coming years; attacks with chemical and radiological materials are also a serious possibility. The spread of missile technology adds a further element of instability and could put Europe at increasing risk.

The most frightening scenario is one in which terrorist groups acquire weapons of mass destruction. In this event, a small group would be able to inflict damage on a scale previously possible only for States and armies.

Regional Conflicts: Problems such as those in Kashmir, the Great Lakes Region and the Korean Peninsula impact on European interests directly and indirectly, as do conflicts nearer to home, above all in the Middle East. Violent or frozen conflicts, which also persist on our borders, threaten regional stability. They destroy human lives and social and physical infrastructures; they threaten minorities, fundamental freedoms and human rights. Conflict can lead to extremism, terrorism and state failure; it provides opportunities for organised crime. Regional insecurity can fuel the demand for WMD. The most practical way to tackle the often elusive new threats will sometimes be to deal with the older problems of regional conflict.

State Failure: Bad governance – corruption, abuse of power, weak institutions and lack of accountability - and civil conflict corrode States from within. In some cases, this has brought about the collapse of State institutions. Somalia, Liberia and Afghanistan under the Taliban are the best known recent examples. Collapse of the State can be associated with obvious threats, such as organised crime or terrorism. State failure is an alarming phenomenon, that undermines global governance, and adds to regional instability.

Organised Crime: Europe is a prime target for organised crime. This internal threat to our security has an important external dimension: cross-border trafficking in drugs, women, illegal migrants and weapons accounts for a large part of the activities of criminal gangs. It can have links with terrorism.

Such criminal activities are often associated with weak or failing states. Revenues from drugs have fuelled the weakening of state structures in several drug-producing countries. Revenues from trade in gemstones, timber and small arms, fuel conflict in other parts of the world. All these activities undermine both the rule of law and social order itself. In extreme cases, organised crime can come to dominate the state. 90% of the heroin in Europe comes from poppies grown in Afghanistan – where the drugs trade pays for private armies. Most of it is distributed through Balkan criminal networks which are also responsible for some 200,000 of the 700,000 women victims of the sex trade world wide. A new dimension to organised crime which will merit further attention is the growth in maritime piracy.

Taking these different elements together – terrorism committed to maximum violence, the availability of weapons of mass destruction, organised crime, the weakening of the state system and the privatisation of force – we could be confronted with a very radical threat indeed.

II. STRATEGIC OBJECTIVES

We live in a world that holds brighter prospects but also greater threats than we have known. The future will depend partly on our actions. We need both to think globally and to act locally. To defend its security and to promote its values, the EU has three strategic objectives:

Addressing the Threats

The European Union has been active in tackling the key threats.

–   It has responded after 11 September with measures that included the adoption of a European Arrest Warrant, steps to attack terrorist financing and an agreement on mutual legal assistance with the U.S.A. The EU continues to develop cooperation in this area and to improve its defences.

–   It has pursued policies against proliferation over many years. The Union has just agreed a further programme of action which foresees steps to strengthen the International Atomic Energy Agency, measures to tighten export controls and to deal with illegal shipments and illicit procurement. The EU is committed to achieving universal adherence to multilateral treaty regimes, as well as to strengthening the treaties and their verification provisions.

–   The European Union and Member States have intervened to help deal with regional conflicts and to put failed states back on their feet, including in the Balkans, Afghanistan, and in the DRC. Restoring good government to the Balkans, fostering democracy and enabling the authorities there to tackle organised crime is one of the most effective ways of dealing with organised crime within the EU.

In an era of globalisation, distant threats may be as much a concern as those that are near at hand. Nuclear activities in North Korea, nuclear risks in South Asia, and proliferation in the Middle East are all of concern to Europe.

In an era of globalisation, distant threats may be as much a concern as those that are near at hand... The first line of defence will be often be abroad. The new threats are dynamic...
Conflict prevention and threat prevention cannot start too early.

Terrorists and criminals are now able to operate world-wide: their activities in central or southeast Asia may be a threat to European countries or their citizens. Meanwhile, global communication increases awareness in Europe of regional conflicts or humanitarian tragedies anywhere in the world.

Our traditional concept of self- defence – up to and including the Cold War – was based on the threat of invasion. With the new threats, the first line of defence will often be abroad. The new threats are dynamic. The risks of proliferation grow over time; left alone, terrorist networks will become ever more dangerous. State failure and organised crime spread if they are neglected – as we have seen in West Africa. This implies that we should be ready to act before a crisis occurs. Conflict prevention and threat prevention cannot start too early.

In contrast to the massive visible threat in the Cold War, none of the new threats is purely military; nor can any be tackled by purely military means. Each requires a mixture of instruments. Proliferation may be contained through export controls and attacked through political, economic and other pressures while the underlying political causes are also tackled. Dealing with terrorism may require a mixture of intelligence, police, judicial, military and other means. In failed states, military instruments may be needed to restore order, humanitarian means to tackle the immediate crisis. Regional conflicts need political solutions but military assets and effective policing may be needed in the post conflict phase. Economic instruments serve reconstruction, and civilian crisis management helps restore civil government. The European Union is particularly well equipped to respond to such multi-faceted situations.

Building Security in our Neighbourhood

Even in an era of globalisation, geography is still important. It is in the European interest that countries on our borders are well-governed. Neighbours who are engaged in violent conflict, weak states where organised crime flourishes, dysfunctional societies or exploding population growth on its borders all pose problems for Europe.

Enlargement should not create new dividing lines in Europe.
Resolution of the Arab/Israeli conflict is a strategic priority for Europe

The integration of acceding states increases our security but also brings the EU closer to troubled areas. Our task is to promote a ring of well governed countries to the East of the European Union and on the borders of the Mediterranean with whom we can enjoy close and cooperative relations.

The importance of this is best illustrated in the Balkans. Through our concerted efforts with the US, Russia, NATO and other international partners, the stability of the region is no longer threatened by the outbreak of major conflict. The credibility of our foreign policy depends on the consolidation of our achievements there. The European perspective offers both a strategic objective and an incentive for reform.

It is not in our interest that enlargement should create new dividing lines in Europe. We need to extend the benefits of economic and political cooperation to our neighbours in the East while tackling political problems there. We should now take a stronger and more active interest in the problems of the Southern Caucasus, which will in due course also be a neighbouring region.

Resolution of the Arab/Israeli conflict is a strategic priority for Europe. Without this, there will be little chance of dealing with other problems in the Middle East. The European Union must remain engaged and ready to commit resources to the problem until it is solved. The two state solution – which Europe has long supported – is now widely accepted. Implementing it will require a united and cooperative effort by the European Union, the United States, the United Nations and Russia, and the countries of the region, but above all by the Israelis and the Palestinians themselves.

The Mediterranean area generally continues to undergo serious problems of economic stagnation, social unrest and unresolved conflicts. The European Union's interests require a continued engagement with Mediterranean partners, through more effective economic, security and cultural cooperation in the framework of the Barcelona Process. A broader engagement with the Arab World should also be considered.

AN INTERNATIONAL ORDER BASED ON EFFECTIVE MULTILATERALISM

In a world of global threats, global markets and global media, our security and prosperity increasingly depend on an effective multilateral system. The development of a stronger international society, well functioning international institutions and a rule-based international order is our objective.

We are committed to upholding and developing International Law. The fundamental framework for international relations is the United Nations Charter. The United Nations Security Council has the primary responsibility for the maintenance of international peace and security. Strengthening the United Nations, equipping it to fulfil its responsibilities and to act effectively, is a European priority.

Our security and prosperity increasingly depend on an effective multilateral system. We are committed to upholding and developing International Law.
The fundamental framework for international relations is the United Nations Charter.

We want international organisations, regimes and treaties to be effective in confronting threats to international peace and security, and must therefore be ready to act when their rules are broken.

Key institutions in the international system, such as the World Trade Organisation (WTO) and the International Financial Institutions, have extended their membership. China has joined the WTO and Russia is negotiating its entry. It should be an objective for us to widen the membership of such bodies while maintaining their high standards.

One of the core elements of the international system is the transatlantic relationship. This is not only in our bilateral interest but strengthens the international community as a whole. NATO is an important expression of this relationship.

Regional organisations also strengthen global governance. For the European Union, the strength and effectiveness of the OSCE and the Council of Europe has a particular significance. Other regional organisations such as ASEAN, MERCOSUR and the African Union make an important contribution to a more orderly world.

It is a condition of a rule-based international order that law evolves in response to developments such as proliferation, terrorism and global warming. We have an interest in further developing existing institutions such as the World Trade Organisation and in supporting new ones such as the International Criminal Court. Our own experience in Europe demonstrates that security can be increased through confidence building and arms control regimes. Such instruments can also make an important contribution to security and stability in our neighbourhood and beyond.

The quality of international society depends on the quality of the governments that are its foundation. The best protection for our security is a world of well-governed democratic states. Spreading good governance, supporting social and political reform, dealing with corruption and abuse of power, establishing the rule of law and protecting human rights are the best means of strengthening the international order.

Trade and development policies can be powerful tools for promoting reform. As the world's largest provider of official assistance and its largest trading entity, the European Union and its Member States are well placed to pursue these goals.

Contributing to better governance through assistance programmes, conditionality and targeted trade measures remains an important feature in our policy that we should further reinforce. A world seen as offering justice and opportunity for everyone will be more secure for the European Union and its citizens.

A number of countries have placed themselves outside the bounds of international society. Some have sought isolation; others persistently violate international norms. It is desirable that such countries should rejoin the international community, and the EU should be ready to provide assistance. Those who are unwilling to do so should understand that there is a price to be paid, including in their relationship with the European Union.

III. POLICY IMPLICATIONS FOR EUROPE

The European Union has made progress towards a coherent foreign policy and effective crisis management. We have instruments in place that can be used effectively, as we have demonstrated in the Balkans and beyond. But if we are to make a contribution that matches our potential, we need to be more active, more coherent and more capable. And we need to work with others.

More active in pursuing our strategic objectives. This applies to the full spectrum of instruments for crisis management and conflict prevention at our disposal, including political, diplomatic, military and civilian, trade and development activities. Active policies are needed to counter the new dynamic threats. We need to develop a strategic culture that fosters early, rapid, and when necessary, robust intervention.

We need to develop a strategic culture that fosters early, rapid and when necessary, robust intervention.

As a Union of 25 members, spending more than 160 billion Euros on defence, we should be able to sustain several operations simultaneously. We could add particular value by developing operations involving both military and civilian capabilities.

The EU should support the United Nations as it responds to threats to international peace and security. The EU is committed to reinforcing its cooperation with the UN to assist countries emerging from conflicts, and to enhancing its support for the UN in short-term crisis management situations.

We need to be able to act before countries around us deteriorate, when signs of proliferation are detected, and before humanitarian emergencies arise. Preventive engagement can avoid more serious problems in the future. A European Union which takes greater responsibility and which is more active will be one which carries greater political weight.

More Capable. A more capable Europe is within our grasp, though it will take time to realise our full potential. Actions underway – notably the establishment of a defence agency – take us in the right direction.

To transform our militaries into more flexible, mobile forces, and to enable them to address the new threats, more resources for defence and more effective use of resources are necessary.

Systematic use of pooled and shared assets would reduce duplications, overheads and, in the medium-term, increase capabilities.

In almost every major intervention, military efficiency has been followed by civilian chaos. We need greater capacity to bring all necessary civilian resources to bear in crisis and post crisis situations.

Stronger diplomatic capability: we need a system that combines the resources of Member States with those of EU institutions. Dealing with problems that are more distant and more foreign requires better understanding and communication.

Common threat assessments are the best basis for common actions. This requires improved sharing of intelligence among Member States and with partners.

As we increase capabilities in the different areas, we should think in terms of a wider spectrum of missions. This might include joint disarmament operations, support for third countries in combating terrorism and security sector reform. The last of these would be part of broader institution building.

The EU-NATO permanent arrangements, in particular Berlin Plus, enhance the operational capability of the EU and provide the framework for the strategic partnership between the two organisations in crisis management. This reflects our common determination to tackle the challenges of the new century.

More Coherent. The point of the Common Foreign and Security Policy and European Security and Defence Policy is that we are stronger when we act together. Over recent years we have created a number of different instruments, each of which has its own structure and rationale.

The challenge now is to bring together the different instruments and capabilities: European assistance programmes and the European Development Fund, military and civilian capabilities from Member States and other instruments. All of these can have an impact on our security and on that of third countries. Security is the first condition for development.

Diplomatic efforts, development, trade and environmental policies, should follow the same agenda. In a crisis there is no substitute for unity of command.

Better co-ordination between external action and Justice and Home Affairs policies is crucial in the fight both against terrorism and organised crime.

Greater coherence is needed not only among EU instruments but also embracing the external activities of the individual member states.

Coherent policies are also needed regionally, especially in dealing with conflict. Problems are rarely solved on a single country basis, or without regional support, as in different ways experience in both the Balkans and West Africa shows.

Working with partners There are few if any problems
we can deal with on our own. The threats described
above are common threats, shared with all our closest
partners. International cooperation is a necessity. We
need to pursue our objectives both through multilateral
cooperation in international organisations and through
partnerships with key actors.

*Acting together, the European
Union and the United States
can be a formidable force for
good in the world.*

The transatlantic relationship is irreplaceable. Acting together, the European Union and the United
States can be a formidable force for good in the world. Our aim should be an effective and balanced
partnership with the USA. This is an additional reason for the EU to build up further its capabilities and increase its coherence.

We should continue to work for closer relations with Russia, a major factor in our security and prosperity. Respect for common values will reinforce progress towards a strategic partnership.

Our history, geography and cultural ties give us links with every part of the world: our neighbours
in the Middle East, our partners in Africa, in Latin America, and in Asia. These relationships are an
important asset to build on. In particular we should look to develop strategic partnerships, with
Japan, China, Canada and India as well as with all those who share our goals and values, and are
prepared to act in their support.

Conclusion

This is a world of new dangers but also of new opportunities. The European Union has the potential to make a major contribution, both in dealing with the threats and in helping realise the
opportunities. An active and capable European Union would make an impact on a global scale. In
doing so, it would contribute to an effective multilateral system leading to a fairer, safer and more
united world.

Annex 4

COMMISSION OF THE EUROPEAN COMMUNITIES

Brussels, 19.3.2004
SEC(2004) 332

COMMISSION STAFF WORKING PAPER
European Security Strategy

FIGHT AGAINST TERRORISM

In December 2003, the European Council asked the Presidency and SG/HR, in co-ordination with the Commission to present concrete proposals for the implementation of the European security strategy in four areas including the fight against terrorism (para. 85).

The Commission welcomes the opportunity to contribute to the further development of EU policy in the fight against terrorism, also in the light of the terrorist atrocities in Spain on 11 March 2004. As recognised in the ESS, terrorism is not a threat which can be tackled by purely military means. Other policies can and do have a role to play.

A – The Commission approach

The EU's basic objective in the fight against terrorism is to ensure that its citizens have the ability to live in freedom, peace and safety. To achieve this objective we must ensure a high level of security within the EU while at the same time promoting security, stability and prosperity in third countries.

Achieving this implies action, together with partner countries, to eliminate or reduce the threat of terrorist attack whether to citizens themselves, to essential services (such as water supplies, energy, transport and communications) or production systems (agro-food and process industries) as well as to establish mechanisms (surveillance, early warning, alert and response systems and procedures) to deal effectively and efficiently with the consequences of any attacks. Action must also be taken to address the root causes of insecurity and the factors which contribute to the emergence of terrorism. Steps aimed at enhancing security must be taken without prejudice to individual rights and freedoms and the openness and tolerance of our societies must be maintained. At the same time EU actions aim to strengthen governance, including the rule of law, and to encourage the development of sound institutions both within the Union and in third countries.

Terrorism:

* takes advantage of this era of more open borders and integrated economies;
* undermines the openness and tolerance of societies;
* poses challenges to the core EU objectives of the promotion of free movement of persons, goods, services and capital; and
* makes evident the intrinsic link between internal and external security.

The challenge is to benefit from the advantages of free movement, whilst minimising the security threats and to handle the fight against terrorism within a wider framework of action. Security within the EU cannot be achieved at the cost of creating an inward-looking Union. The EU approach is therefore to strengthen internal security in a co-ordinated and multidisciplinary manner, and to promote stability and security beyond our borders whilst avoiding new dividing lines, particularly with the near neighbours.

Numerous EU policies contribute to the fight against terrorism, but have not been developed or designated specifically as counter-terrorism actions. This is also true for actions at the EU and Member State level. Many of the mechanisms and actions necessary to combat terrorism are the same as those needed to tackle other forms of serious and organised crime. Strengthened police, customs and judicial cooperation help combat organised criminal groups as well as terrorists. Effective anti-money laundering measures help cut off funds to organised crime and terrorism. Mechanisms necessary to protect communications infrastructure against terrorist attacks are the same as those to protect against cyber-crime more generally. Health security procedures and alert mechanisms are as necessary for natural health pandemics as for bio-terrorism. The Community civil protection mechanism deals with the response to natural disasters as well as man-made ones such as terrorist attacks. Effective border controls are a defence against drug and human trafficking as well as against the illegal transport of WMD and nuclear devices or other terrorist activities. Using our external programmes for the promotion of good governance including institutional capacity building, fighting terrorism and corruption and improving transparency is essential for overall development and economic growth. But even if they were not designed with counter-terrorism as their primary objective, all these actions constitute a significant element of the EU's counter-terrorism activity. As indicated in the Communication on the next Financial Perspectives (COM(2004)101 final) the Commission expects work in these areas to be an increasingly important element of EU action in the years ahead.

The key to the effectiveness of the EU approach is for all of our actions to be implemented in a co-ordinated and comprehensive manner, within an agreed framework.

The fight against terrorism involves a plethora of players and many different instruments, both at national and EU level. The key to pulling all these strands together is effective coordination. For its part, the Commission intends to reinforce its internal coordinating mechanisms in order to manage the many crosscutting issues in a coherent manner.

B – Action under way

The first responsibility for combating terrorism lies with the Member States. Action at the EU level, by the Community and/or by Member States collectively, has focused on those fields where it can provide added value to the efforts made by individual Member States. Examples of these actions are set out below.

1. JUSTICE AND HOME AFFAIRS

The objective in the area of Justice and Home Affairs is to establish an area of freedom, security and justice within the EU whilst sharing our capacities and values with third countries to strengthen global stability and security. Galvanised by the events of 11 September 2001, a range of urgent measures were set out at the Justice and Home Affairs Council of 20 September 2001, covering: judicial cooperation; cooperation between police and intelligence services; financing of terrorism; measures at borders; and improved cooperation with the United States. However, it should be recalled that the EU was already mindful of the internal and external threat posed by terrorism. This was illustrated by references to the fight against terrorism in the Treaty of Amsterdam and other key documents. This enabled the Commission to present relevant proposals swiftly, such as the European Arrest Warrant. A number of additional measures as outlined below, both in the first and third pillar, have served to develop justice and home affairs policies whilst contributing to the fight against terrorism.

Prevention and fight against terrorism remains a top priority and requires increased efforts. Qualitative and quantitative improvement of the exchanges of information must be sought. It is essential, in the fight against terrorism, that the judicial authorities and law enforcement agencies concerned obtain the most complete and up-to-date information at any time of the procedure. The setting up of effective mechanisms for exchange of information on convictions and prohibitions will constitute a means for fighting against infiltration of terrorist groups. It represents a major element for avoiding infiltration of terrorist groups in legal activities in the objective to fight against the financing of terrorism.

In order to be fully effective in the fight against financing of terrorism, the links between terrorism and other forms of criminality need to be addressed and the fight against organised crime strengthened. The adoption of measures making it possible to identify the holders and true beneficiaries of bank accounts would be a valuable tool in the fight against the financing of terrorism. In general greater financial transparency constitutes a crucial means of fighting against terrorist financing. In this context, measures to address the use of illegal alternative remittance systems and cash carriers as well as the use of non profit organizations for financing acts of terrorism or terrorist groups are challenges for the future.

a) Border Security

Border and travel security is rapidly becoming one of the most important elements in the fight against terrorism, both at EU and multilateral level and in relations with the US. One of the primary tools that the EU is developing is the integrated border management strategy. The Union and the Member States have developed a wide range of measures including improved security features of visas and travel documents, and strengthened controls and surveillance of external borders through improved coordination and joint operations.

Border management

Efficient control and surveillance of the external borders is a prerequisite for maintaining the internal security of Member States in an area in which internal border controls are lifted. In November 2003 the Commission presented a proposal for a Council Regulation establishing a European Agency for the Management of Operational Co-operation at the External Borders of the Member States of the European Union. The purpose of the Agency is to co-ordinate operational activities of Member States at the external borders (including, where relevant, with third countries) and facilitate the application of the Schengen acquis in order to ensure a high and uniform level of control of persons at and surveillance of the external borders. These efforts will be closely coordinated with those under way to establish a European coordinated policy and activity for Coast Guard services whose duties shall be to enforce the law of the sea and all relevant European legislation in EU territorial waters.

Document Security

The Thessaloniki European Council called for a coherent approach on **biometric identifiers** which would result in harmonised standards for documents for third country nationals and EU citizens' passports. Starting with visas, the Commission adopted two proposals, which aim to integrate biometric identifiers in the uniform format for visas and the uniform format for residence permits of third country nationals. Member States will be required to integrate two biometric identifiers into the visa and the residence permit for third country nationals.

The Commission has also presented a proposal on the harmonisation of security features, including biometrics, of the EU citizen's passport. This proposal covers improved security of the passport by harmonising and making legally binding common security features. This work also feeds into multilateral initiatives to spread best practice on document security such as those being developed within ICAO and G8.

Information Systems

As part of the 'Comprehensive Plan to Combat Illegal Migration and Trafficking of Human Beings' adopted by the JHA Council on 28 February 2002 on the basis of the Commission's Communication on illegal immigration of 15 November 2001, a European **Visa Information System** (VIS) was proposed. The primary objective of the VIS is to support the common visa and migration policy. However, it should also contribute towards internal security and to combating terrorism by enabling the instant verification of visas and identification of visa holders. As advised by the Council it will also take over the function of the VISION network for consulting the central authorities, referred to in Article 17 (2) of the Schengen Convention, which is currently integrated in the present Schengen Information System. This network allows checking visa applications against national terrorist watchlists. Similarly the new version of the Schengen Information System, **SIS II**, will contribute to the fight against terrorism by supporting police and judicial cooperation.

b) Criminal Law Instruments

The aim is to put in place for the first time legal frameworks that provide Member States with EU instruments to create a common judicial area. These instruments establish minimum legal standards, denying safe havens, and simplify judicial cooperation through mutual recognition of judicial decisions based on mutual trust between national authorities.

Framework Decisions on combating terrorism and on the European Arrest Warrant were adopted on 13 June 2002, as key elements to achieving the area of freedom, security and justice and to the EU's fight against terrorism. The **Framework Decision on Combating Terrorism** ensures that terrorists receive appropriate punishment in all Member States, avoiding safe havens, by establishing a common EU definition of a 'terrorist offence' and setting common minimum sentences. The European Arrest Warrant replaces classic extradition by an entirely judicial and simplified procedure, adopting the principle of mutual recognition of judicial decisions, based upon a high degree of mutual trust and cooperation. With the European Arrest Warrant, terrorists will no longer be able to abuse extradition procedures to avoid prosecution, as they can be swiftly arrested and surrendered no matter where they travel within the EU. Other mutual recognition instruments, such as the **Framework Decision on execution of orders Freezing Assets or Evidence**, will also help fight terrorism, for instance with freezing orders being executed without the delay inherent in traditional mutual assistance regimes.

c) Operational capacities

The EU has significantly developed its operational arm over the last few years. Europol and Eurojust are playing a key role in the fight against terrorism both by facilitating law enforcement cooperation and information exchange and developing new instruments at the EU level, such as joint threat assessments. This effort needs to be stepped up further.

Every six months the Council assesses the terrorist threat and keeps an updated common list identifying the most significant terrorist organisations. The EU Police Chiefs Task Force and the heads of EU Counter Terrorism Units meet regularly in order to exchange intelligence and experiences in the fight against terrorism.

Europol has been given a central role in the fight against terrorism, following 11 September 2001, particularly through the establishment of its Counter-Terrorism Task Force which brought together experts from various law enforcement and intelligence services. Following the expiration of the CTTF's mandate, Europol's Serious Crime Unit has taken on counterterrorism work, including collecting, sharing and analysing information concerning the threat of international terrorism and the production of an annual "Situation and Trends Report on Terrorist Activity in the EU". EUROPOL and the Commission are planning EU Joint Training for Law Enforcement and Public Health Officials on Interaction of Criminal and Epidemiological Investigations beginning in April 2004 to strengthen the response to future terrorist attacks involving biological agents.

The Commission is developing ideas for an EU information and communication policy which will build on the Dublin Declaration of November 2003 that was endorsed by the information JHA Council of January 2004. The aim is to set out markers for the establishment for intelligence-led law enforcement and to promote effective national criminal intelligence systems which are compatible at EU level and allow for the effective access, analysis, and use of data. This policy aims at facilitating the detection of threats to public order and security, to avert security risks, and to fight organised crime throughout the Union, including through enhanced access to data not produced for law enforcement purposes. It will be accompanied by a legislative initiative on the processing and protection of personal data used by law enforcement and will, furthermore, contribute to international efforts in the fight against terrorism and organised crime.

Eurojust, established in 2002 as an independent body composed of magistrates from EU Member States, aims to improve coordination and cooperation between investigators and prosecutors dealing with serious international crime including terrorism and has convened meetings on how to improve judicial cooperation to fight terrorism. Member States are obliged to designate a Eurojust national correspondent for terrorist matters, in order to enhance its counter-terrorist work.

Joint Investigation Teams, established by the Framework Decision of 13 June 2002 on combating terrorism, will provide enhanced cooperation in investigating cross-border crime, in particular terrorist offences involving any of the persons, groups or entities mentioned in the list annexed to Common Position 2001/931/CFSP. A Council Recommendation has also been adopted to set up Multi-national ad hoc teams for exchanging information on terrorists in the pre-criminal investigative phase.

d) Co-operation with United States

In the JHA field, particular attention has been paid to developing cooperation with the US. Unprecedented levels of law enforcement and judicial cooperation have been developed. A cooperation agreement and an agreement concerning data protection have been signed between Europol and US. In addition EU and US have concluded agreements on extradition and mutual legal assistance. US contacts with Eurojust have also been reinforced, and a range of other new areas of cooperation developed including with the Police Chiefs Task Force.

2. TERRORIST FINANCING

Terrorists need financial resources to operate. A key factor in the effectiveness of their operations is the ability to move money efficiently through the global financial system. One of the objectives of EU actions is therefore to make it impossible for terrorists to acquire and use funding for their activities. At the EU level, a range of legislative and operational measures have been adopted, some of which aim to counter various criminal activities including terrorism and others of which are specifically aimed at combating the financing of terrorism. The EU has responded quickly both in supporting and implementing action connected with UN Security Council Resolutions inter alia by adopting Community Regulations ordering the freezing of all funds and assets of certain persons, groups and entities suspected of terrorism or financing of terrorism as well as prohibiting making funds and assets available to such persons, groups or entities. In order to facilitate the application of the freezing measures, the Commission and the European banking sector are establishing an electronic database of all targeted persons and entities. The EU has also improved its anti-money laundering measures by adopting a second anti-money laundering Directive and it was agreed that all offences linked to the financing of terrorism should be money laundering predicate offences. In addition, through its participation in relevant international organisations and fora, such as the Financial Action Task Force, the Commission supports global efforts to make the international financial system less vulnerable to abuse by terrorists.

Customs also contributes to the fight against money laundering. As the provisions of the money laundering directive begin to bite, criminals and terrorists are likely to turn to cash as an easier way of moving funds around. The adoption by the Council of the Commission proposal to introduce controls on cash movements by customs at the external frontier would transform the present fragmented approach into a common, simple and rapid first defence mechanism.

Terrorist financing, however, cannot be addressed in isolation. There is growing evidence of the links between terrorism and other forms of organised crime. We therefore need to develop our understanding of these links as well as policies to address them.

3. TRANSPORT SECURITY

In both the maritime and aviation sectors EU regulations have been enacted which make mandatory a number of security measures on aircrafts and ships and in airports and harbours. The aviation regulation has been in force since July 2003 while the maritime measures will have to be implemented in all ports and ships worldwide by July 2004. Two new European Commission inspectorates will investigate the implementation of those measures in all the EU Member States. Close cooperation has been maintained with a number of trading partner countries, including the USA with whom regular coordination meetings take place. A cooperation group has recently initiated discussion on research projects in this area. In addition, new legislation on security in ports has been presented for approval by the Commission to the other EU institutions.

Beyond these security measures dealing with ground side of transportation great attention is being paid to the threat of using civil aircraft as a weapon or unlawful vehicle. Implementation of the Single European Sky rules will develop civil-military cooperation in managing airspace and controlling air traffic flow. It provides a strong impetus to develop additional measures combining civil and military actions to prevent and react efficiently to this sort of threat.

The Commission has also issued a Directive to allow Member States to issue motor vehicle registration documents under the format of smart cards as an alternative to paper documents; this will help to considerably reduce fraud. Further, the Commission has proposed that provisions aimed at increasing security (covering staff training, safe storage, design of safety plans, and identity documents for staff) be introduced in international regulations governing the transport of dangerous goods by rail, road and waterways. After adoption, these provisions will become Community law.

A public consultation document has been launched concerning future proposal expected later this year, on multi-modal security to secure and make more transparent the transport of cargo between the factory gate and the consumer or the export point. This subject is of primary interest to the transport and energy sector, and many new initiatives covering a number of subjects of key security importance such as urban transport and orphan nuclear sources are also being studied.

4. CRITICAL INFRASTRUCTURE PROTECTION

With the rapid development of an increasingly networked world, protection of information infrastructures is crucial to the correct functioning of modern society. The impact of possible terrorist attacks on these infrastructures will have devastating affects for all economic sectors e.g. energy, communications, transportation and water supplies. The EU is developing a multi-faceted approach, enhancing the legal framework (electronic communications legal instruments such as the 'telecom package'); developing policies on cyber-crime (Framework Decision on attacks against information systems) and improving prevention mechanisms.

The electricity and gas markets are increasingly being opened to competition in the same way as communication services are. Energy is considered to be a special product, of which the security of supply is a political priority. Nuclear installations and other key industries are other examples of infrastructures requiring a high level of security.

Though networks can be, and often are, owned by the private sector, all Member States regulate the economic behaviour of the sector. Currently the security and safety of energy distribution networks is overseen by Member States mostly in accordance with local rules and regulations. Given the increasing interdependence of European national energy markets, the EU dimension of security and safety in energy transfer should be strengthened substantially.

As a first concrete step in this area the Commission has launched preparations of common guidelines for managing safety and operation standards in European electricity network operation, as proposed by the Florence Forum of electricity network regulators in their 10th meeting. A coordination of European Security services and of European Transport authorities is necessary to develop a coordination framework in order to harmonise standards and levels of protection of the key energy and transport infrastructures.

5. CUSTOMS/TRADE ISSUES

Effective means are needed to control the flow of potentially harmful goods across our frontiers without unduly hampering legitimate trade. To secure the traffic coming towards the EU and to enable a pro-active approach in protecting EU citizens, close co-operation with partner customs administrations world-wide is an essential element in securing the global supply chain. The U.S. Container Security Initiative is one example of how customs administrations can co-operate to improve security in logistical processes. This exercise however needs to be extended to all exporting ports in order to be meaningful. Following the initialling of an EC-US Agreement to ensure co-operation on CSI and related matters, discussions are continuing with other third countries (e.g. India, China, Hong Kong, Canada, and New Zealand). The aim would be to secure the logistical supply chain by expanding existing or future customs co-operation agreements to cover transport security.

At the end of July 2003, the Commission presented a package, consisting of a Communication on the role of customs in the integrated management of external borders and the consequent proposed change of the Community Customs Code to introduce a common approach to risk management, introducing security aspects in customs controls. Work already underway to implement these security measures should be accelerated.

As well as ensuring adequate control of goods coming into the EU, action is required in parallel to ensure that nothing is exported which might be used to commit terrorist attacks. Regulation 1334/2000 set up the EU regime for the control of exports of dual-use items and technology. It also introduces controls on intangible transfers of technology for exports outside the European Union. The regulation's scope is limited to licensing and the modalities of dual–use exports from the EU. It does not address most of the issues related to enforcement of export controls which rests with Member States.

6. HEALTH SECURITY

The bio-terrorist attacks in the US in the autumn of 2001 and Belgium in January 2003, as well as evidence from law enforcement operations (e.g. the London ricin seizure) demonstrate that the risk of attack from biological and chemical agents is a very real one. In response to this threat, the Commission has undertaken a series of actions in a range of policy areas. A Health Security Committee was established in November 2001; a programme of co-operation in the EU on preparedness and response to biological and chemical agent attacks (health security) was drawn up in December 2001 and a Task force on health security was set up with seconded national experts in May 2002. A communication (COM (2003) 320) on progress with the implementation of the health security programme was published on 2 June 2003.

The health security programme aims to ensure an EU-wide capability for the timely detection and identification of biological and chemical agents in laboratories, the rapid and reliable determination and diagnosis of relevant human disease cases, the availability of medicines, co-ordination of emergency plans and the drafting and dissemination of rules and guidance on facing-up to attacks from the health point of view. Examples of actions with MS, in coordination with other EU actions, and involving international initiatives include: the coordination and evaluation of MS' smallpox plans; modelling of outbreaks and data for simulations; the establishment of a secure 24 hour/7 day-a-week rapid alert system (RASBICHAT) for deliberate releases of biological and chemical agents which links the members of the Health Security Committee and permanent contact points in all the Member States with the Commission and connects to other EU alert systems; monitoring of Web-based information to provide advance warning of suspicious circumstances or outbreaks; the establishment of a network of high security laboratories; the development of a framework for an Expert Directory with information on relevant expertise in the different MS and the development of strategies for securing adequate supplies of vaccines and anti-virals.

In parallel, the Commission is participating in international health security initiatives such as the Global Health Security Action Initiative agreed by the G7 and Mexican Health Ministers and Commissioner Byrne in November 2001 which has similar goals to those of the EU cooperation (collaboration on smallpox emergency plans and training, laboratory detection techniques, risk management and communication, chemical incident preparedness, patient isolation techniques). The WHO is fully associated in these activities.

7. CIVIL PROTECTION

Following the request made in December 2001 by the European Council, the programme to improve co-operation in the EU for preventing and limiting the consequences of chemical, biological, radiological or nuclear terrorist threats (the CBRN programme) was adopted by the Commission on 21 November 2002 and by the Council on 20 December 2002. This programme sets out the strategic objectives that need to be addressed in order to improve the protection of the population, the environment, the food chain and property against CBRN threats and attacks and describes where there is a need for further action. In December 2003 the first annual report on the programme was presented to the Council. This report includes, for each of the strategic objectives of the programme, the new initiatives and measures taken by the Commission as well as those that are planned. On civil protection, the report covers in particular the work done in the context of the implementation of the Community civil protection mechanism established under Council Decision 2001/792/EC, Euratom adopted on 23 October 2001. This includes the organisation of several CBRN exercises.

8. EXTERNAL ACTION

The Commission considers the main objective of EU external action in the fight against terrorism to be to promote the implementation of international norms and legal instruments relevant to the fight against terrorism, through targeted political dialogue and technical assistance as well as through co-operation in international and regional organisations. This requires making use of all the policies and instruments of the EU's external action in a holistic and coherent way whilst also fully respecting other external policy objectives.

The fight against terrorism continues to be an important element in the EU's **relations with third countries**. The EC has an extensive track record in the provision of **technical assistance** relevant to the fight against terrorism (e.g., customs law and practice, immigration law and practice, police and law enforcement, financial law and practice, judicial capacity building – all areas identified in UNSCR 1373 as essential areas for an effective defence against terrorism) notably through assistance projects on Justice and Home Affairs. These programmes, initially developed to help bring the acceding countries up to EU standards are now a major part of the CARDS and TACIS programmes and are also of growing importance within the MEDA programme where, at the request of the countries concerned, counterterrorism training for police and judiciary is an important part of the MEDA regional JHA programme. In addition, the EU has initiated a number of specific, more targeted counterterrorism projects initially in the Philippines and Indonesia, as well as ASEAN at the regional level, where Rapid Reaction Mechanism (RRM) funds have been used to kick-start projects in the areas of terrorist financing and border management. Follow-up actions will be funded in the longer term under the normal country or regional programmes. Similar actions are under preparation for Pakistan. RRM funds have also been used to fund police reform and border management projects in Central Asia (the former in co-operation with the OSCE), both with an important counter-terrorism element. Further use of RRM funds for counter-terrorism projects remains under consideration.

EC /EU Partnership and Co-operation Agreements with third countries provide valuable frameworks for comprehensive strategies that can help address the root causes of insecurity and which may contribute to the emergence of terrorism. The Cotonou Partnership Agreement provides a good example of an effective and integrated framework through which the EU can address not only poverty reduction, corruption and human rights but also peace-building, security, and root causes of conflict in the political dialogue with partner countries. These comprehensive partnership and co-operation agreements also provide the framework for specific technical assistance to assist third countries in the implementation of UNSCR 1373.

Development assistance has an impact on the environment that terrorist groups can exploit. It can erode the support base for terrorist networks and movements (through its focus on poverty reduction, land reform, governance, fight against corruption, the promotion of participatory development processes). **Governance** is a key component of policies and reform for poverty reduction, democratization and global security. Governance failures with roots in poverty and inequality are in many cases key factors contributing to terrorism. **Fighting corruption** and **improving transparency** are also crucial elements in a strategy to fight terrorism. Corruption undermines the government's credibility and the legitimacy of democracy. The EU is actively supporting interventions contributing to good governance and increased transparency in partner countries.

Anti-terrorism clauses in EU agreements with third countries are another important element of the EU's external action in the fight against terrorism. Such clauses have been included in agreements concluded with Algeria, Lebanon, Chile, Croatia, FYROM, Andean Community and the San Jose countries and are under negotiation in agreements with MERCOSUR, Iran, Syria and the GCC. In the forthcoming revision of the Cotonou Partnership Agreement, the EU is proposing the introduction of specific new provisions on co-operation in the field of counter-terrorism. This is intended to contribute to country owned agendas on security and counter terrorism, and to the effectiveness of the fight against terrorism at the national, regional and global levels.

9. SAFEGUARDING INDIVIDUAL RIGHTS AND FREEDOMS AND COMBATING RACISM

The EU is founded on the principles of liberty, democracy, respect for human rights and fundamental freedoms and the rule of law. The right to equality before the law and the protection of all persons from discrimination, together with the respect and promotion of the rights of minorities is essential to the proper functioning of democratic societies. We must therefore ensure that vulnerable minority communities within the EU are protected and their individual rights respected in the context of implementation of counter-terrorism policies.

After the terrorist attacks on 11 September 2001, the European Monitoring Centre on Racism and Xenophobia (EUMC), drew attention to the finding that Islamic communities and other vulnerable groups had become the targets of increased hostility.

The Centre's Islamophobia report is an important vehicle for drawing attention to the potential impact of counter-terrorism action on human rights, social and community cohesion and the successful integration of minority communities. The Centre has also outlined action at the local level to integrate Islamic communities under a community cohesion and social inclusion framework in three areas - employment, education and access to public services. In addition, the Centre works with the media in an effort to encourage balanced reporting and to avoid stoking up prejudices and/or fuelling tension within communities.

C – Priorities for future action

Since September 11th the EU has developed an impressive range of policies and instruments which contribute to the fight against terrorism, as indicated in the EU Action Plan against terrorism and the "anti-terrorism roadmap". Much has already been done, as mandated in the initial Action Plan. The key priority now is to ensure full implementation of what has already been decided and to consider possible new initiatives so as to fill any gaps in the Union's counter-terrorism toolbox. The Commission is determined to contribute effectively to this endeavour in the areas of its competence. Progress is needed in particular in the following areas.

JHA

Future policy and operational developments already envisaged in a number of JHA fields will contribute further to the fight against terrorism; we must take full advantage of the potential contribution of these and existing instruments.

- We should **monitor and support the comprehensive and effective implementa-tion of existing legislative instruments,** namely: Framework Decision on com-bating terrorism; European Arrest Warrant; and Framework Decision on execution of orders freezing assets or evidence;

- There will be opportunities **to explore new initiatives to improve co-operation in light of the results of the evaluation of Member States' legal systems and their implementation at national level in the fight against terrorism;**

- We need to further **explore the potential of new tools** with a dual or multiple character such as the Visa Information System to contribute towards combating terrorism;

- We need to support full potential being made of capacities already provided for, such as the **establishment of joint investigation teams** in the area of police co-operation.

- We should develop **markers** for the establishment of intelligence-led law enforce-ment and promote effective national criminal intelligence systems which are com-patible at EU level and allow for the effective access to, analysis and use of data.

- We should **develop cooperation with the private sector, through the establishment of public-private partnerships,** to improve protection of information infrastructures.

- In order to enhance the effectiveness of **Eurojust's work,** all Member States should implement the Eurojust Decision. In addition, all Member States should designate a Eurojust national correspondent for terrorist matters.

- we should agree new instruments such as the Commission's proposal for a **European Evidence Warrant** to make cross-border obtaining of evidence clearer, faster and with appropriate safeguards. In due course the EU should create a comprehensive system, based on mutual recognition, for obtaining and using evidence.

Fight against Terrorism Financing

In order to develop further a comprehensive approach to prevent the financing of terrorism and the abuse of the financial system by terrorists, as well as addressing the linkages between financing of terrorism and organised crime, we should:

- Implement the relevant **FATF recommendations,** including in particular those aimed at preventing the use of informal financial remittance systems and of char-ities and other nonprofit organizations for the purposes of the financing of terror-ism;

- Adopt measures making it possible to **identify the holders and true beneficiaries of bank accounts** as a tool in the fight against the financing of terrorism and money laundering. This information should be accessible to judicial authorities and law enforcement agencies; and

- Create effective mechanisms to address the use of **cash movements** by terrorists to avoid controls on electronic financial transactions.

Customs

- Foster co-operation with neighbouring states and major trading partners to ident-ify and address **high risk areas.**

- Promote **co-operation and information sharing** with other agencies, particularly those acting at the border, (police, immigration, veterinary, transport etc.) to help identify and deal with high risk movements.

- Promote consistent and effective **security arrangements** for goods at all points of the external borders of the Union. This will require more resources; both human and technical (risk management systems, radiation detectors, non-intrusive inspection equipment etc.).

- Ensure suitable **crisis planning** is in place for handling consignments suspected of being linked to terrorism (WMD, explosives, biological devices etc.).

Health Security

The Health Security strategy aims at strengthening preparedness and response capacity in the Member States and co-ordination of counter-measures in the European Union. To achieve this, priority will be given to:

- the further implementation of the Council and Parliament Decision 2119/98/EC establishing a Community Network for the **epidemiological surveillance and control of communicable** disease in the Community (24/09/1998), to install an effective a system of prior information and consultation between the Member States about countermeasures to be taken in case of public health threats; and

- **the adoption of a Community Generic Preparedness and Response plan for Public Health threats and events of EU concern, as requested** by the Health Council on 6 May and again on 2 June 2003 following the SARS outbreak.

Transport and energy security

Activities already under way will be maintained, reinforced and structured with the aim of **ensuring appropriate security in each transport and energy mode**. The Corps of Inspectors in the nuclear, aviation and maritime sector will guarantee the enforcement of the legislation adopted in these fields; adoption of further security related legislation may require additional enforcement/inspection mechanisms. We expect to see extensive recourse to satellite technology (positioning and telecommunications) in order to assist the enforcement agencies and organisations in better targeting their inspections, using in addition comparisons between transport data made available by operators and the intelligence gained by the inspectors through their own experience or as a result of coordination with trading partners agencies. The same technology will assist users in moving faster with less controls and more comfort. Research will be needed to develop new tools to be put at the disposal of both users and enforcement agencies; thematic networks will need to be established in order to compare notes between Member States operators of public services and to develop common reflexes and attitudes in the pursuit of greater security.

Use of passenger travel data

The Commission will pursue as a matter of priority the discussions that have been started with Member States and other relevant parties, e.g. Europol, with a view to making a first proposal by the middle of 2004 outlining an EU approach to the use of travellers' data for border and aviation security and other law enforcement purposes. Such a policy framework will need to strike a balance between security concerns on the one hand and data protection and other civil liberties on the other.

Civil Protection

Activities in this field are essentially based on the Civil Protection Community Mechanism established under Council decision 792/2001 of 23 October 2001. In this context, work on strengthening preparedness at EU level to deal with the consequences of potential CBRN threats will continue to be a priority. It will include in particular:

- The full integration of the content of the **database of military assets and capabilities** into the Community Mechanism, as agreed by the GAERC Council in its 8 December 2003 Conclusions;

- Further development of the EU work on **CBRN threats**, including the organisation of specific full-scale exercises and other appropriate initiatives in order to test and further improve the level of preparedness and interoperability of available capabilities.

Moreover, prospects for cooperation on civil protection with relevant international organisations and third countries will continue to be explored

Research and technological development

In an increasingly technological and knowledge-based world, the EU needs **excellence in research and technological development** in order to tackle effectively the new security challenges and in particular terrorism. The Commission is developing a long-term vision and strategic agenda in security-related research and is preparing the way for a full-fledged European Security Research Programme after 2006. Therefore the Commission has launched in 2004 a Preparatory Action entitled "Enhancement of the European industrial potential in the field of security research" with funding of €65 million foreseen over three years (2004–2006) to support projects through open calls. One of five priority missions to be addressed is the protection against terrorism, including biological and chemical attacks. Other priority missions are: surveillance of EU borders and technologies to tag, track and trace goods; optimising security and protection of networked systems such as electricity and communication networks from attacks; coordination between emergency services and getting emergency services' equipment to work together; and enhancing crisis management.

External action

The EU needs to **engage more effectively with third countries**, especially those countries of particular significance to the fight against terrorism (those where we have evidence of a terrorist threat or of specific terrorist activity such as recruitment or training, those who are direct or indirect sources of terrorist financing etc). We need to use the information we already have, whether from threat assessments from various sources or the more general EU Crisis Prevention Watch List exercise to identify countries representing a potential threat and target our political dialogue accordingly. The anti-terrorism clauses in agreements with third countries should be followed up and the related provisions on cooperation implemented, underpinned by technical assistance as appropriate.

The need for assistance to help third countries meet international counter-terrorism standards remains immense. The EU should be prepared to **offer more and better targeted technical assistance** in cooperation with the UNCTC and other relevant international and regional organisations. The EU can provide valuable support by more effectively taking into consideration counter-terrorism as an integral part of the programming cycle of its assistance to the countries affected. This must be done in partnership with the countries concerned, since ownership and shared responsibility are keys to successful cooperation. The implementation of UNSCR 1373 should be systematically taken into account in the dialogue with countries which request such assistance. The objective would be to enable a more flexible response to identified needs. The possibility of launching further CFSP Joint Actions to provide direct assistance in the field of counter-terrorism could also be considered (as was done in the context of the EU Special Adviser on Security Issues to the Palestinian Authority).

Better co-ordination of EU and Member States' assistance programmes in this area is also essential, including at local level in accordance with existing guidelines. Better information is needed not just on assistance already being provided by Member States but also on what is being planned in order to avoid duplication. There is also a need for more exchange of information, analysis and **more effective cooperation with other donors** regarding approaches to difficult partnerships and action to address the root causes of terrorism. It is important not to leave these partners behind but to find alternative approaches to cooperation, given the potentially negative consequences for security of isolating a country and leaving extremism and terrorism growing in so-called failed states. Better sequencing of governance, peace and security, linking relief, rehabilitation and development (LRRD) interventions on the basis of a holistic approach to both policy implementation and policy development would make a more effective contribution to increased short and medium term security and the prevention of terrorism.

More action is needed to **foster greater inter-cultural understanding**, especially between the EU and regions in the world where terrorism has a particular resonance. Inter-cultural dialogue, organised within the framework of the Asia-Europe Foundation (ASEF), the envisaged Euro-Med Foundation for the dialogue of culture and civilisations and beyond, could contribute to a climate of dialogue and, if possible, increased mutual understanding on sensitive issues such as the definition of terrorism, violence, "right of resistance", Jihad etc. Initiatives should be considered targeting, for example, selected academic multipliers, thinktanks, and religious leaders who are deemed to be able to influence public opinion in the countries. Such action could also be conducive to an enhanced dialogue with Islamic countries in the context of the ongoing negotiations at the UN for a comprehensive Convention against terrorism.

This might be complemented by specific **bilateral dialogues** with countries representing and/or being linked to an important part of the population in the EU (for example: Northern Africa, Bosnia and Herzegovina etc). Such bilateral dialogue would equally include topics related to racism, xenophobia or other problems ethnic or national minorities are often confronted with, including within the EU.

Safeguarding individual rights and freedoms and combating racism

Greater priority needs to be given to the adoption of the **Framework Decision on combating racism and xenophobia** and its importance in the context of a balanced approach to countering terrorism and protecting vulnerable minority communities from the interplay between race and terrorism. Further action is needed to promote inclusiveness and protect minorities within the EU who might be unjustifiably targeted by counter-terrorist policies or at risk from a backlash in the event of a major terrorist incident. This might include exchange of information and best practices in educational and social policies, policing and antidiscrimination policies as well as on approaches for integrating minority communities, and dealing with individuals or groups whose aim is to promote racism, xenophobia or religious hatred within the EU. The EU also needs to continue its support for inter-community dialogue. The EU has initiated action in many of these fields in different contexts. These need to be drawn together in a concerted way and their benefits in a counter terrorism framework acknowledged.

Annex 5

COUNCIL OF THE EUROPEAN UNION

Brussels, 18 November 2004

14797/04

LIMITE

COSDP 694
PESC 987

"A" ITEM NOTE

from: Coreper

to: Council

Subject : Conceptual Framework on the ESDP dimension of the fight against terrorism

1. In June 2004, the European Council, within the context of the report on the implementation of the Declaration on combating terrorism, requested the Political and Security Committee to elaborate the conceptual framework identifying the main elements of the ESDP dimension of the fight against terrorism, including preventive aspects. The EU Plan of action on combating terrorism also reflected this request.

2. On 8 October 2004, the Secretariat submitted to the Political and Security Committee a draft Conceptual Framework (doc. 13234/04), which was subsequently discussed in the PSC meetings of 19 and 28 October, as well as of 3 and 9 November 2004.

3. At its meeting of 9 November 2004, the Political and Security Committee noted the EUMC and CIVCOM advices regarding the Conceptual Framework on the ESDP dimension of the fight against Terrorism and agreed the text set out in document 13234/4/04 REV 4.

4. The Commission has drawn attention to its request to delete the word "including" in paragraph 19.d.

5. This document should also be seen in the light of the "Hague Programme" (doc. 13993/04). 6. Coreper approved the text at annex on 18 November 2004 and recommended that Council approve it in view of the December European Council.

CONCEPTUAL FRAMEWORK ON THE EUROPEAN SECURITY AND DEFENCE POLICY (ESDP) DIMENSION OF THE FIGHT AGAINST TERRORISM

A. General

1.   The European Council has called for work to be rapidly pursued on the contribution of ESDP to the fight against terrorism on the basis of actions taken since the Seville declaration. In this regard the Report to the June 2004 European Council on the implementation of the Declaration on combating terrorism[1] requested the Political and Security Committee to elaborate the conceptual framework identifying the main elements of the ESDP dimension of the fight against terrorism, including preventive aspects. The EU Plan of action on combating terrorism also reflected this request[2]. The European Security Strategy and the Declaration on combating terrorism, which includes the Declaration on Solidarity against terrorism, laid the foundations of this framework.

2.   As indicated in the European Security Strategy, global terrorism, often nourished by violent extremism ready to use unlimited violence in a context of increasingly open borders, poses a growing strategic threat to the whole of Europe, which is both a target and a base for such terrorism. The most frightening scenario is one in which terrorist groups acquire weapons of mass destruction. Dealing with terrorism may require a comprehensive approach based on intelligence, police, judiciary, military and other means. In failed states, military instruments may be needed to restore order, humanitarian means to tackle the immediate crisis. Regional conflicts need political solutions but military assets and effective policing may be needed in the post conflict phase. Civilian crisis management helps restore civil government. The European Union is particularly well equipped to respond to such multi-faceted situations, including with its civilian and military crisis management operations.

3.   The Declaration on Combating terrorism, adopted by the European Council in March 2004, welcomed the political commitment of Member States to act jointly against terrorist acts, in the spirit of the solidarity clause contained in article I-43 of the draft treaty establishing a Constitution for Europe. The declaration on Solidarity against terrorism specifies that, if one of the Member States is the victim of a terrorist attack, the Member States shall mobilise all instruments at their disposal, including military resources:
–   to prevent the terrorist threat in the territory of one of them;
–   to protect democratic institutions and the civilian population from any terrorist attack;
–   to assist a Member State in its territory at the request of its political authorities in the event of a terrorist attack.

4.   This document addresses the ESDP dimension of the fight against terrorism, including preventive aspects, in accordance with art 17.2 of the TEU and in the spirit of Article III-309 of the draft treaty establishing a Constitution for Europe. It also considers other ways in which assets can contribute in a concerted way to European efforts in this context.

B. Basic Principles

5. The following six basic principles apply:
–   solidarity between EU Member States;
–   voluntary nature of Member States' contributions;
–   clear understanding of the terrorist threat and full use of available threat analysis;

---

1 doc. 10585/04, Declaration on Combating terrorism.
2 doc. 10586/04, EU Plan of Action on Combating Terrorism, action 3.7.

- cross pillar co-ordination in support of the EU common aim in the fight against terrorism;
- co-operation with relevant partners;
- complementary nature of the ESDP contribution, in full respect of Member States' responsibilities in the fight against terrorism and with due regard to appropriateness and effectiveness considerations.

6. As indicated in the Declaration on combating terrorism, terrorism will only be defeated by solidarity and collective action. The voluntary nature of Member States' contributions is one of the fundamental principles of the EU capability development process. When it comes to a terrorist attack against one of the Member States the Declaration on solidarity against terrorism states that Member States shall mobilise all instruments at their disposal, including military resources. It shall be for each Member State to choose the most appropriate means to comply with this solidarity commitment; ways of pooling, sharing or co-ordinating often scarce resources in this field should be sought.

7. The recent wave of terrorism arises from complex causes. Such a multifaceted threat can be addressed only by applying the full spectrum of instruments at the disposal of the European Union and its Member States. Effective and swift cross pillar co-ordination is therefore essential.

8. The EU Counter-Terrorism Coordinator will contribute to ensure that the efforts in the field of ESDP are developed in a coordinated way with the overall EU framework.

9. In line with the Presidency Conclusions to the June 2004 European Council, the Union will continue to develop initiatives for closer co-operation with international organisations and to maintain the closest possible co-ordination with the United States and other partners.

C. Main areas of action

10. In response to crises, the Union can mobilise a vast range of both civilian and military means and instruments, thus giving it an overall crisis-management and conflict-prevention capability in support of the objectives of the Common Foreign and Security Policy. This facilitates a comprehensive approach to prevent the occurrence of failed states, to restore order and civil government, to deal with humanitarian crises and prevent regional conflicts. By responding effectively to such multifaceted situations, the EU already makes a considerable contribution to long term actions for the prevention of terrorism.

11. The European Security and Defence Policy, which encompasses civilian and military crisis management operations under Title V of the TEU, as well as other EU efforts, can contribute further to the fight against terrorism, either directly or in support of other instruments. There are four main areas of action:
- prevention;
- protection;
- response/consequence management;
- support to third countries in the fight against terrorism;

In this context, aspects such as the interoperability between military and civilian capabilities in the field of the fight against terrorism and the work on generic scenarios will need to be addressed.

Prevention

12. Prevention is one of the three main objectives identified by the Declaration on solidarity against terrorism, for which all Member States' resources should be mobilised, including military ones.

13. In the framework of an EU-led crisis management operation under Title V of the TEU, pre-

vention of such an asymmetric threat will entail that Member States should ensure that such an operation is supported by the necessary level of information gathering and effective intelligence. Scenarios involving maritime and airspace control-type operations should be envisaged.

Protection

14. Protection, including force protection, is a fundamental aspect of any crisis management operation. In the case of a terrorist threat, protection should minimise the vulnerabilities of EU personnel, materiel, assets and, as appropriate, possible key civilian targets, including critical infrastructure, in the area of operations.

Response/consequence Management

15. Addressing the effects of an attack is a field where civilian and military means can have either a direct or a supporting role.

16. In the context of a crisis management operation under Title V of the TEU, the EU-led force on the ground will be more rapidly available for consequence management, in most cases together with the local authorities. Therefore, in full compliance with the objectives of the mission, the EU-led force should be ready to "fill the gap" with military and civilian capabilities while waiting for an expected international civil protection support at high readiness.

17. Within the EU, military means (in accordance with national regulations) could also have a role in support of civilian tools. In this framework, the EU has already taken the necessary steps to make available the content of the database of military assets and capabilities relevant to the protection of civilian populations against terrorist attacks, including CBRN to the Community Civil protection mechanism[3]. In this context, points of contact between the Monitoring and Information Centre and the SITCEN are now established and the database is being updated.

Third countries

18. As indicated by the European Security Strategy, a wider spectrum of ESDP missions might include support to third countries in combating terrorism. The risk of terrorist attacks against deployed ESDP missions should therefore be considered in ongoing work. Separately, the wider issue of the protection of EU citizens in third countries could be further addressed, especially in the case of EU citizens taken hostages by terrorist groups.

D. Action points

19. The following action points are proposed for implementation:

a. Support the development of military capabilities for EU-led crisis management operations by incorporating the terrorist threat in all relevant illustrative scenarios in the framework of the Headline Goal 2010[4]. The development of the corresponding military requirements should be included in the current elaboration of the Requirements Catalogue 2005. Work in this field should take into account possible preventive and protective measures. Possible measures related to prevention of the terrorist threat, including maritime and airspace control-type operations should be considered;

---

3 doc. 6644/4/04.
4 doc. 10586/04, EU Plan of Action on Combating terrorism, action 3.8.

b.   The future Civilian Headline Goal should also give appropriate consideration to the deployment and further development of civilian capabilities (in particular Police, Rule of Law, Civilian Administration and Civil Protection), in order to prevent as well as counter the terrorist threats within the limitations of the mandate;

c.   Defence Intelligence Organisations (working through the Intelligence Division of the EUMS) should support through increased exchanges of intelligence the Joint SITCEN as it implements the SG/HR's report to June European Council on the establishment of an intelligence capacity to cover the range of terrorist threats affecting EU interests both within and outside of the Union;

d.   Elaboration of a detailed report to the Council on modalities procedures and criteria to develop the appropriate level of interoperability between military and civilian capabilities in the framework of protection of civilian populations following a terrorist attack, including in crisis management operations under Title V of the TEU. This report, to be finalised during the first semester of 2005, should contain concrete proposals based on lessons-learned from real life incidents and planning scenarios taking into account best practices;

e.   Improve protection of all personnel, material and assets deployed for crisis management operations under Title V of the TEU, including, as appropriate, the ability to protect possible key civilian targets, including critical infrastructure, in the area of operations within available means and capabilities and on a case by case basis based on the threat analysis. The PSC should provide preliminary recommendations to the Council by the 2005 June European Council, also fostering ongoing work in the ECAP NBC Project Group, notably on an NBC Centre of Competence, including civilian expertise;

f.   Consolidate ongoing work in view of deepening and widening the content of the military database of military assets and capabilities relevant to the protection of civilian populations against terrorist attacks, including CBRN.[5] Special attention should be given to all possible instruments for assistance to victims. In this framework, a bidding process to incorporate Member States voluntary contributions in an addendum to the current Force Catalogue was launched. The PSC, based on an EUMC preliminary detailed analysis, should identify a set of pragmatic recommendations to the Council on the role of this database in the wider context of the Headline Goal 2010 and on possible further more systematic updates. Equally, PROCIV should also be involved in the respective area of competence;

g.   In the context of support to third countries in combating terrorism, specific measures could entail the development of appropriate co-operation programmes to promote trust and transparency, the support in planning activities related to the fight against terrorism including consequence management or support in training and exercises;

h.   Conceptual work on consular co-operation and evacuation of EU citizens in third countries should continue in the relevant working groups. These cases could be included in the relevant scenarios of HLG 2010, as well as in EU exercises;

i.   Develop a visible and effective rapid response protection[6] capability to be included as protection component of EU-led crisis management operations under Title V of the TEU. Such capacity, to be voluntarily contributed by Member States, would allow an immediate reaction in the affected area in the immediate aftermath of a possible terrorist attack, in most cases in support of local authorities and pending the arrival of further expected aid from the international community[7]. This capacity would deal with all aspects of protection. In order to maximise effective use of available resources, Member States should consider the possibility of sharing and pooling assets. When appropriate through this initiative, Member States could

---

5 doc. 10586/04, EU Plan of Action on Combating terrorism, actions 5.2.2 and 5.2.3.
6 Protection as defined in section C.
7 This would normally be a matter of hours.

also consider further contributing to the Community Civil Protection Mechanism. The PSC should address the issue of the interaction of this ESDP rapid reaction protection capability with other EU existing instruments and elaborate a concept by June 2005;

j. Relevant aspects of the March Declaration on Solidarity against terrorism should also be exercised and considered for inclusion in the EU exercise programme, as appropriate;

k. Sponsor an ISS Seminar on the ESDP contribution to the fight against terrorism in the wider context of the EU approach in this field, to be held not later than March 2005. Participation in the seminar would be open to representatives and high level experts (national crisis coordinators, academics, etc) of key partners, such as the US, the UN and NATO. This brainstorming would feed a discussion in PSC on possible further measures on the ESDP contribution to the fight against terrorism;

l. Seek ways of co-operating with NATO[8] in the fields of:
–   non-binding guidelines and minimum standards for the protection of the civilian population against CBRN risks;
–   framework agreement on the facilitation of cross border transport;
–   identification of the relevant national points of contact, with a view to creating a common database of points of contact;
–   cross-participation, on a case-by case basis, in each other's consequence management exercises, as observers.

---

8 doc. 10586/04, EU Plan of Action on Combating terrorism, action 5.1.

Annex 6

COUNCIL OF THE EUROPEAN UNION

Brussels, 24 November 2005

14781/1/05
REV 1

LIMITE

JAI 452
ENFOPOL 164
COTER 81

"I/A" ITEM NOTE

from : Presidency
to : COREPER/Council
No. prev. doc. : 14347/05 JAI 414 ENFOPOL 152 COTER 69

Subject: The European Union Strategy for Combating Radicalisation and Recruitment to Terrorism

1.   Terrorism is a threat to all States and to all peoples. It poses a serious threat to the security of the European Union and the lives of its citizens. The European Union remains determined to tackle this scourge. Doing so requires a comprehensive response. We must reduce the threat: by disrupting existing terrorist networks and by preventing new recruits to terrorism. And we must reduce our vulnerability to attack: by better protecting potential targets and improving our consequence management capabilities.

2.   To enhance our policies to prevent new recruits to terrorism, at the European Council of 17 December 2004 we agreed to elaborate a strategy and action plan to address radicalisation and recruitment to terrorism. This strategy builds on the considerable work since the 25 March 2004 European Council Declaration on Combating Terrorism, including the Commission Communication on Terrorist Recruitment: addressing the factors contributing to violent radicalisation. It outlines how the Union and Member States will combat radicalisation and recruitment into terrorism. It will form part of a broader EU Counter-Terrorism strategy and Action Plan that the European Council will be asked to endorse by the end of 2005.

The Challenge

3.   Radicalisation and recruitment to terrorism are not confined to one belief system or political persuasion. **Europe has experienced different types of terrorism in its history**. But the terrorism perpetrated by Al-Qa'ida and extremists inspired by Al-Qa'ida has become the main terrorist threat to the Union. While other types of terrorism continue to pose a serious threat to EU citizens, the Union's response to radicalisation and recruitment focuses on this type of terrorism.

4.   The vast majority of Europeans, irrespective of belief, do not accept extremist ideology. Even

amongst the small number that do, only a few turn to terrorism. The decision to become involved in terrorism is an individual one, even though the motives behind such a decision are often similar. There can be no excuse or impunity for such actions, but it is our responsibility to identify and counter the ways, propaganda and conditions through which people are drawn into terrorism and consider it a legitimate course of action.

5. Addressing this challenge is beyond the power of governments alone. Al-Qa'ida and those inspired by them will only be defeated with the engagement of the public, and especially Muslims, in Europe and beyond. The overwhelming majority of people espouse the values of peace and tolerance. The European Union rejects any justification for terrorism, religious or otherwise. The Union welcomes the strong stance that the people of Europe and beyond, including Muslims, have taken to reject terrorism and urges them not to relent in their condemnation.

Our Response

6. To counter radicalisation and terrorist recruitment, the EU resolves to:

- disrupt the activities of the networks and individuals who draw people into terrorism;
- ensure that voices of mainstream opinion prevail over those of extremism;
- promote yet more vigorously security, justice, democracy and opportunity for all.

7. Throughout we will ensure that we do not undermine respect for fundamental rights. To ensure our responses remain effective and appropriate, we will work to develop our understanding of the problem. In doing this, we will engage in dialogue with governments which have faced this problem, academic experts and Muslim communities in Europe and beyond.

Disrupting the activities of the networks and individuals who draw people into terrorism

8. There are practical steps an individual must take to become involved in terrorism. The ability to put ideas into action has been greatly enhanced by globalisation: ease of travel and communication and easy transfer of money mean easier access to radical ideas and training. The Internet assists this facilitation and provides a means for post-attack justification.

9. We need to spot such behaviour by, for example, community policing, and effective monitoring of the Internet and travel to conflict zones. We should build our expertise by exchanging national assessments and analyses. We also need to disrupt such behaviour. We will limit the activities of those playing a role in radicalisation including in prisons, places of education or religious training, and worship, and by examining the issues around admittance and residence of such individuals. We will develop our work to prevent individuals gaining access to terrorist training, targeting especially those who travel to conflict zones. We must put in place the right legal framework to prevent individuals from inciting and legitimising violence. And we will examine ways to impede terrorist recruitment using the Internet. We will pursue political dialogue and target technical assistance to help others outside the EU to do the same.

Ensuring that voices of moderation prevail over those of extremism

10. There is propagation of a particular extremist worldview which brings individuals to consider and justify violence. The core of the issue is propaganda which distorts conflicts around the world as a supposed proof of a clash between the West and Islam and which claims to give individuals both an explanation for grievances and an outlet for their anger. This diagnosis distorts perceptions of Western policies and increases suspicions of hidden agendas and double standards.

11. We need to empower moderate voices by engaging with Muslim organisations and faith

groups that reject the distorted version of Islam put forward by Al-Qa'ida and others. We need to support the availability of mainstream literature, seek to encourage the emergence of European imams and enhance language and other training for foreign imams in Europe. We need to get our own message across more effectively. We will co-ordinate and enhance our efforts to change the perceptions of European and Western policies particularly among Muslim communities, and to correct unfair or inaccurate perceptions of Islam and Muslims. We should also develop a non-emotive lexicon for discussing the issues in order to avoid linking Islam to terrorism. We must ensure that by our own policies we do not exacerbate division.

Promoting yet more vigorously security, justice, democracy and opportunity for all

12. There is a range of conditions in society which may create an environment in which people can more easily be radicalised. Such factors do not necessarily lead to radicalisation, but may make the radical message more appealing both to those who suffer them and those who identify with their suffering. These conditions may include poor or autocratic governance; states moving from autocratic control via inadequate reform to partial democracy; rapid but unmanaged modernisation; and lack of political and economic prospects, unresolved international and domestic strife; and inadequate and inappropriate education or cultural opportunities for young people. Within the Union, most of these factors are not present, but within individual segments of the population they may apply and there may also be issues of identity in immigrant communities.

13. We must eliminate the structural factors supporting radicalisation both within the Union and outside it. As part of our response, within the Union we must target inequalities and discrimination where they exist and promote inter-cultural dialogue, debate, and, where appropriate, long term integration. Outside Europe, we must promote good governance, human rights, democracy, as well as education and economic prosperity, through our political dialogue and assistance programmes. And we must work to resolve conflict.

Increasing our understanding and developing our response appropriately

14. Radicalisation of certain Muslim individuals in Europe is a relatively recent phenomenon. Even those areas of Europe where radicalisation is not a major issue at present, or where large Muslim communities do not exist, could become targets for extremists. The EU will continue to develop its collective understanding of the issues, listening to Muslims, and others, comparing national situations and establishing a European picture. The response will need to evolve in line with the situation in Europe and beyond. To ensure that our approach remains up to date we will review progress annually.

Delivering the Strategy

15. Member States will work, individually and together, with the support of the European Commission and other European Union bodies to deliver this strategy. The key to our success will be the degree to which non-governmental groups – communities, religious authorities and other organisations – across Europe play an active part in countering the rhetoric of the extremists and highlighting their criminal acts.

16. The challenge of combating radicalisation and terrorist recruitment lies primarily with the Member States, at a national, regional and local level. They set the social, education, and economic policies that can foster equality and inclusion within mainstream society. It is they who determine foreign, defence and security policies, and the manner in which these are publicly communicated. It is their Parliaments and people to whom Governments are accountable for these policies. The challenge of radicalism and means to counter it vary greatly in each Member State. This strategy allows Member States to take forward work at national level

based on a common understanding of the factors and of principles and actions for countering them.

17. Work at the pan-European level can provide an important framework. Member States are able to co-ordinate their policies; share information about responses developed at national level; determine good practice; and work together to come up with new ideas. The Commission supports this through channelling its policies effectively, including through the investment of funds for research, the organisation of conferences, support for education and inter-cultural engagement, and monitoring at the pan-EU level.

18. Work beyond Europe can be undertaken through the instruments, mechanisms and processes that the EU has established with individual countries and regional organisations, including through political dialogue and assistance programmes.

Annex 7

**COUNCIL OF THE
EUROPEAN UNION**

Brussels, 30 November 2005

14469/4/05
REV 4

LIMITE

JAI 423
ECOFIN 353
TRANS 234
RELEX 639
ECO 136
PESC 1010
COTER 72
COSDP 810
PROCIV 174
ENER 172
ATO 103

NOTE

from:	Presidency and CT Co-ordinator
to:	Council/European Council
No. prev. doc.:	14469/3/05 REV 3 JAI 423 ECOFIN 353 TRANS 234 RELEX 639 ECO 136 PESC 1010 COTER 72 COSDP 810 PROCIV 174 ENER 172 ATO 103

Subject: The European Union Counter-Terrorism Strategy

This document is being forwarded to the Council for agreement and will then be transmitted to the European Council for adoption.

* * *

THE EUROPEAN UNION COUNTER-TERRORISM STRATEGY

PREVENT   PROTECT   PURSUE   RESPOND

The European Union's strategic commitment:
To combat terrorism globally while respecting human rights,
and make Europe safer, allowing its citizens to live in an area of freedom, security and justice

---

The EU 's Counter-Terrorism Strategy covers four strands of work, fitting under its strategic commitment:

STRATEGIC COMMITMENT

To combat terrorism globally while respecting human rights, and make Europe safer, allowing its citizens to live in an area of freedom, security and justice

PREVENT	PROTECT	PURSUE	RESPOND
To prevent people turning to terrorism by tackling the factors or root causes which can lead to radicalisation and recruitment, in Europe and internationally	To protect citizens and infrastructure and reduce our vulnerability to attack, including through improved security of borders, transport and critical infrastructure	To pursue and investigate terrorists across our borders and globally; to impede planning, travel, and communications; to disrupt support networks; to cut off funding and access to attack materials, and bring terrorists to justice	To prepare ourselves, in the spirit of solidarity, to manage and minimise the consequences of a terrorist attack, by improving capabilities to deal with: the aftermath; the co-ordination of the response; and the the needs of victims

Member States have the primary responsibility for combating terrorism, and the EU can add value in four main ways:

THE EUROPEAN UNION ADDS VALUE BY

STRENGTHENING NATIONAL CAPABILITIES	FACILITATING EUROPEAN COOPERATION	DEVELOPING COLLECTIVE CAPABILITY	PROMOTING INTERNATIONAL PARTNERSHIP
Using best practice, and sharing knowledge and experiences in order to improve national capabilities to prevent, protect against, pursue and respond to terrorism, including through improved collection and analysis of information and intelligence	Working together to share information securely between Member States and Institutions. Establishing and evaluating mechanisms to facilitate cooperation including between police and judicial authorities, through legislation where necessary and appropriate	Ensuring EU level capacity to understand and make collective policy responses to the terrorist threat, and making best use of the capability of EU bodies including Europol, Eurojust, Frontex, the MIC and the SitCen	Working with others beyond the EU, particularly the United Nations, other international organisations and key third countries, to deepen the international consensus, build capacity and strengthen cooperation to counter terrorism

CROSS-CUTTING
CONTRIBUTIONS

PREVENT   **PROTECT**   **PURSUE**   **RESPOND**

The EU should pursue its goals in a democratic and accountable way.
Political oversight of the Strategy and regular follow-up will be essential:

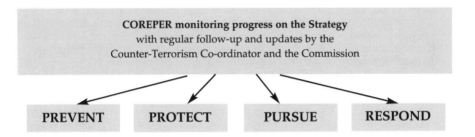

EUROPEAN COUNCIL: POLITICAL OVERSIGHT

THE HIGH-LEVEL POLITICAL DIALOGUE ON COUNTER-TERRORISM
COUNCIL - EUROPEAN PARLIAMENT- COMMISSION
Meeting once per Presidency to ensure inter-institutional governance

COREPER monitoring progress on the Strategy
with regular follow-up and updates by the
Counter-Terrorism Co-ordinator and the Commission

PREVENT   **PROTECT**   **PURSUE**   **RESPOND**

THE EU COUNTER-TERRORISM STRATEGY

PREVENT   PROTECT   PURSUE   RESPOND

STRATEGIC COMMITMENT

To combat terrorism globally while respecting human rights, and make Europe safer, allowing its
citizens to live in an area of freedom, security and justice

INTRODUCTION

1. Terrorism is a threat to all States and to all peoples. It poses a serious threat to our security, to
    the values of our democratic societies and to the rights and freedoms of our citizens, especially
    through the indiscriminate targeting of innocent people. Terrorism is criminal and unjustifi-
    able under any circumstances.

2. The European Union is an area of increasing openness, in which the internal and external
    aspects of security are intimately linked. It is an area of increasing interdependence, allowing
    for free movement of people, ideas, technology and resources. This is an environment which
    terrorists abuse to pursue their objectives. In this context concerted and collective European
    action, in the spirit of solidarity, is indispensable to combat terrorism.

3. The four pillars of the EU's Counter-Terrorism Strategy - prevent, protect, pursue, and
    respond – constitute a comprehensive and proportionate response to the international terror-
    ist threat. The Strategy requires work at national, European and international levels to reduce
    the threat from terrorism and our vulnerability to attack. The Strategy sets out our objectives
    to prevent new recruits to terrorism; better protect potential targets; pursue and investigate

members of existing networks and improve our capability to respond to and manage the consequences of terrorist attacks. This Strategy takes into the next phase the agenda of work set out at the March 2004 European Council in the wake of the Madrid bombings.

4.   Across the four pillars of the Union's Strategy a horizontal feature is the Union's role in the world. As set out in the European Security Strategy, through its external action the European Union takes on a responsibility for contributing to global security and building a safer world. Acting through and in conjunction with the United Nations and other international or regional organisations, the EU will work to build the international consensus and promote international standards for countering terrorism. The EU will promote efforts in the UN to develop a global strategy for combating terrorism. Continuing to make counter-terrorism a high priority in dialogue with key partner countries, including the USA, will also be a core part of the European approach.

5.   Given that the current international terrorist threat affects and has roots in many parts of the world beyond the EU, co-operation with and the provision of assistance to priority third countries – including in North Africa, the Middle East and South East Asia – will be vital. Finally, working to resolve conflicts and promote good governance and democracy will be essential elements of the Strategy, as part of the dialogue and alliance between cultures, faiths and civilisations, in order to address the motivational and structural factors underpinning radicalisation.

PREVENT

6.   In order to prevent people from turning to terrorism and to stop the next generation of terrorists from emerging, the EU has agreed a comprehensive strategy and action plan for combating radicalisation and recruitment into terrorism. This strategy focuses on countering radicalisation and recruitment to terrorist groups such as Al Qaeda and the groups it inspires, given that this type of terrorism currently represents the main threat to the Union as a whole.

7.   Terrorism can never be justified. There can be no excuse or impunity for terrorist acts. The vast majority of Europeans, irrespective of belief, do not accept extremist ideologies. Even amongst the small number that do, only a few turn to terrorism. The decision to become involved in terrorism varies from one individual to another, even though the motives behind such a decision are often similar. We must identify and counter the methods, propaganda and conditions through which people are drawn into terrorism.

8.   The challenge of combating radicalisation and terrorist recruitment lies primarily with the Member States, at a national, regional and local level. However, EU work in this field, including the contribution of the European Commission, can provide an important framework to help co-ordinate national policies; share information and determine good practice. But addressing this challenge is beyond the power of governments alone and will require the full engagement of all populations in Europe and beyond.

9.   There are practical steps an individual must take to become involved in terrorism. The ability to put ideas into action has been greatly enhanced by globalisation: ease of travel, transfer of money and communication - including through the internet - mean easier access to radical ideas and training. We need to spot such behaviour for example through community policing and monitoring travel to conflict zones. We also need to disrupt such behaviour by: limiting the activities of those playing a role in radicalisation; preventing access to terrorist training; establishing a strong legal framework to prevent incitement and recruitment; and examining ways to impede terrorist recruitment through the internet.

10. The propagation of a particular extremist worldview brings individuals to consider and justify violence. In the context of the most recent wave of terrorism, for example, the core of the issue is propaganda which distorts conflicts around the world as a supposed proof of a clash between the West and Islam. To address these issues, we need to ensure that voices of mainstream opinion prevail over those of extremism by engaging with civil society and faith groups

that reject the ideas put forward by terrorists and extremists that incite violence. And we need to get our own message across more effectively, to change the perception of national and European policies. We must also ensure that our own policies do not exacerbate division. Developing a non-emotive lexicon for discussing the issues will support this.

11. There is a range of conditions in society which may create an environment in which individuals can become more easily radicalised. These conditions include poor or autocratic governance; rapid but unmanaged modernisation; lack of political or economic prospects and of educational opportunities. Within the Union these factors are not generally present but in individual segments of the population they may be. To counter this, outside the Union we must promote even more vigorously good governance, human rights, democracy as well as education and economic prosperity, and engage in conflict resolution. We must also target inequalities and discrimination where they exist and promote inter-cultural dialogue and long-term integration where appropriate.

12. Radicalisation and recruitment is an international phenomenon. There is much we can do with our partners overseas to assist them in combating radicalisation, including through co-operation and assistance programmes with third countries and work through international organisations.

13. Key priorities for 'Prevent' are to:

- Develop common approaches to spot and tackle problem behaviour, in particular the misuse of the internet;
- Address incitement and recruitment in particular in key environments, for example prisons, places of religious training or worship, notably by implementing legislation making these behaviours offences;
- Develop a media and communication strategy to explain better EU policies;
- Promote good governance, democracy, education and economic prosperity through Community and Member State assistance programmes;
- Develop inter-cultural dialogue within and outside the Union;
- Develop a non-emotive lexicon for discussing the issues;
- Continue research, share analysis and experiences in order to further our understanding of the issues and develop policy responses.

PROTECT

14. Protection is a key part of our Counter Terrorism Strategy. We must strengthen the defences of key targets, by reducing their vulnerability to attack, and also by reducing the resulting impact of an attack.

15. While Member States have the primary responsibility for improving the protection of key targets, the interdependency of border security, transport and other cross-border infrastructures require effective EU collective action. In areas where EU-level security regimes exist, such as border and transport security, the EU and European Commission in particular have played an important role in raising standards. Further work between Member States, with the support of the European institutions, will provide an important framework in which Member States are able to co-ordinate their policies, share information about responses developed at national level, determine good practice, and work together to develop new ideas.

16. We need to enhance protection of our external borders to make it harder for known or suspected terrorists to enter or operate within the EU. Improvements in technology for both the capture and exchange of passenger data, and the inclusion of biometric information in identity and travel documents, will increase the effectiveness of our border controls and provide greater assurance to our citizens. The European Borders Agency (Frontex) will have a role in providing risk assessment

as part of the effort to strengthen controls and surveillance at the EU's external border. The establishment of the Visa Information System and second generation Schengen Information System will ensure that our authorities can share and access information and if necessary deny access to the Schengen area.

17.   We also must work collectively to raise standards in transport security. We must enhance the protection of airports, seaports, and aircraft security arrangements in order to deter terrorist attacks and address the vulnerabilities in domestic and overseas transport operations. These measures will be developed by a combination of specific assessments of threat and vulnerability, the implementation of agreed EU legislation on aviation and maritime security, and the agreement of revised EU legislation on aviation security. There is also scope for working together to increase road and rail security. To support work in all of these fields, EU research and development policy including the European Commission's R&D programmes should continue to include security related research in the context of terrorism.

18.   Reducing the vulnerability across Europe of critical infrastructure to physical and electronic attack is essential. To further enhance our protection, we agreed to establish a Programme of work aimed at improving the protection of critical infrastructure across Europe. We will continue work to this end, developing an all hazard approach which recognises the threat from terrorism as a priority.

19.   We must also ensure that our collective work, and particularly EU research efforts, contribute to developing methodologies for protecting crowded places and other soft targets from attacks.

20.   Internationally, we must work with partners and international organisations on transport security, and non-proliferation of CBRN materials and small arms/light weapons, as well as provide technical assistance on protective security to priority third countries as a component of our wider technical assistance programmes.

21.   Key priorities for 'Protect' are to:

•   Deliver improvements to the security of EU passports through the introduction of biometrics;
•   Establish the Visa Information System (VIS) and the second generation Schengen Information System (SISII);
•   Develop through Frontex effective risk analysis of the EU's external border;
•   Implement agreed common standards on civil aviation, port and maritime security;
•   Agree a European programme for critical infrastructure protection;
•   Make best use of EU and Community level research activity.

PURSUE

22.   We will further strengthen and implement our commitments to disrupt terrorist activity and pursue terrorists across borders. Our objectives are to impede terrorists' planning, disrupt their networks and the activities of recruiters to terrorism, cut off terrorists' funding and access to attack materials, and bring them to justice, while continuing to respect human rights and international law.

23.   As agreed in the Hague Programme, when preserving national security, Member States will also focus on the security of the Union as a whole. The Union will support the efforts of Member States to disrupt terrorists by encouraging the exchange

of information and intelligence between them, providing common analyses of the threat, and strengthening operational co-operation in law enforcement.

24. At national level the competent authorities need to have the necessary tools to collect and analyse intelligence and to pursue and investigate terrorists, requiring Member States to update their policy response and legislative provisions where necessary. In this respect our common aim is to follow up and take full account of the recommendations identified during the EU's peer evaluation process. Member States will report back on how they have improved their national capabilities and machinery in light of these recommendations.

25. Developing a common understanding of the threat is fundamental to developing common policies to respond to it. The Joint Situation Centre's assessments, based on the contributions of national security and intelligence agencies and Europol, should continue to inform decisions across the range of the EU's policies.

26. Instruments such as the European Arrest Warrant are proving to be important tools in pursuing and investigating terrorists across borders. Priority should now be given to other practical measures in order to put into practice the principle of mutual recognition of judicial decisions. A key measure is the European Evidence Warrant, which will enable Member States to obtain evidence from elsewhere in the EU to help convict terrorists. Member States should also improve further the practical co-operation and information exchange between police and judicial authorities, in particular through Europol and Eurojust. In addition, Joint Investigation Teams should be established where necessary for cross-border investigations. Evaluation of the implementation of legislative measures will be important and will inform further work, and Member States should ensure that they implement agreed European measures as well as ratify relevant international Treaties and Conventions, to ensure an appropriate legislative response to the threat.

27. To move from ad hoc to systematic police co-operation, one important step will be developing and putting into practice the principle of availability of law enforcement information. In addition, the development of new IT systems such as the Visa Information System and the next generation Schengen Information System, while safeguarding data protection, should provide improved access to those authorities responsible for internal security thereby widening the base of information at their disposal. Consideration should also be given to developing common approaches to the sharing of information on potential terrorists and on individuals deported for terrorism-related offences.

28. Terrorists must also be deprived of the means by which they mount attacks – whether directly (eg weapons and explosives) or indirectly (eg false documentation to enable undetected travel and residence). Their ability to communicate and plan undetected should be impeded by measures such as the retention of telecommunications data. They must also be deprived as far as possible of the opportunities offered by the Internet to communicate and spread technical expertise related to terrorism.

29. Creating a hostile operating environment for terrorists also means tackling terrorist financing. The EU has already put in place provisions for freezing terrorist assets. The next stage is to implement the EU-wide legislation concerning money laundering and cash transfers, and to agree steps to impede money (wire) transfers by terrorists. In addition, tackling the misuse of the non-profit sector remains a priority. We must also ensure that financial investigation is an integral part of all terrorism investigations. These measures and others which build on the Financial Action Task Force's recommendations, form part of the EU's comprehensive strategy for combating terrorist financing. A review of the EU's performance against terrorist financing is currently being conducted to ensure our approach is kept up to date.

30.   Much of the terrorist threat to Europe originates outside the EU. 'Pursue' must therefore also have a global dimension. The EU will work to reinforce the international consensus through the United Nations and other international bodies and through dialogue and agreements (which include counter-terrorism clauses) with key partners, and will work for agreement of a UN Comprehensive Convention against Terrorism. Assistance will be provided to priority countries to help them introduce and implement the necessary mechanisms to disrupt terrorism, in coordination with the work of other donors.

31.   Key priorities on 'Pursue' are to:

•   Strengthen national capabilities to combat terrorism, in light of the recommendations of the peer evaluation of national anti-terrorism arrangements;
•   Make full use of Europol and Eurojust to facilitate police and judicial cooperation, and continue to integrate the Joint Situation Centre's threat assessments into CT policy making;
•   Further develop mutual recognition of judicial decisions, including by adopting the European Evidence Warrant;
•   Ensure full implementation and evaluation of existing legislation as well as the ratification of relevant international Treaties and Conventions;
•   Develop the principle of availability of law enforcement information;
•   Tackle terrorist access to weapons and explosives, ranging from components for homemade explosive to CBRN material;
•   Tackle terrorist financing, including by implementing agreed legislation, working to prevent the abuse of the non-profit sector, and reviewing the EUs overall performance in this area;
•   Deliver technical assistance to enhance the capability of priority third countries.

RESPOND

32.   We cannot reduce the risk of terrorist attacks to zero. We have to be able to deal with attacks when they occur, recognising that attacks can have effects across EU borders. The response to an incident will often be similar whether that event is natural, technological or man-made, hence the response systems in place to manage the consequences of natural disasters may also be used to alleviate the effects on citizens in the aftermath of a terrorist attack. Our response to any such events should make full use of the existing structures, including the Civil Protection Mechanism, which the EU has developed to respond to other major European and international crises, and be co-ordinated with the action of other international organisations involved.

33.   In the event of an incident with cross border effects there will be a need for rapid sharing of operational and policy information, media co-ordination and mutual operational support, drawing on all available means, including military resources. The ability of the EU to take consistent or collective action will also be essential to an effective and efficient response. The development of EU crisis co-ordination arrangements, supported by the necessary operational procedures, will help ensure the coherence of the EU response to terrorist attacks.

34.   Member States have the lead role in providing the emergency response to a terrorist incident on their territory. Nevertheless, there remains a need to ensure that the EU collectively, supported by the European Institutions including the Commission, has the capability to respond in solidarity to an extreme emergency which might overwhelm the resources of a single Member State, and could constitute a serious risk to the Union as a whole. Reviewing and revising the current

framework for mutual support – the Community Mechanism for civil protection – is important in ensuring this safeguard.

35. Developing a risk based approach to capability assessment – focusing on preparing for those events which are judged most likely to occur, and which would have the greatest impact – will enable Member States to develop their capabilities to respond in the event of an emergency. The shared EU database listing the resources and assets which Member States might be able to contribute to dealing with such events in other Member States or overseas complements this work.

36. The solidarity, assistance and compensation of the victims of terrorism and their families constitutes an integral part of the response to terrorism at national and European level. Member States should ensure that appropriate compensation is available to victims. Through sharing of best practice on national arrangements, and the development of contact between national victims' associations, the European Commission will enable the EU to take steps to enhance the support offered to those who most suffer from terrorist attacks.

37. Internationally, there is a need to provide assistance to EU citizens in third countries and to protect and assist our military and civilian assets on EU crisis management operations. We should also ensure that our work on disaster response is closely co-ordinated with related work in international organisations and in particular the United Nations. Finally, the technical assistance provided by the EU to priority third countries will need to factor in assistance on managing the consequences of terrorist attacks.

38. Key priorities on 'Respond' are to:

- Agree EU Crisis Co-ordination Arrangements and the supporting operational procedures for them;
- Revise the legislation on the Community Mechanism for civil protection;
- Develop risk assessment as a tool to inform the building of capabilities to respond to an attack;
- Improve co-ordination with international organisations on managing the response to terrorist attacks and other disasters;
- Share best practice and develop approaches for the provision of assistance to victims of terrorism and their families.

DEMOCRATIC ACCOUNTABILITY

39. The European Council will review progress on the Strategy once every six months.

40. Once per Presidency, and ahead of the European Council's review of progress, a High Level Political Dialogue on Counter-Terrorism, bringing together the Council, European Commission, and European Parliament, will meet to allow the three Institutions to consider progress together and promote transparency and balance in the EU's approach.

41. This Strategy will be complemented by a detailed Action Plan listing all the relevant measures under the four strands of this strategy. This will allow for detailed progress to be monitored on a regular basis by the Committee of Permanent Representatives, with regular follow-up and updates from the Counter-Terrorism Co-ordinator and the European Commission.

Annex 8

COMMISSION OF THE EUROPEAN COMMUNITIES

Brussels, 12.12.2006
COM(2006) 786 final

COMMUNICATION FROM THE COMMISSION

on a European Programme for Critical Infrastructure Protection

(Text with EEA relevance)

1. BACKGROUND

The European Council of June 2004 asked for the preparation of an overall strategy to protect critical infrastructure. The Commission adopted on 20 October 2004 a Communication on Critical Infrastructure Protection in the Fight against Terrorism which put forward suggestions on what would enhance European prevention, preparedness and response to terrorist attacks involving Critical Infrastructures (CI).

The Council conclusions on "Prevention, Preparedness and Response to Terrorist Attacks" and the "EU Solidarity Programme on the Consequences of Terrorist Threats and Attacks" adopted by Council in December 2004 endorsed the intention of the Commission to propose a European Programme for Critical Infrastructure Protection (EPCIP) and agreed to the setting up by the Commission of a Critical Infrastructure Warning Information Network (CIWIN).

In November 2005, the Commission adopted a Green Paper on a European Programme for Critical Infrastructure Protection (EPCIP) which provided policy options on how the Commission could establish EPCIP and CIWIN.

The 2005 December Justice and Home Affairs (JHA) Council Conclusions on Critical Infrastructure Protection called upon the Commission to make a proposal for a European Programme for Critical Infrastructure Protection.

This Communication sets out the principles, processes and instruments proposed to implement EPCIP. The implementation of EPCIP will be supplemented where relevant by sector specific Communications setting out the Commission's approach concerning particular critical infrastructure sectors[1].

2. PURPOSE, PRINCIPLES AND CONTENT OF EPCIP

2.1. The objective of EPCIP

The general objective of EPCIP is to improve the protection of critical infrastructures in the EU. This objective will be achieved by the creation of an EU framework concerning the protection of critical infrastructures which is set out in this Communication.

---

[1] The Commission intends to put forward a Communication on Protecting Europe's Critical Energy and Transport Infrastructure.

2.2. Types of threats to be addressed by EPCIP

While recognising the threat from terrorism as a priority, the protection of critical infrastructure will be based on an all-hazards approach. If the level of protective measures in a particular CI sector is found to be adequate, stakeholders should concentrate their efforts on threats to which they are vulnerable.

2.3. Principles

The following key principles will guide the implementation of EPCIP:

• **Subsidiarity** – The Commission's efforts in the CIP field will focus on infrastructure that is critical from a European, rather than a national or regional perspective. Although focusing on European Critical Infrastructures, the Commission may where requested and taking due account of existing Community competences and available resources provide support to Member States concerning National Critical Infrastructures.

• **Complementarity** – the Commission will avoid duplicating existing efforts, whether at EU, national or regional level, where these have proven to be effective in protecting critical infrastructure. EPCIP will therefore complement and build on existing sectoral measures.

• **Confidentiality** – Both at EU level and MS level, Critical Infrastructure Protection Information (CIPI) will be classified appropriately and access granted only on a need-to-know basis. Information sharing regarding CI will take place in an environment of trust and security.

• **Stakeholder Cooperation** – All relevant stakeholders will, as far as possible, be involved in the development and implementation of EPCIP. This will include the owners/operators of critical infrastructures designated as ECI as well as public authorities and other relevant bodies.

• **Proportionality** – measures will only be proposed where a need has been identified following an analysis of existing security gaps and will be proportionate to the level of risk and type of threat involved.

• **Sector-by-sector approach** – Since various sectors possess particular experience,expertise and requirements with CIP, EPCIP will be developed on a sector-by-sector basis and implemented following an agreed list of CIP sectors.

2.4. The EPCIP framework

The framework will consist of:

• A procedure for the identification and designation of European Critical Infrastructures (ECI), and a common approach to the assessment of the needs to improve the protection of such infrastructures. This will be implemented by way of a Directive.

• Measures designed to facilitate the implementation of EPCIP including an EPCIP Action Plan, the Critical Infrastructure Warning Information Network (CIWIN), the use of CIP expert groups at EU level, CIP information sharing processes and the identification and analysis of interdependencies.

• Support for Member States concerning National Critical Infrastructures (NCI) which may optionally be used by a particular Member State. A basic approach to protecting NCI is set out in this Communication.

• Contingency planning.

• An external dimension.

• Accompanying financial measures and in particular the proposed EU programme on "Prevention, Preparedness and Consequence Management of Terrorism and other Security Related Risks" for the period 2007-2013, which will provide funding opportunities for CIP related measures having a potential for EU transferability.

Each of these measures is addressed below.

2.5. The CIP Contact Group

An EU level mechanism is required in order to serve as the strategic coordination and cooperation platform capable of taking forward work on the general aspects of EPCIP and sector specific actions. Consequently, a CIP Contact Group will be created.

The CIP Contact Group will bring together the CIP Contact Points from each Member State and will be chaired by the Commission. Each Member State should appoint a CIP Contact Point who would coordinate CIP issues within the Member State and with other Member States, the Council and the Commission. The appointment of the CIP Contact Point would not preclude other authorities in the Member State from being involved in CIP issues.

3. EUROPEAN CRITICAL INFRASTRUCTURES (ECI)

European Critical Infrastructures constitute those designated critical infrastructures which are of the highest importance for the Community and which if disrupted or destroyed would affect two or more MS, or a single Member State if the critical infrastructure is located in another Member State. This includes transboundary effects resulting from interdependencies between interconnected infrastructures across various sectors. The procedure for the identification and designation of European Critical Infrastructures (ECI), and a common approach to the assessment of the needs to improve the protection of such infrastructures will be established by means of a Directive.

4. MEASURES DESIGNED TO FACILITATE THE DEVELOPMENT AND IMPLEMENTATION OF EPCIP

A number of measures will be used by the Commission to facilitate the implementation of EPCIP and to further EU level work on CIP.

4.1. EPCIP Action Plan

EPCIP will be an ongoing process and regular review will be carried out in the form of the EPCIP Action Plan (Annex). The Action Plan will set out the actions to be achieved along with relevant deadlines. The Action Plan will be updated regularly based on the progress made.

The EPCIP Action Plan organizes CIP related activities around three work streams:

• Work Stream 1 which will deal with the strategic aspects of EPCIP and the development of measures horizontally applicable to all CIP work.

• Work Stream 2 dealing with European Critical Infrastructures and implemented at a sectoral level.

• Work Stream 3 which will support the Member States in their activities concerning National Critical Infrastructures.

The EPCIP Action Plan will be implemented taking into account sector specificities and involving, as appropriate, other stakeholders.

4.2. Critical Infrastructure Warning Information Network (CIWIN)

The Critical Infrastructure Warning Information Network (CIWIN) will be set up through a separate Commission proposal and due care will be taken to avoid duplication. It will provide a platform for the exchange of best practices in a secure manner. CIWIN will complement existing networks and could also provide an optional platform for the exchange of rapid alerts linked to the Commission's ARGUS system. The necessary security accreditation of the system will be undertaken in line with relevant procedures.

4.3. Expert groups

Stakeholder dialogue is crucial for improving the protection of critical infrastructures in the EU. Where specific expertise is needed the Commission may therefore setup CIP expert groups at EU level to address clearly defined issues and to facilitate public-private dialogue concerning critical infrastructure protection. Expert groups will support EPCIP by facilitating exchanges of views on related CIP issues on an advisory basis. These expert groups constitute a voluntary mechanism in which public and private resources are blended to achieve a goal or set of goals judged to be of mutual benefit both to citizens and the private sector.

CIP expert groups will not replace other existing groups already established or which could be adapted to fulfil the needs of EPCIP, nor will they interfere with direct information exchanges between industry, the MS authorities and the Commission.

An EU level CIP expert group will have a clearly stated objective, a timeframe for the objective to be achieved and clearly identified membership. CIP Expert Groups will be dissolved following the achievement of their objectives.

Specific functions of CIP expert groups may vary across CI sectors depending on the unique characteristics of each sector. These functions may include the following tasks:

• Assist in identifying vulnerabilities, interdependencies and sectoral best practices;

• Assist in the development of measures to reduce and/or eliminate significant vulnerabilities and the development of performance metrics;

• Facilitating CIP information-sharing, training and building trust;

• Develop and promote "business cases" to demonstrate to sector peers the value of participation in infrastructure protection plans and initiatives;

• Provide sector-specific expertise and advice on subjects such as research and development.

4.4. The CIP information sharing process

The CIP information sharing process among relevant stakeholders requires a relationship of trust, such that the proprietary, sensitive or personal information that has been shared voluntarily will not be publicly disclosed and that that sensitive data is adequately protected. Care must be taken to respect privacy rights.

Stakeholders will take appropriate measures to protect information concerning such issues as the security of critical infrastructures and protected systems, interdependency studies and CIP related vulnerability, threat and risks assessments. Such information will not be used other than for the purpose of protecting critical infrastructure. Any personnel handling classified information will have an appropriate level of security vetting by the Member State of which the person concerned is a national.

In addition, CIP information exchange will recognize that certain CIP information, though unclassified, may still be sensitive and therefore needs to be treated with care.

CIP information exchange will facilitate the following:

• Improved and accurate information and understanding about interdependencies, threats, vulnerabilities, security incidents, countermeasures and best practices for the protection of CI;

• Increased awareness of CI issues;

• Stakeholder dialogue;

• Better-focused training, research and development.

4.5. Identification of interdependencies

The identification and analysis of interdependencies, both geographic and sectoral in nature, will be an important element of improving critical infrastructure protection in the EU. This ongoing process will feed into the assessment of vulnerabilities, threats and risks concerning critical infrastructures in the EU.

5. NATIONAL CRITICAL INFRASTRUCTURES (NCI)

With due regard to existing Community competences, the responsibility for protecting National Critical Infrastructures falls on the NCI owners/operators and on the Member States. The Commission will support the Member States in these efforts where requested to do so.

With a view to improving the protection of National Critical Infrastructures each Member State is encouraged to establish a National CIP Programme. The objective of such programmes would be to set out each Member State's approach to the protection of National Critical Infrastructures located within its territory. Such programmes would at a minimum address the following issues:

• The identification and designation by the Member State of National Critical Infrastructures according to predefined national criteria. These criteria would be developed by each Member State taking into account as a minimum the following qualitative and quantitative effects of the disruption or destruction of a particular infrastructure:

• Scope - The disruption or destruction of a particular critical infrastructure will be rated by the extent of the geographic area which could be affected by its loss or unavailability.

• Severity - The consequences of the disruption or destruction of a particular infrastructure will be assessed on the basis of:

–   Public effect (number of population affected);
–   Economic effect (significance of economic loss and/or degradation of products or
        services);
–   Environmental effect;
–   Political effects;
–   Psychological effects;
–   Public health consequences.

Where such criteria do not exist, the Commission will assist a Member State, at its request, in their development by providing relevant methodologies.

• The establishment of a dialogue with CIP owners/operators.
• Identification of geographic and sectoral interdependencies.
• Drawing-up NCI related contingency plans where deemed relevant.
• Each Member State is encouraged to base its National CIP Programme on the common list of CI sectors established for ECI.

The introduction of similar approaches to the protection of NCI in the Member States would contribute to ensuring that CI stakeholders throughout Europe benefit from not being subjected to varying frameworks resulting in additional costs and that the Internal Market is not distorted.

6. CONTINGENCY PLANNING

Contingency planning is a key element of the CIP process so as to minimize the potential effects of a disruption or destruction of a critical infrastructure. The development of a coherent approach to the elaboration of contingency plans addressing such issues as the participation of owners/operators of critical infrastructure, cooperation with national authorities and information sharing among neighbouring countries should form an important element of the implementation of the European Programme for Critical Infrastructure Protection.

7. EXTERNAL DIMENSION

Terrorism, other criminal activities, natural hazards and other causes of accidents are not constrained by international borders. Threats cannot be seen in a purely national context. Consequently, the external dimension of Critical Infrastructure Protection needs to be fully taken in to account in the implementation of EPCIP. The interconnected and interdependent nature of today's economy and society means that even a disruption outside of the EU's borders may have a serious impact on the Community and its Member States. Equally true, the disruption or destruction of a critical infrastructure within the EU may have a detrimental effect on the EU's partners. Finally, working toward the goal of increasing the protection of critical infrastructure within the EU will minimize the risk of the EU economy being disrupted and thereby contribute to the EU's global economic competitiveness.

Consequently, enhancing CIP cooperation beyond the EU through such measures as sector specific memoranda of understanding (e.g. on the development of common standards, undertaking joint CIP related studies, identification of common types of threats and exchanging best-practices on protection measures) and encouraging the raising of CIP standards outside of the EU should therefore be an important element of EPCIP. External cooperation on CIP will primarily focus on the EU's neighbours. Given however the global interconnectedness of certain sectors including ICT and financial markets, a more global approach would be warranted. Dialogue and the exchange of best practices should nevertheless involve all relevant EU partners and international organizations. The Commission will also continue promoting improvements in the protection of critical infrastructures in non-EU countries by working with G8, Euromed and European Neighbourhood Policy partners through existing structures and policies, including the "Instrument for Stability".

8. ACCOMPANYING FINANCIAL MEASURES

The Community programme "Prevention, Preparedness and Consequence Management of Terrorism and other Security Related Risks" for the period 2007-2013 will contribute to the implementation of EPCIP.

Within the general objectives, and unless covered by other financial instruments, the programme will stimulate, promote and develop measures on prevention, preparedness and consequence management aimed at preventing or reducing all security risks, in particular risks linked with terrorism, where appropriate based on comprehensive threat and risk assessments.

Funding under the programme, by way of grants and Commission initiated actions, will be used in particular toward the development of instruments, strategies, methodologies, studies, assessments and activities/measures in the field of the effective protection of critical infrastructure (at both EU and MS levels).

ANNEX

EPCIP Action Plan

Work Stream 1. Consecutive EPCIP strategies

Work stream 1 will serve as the strategic platform for overall EPCIP coordination and cooperation through the EU CIP Contact Group.

Phase 1

Action	Actor	Timeframe
Identification of priority sectors for action (The transport and energy sectors will be among the first priorities)	Commission	As soon as possible and thereafter on an annual basis
Development of common CI sector-based working definitions and terminology	Commission, MS and other stakeholders where relevant	at the latest one year following the entry into force of the ECI Directive
Elaboration of general criteria to be used in identifying ECI	Commission, MS and other stakeholders where relevant	at the latest one year following the entry into force of the ECI Directive
Creation of an inventory of existing national, bilateral and EU critical infrastructure protection programmes	Commission, MS	ongoing
Creation and agreement on guidelines on collection and use of sensitive data between stakeholders	Commission, MS, and other stakeholders where relevant	ongoing
Collection of CIP related best practices, risk assessment tools and methodologies	Commission, MS and other stakeholders where relevant	ongoing
Commissioning studies concerning interdependencies	Commission, MS and other stakeholders where relevant	ongoing

Phase 2

Action	Actor	Timeframe
Identification of gaps where Community initiatives would have added-value	Commission, MS and other stakeholders where relevant	ongoing
Where relevant, setting up of CIP sector based expert groups at EU level	Commission, MS and other stakeholders where relevant	ongoing
Identification of proposals for CIP actions that could be funded at EU level	Commission, MS	ongoing
Initiation of EU funding for CIP actions	Commission	ongoing

Phase 3

Action	Actor	Timeframe
Initiation of cooperation with 3rd countries and international organisations;	Commission, MS	ongoing

Work Stream 2. Protection of European critical infrastructure (ECI)

Work stream 2 will focus on reducing the vulnerability of ECI.

Phase 1

Action	Actor	Timeframe
Elaboration of sector specific criteria to be used in identifying ECI	Commission, MS and other stakeholders where relevant	at the latest one year following the entry into force of the ECI Directive

Phase 2

Action	Actor	Timeframe
Identification and verification on a sectorby- sector basis of CI likely to qualify as ECI	Commission, MS	at the latest one year after the adoption of the relevant criteria and thereafter on an ongoing basis
Designation of ECI	Commission, MS	ongoing
Identification of vulnerabilities, threats and risks to particular ECI including the establishment of Operator Security Plans (OSPs) at the latest one year after designation as ECI	Commission, MS, ECI owners/operators (generic report to Commission)	at the latest one year after designation as ECI
Assessment of whether protection measures are needed and whether EU level measures are required	Commission, MS and other stakeholders where relevant	at the latest 18 months after designation as ECI
Assessment of the approach of each Member State to alert levels concerning infrastructure designated as ECI. Launching of a feasibility study on calibrating or harmonizing such alerts.	Commission, MS	ongoing

Phase 3

Action	Actor	Timeframe
Development and adoption of proposals for minimum protection measures concerning ECI	Commission, MS, ECI owners/ operators	following the assessment of whether protection measures are needed and whether EU level measures are required
Implementation of minimum protection measures	MS, ECI owners/ operators	ongoing

Work Stream 3. Support concerning NCI

Work Stream 3 is an intra-Member State work stream to assist the Member States in the protection of NCI.

Phase 1

Action	Actor	Timeframe
Exchange of information on the criteria used to identify NCI	MS (Commission may assist where requested)	ongoing

Phase 2

Action	Actor	Timeframe
Identification and verification on a sector-by-sector basis of CI likely to qualify as NCI	MS and other stakeholders where relevant	ongoing
Designation of particular CI as NCI	MS	ongoing
Analysis of existing security gaps in relation to NCI on a sector-by-sector basis	MS and other stakeholders where relevant (Commission may assist where requested)	ongoing

Phase 3

Action	Actor	Timeframe
Establishment and development of National CIP Programmes	MS (Commission may assist where requested)	ongoing
Development of specific protection measures for each NCI	MS, NCI (Commission may assist where requested)	ongoing
Monitoring that owners/operators carry out the necessary implementation measures	MS	ongoing

Annex 9

MEMO/07/98
Brussels, 12 March 2007

Commission Activities in the Fight against Terrorism

I. Past (since 2004) and future Commission activities in the fight against terrorism

A) *Prevention, preparedness and response to terrorist attacks*

Achieved

Communications

– Green Paper on detection and associated technologies in the work of law enforcement, customs and other security authorities (September 2006)
– Communication on ensuring greater security of explosives, detonators, bombmaking equipment and fire-arms (July 2005)
– Communication on improving Community Civil Protection Mechanism (Apr 2005)
– Communication on prevention, preparedness and response to terrorist attacks (Oct 2004)
– Communication on Critical Infrastructure Protection in the fight against terrorism (Oct 2004)
– Communication on preparedness and consequence management in the fight against terrorism (Oct 2004)
– Communication and a possible proposal for a legal instrument on supply chain security
– Communication addressing violent radicalisation and recruitment of terrorists
– Communication on European Programme for Critical Infrastructure Protection (EPCIP)
– Communication on Building Solidarity Through Mutual Assistance: Report on the assessment of civil protection assistance available through the Community Civil Protection Mechanism in case of major terrorist attacks in the Union (EU Restricted)
– Green paper on European Programme for Critical Infrastructure Protection (EPCIP)
– Communication on a Strategy for a secure Information Society – "Dialogue, partnership and empowerment" (May 2006)

Adopted legislation

– Council Framework Decision of 24.02.2005 on Attacks against Information Systems
– Regulation n° 68/2004 of 15 January 2004 amending Regulation (EC) n° 622/2003 laying down measures for the implementation of the common basic standards on aviation security
– Commission Regulation (EC) n° 781/2005 of 25 May 2005 amending Regulation (EC) n° 622/2003 laying down measures for the implementation of the common basic standards on aviation security

– Commission Regulation (EC) N°857/2005 of 6 June 2005 amending Regulation (EC) n° 622/2003 laying down measures for the implementation of the common basic standards on aviation security
– Commission Regulation (EC) n° 1138/2004 of 21 June 2004 establishing a common definition of critical parts of security restricted areas at airports
– Council Directive 2004/82/EC of 29 April 2004 on the obligation of carriers to communicate passenger data
– Commission Regulation (EURATOM) 302/2005 of 8.2.2005 on the application of EURATOM safeguards
– Security amendments to the Community Customs Code that relate to checks on the flow of goods by introducing a system of pre-arrival and pre-departure declarations and by using an improved system of data communication and information sharing between Member States (adopted in April 2005 – Regulation (EC) No. 648/2005).
– Council Decision approving the conclusion of the Convention on Early Notification of a Nuclear Accident
– Commission Decision for accession to the Convention on Early Notification of a Nuclear Accident

Proposed legislation

– Proposal for a regulation establishing a rapid response and preparedness instrument for major emergencies [COM(2005)113]
– Proposal for a directive on enhancing port security [COM(2004) 76 of 10 February 2004]
– Implementing regulation to the Security amendments to the Community Customs Code.
– Proposals for a complete modernisation of the customs code and a Decision on e-customs
– Proposal for a Directive on a European Programme for the protection of critical infrastructure

Report

– Report to the Council on modalities procedures and criteria to develop the appropriate level of interoperability between military and civilian capabilities in the framework of protection of civilian populations following a terrorist attack, including in crisis management operations under Title V of the TEU
– Report on "The Impact of 7 July 2005 Bombs Attack on Muslim Communities in the EU" by the European Monitoring Centre (EUMC)
– Report on recruitment to terrorism including the possible adoption of an agreed set of recommendations
– Report on transport security including financing issues.

Other

– Council decision establishing the specific programme "Prevention, Preparedness and Consequence Management of Terrorism" for the period 2007-2013 (framework programme on "Security and Safeguarding Liberties" for the period 2007-2013")
– Establishment of an Expert Group on Violent Radicalisation
– Establishment of the High Level Group on Minorities
– The Programme on Health, Security aims at setting up EU cooperation and mutual assistance against biological or chemical attacks
– Establishment by the Community Civil Protection Mechanism of procedures for early warning, alert and activation of response through the central MIC
– RAS-BICHAT rapid alert system for deliberate releases of biological and chemical agents, improved co-operation with other alert mechanisms
– Set up of a RASCHEM – exchange of information and warnings between Poison Control Centres
– MediSYS, monitoring of Web-based information to provide advance, real-time, warning of suspicious circumstances or outbreaks
– Guidance on General preparedness and response planning and integration of EU dimension in all national health emergency plans is being prepared
– HEOF – Health emergency operations facility: improvement of the current crisis and communication centre
– Establishment of a secure general rapid alert system (ARGUS)
– Commission financing decision – Pilot Project 'Fight against terrorism' (2005 and 2006)

– Financial decision on a pilot project terrorism aiming at inter-linkage of Commission crisis management structures and Member States' relevant law enforcement agencies

To Do

Communication

– Communication on security measures in various transport modes including their financing
– Green Paper on Bio-Preparedness and Food Defence
– EU Action plan to improve the security of explosives and detonators

Commission Decisions

– Commission decision for adoption of the IAEA Convention on early notification of a nuclear accident by the European Atomic Energy Community
– Commission Decision for adoption of the IAEA Convention on Assistance in the case of a nuclear Accident or radiological emergency by the European Atomic Energy Community
– development of a legal framework to counter the dissemination of terrorist propaganda and bomb-making and other terrorism expertise through the internet – Communication on a strategy for a secure Information
– Communication on witness protection for the cooperation with counter-terrorism investigations

Proposed legislation

– Proposal for a Council directive on the supervision and control of shipments of radioactive waste and spent fuel
– Proposal for a directive on security in the intermodal transportation chain (transportation of goods)
– Proposal for a Directive on regulating the alternative remittance system (inter alia FATF SR VI)
– Development of a legal framework to remove illegal material from the internet – Revision of Regulation 2320/2002 reinforcing common standards on aviation security.

Report

– EU profile on counter-terrorism for CODEXTER – an ad hoc Committee of Experts on Terrorism in the Council of Europe (jointly with the Council)
– First report on the state of play of research in the field of radicalization and recruitment by the Expert Group on Violent Radicalisation
– Second report on manifestations, trends and dynamics of radicalisation processes by the Expert Group on Violent Radicalisation.
– Report (II) based on the implementation of the Framework Decision on Combating Terrorism
– Report on the assessment of civil protection assistance through the Mechanism in case of major terrorist attack in the EU, including the medical resources required to respond to a bio-terrorist attack.
– Second Report evaluating the implementation of the Framework Decision of 13 June 2002 on combating terrorism.

Other

– Reinforce the protection of European citizen abroad
– Implement EU Crisis Coordination arrangements to share information
– The Cooperation part of the Commission proposal for the 7th RTD Framework Programme (FP7), will include a Security and Space theme

B) Victims of terrorism

Achieved

– A memorial report dedicated to the victims of terrorism (Feb 2005)

– 2 pilot projects approved by the EP, allowing the Commission to spend 3M€ on projects aimed at improving the situation of victims of terrorism
– Preparatory action approved by the EP, allowing the Commission to spend 1.8 million on terrorism
– As part of the Civil Justice programme, a further 2M€ will be spent on projects assiting the victims of terrorism
– Council directive 2004/80/EC of 29 April 2004 relating to compensation to crime victims

C) Fight against financing of terrorism

Achieved

Communication

– Communication on the Prevention of and fight against organised crime in the financial sector COM(2004) 262
– Communication on the prevention of and the fight against terrorist financing through measures to improve the exchange of information, to strengthen transparency and enhance the traceability of financial transactions COM(2004) 700
– Communication COM(2005) 620 on "the prevention and fight against terrorist financing through enhanced level national level coordination and greater transparency of the non-profit sector" setting out (i) best practice advice in cooperation structures and the exchange of financial intelligence and (ii) putting forward a Recommendation to the MS and a framework for a Code of Conduct for NPOs to enhance transparency within the non-profit sector

Other

EU Joint Strategy Paper on Counter Terrorist Financing; "The fight against terrorist financing" presented by Secretary General/ High Representative and Commission to the European Council. 16089/04 of 14th December 2004

Adopted legislation

– Council Decision on co-operation among financial intelligence units (FIUs) of October 2000 (2000/642/JHA)
– Framework Decision of 26 June 2001 (2001/500/JHA) on money laundering, the identification, tracing, freezing, seizing and confiscation of instrumentalities and the proceeds of crime
– Council Act of 16 October 2001 establishing, in accordance with Article 34 of the Treaty on European Union, the Protocol to the Convention on Mutual Assistance in Criminal Matters between the Member States of the European Union (2001/C 326/01, OJ C326 of 21 November 2001)
– Directive 2001/97/EC of 4 December 2001 amending Council Directive 91/308/EEC on prevention of the use of the financial system for the purpose of money laundering
– Council Decision of 6 December 2001 extending Europol's mandate to deal with serious forms of international crime listed in the Annex to the Europol Convention (2001/C 362/01; OJ C 362 of 18 December 2001)
– Council Common Position of 27 December 2001 on combating terrorism (2001/930/CFSP; OJ L 344 of 28 December 2001)
– Council Common Position of 27 December 2001 on the application of specific measures to combat terrorism (2001/931/CFSP; OJ L 344 of 28 December 2001)
– Council Regulation (EC) No 2580/2001 of 27 December 2001 on specific restrictive measures directed against certain persons and entities with a view to combating terrorism (OJ L 344 of 28 December 2001)
– Council Decision of 27 December 2001 establishing the list provided for in Article 2(3) of Council Regulation (EC) No 2580/2001 on specific restrictive measures directed against certain persons and entities with a view to combating terrorism (2001/927/EC; OJ L 344 of 28 December 2001)
– Council Common Position of 27 May 2002 concerning restrictive measures against Usama bin Laden, members of the Al-Qaida organisation and the Taliban and other individuals, groups,

undertakings and entities associated with them and repealing Common Positions 96/746/CFSP, 1999/727/CFSP, 2001/154/CFSP and 2001/771/CFSP (2002/402/CFSP; OJ L 139 of 29 May 2002)
– Council Regulation (EC) No 881/2002 of 27 May 2002 imposing certain specific restrictive measures directed against certain persons and entities associated with Usama bin Laden, the Al-Qaeda network and the Taliban, and repealing Council Regulation (EC) No 467/2001 prohibiting the export of certain goods and services to Afghanistan, strengthening the flight ban and extending the freeze of funds and other financial resources in respect of the Taliban of Afghanistan (OJ L 139 of 29 May 2002)
– Directive on Insider Trading and Market Manipulation (Market Abuse) (2003/6 of 28 January 2003; OJ L 96 of 12 April 2003) and its implementing measures (Commission Directives 2004/72/EC; 2003/124/EC; 2003/125/EC)
– Ratification of international conventions in accordance with UN SC Resolution 1373 (2001)
– Council Framework Decision 2003/577/JHA of 22 July 2003 on the execution in the European Union of orders freezing property or evidence (OJ L 196/45 of 2nd of August 2003)
– Framework Decision of 20 September 2005 on the exchange of information and cooperation concerning terrorist offences (2005/671/JHA)
– Regulation of 26th October 2005 on controls on cash entering or leaving the Community (Regulation (EC) No. 1889/2005)
– Council Framework Decision 2006/783/JHA of 6 October 2006 on the application of the principle of mutual recognition to confiscation orders (OJ L 328/59 of 24th November 2006)
– Directive of 26th October 2005 on the prevention of the use of the financial system for the purpose of money laundering and terrorist financing (also known as the Third Money Laundering Directive), (OJ L 309 of 25th November 2005; entered into force 15 December 2005).
– Regulation (EC) No 1781/2006 of the European Parliament and of the Council of 15 November 2006 on information on the payer accompanying transfers of funds (OJ L 345/ of 8th December 2006)

Proposed legislation

– Commission proposal for a Directive on a New Legal Framework for Payments in the Internal Market (regulating inter alia alternative remittance systems, in compliance with Financial Activities Task Force SR VI)
– Draft Council Decision concerning cooperation between Asset Recovery Offices of the Member States in the field of tracing and identification of proceeds from, or other property related to, crime

Reports

– A follow-up based on Article 6 of the Council Framework Decision of 26 June 2001 on money laundering, the identification, tracing, freezing, seizing and confiscation of instrumentalities and the proceeds of crime; COM(2006) 72 of 21st February 200

Other

– Establishment of intelligence capacity in relation to terrorist financing within SitCen to inform the work of relevant bodies
– Study on EU's performance on Terrorist Financing in particular in respect of Financial Activities Task Force (FATF) special recommendations and act on recommendations awarded in April 2006. Study was completed in February 2007.

To Do

– Implement the Third Money Laundering Directive. Member States shall comply with the Directive by 15 December 2007. The Commission adopted implementing measures to the 3rd AML Directive: Commission Directive 2006/70/EC of 1 August 2006 laying down implementing measures for Directive 2005/60/EC of the European Parliament and of the Council as regards the definition of politically exposed person and the technical criteria for simplified customer due diligence procedures and for exemption on grounds of a financial activity conducted on an occasional or very limited basis (OJ L 214/29 of 4th August 2006). Furthermore, the Commission is organising transposition meetings with Member States.

– Initiate outreach programmes to EU financial private sector to coordinate procedures to combat terrorist financing.
– Implement Regulation (EC) No. 1889/2005 of 26 October 2005 on controls of cash or leaving the Community.
– Implement Regulation (EC) No. 1781/2006 of 15 November 2006 on information on the payer accompanying transfers of funds
– Further conduct dialogue with the non-profit sector on the implementation of requirements laid down in the Communication COM(2005) 620 and the FATF Interpretative Note to Special Recommendation VIII.
– Encourage follow-up to Peer Evaluation round addressing national machinery relevant to coordination and information exchanges structures in context of counter terrorist financing work.
– Together with Counter Terrorism Coordinator produce new EU Counter Terrorism Strategy in 2007.
– Promote use of financial intelligence in all counter terrorist investigations through on-going work to highlight and encourage greater focus on financial investigation as a law enforcement technique.

D) Police matters, data and information exchange

Achieved

Communication

– Communication: Towards enhancing access to information by law enforcement agencies (Jun 2004)
– Communication on measures to be taken to combat terrorism and other forms of serious crime, in particular to improve exchanges of information
– Communication on improved effectiveness, enhanced interoperability and synergies among European databases in the area of Justice and Home Affairs

Adopted legislation

– Framework Decision on combating terrorism
– Framework Decision to replace Joint Action 1998/733/JHA on Criminal Organisations
– Council Decision on the exchange of information and co-operation concerning terrorist offences
– Framework Decision on simplifying the exchange of information and intelligence between law enforcement authorities of the Member States, in particular as regards serious offences including terrorist acts
– Directive on the retention of telecommunications traffic data – Council Decision on the implementation of specific measures for police and judicial cooperation to combat terrorism in accordance with Article 4 of Common Position 2001/931/CFSP
– Council Common Position 2005/69/JHA of 21.01.2005 on exchanging certain data with Interpol
– Council Decision establishing the European Police College (CEPOL)
– Framework Decision on Joint Investigation Teams
– Council Decision of 20 September 2005 establishing the European Police College (CEPOL)
– Council Decision of 12 February 2007 establishing the Specific Programme "Prevention of and Fight against Crime" for the period 2007 to 2013, as part of General Programme on Security and Safeguarding Liberties (2007/125/JHA, OJ L 58 of 24 February 2007)

Proposed legislation

– Draft Framework Decision on information exchange under the principle of availability
– Draft Framework Decision on the processing of personal data in the framework of police and judicial cooperation
– Proposal for a Council Decision on Europol

Report

– Interim report on the outcome of the process of peer evaluation on national arrangements in the fight against terrorism in the 15 Member States

– Final report on the outcome of the process of peer evaluation on national arrangements in the fight against terrorism covering the new Member States
– Report from the Commission on the legal transposition of Council Decision of 28 February 2002 setting up Eurojust, with a view to reinforcing the fight against serious crime
– Report on the Terrorist attacks in Madrid from a law enforcement perspective
– Report on the implementation of the Framework decision on Joint Investigation Teams
– Joint report by CEPOL and Europol on what Counter-Terrorism related training they have so far provided and what more could be done
– First Report evaluating the implementation of the Framework Decision of 13 June 2002 on combating terrorism of 8 June 2004.

Other

– The drawing up of common lists containing the most significant terrorists and terrorist organisations, which are regularly and appropriately updated
– All Member States are connected to the Bureau de Liaison
– Implementation of the Europol Information System (available in the 25 Member states since 10 October 2005)
– Development of the European Crime Intelligence Model with the assistance of the Police Chiefs Task Force
– Europol/Eurojust Agreement (effective from 10 June 2004)
– Setting up of the Counter-Terrorism Task Force (CTTF) (Europol)
– Establishments of links between SitCen and Europol
– All Member States have designated their Eurojust national correspondent for terrorist matters
– COUNCIL RECOMMENDATION of 27 April 2006 on the drawing up of agreements between police, customs and other specialised law enforcement services in relation to the prevention and combating of crime (OJ C 124 of 25.5.2006, p 1)

To Do

Communications

– Communication: Towards a general policy on the fight against cyber crime (including a description of a number of actions aiming at improving operational law enforcement cooperation, i.a. against cyber terrorism)

Proposed legislation

– Proposal on a European policy for the use of passenger name records (PNR)
– Proposal for a directive on the use of Passenger Name Records (PNR) for law enforcement purposes
– Proposal for a Council decision on access to the Visa Information System by authorities competent for internal security matters

E) Judicial and criminal matters

Achieved

Communications

– White Paper on exchanges of information on convictions and the effect of such convictions in the European Union (January 2005)

Adopted legislation

– Framework Decision on the European Arrest Warrant
– Framework Decision on the Confiscation of crime related proceeds, instrumentalities and property

– Council Decision 2005/876/JHA of 21 November 2005 on the exchange of information extracted from the criminal record
– Draft Framework Decision on a European Evidence Warrant (political agreement reached in the Council).

Proposed legislation

– Proposal for a framework decision on the fight against organised crime [COM (2005)6 of 19.01.2005] to replace joint action 1998/733/JHA
– Proposal for a Council framework decision on taking account of convictions in the Member States of the European Union in the course of new criminal proceedings [COM(2005)91 of 17.03.2005]
– Draft Framework Decision on the application of the principle of mutual recognition to Confiscation Orders (when the remaining national parliamentary reservation is lifted).
– Proposal for a Council framework decision on the organisation and content of the exchange of information extracted from criminal records between Member States.

Reports

– Report by Eurojust on the measures the unit has implemented since December 2004 in the fight against terrorism
– Report on the transposition by the Member States of the Framework Decision on the Execution in the EU of orders freezing Property or Evidence

Other

– Convention on Mutual Assistance in Criminal Matters and its Protocol
– All Member States have designated their Eurojust national correspondent for terrorist matters
– Network on national experts on Joint Investigation Teams established

To Do

– Communication on the feasibility of an index of non EU nationals convicted in an EU Member State

Report

– A follow-up report on the decision establishing Eurojust
– A revised report on the European arrest warrant

F) Borders

Achieved

Adopted legislation

– Council Regulation (EC) n° 2007/2004 of 26 October 2004 establishing a European Agency for the Management of Operational Cooperation at the External Borders of the Member States of the European Union
– Council regulation on the introduction of new functions for the Schengen Information System
– Council decision of 8 June 2004 establishing the Visa Information System (VIS)
– Regulation (EC) n° 724/2004 amending Regulation (EC) No 1406/2002 establishing a European Maritime Safety Agency
– Regulation (EC) n° 725/2004 on enhancing ship and port facility security
– Council Directive 2004/82/EC on the obligation of carriers to communicate passenger data
– Commission Regulation EC 884/2005 laying down procedures for conducting Commission inspections in the field of maritime security

Proposed legislation

– Proposal for a regulation concerning Visa Information System and the exchange of data between Member States on short-stay visas
– Proposal for a Council decision on the establishment, operation and use of the second generation Schengen Information System (SIS II)
– Proposal for a regulation on the establishment, operation and use of the second generation Schengen Information System (SIS II)
– Proposal for a Regulation regarding access to the Second Generation Schengen Information System (SIS II) by the services in the Member States responsible for issuing vehicle registration certificates
– Proposal for a regulation laying down provisions for the implementation of Council Regulation (EEC) No 2913/92 establishing the Community Customs Code. The recently published preliminary draft proposal aims at defining the necessary amendments that must be made to Commission Regulation (EEC) No 2454/93, consequent to the amendments made to Council Regulation 92/2913 (EEC), by Regulation (EC) 648/2005 of the European Parliament and Council, OJ L 117, 04.05.2005, p.13. The deadline for response to the open consultation related to the above mentioned proposal was 16th September 2005.
– Council decision n° 2004/512/EC establishing the Visa Information System (VIS)
– Regulation (EC) n° 648/2005 amending Council Regulation (EEC) No 2913/92 establishing the Community Customs Code
– Implementing Regulation to the security amendments of the Community Customs Code (Regulation EC no. 648/2005)
– Proposal for a complete modernisation of the custom code introducing the supporting IT system.

Report

– Report from study of the role of Customs in the Member States in relation to security/anti-terrorism at EU Borders (approved by CCWG, 10238/04)

Other

– Strategy for Customs Cooperation and related work plan
– Statement of support for the Proliferation Security Initiative
– The Borders Code

To Do

Communication

– Communication on enhanced interaction between VIS, SISII and EURODAC

Proposed legislation

– Develop and implement a common EU approach to the exchange and analysis of passenger information: agree Directive on airline passenger name records.
– Regulation of the European Parliament and of the Council concerning the VIS and the exchange of data on short stay-visas.

G) Security research

The Commission has launched new research initiatives to improve the security of EU citizens. Security makes a timely entry into the list of research themes to be undertaken swiftly, in order to respond to highly societal demand in the face of new security challenges. For more details see MEMO/05/116.

Activities

– The Commission proposal for the 7th RTD Framework Programme includes Security Research as a new theme. Security Research is composed of four vertical priorities and three transversal priorities.

Vertical priorities

– Protection against terrorism and crime: delivering technology solutions for threat (e.g. CBRN) awareness, detection, prevention, identification, protection, neutralisation and containment of effects of terrorist attacks and organised crime.
– Security of infrastructures and utilities: analysing and securing existing and future public and private critical/networked infrastructure (e.g. in transport, energy, ICT), systems and services (including financial and administrative services).
– Border security: focusing on technologies and capabilities to enhance the effectiveness and efficiency of all systems, equipment, tools and processes required for improving the security of Europe's land and coastal borders, including border control and surveillance issues.
– Restoring security in case of crisis: focusing on technologies in support of diverse emergency management operations (such as civil protection, humanitarian and rescue tasks, support to CFSP), and on issues such as interorganisational co-ordination and communication, distributed architectures and human factors.

Transversal priorities

– Security Systems Integration & Interoperability
– Technologies to enhance interoperability of systems, equipment, services & processes
– Organisation, protection of confidentiality & integrity of information, traceability of transactions, processing
– Security and Society
– Socio economic aspects related to crime, perception of security, ethics, privacy, societal foresight
– Safeguarding privacy & liberties, vulnerabilities, new threats, management & impact assessment of consequences
– Security Research Coordination & Structuring
– Coordination of security research efforts, development of synergies (civil/security/defence), legal conditions, use of infrastructures

Achieved

– Commission proposal to increase funding for security research projects from 2007. The Commission proposes a common budget allocation in the 7th RTD Framework Programme (2007-2013) for Security and Space related research activities of € 408 Mio per year. The evaluation of the last call for proposals of the preparatory action in the field of security research (2004-2006) took place in June 2006. Contract negotiations will take place in autumn 2006.
– ESRAB (the European Security Research and Advisory Board) finalised its report, advising the Commission on the content and the implementation of security research in FP7. The report will be available towards the end of September 2006. It will be the basis for the work programme of security research within FP7.
– Inventory and analysis of on-going research activities in the field of biological and chemical terrorism and identification of gaps and needs in scientific knowledge and research priorities which contribute to define annual research work programmes and priorities (updated 2005)
– Selection Funding of five projects (Scientific Support to Policies) in the area of biological and chemical terrorism within the scope of the 6th Framework Programme for Research (2002-2006)
– The 2002 CBRN-programme (Doc. 1427/02) was replaced by the 2004 Solidarity Programme.

To Do

– Launch of three further Scientific Support to Policies projects in the area of biological and chemical terrorism in the second half of 2005

– Ensure full implementation of the EU Health Security Strategy and CBRN Programme.
– Based on the ESRAB report, the 1st Work programme for Security Research within FP7 is being prepared for adoption towards the end 2006 to enable a timely launch of the call for proposals during the 1st semester 2007.

II. Call on member states:

A) To allow adoption of instruments on which political agreement has been reached but which are subject to a parliamentary reserve

– Proposal for a Council framework decision on the application of mutual recognition to confiscation orders (parliamentary reserve by one MS; political agreement reached 6 June 2004)
– Proposal for a Council decision on the exchange of information and cooperation concerning terrorist offences (reserves by four MS)
– Proposal for a Council decision on the exchange of information extracted from the criminal record (political agreement in February 2005; reserve by one MS)
– Recommendation to Member States on a Framework for a Code of Conduct

B) To ratify

– All UN conventions and protocols addressing terrorism
– The Convention on mutual assistance in criminal matters between the Member States of the EU of 29 May 2000 and the Protocol of 16 October 2001 to this Convention.

C) To transpose or to correct errors in transposition of acts, deadlines of which have expired

– To ensure that the Framework Decision of 13 June 2002 on the European Arrest Warrant and the surrender procedures between Member States is transposed correctly, notably on the basis of the Commission report based on Article 34 of this Council Framework Decision (COM (2005)63 of 23.02.2005), and to inform the Commission and the General Secretariat of the Council accordingly by March 2006, following the conclusions of the JHA Council of 2.06.2005.
– To ensure that the Council Framework Decision of 13 June 2002 on joint investigation teams is transposed and to correct errors in transposition.
– To implement and correct implementation of framework decisions outlined in the Action Plan on Terrorism (e.g., the Framework Decision on Combating Terrorism – 6 MS to provide information; 2 MS to provide texts of legislation)
– To implement the Framework Decision on Money Laundering (2001/500/JHA of 26 June 2001), to take account of the first Commission report of 5 April 2004 and to inform the Commission and Council Secretariat General accordingly before the end of July 2005
– To inform regularly the Commission and the Council Secretariat General about implementation of the Framework Decisions outlined in the Action Plan on Terrorism
– To provide the Commission with texts of legislation in respect to the Framework Decisions outlined in the Action Plan on Terrorism

IV. International dimension

– Promotion of the implementation of relevant international norms and legal instruments, through targeted technical assistance, political dialogue and cooperation in international and regional organisations. Actions taken to combat terrorism are balanced against the need to protect individual rights and freedoms.
– Support for the United Nations, including regular contacts and meetings with UN bodies, particularly the Counter-Terrorism Committee (CTC) the Counter- Terrorism Executive Directorate (CTED), the 1267 Sanctions Committee and UNODC (Office for the fight against Drugs and Crime).

– Action in favour of the adoption and implementation of UN instruments; and in support for development of a comprehensive UN Convention against Terrorism and a global counter-terrorism strategy.
– Working with international and regional organisations.
– Development of technical assistance. The Community provides counterterrorism related assistance to help countries implement UNSCR 1373 (2001),which is handled from within regular Community assistance programmes.
– Counter-terrorism is a key element of political dialogue and counter-terrorism clauses are included in agreements with third countries.
– Reinforcement of the protection of European citizens in third countries – in April 2005, the Commission proposed to make the MIC available to facilitate and support consular cooperation in the event of major emergencies in third countries, affecting EU citizens.
– The follow up to the Container Security Initiative (CSI)

INDEX

The annexes are not indexed